The Wines of the Loire, Alsace and Champagne

THE WINES OF
THE LOIRE
ALSACE AND
CHAMPAGNE

HUBRECHT DUIJKER

FOREWORD BY
Hugh Johnson

Photography by Jan Jonker and Hubrecht Duijker

MITCHELL BEAZLEY

To my parents

Some commonly used terms

Appellation. Short for *appellation d'origine contrôlée*: legally protected designation of wine from a named and prescribed area.
Cave. Cellar, usually underground.
Caveau. Café specializing in wine; sometimes also an unpretentious restaurant.
Chaptalization. The addition of legally prescribed amounts of sugar to grape must to increase the alcoholic content of wine.
Confrérie. A wine fraternity.
Cuve. Fermentation or storage vat or tank of wood, concrete, steel, stainless steel, glass fibre or other synthetic material.
Cuvée. Literally a vatful of wine. Usually, however, it indicates a blend of wines, generally from the same grape variety and of the same vintage; and in Champagne it also means the first pressing and the resultant wine.

Demi-muid. Large wooden vat.
Domaine. Wine estate.
Fermentation malolactique. Malolactic fermentation that breaks down acids in the wine. Essential for red wines, optional for white.
Macération carbonique. Process in which fermentation takes place within uncrushed grapes placed in carbon dioxide, resulting in fragrant wines that are quickly drinkable (Beaujolais Primeur, for example).
Must. Unfermented grape juice.
Négociant. Shipper; wine producer and dealer; firm performing these functions.
Oenology (enology). Science of wine-making. Hence oenologist, a wine scientist or technician.
Phylloxera. Parasite that destroyed nearly all the European vineyards around the turn of the century.
Rendement. Yield; the amount of wine, normally measured in hectolitres, produced by a

Contents

Art direction: Van Sambeek & Watano, Amsterdam
Photography: Jan Jonker and Hubrecht Duijker
Maps: Otto van Eersel
Jacket photo: front Van Sambeek & Watano, Amsterdam

First impression 1981

English translation by Danielle de Froidmont Associates

ISBN 0 85533 470 3

Printed in the Netherlands

Typeset and prepared by T&O Graphics and Taylor Jackson Designs Ltd, Lowestoft, Suffolk

First published in the U.K. by
Mitchell Beazley, London
Artists House
14-15 Manette Street
London W1V 5LB

© 1981 by Het Spectrum B.V.
English translation © Mitchell Beazley Publishers 1983

particular vineyard, grape, commune or district. For quality wines there is always a legally prescribed maximum, which may be revised upwards by not more than 20% in a given year depending on the success of the vintage.

Soutirage. Drawing off; transference of wine to a clean vat.

Terroir. A somewhat earthy taste derived from the soil where a particular wine has grown.

Vignoble. Vineyard.

Vin délimité de qualité supérieure (VDQS). Wine from a legally prescribed and protected named area, a little below the quality of the *appellation contrôlée* category.

Vinification. The wine-making process.

Viticulteur. Wine grower.

Acreages

In this book there are many references to the acreages of districts, villages and vineyards. The latest figures at the time of writing have been given; obviously these may be subject to slight changes.

Labels

Wine producers sometimes change their labels; it can also happen that the same wine is sold under different labels. The reader should bear this in mind when looking for a wine mentioned in this book.

Foreword

Regular visitors to the wine regions of France soon become aware that, contrary to British folk-lore, we are not the only, nor even the most active, northern investigators of these Elysian fields. Holland and Belgium, small though they are in man-power, are rich, critical and even fanatical followers of French wine at every level.

For several years now I have been bumping into a young Dutch writer whose reception by the (often hard-boiled) French producers has impressed me. They like him. They open their bottles, estate records, and even their homes to him. I think it is his cool candour they admire: not always the easiest attitude when tasting the grower's pride under his gaze.

Hubrecht Duijker, this cool young man, has spent the greater part of the last decade in France, methodically tasting, interviewing and photographing to make the most complete album of France and its better wine growers that anyone has yet produced. The first volumes, on Bordeaux, were rapturously received by the Bordeaux growers — not the easiest fraternity to please. The two later volumes, on Burgundy, and on the trio of Alsace, Champagne and the Loire, have had the same reception. Translated into French they have sold like buns.

Hubrecht was kind enough to tell me, when we first met five years ago in Amsterdam, that my World Atlas of Wine was his first inspiration. I am very happy, having read and profited by his books, to have sparked something so thorough, so graphic, and so enjoyable. Duijker's books are the perfect armchair journey through my favourite French provinces: the ideal appetizer to their incomparable wines.

Hugh Johnson
London

Introduction

After writing my books on Bordeaux and Burgundy I could not resist the temptation to embark on a similarly detailed account of other French wine regions. For years I have been in love with two northern French regions and their wines, Champagne and Alsace. I visited the former on my first wine journey, the latter not long afterwards. Since then I have tried to travel around both regions at least once a year. Later I discovered the Loire valley, fascinating for its wealth of wines as well as its splendid châteaux. The Loire, Alsace and Champagne are all described in this book. What they have in common is their situation, in the northern half of France, and the fact that they produce mainly white wines (although, of course, the Loire also makes a great deal of rosé and red). In almost all other respects these regions vary greatly, and for that reason each is treated differently here. The description of the Loire is centred on its districts and *appellations*; Alsace is dealt with village by village; and in the Champagne the accent is on the shippers. In fact, *The Wines of the Loire, Alsace and Champagne* is three books in one.

Although I had already journeyed around these areas many times, I visited them again especially for this work. My travels lasted for about three months, during which time, usually for six days a week, and from early morning to dusk, I was out visiting hundreds of wine producers — growers, cooperatives and shippers. Not only did I gather invaluable information from them, but I was also able to taste all their best and most representative wines. At home, too, dozens of Dutch importers kindly allowed me to taste their Loire and Alsace wines, and their champagnes. From some two to three thousand wines that I tasted I have selected the most interesting, and these the reader will find, complete with label and description, set out above the relevant chapters. My choice is, of course, strictly personal, and not intended to be comprehensive. Nevertheless, I am confident that it will point the reader to at least some of the best wines of each region.

In perusing this book and its illustrations the reader will become ever more aware — as I have done — of the extent to which wine is interwoven with cultural forms of all kinds, with history, traditions, gastronomy, the landscape, soil and climate — and with people. I have the most pleasant recollections of the many people I met during my travels. There is truth in Théophile Gautier's words: 'Wine makes sudden friendship blossom.'

In writing this book, I approached many individuals and institutions; in nearly all instances cooperation was immediately forthcoming. Regrettably, it is impossible to name them all, but a few must be singled out for special mention. I owe a great debt of gratitude to two fellow countrymen, Kees Veenenbos and Alex Wilbrenninck, who work in the wine trade in the Loire. Then there were Robin and Judith Yapp: these British wine buyers and authors introduced me to many excellent growers. In Alsace I received tremendous help from the Comité Interprofessionnel du Vin d'Alsace and its director, Pierre Bouard. And my sincere thanks are due to the Comité Interprofessionnel du Vin de Champagne for splendid assistance in that region. Finally, I would like to mention Sopexa, the French information bureau for agricultural produce, whose cooperation I have greatly appreciated.

Hubrecht Duijker
Abcoude, Netherlands

The Loire

The Loire is the longest river in France. On its 635-mile course from the Ardèche, where it rises as a clear tumbling mountain stream, down to the Atlantic, which it enters as a broad, grey-brown mass of water, it flows through 12 *départements* and a wider diversity of landscapes. Following the Loire, you encounter immense woods, countless orchards, fertile fields and a great variety of vineyards.

Besides encountering almost every facet of French agriculture along the Loire, you also become acquainted with important aspects of the nation's culture. The Loire valley is suffused with the Renaissance, that period of revival and of a new, more secular view of the world which, at the end of the 15th and the beginning of the 16th century, found such remarkable expression, especially in art and architecture: in no other river valley will you find so many châteaux. Moreover, along the Loire and its tributaries (the Cher, Indre, Loir, Sarthe, Mayenne and many others) lie a number of towns intimately associated with French history — Angers, Saumur, Tours, Blois, Beaugency, Orléans, Gien. Most have town centres full of atmosphere, sometimes still medieval.

Flowers and fruit

The valley of the Loire is at its most beautiful in May and June, when the sky is

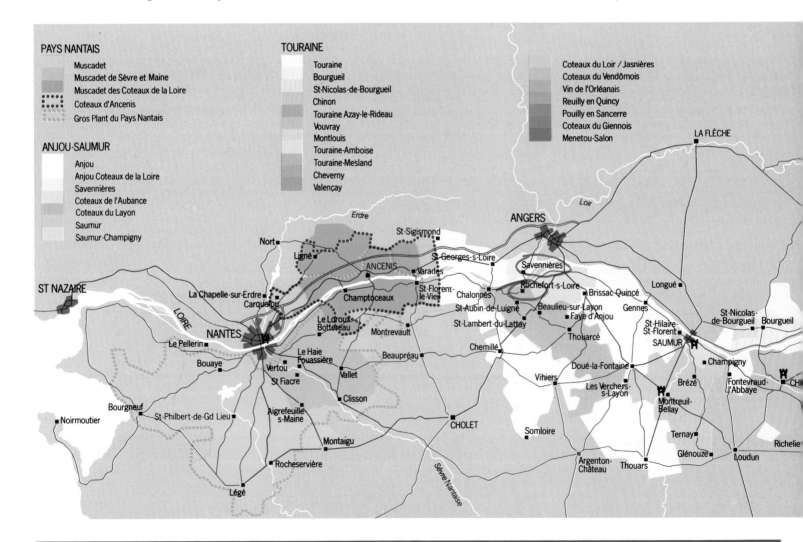

Opposite page, above:
The Loire in the soft glow of
dusk. This photo was taken near
Ancenis.

Below:
Map of the Loire valley showing
the most important wine
districts. All are discussed in the
following chapters, working
upstream from Muscadet.

As in many other wine districts,
it was the monks who actually
developed viticulture in the
Loire.

Because the sea winds blow
deep inland through the river
valleys, many sailing ships used
to navigate the Loire, and many
windmills stood on its banks.

The Loire was formerly
connected with the Seine, and
thus Paris.

Some of the ancient produce of
the Loire valley, saffron,
coriander, liquorice, anise, silk,
flax and mulberries — has
largely or wholly disappeared.

One of the shortest Loire
tributaries is the Maine, at
Angers. Less than 6 miles long,
the Maine receives the waters of
the Loire, Sarthe and Mayenne.
The Angers Maine should not be
confused with that of the
Muscadet district of Maine et
Sèvre.

The Loire valley has about
105,000 acres of denominated
vineyards (appellation contrôlée
and VDQS) that give an average
of 18,350,000 cases a year. About
twice as much vin de table is
produced in the region, but this
quantity seems to be decreasing.

The Loire

clear and the flowers are out. In June, for
example, there are no fewer than 250,000
rose bushes in bloom in the Parc de la Source
in Olivet, near Orléans. Elsewhere in the
valley you see tulips, irises, geraniums, lilies,
azaleas, rhododendrons, dahlias, camellias
and hortensia; and the fruit trees are also
then in blossom. The Loire region is not only
the home of the famous Reine Claude apple,
named after the wife of Francis I, but it also
produces many pears — including the rather
tart quince — cherries and plums. The region
likewise grows melons, peaches, currants,
raspberries, strawberries, nuts and large
quantities of mushrooms. All this is possible
because of a mild climate. The soft sea air is
blown deep inland, about as far as Orléans,
along the valleys of the Loire and its
tributaries. In addition to spring, autumn is
a good time to visit the Loire. The leaves of
the trees and vines are tinted gold and the air
takes on a warm haze.

The châteaux

It has been said that the Loire is a queen and
has been loved by kings. French monarchs,
keen huntsmen all, were deeply attracted by
the extensive forests of the Loire valley; so
here they built their fine châteaux. The great
period of château building began after the
English had finally been driven from the
Loire and from France (Joan of Arc having
pointed the way in 1429 with her victory at

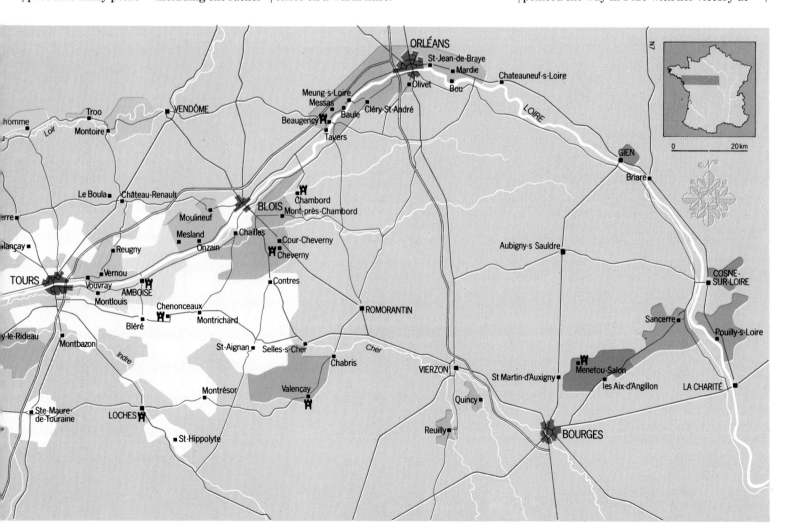

Orléans). The king at that time was Charles VII. He was followed in 1461 by Louis XI, builder of the château of Langeais. In 1483 Charles VIII came to the throne. He started work on the imposing château of Amboise. This monarch met a tragic end in 1498 when he hit his head against an archway, dying the same day. Louis XII, who succeeded him, was largely responsible for the splendid château of Blois. The French Renaissance reached its zenith under Francis I, who reigned from 1515 to 1547. He built Chambord, the most massive of the Loire châteaux, with 440 rooms.

Architectural styles

Other châteaux built entirely or mainly during the Renaissance are those of Azay-le-Rideau, very pure in its style; Châteaudun, with some 12th-century parts; Chaumont, high above the Loire near Amboise; Chenonceau, built over the Cher and given by Henry II in 1547 to his mistress Diane de Poitiers, 20 years older than himself; Ussé, which acquired its present form in the 17th century; and Villandry, world-famous for its beautiful gardens. The Classical style is found in châteaux dating from the 17th and 18th centuries, such as Cheverny and Valençay. In both the Renaissance and the succeeding Classical period, a château served purely peaceful purposes as a country residence. A medieval castle, however, was primarily a fortress and its architecture was therefore sober, even grim. Examples are Angers, Chinon, Loches, Montreuil-Bellay and Sully.

A trade route

The Loire region has of course been more than a mere playground for French monarchs and nobility. As elsewhere in France, the common man had to work hard for his daily bread; or, as the writer Michelet put it: 'The Loire valley is a monk's habit with a golden fringe.' Today the Loire is barely navigable, whereas formerly it was France's most important waterway. Vast

quantities of goods and produce were carried in flat-bottomed boats from central and southern France to Orléans and thence to Paris. Included among such commodities was wine.

In 1820, for example, the books of a wine merchant in Saint-Thibault, near Sancerre, recorded that he had shipped 4,340 *pièces* (some 190,300 gallons) of wine, valued at 4,340,000 gold francs, to a single customer. This quantity represents one-seventh to one-sixth of the total production of Sancerre today. The heavy traffic on the Loire is clearly demonstrated by another statistic: in the year 1834, a total of 19,177 craft were counted on the stretch south of Orléans alone, an average rate of about 50 a day. Nowadays, industry complements the incomes derived from arable and stock farming in the Loire valley, and the contrast between gracious châteaux and modern installations can be quite staggering. A striking instance of this occurs if you follow the right bank of the river upstream to Saumur; here, on the opposite bank, you will see a magnificent castle dating from the 14th, 15th and 16th centuries, then shortly afterwards the futuristic outlines of the country's first nuclear reactor.

La Loire gastronomique

In writing this book I have made several journeys along the course of the Loire, covering hundreds of miles. In doing so I have gained a good idea of what the region has to offer in the culinary sphere. My memories of the valley, therefore, are not confined to its châteaux, towns and villages, but include the aroma and taste of countless dishes. I have dined very simply on special smoked mussels at an alfresco meal served by Louis Métaireau; and I discovered an anonymous restaurant next door to the butcher in Beaulieu-sur-Layon, where about 60 people tucked into a nourishing menu of *crudités*, chicken, cheese and fruit. I have visited restaurants emblazoned with Michelin stars: and at the *Auberge des Templiers*, Les Bézards, I ate splendidly

mellow smoked Loire salmon, a fish that was also served at the *Barrier* in Tours. I have feasted on eels, usually grilled, and pike, with *beurre blanc* sauce, which is very characteristic of the region. This is made from butter, shallots and vinegar or dry white wine. Other specialities of the Loire are the many kinds of goat's milk cheese; asparagus, especially in Touraine; *rillettes*, usually thin strips of pork slowly cooked right through in its own juices, then served with the fat poured over it; *rillons*, cubes of pork prepared and served in the same way

The Loire

except that the meat is fried up again (both these recipes come from Tours); and *rillauds* or *rillots*, from Anjou, similar to *rillettes*, but with added caramel, the meat being served hot rather than cold.

Many varieties of grape

My memories of wine are, nevertheless, even more vivid than my gastronomic impressions. The Loire valley produces an incredible number of different wines from a plentiful variety of grapes. The reason why it possesses such a rich and subtle range is because varieties have been brought here from almost every corner of France. The most important grape varieties, beginning with the white, are:

Chenin Blanc or *Pineau de la Loire*. The most characteristic of all Loire grapes and native to the region. Gives very diverse wines, from chalk-dry to luxuriantly sweet.

Sauvignon. Probably imported from the southwest. Produces fresh-tasting wines, often with a marked bouquet in which asparagus, fennel, grass, fruit and flowers can be discerned, as well as a slight aroma of musk.

Chardonnay or *Auvernat Blanc*. A noble grape from Burgundy that gives gentle, expansive wines.

Pinot Gris, Malvoisie, Pinot Beurot or *Tokay d'Alsace*. A less productive variety that makes generally robust, supple wines, from dry to semi-sweet.

Pineau Menu, Menu Pineau or *Arbois*. Related to the Chenin Blanc, of slightly lesser quality, but more resistant to bad weather.

Muscadet or *Melon de Bourgogne*. A hardy, frost-resistant grape, related to the Gamay Noir à Jus Blanc of Beaujolais. The basis of all Muscadets.

Gros Plant, Folle Blanche or *Picpoul*. Productive, simple variety that in Armagnac and elsewhere provides a thin wine for distilling.

Romorantin. Planted only in Touraine, but originally from Burgundy. Important in Cheverny.

The following black varieties are encountered in the Loire:

Gamay Noir à Jus Blanc. Of Beaujolais origin; common in the Loire valley.

Cabernet Franc or *Breton*. A grape imported from Bordeaux, milder, more congenial, less distinguished than Cabernet Sauvignon.

Cabernet Sauvignon. Produces harder, more astringent wines than Cabernet Franc and is much less common along the Loire. A classic Bordeaux grape.

Malbec or *Cot*. Usually ripens earlier than the Cabernets. Richly coloured wines with a lot of tannin. Much planted in the Cahors district.

Pinot Noir or *Auvernat Rouge*. All the great red Burgundies are made from this. Not always a success in the Loire.

Pinot Meunier, Meunier or *Gris Meunier*. Fairly productive, rather rustic grape from Champagne. Along the Loire it is especially prevalent around Orléans.

Groslot or *Grolleau*. An original native Loire grape from around the Langeais district. The basis of Rosé d'Anjou and other rosés.

Pineau d'Aunis or *Chenin Noir*. Aunis is a village in the neighbourhood of Saumur. This grape makes mostly fresh, dry rosés, with an occasional red wine.

Opposite page, above left:
The very classic Loire
combination of pike with a
beurre blanc, as served at
numerous restaurants in the
region.

Opposite page, above right:
Salmon are caught in the Loire.
A portion of delicious smoked
salmon at the excellent Auberge
des Templiers restaurant, Les
Bézards.

Below:
With Angers, Azay-le-Rideau,
Blois, Chenonceau and Loches,
the château of Chambord is
among the most beautiful in the
Loire valley. Building began in
1519 under Francis I. It took so
long and cost so much that the
king was often forced to raise
money in unlawful ways, such as
by plundering churches. After
Francis I, Henry II continued
the work. Chambord is the
biggest of all the Loire châteaux,
with 440 rooms and 365
chimneys. Around the château
is an extensive park with over
11,000 acres of woods where
Francis I used to hunt with his
hundreds of hounds and 300
falcons. A 20-mile wall, the
longest in France, was built
around the park. The château is
virtually without furniture.

Left:
The château of Montreuil-
Bellay, situated above the
village of the same name, dates
mainly from the 14th century. In
the grounds are a Gothic church
(one of the three belonging to the
village), remains of old
fortifications, a small park and a
well 990 feet deep. The château
produces its own wine: its label
and a description are included in
the Saumur chapter, page 32.

Other châteaux well worth
visiting are Amboise,
Beaugency, Chaumont,
Cheverny, Chinon, Langeais,
Saumur, Ussé, Valençay,
Vendôme and Villandry.

The Loire

An astonishing range of wines

These grapes, and a few other less commonly
grown varieties, produce an amazing
diversity of wines along the banks of the
Loire and its tributaries, on many different
types of soil and in various climatic
conditions. There are still, *pétillant* or
sparkling wines; white, red or rosé; dry, semi-
sweet or very sweet. You will get to know
them in detail in the ensuing chapters,
following the Loire upstream from its
estuary. All *appellations contrôlées* of any
importance are described, and also numbers
of wines of the VDQS category (*vin délimité
de qualité supérieure*). My criterion in the
choice of districts and wines has been that
they can reasonably be regarded as lying
within the valley of the Loire: for example,
Jasnières, Coteaux du Vendômois, Valençay
and Côtes du Forez are included, but Haut-
Poitou, Saint-Pourçain-sur-Sioule and Côtes
d'Auvergne are not.

I am sure that the text and illustrations of
this book will enable the reader to make
stimulating discoveries, later reinforced, it
is to be hoped, by a personal expedition,
glass in hand, to the Loire. I would also like
to think that the following pages may dispel
some of those persistent misunderstandings
about the region: that Anjou produces only
cheap rosés; or the much-publicized idea that
the wines of Savennières are semi-sweet in
taste; or that the best Reuilly wine is the
white, not the rosé; and that red Bourgueil
has to be drunk young. *Bon voyage!*

Below left:
Château la Noë at Vallet. It is occupied by its owner, Count Jean de Malestroit, who has written novels, and a book about Nantes. Around the château — one of the few in Muscadet — are 148 acres of vineyards, of which 30 acres are cultivated by the count.

Below right:
Louis Métaireau (with spectacles) receives a situation report during the grape harvest.

Opposite page, below left:
Picking the Muscadet grape.

Opposite page, below right:
Near Saint-Hilaire; the landscape of Muscadet, where some 9,000 wine growers cultivate about 23,000 acres. Wine firms control approximately one-third of production through contracts and ownership of vineyards.

The village of Vallet has a Maison du Muscadet where wines from local growers can be tasted and bought. The village is about to lose some 250 acres to a new motorway, out of a total 2,500 acres of vineyards.

Like Bordeaux, the Muscadet uses a 50-gallon wooden barrel, the barrique.

The Sur Lie legislation of 1977 stipulates that the wine must spend only one winter in the cuve or vat, that at bottling it should still be on the lie remaining from vinification, and that it should be bottled before 1 July. An analysis is also required.

An example of good Muscadet without further definition: the wine from the Domaine des Herbauges. Wine grower Luc Choblet cultivates about 50 acres. Bottled sur lie, this Muscadet does not possess great breeding or richness, but has a pleasant, quite lively, fresh taste.
A rather better wine is made by Armund Guérin and his son Daniel of the Domaine de la Forchetière at Courcoué-sur-Logne: a gentle, fragrant, sound, very congenial Muscadet from about 17 acres.

Jacques Guindon and his son Pierre grow Muscadet des Coteaux de la Loire on some 34 acres in Saint-Géréon near Ancenis, on the right bank of the Loire. Their wine is bottled sur lie, and is at the top of its appellation. I particularly like its taste. At its best it is full, almost juicy, and fruity. The bouquet, however, is generally not quite so good. Another good Muscadet des Coteaux de la Loire is Domaine des Joutières from Aubert Frères.

My favourite Muscadets are from Louis Métaireau. They leave all others behind for breeding, purity and absolute class. They are made by nine independent growers who cultivate a total of 180 acres. Together they select the best wines from all nine (usually 300,000 from 600,000 bottles). From these there is a further selection of the best Muscadet, especially for restaurateurs, and it is given an ornate label and the title Coupe 'Louis Métaireau'. Full-bodied, lightly sparkling, excellent.

In 1972 Louis Métaireau and seven of his nine growers bought the Grand Mouton estate in Saint-Fiacre. This contains many old vines, some in rows more than half a mile long, and covers 67 acres. Thanks to its excellent situation, the first grapes of Sèvre et Maine are often picked here. The wine is excellent, almost delicate in bouquet, elegant and lightly sparkling, perfect in its balance. Less full-bodied than the Coupe 'Louis Métaireau'.

Muscadet

The district of origin of Muscadet is *le pays nantais,* the area around Nantes. Most of the vineyards lie southeast of the town, but vines also flourish to the south and southwest, and to the east and northeast. The Loire virtually ends its long river course at Nantes: from here it is only another 30 miles down to the Atlantic.

The vine has been cultivated here since Roman times. Until the 17th century mainly black grapes were planted. From 1639 these began gradually to be replaced by white varieties — at the insistence of the Dutch. They were looking for a light white wine suitable for distilling. Hitherto they had imported a wine of this type from the Charente, but the duty there had become too high. The duchy of Brittany, to which Nantes and its environs belonged, was still independent and levied no taxes on the export of wine. Before the arrival of the Dutch, the wines of Nantes had been poor, and none were exported. This situation changed dramatically under Dutch influence. In 1664 a Nantes merchant noted: 'The Dutchmen have introduced a certain custom, whereby the wines are bottled, transferred, sulphurized and reinforced, by which means they are better preserved in transport and can be sold in the northern countries.'

A destructive winter

The Dutch were so successful with their methods that later a king of France had to prohibit any more arable land being given over to wine-growing. There are still many names of Dutch origin in Nantes and the surrounding district, and the Château de Goulaine, now a historic monument, once even had a Dutch owner.

The change from red to white wine did not really get under way until the unimaginably severe winter of 1709, which destroyed all the vines and even froze sea water. In the following 30 years practically the whole wine-growing area was replanted with white grape varieties. One of these — already present in the district for half a century — was to predominate. It came from Burgundy and was originally called the Melon de Bourgogne; in Nantes it was dubbed the Muscadet. Experts from Burgundy helped with the planting — there is a hamlet called Bourguignon in the Vallet district.

The Muscadet is a very frost-resistant variety that usually ripens before October. Because it ripens quickly it has to be harvested in a short time — within a week or two. The Muscadet is closely related to the Gamay à Jus Blanc from which all red Beaujolais is made.

Growing popularity

Until the beginning of this century Muscadet was drunk mainly in its own district, particularly in the numerous cafés

Robert, 11th Marquis of Goulaine, owns the splendid Château de Goulaine in Sèvre et Maine, a listed monument. He has almost 100 acres of vineyards producing approximately 150,000 bottles of Sur Lie. Muscadet Marquis de Goulaine is a stylish, refined wine of good quality. A superior version — deeper, more rounded, — is La Cuvée du Millénaire, which carries a black label. Only 10,000 to 15,000 bottles become available annually.

Jean Dabin and his son François cultivate 62 acres mainly in Saint-Fiacre. Their best vineyard is the Domaine de Gras-Moutons, 20 steep acres. The wine ferments in large barrels of oak reinforced with stainless steel, which Dabin, originally a cooper by trade, designed and made himself. The Gras-Moutons is a subtle Muscadet, full of character with a fine aftertaste. It can mature for a year. Exactly the same wine is sold with a black label at a higher price.

Joseph Hallereau lives near Vallet and has bottled his wine sur lie since 1947: he terms himself the 'inventor' of the process. His vineyard, of almost 50 acres, is two-thirds planted with Muscadet. The quality of the wine can vary as each importer makes his own selection from the available vats. The best Muscadet from Hallereau has an elegant taste, is full and rounded in the mouth and has a good aftertaste; but, as mentioned, lesser qualities also occur.

Château la Noë lies in the middle of a large park near Vallet, and is occupied by its novelist owner Count Jean de Malestroit. The 148-acre vineyard of this imposing château is mostly 'share-cropped' by about 20 wine growers. The count cultivates 30 acres himself and receives the grapes from a further 35. The wine is outstanding and aromatic, at least for a Muscadet; rather old-fashioned, but, in my opinion, good.

The house of Chéreau-Carré is the exclusive distributor of wines from six estates belonging to the Chéreau and Carré families, 272 acres in all. These are wines that mature remarkably well, usually three to five years. I find the best wines are those from the Domaine de Chasseloir (62 acres, including 10 acres planted with old vines of the rare Comte Leloup de Chasseloir variety), Domaine du Bois Bruley (42 acres) and Grand Fief de Cormeraie (12 acres). None of the wines are filtered.

Michel Chiron and his son Philippe together work 45 acres a few miles from Mouzillon. Their Muscadet from the Clos des Roches Gaudinières is made exclusively from the juice of the first pressing. It is an extraordinarily balanced wine, sometimes with an almost sultry bouquet of spices and a full, pure taste — not too acid, but with abundant freshness. Chiron entertains his guests in a convivial vault where furnishings include an old winepress, an oven and a piano.

Muscadet

of Nantes. In about 1920 a group of wine growers from Saint-Fiacre tried to obtain an *appellation d'origine*. They did not succeed in having their Coteaux de Saint-Fiacre registered, but in 1926 the name Muscadet Grand Cru de Sèvre et Maine was established. Ten years later the district received its first official *appellations contrôlées*: Muscadet de Sèvre et Maine and Muscadet des Coteaux de la Loire. Muscadet, without further definition, was to follow a year later. In the meantime its market expanded beyond its own region: Paris had discovered Muscadet. Since World War II, international tourism and the attractions of the Brittany beaches have contributed greatly to the increasing popularity of Muscadet. Reasonable prices and the growing interest in dry, light white wines have helped as well.

From being a *petit vin* for the townsfolk of Nantes, Muscadet has developed into one of the most popular wines of France, and abroad too it has gained in selling power and respect. Nowadays an average Muscadet vintage amounts to not less than 3,800,000 cases.

Muscadet de Sèvre et Maine

About 85% of the 23,230 acres of Muscadet vineyard is in the Sèvre et Maine district immediately southeast of Nantes. As already mentioned, this district has its own *appellation contrôlée*. It takes its name from the little rivers Sèvre and Maine. Originally the vineyards lay on the valley slopes, but because of the increasing demand for Muscadet, the district has expanded steadily. Now almost 19,800 acres are planted with the Muscadet grape and further growth, to close on 25,000 acres, is expected in the future, both through new planting and by the replacement of the simpler Gros Plant grape (see page 16) by the Muscadet. Because Sèvre et Maine is a large district, the wines display considerable variation. In general, the best come from Vallet and Saint-Fiacre. There is intense rivalry between these two as to which is superior. Vallet (the 't' is pronounced) is called the 'Mecca of Muscadet' by its inhabitants. The soil here is clayey, producing robust wines, initially rather acid. They need more time than other wines to develop; or, as they say locally, 'they need to have seen Easter'. In dry, difficult years, Vallet often produces Muscadet's best wine. Wines resembling · that of Vallet come from Mouzillon, Le Pallet and Chappelle-Heulin. The terrain at Saint-Fiacre is hillier than Vallet, the soil sandier. The result is a suppler wine, but one of excellent quality.

A striking incidental feature of Saint-Fiacre is its Byzantine church, the legacy of a mayor who was fascinated by the Near East.

Guibaud Frères of Mouzillon is a small, agreeable firm that owns or has exclusive contracts with 330 acres of vineyards. Its best-known wine is its own brand Muscadet, Le Soleil Nantais, lively, first-class in taste, elegant in bouquet. The estate wines too have class, particularly those from the Domaine de la Moutonnière (10 acres), belonging to manager-owner Marcel Guilbaud; the Domaine de la Pinfossière (30 acres, a rather more substantial wine); and the Domaine des Laudières (30 acres). Pierre Bellevigne is a subsidiary brand.

The Château de la Cantrie lies in the hamlet of La Cantrie, near Saint-Fiacre. With its 27-acre vineyard, it belongs to the Bossis family. It produces a very good Muscadet Sur Lie, often with a dash of green in the colour and a hint of fruit in the bouquet. The wine usually has a fresh, pure, not too acid or astringent taste, again with a discreet suggestion of fruit and of salt.

André Vinet is a firm that itself owns 25 acres of vineyard, with the monopoly of the crop from a further 136 acres. The best-known estate is the Château la Touche (62 acres) where organic methods are practised (no artificial fertilizer, etc.). The wine enjoys a considerable reputation, but I was not too keen on it: the three years I tasted seemed rather flat and not very lively. Of its sort I prefer Vinet's brand Muscadet Petit Tonneau — vital, fresh and clean in both bouquet and taste.

Château du Cléray — 64 acres Muscadet, 10 acres Gros Plant — belongs to the Sauvion family, wine growers and merchants. An outstandingly lively, elegant, absolutely pure Muscadet is produced here. The Sauvions also carry good wines from a number of exclusive arrangements. Those that most attracted me were the Muscadets from the Château de la Fécumière (17 acres) and the Domaine du Bois-Curé (25 acres). So far as is known, Château du Cléray was the first Muscadet to be shipped to the People's Republic of China.

The Domaine de la Débaudière (22 acres) in Vallet is one of the properties of the firm of Aubert Frères (itself owned by Eschenauer of Bordeaux). It makes a good Muscadet Sur Lie, usually mild of bouquet and quite supple and full of taste. It is not the most refreshing Muscadet, but nonetheless pleasant. This wine house with its craftsmanlike working methods owns a total of 120 acres of vineyards, including some in Anjou. The firm is established in La Varenne, a village on the boundary of the Muscadet des Coteaux de la Loire and Anjou appellations.

In 1975 Anthony de Bascher was killed in a car accident. Since then his 74-acre wine estate of Château la Berrière has been run with great energy by his widow. It lies on the eastern boundary of Sèvre et Maine, in La Chapelle Basse-Mer. La Berrière's Muscadet Sur Lie is not so racé as wines from Vallet and Saint-Fiacre, but possesses a charming personality and a fairly fruity pure taste.

Muscadet

The other districts

As the name suggests, Muscadet des Coteaux de la Loire is situated around the banks of the Loire. The vineyards are on both banks, east of Nantes. Whereas sand, clay and gravel occur in Sèvre et Maine, the soil here is chalky, and the result is a more rustic type of Muscadet. Little of this wine is exported as production amounts to only 5% of that of Sèvre et Maine (a mere 990 acres compared with about 19,800 acres). Both Muscadet de Sèvre et Maine and Muscadet des Coteaux de la Loire have a maximum yield of 40 hectolitres per hectare. This rises to 50 hectolitres for the third and simplest *appellation:* Muscadet. In general this is a rather flat, not very distinguished wine, produced mainly to the south and southwest of Nantes on 1,980 acres of vineyards.

Mild climate

Most Muscadet, and the best, is made in Sèvre et Maine. This, therefore, is the district where I have spent the greater part of my time. It is quite a hilly area, dominated by the vine. In Saint-Fiacre, for example, a larger percentage of land is planted with vines than in any other community in France. The roads here are narrow and winding, the villages small, the churches often massive. There is a lack of good signposting and on many occasions I have lost myself looking for a particular person or estate. Often I have had to ask four or five times to find an individual grower.
The climate is exceptionally mild, so that in parks and gardens you can see magnolias, fig trees, laurels, cedars and sometimes even Mediterranean pines. Viticulture here is primarily a family affair: most holdings (90%) are of less than 5 acres and are therefore worked by the owner and his family. You need 25 acres to be able to live from wine-growing alone; sometimes it is a spare-time activity, alongside a job in the town or village. Families usually cultivate the Gros Plant or Folle Blanche as well (see page 16), or crops other than grapes. The

people have an individualistic attitude to life. Although the land is cut up into small estates, there is no cooperative, as might be expected, in Muscadet Sèvre et Maine, and contract cropping is also rare.

Maximum alcohol content

Muscadet is derived from *musqué*. In fact, a slightly musky aroma is discernible in some Muscadets. For me, however, the true personality of Muscadet is reflected in the clear, beautiful skies in this part of France, washed clean almost continually by a soft, sometimes faintly salt sea breeze. Muscadet is a light, refreshing wine, one of which a grower once said, 'C'est la gaieté'. It is synonymous with uncomplicated pleasure. French legislators have rightly stipulated a *maximum* alcohol content for Muscadet, something that applies to no other wine. It is 12.3°; Muscadet may be no stronger.
In colour a good Muscadet should be very pale, nearly transparent. The bouquet is seldom pronounced, and, according to some, vaguely suggests wild roses. The taste of a good Muscadet will fill the mouth, although it does not have much weight. The character of that taste is dry, but not tart, meagre or immature. Louis Métaireau describes it thus: 'A good Muscadet should be dry but not green.' Finally, Muscadet leaves an extraordinarily fresh, clean impression in the

mouth — sometimes with a very faint hint of vanilla. Never an absolutely great wine, Muscadet nevertheless has considerable merits — especially, for example, as an accompaniment to seafood.

The freshness of Sur Lie

Sur Lie is a special kind of Muscadet, the product of a tradition. The wine growers used to put their best Muscadet aside and the cold of winter was sufficient to make the wine clear. During this season the wine remained in contact with the *lie*, the sediment produced during fermentation. On Easter Monday a little of the wine was drawn off from the cask for tasting. It would

The Domaine de la Tourmaline, of about 74 acres, is in Saint-Fiacre. It is owned and worked by the Gadais brothers, whose wives help in the office. The wine, a Sur Lie, generally needs nine or ten months to develop. After that its taste and bouquet are wonderful. Some fruit in the bouquet, a straightforward taste and a suggestion of terroir in the aftertaste.

During a professional blind tasting, the Muscadet Sur Lie of Marcel-Joseph Guihoux was a surprising discovery, even for the wine importers present. It is a fairly full, gentle Muscadet, not as racé as those of Louis Métaireau, but nevertheless of outstanding quality. It has an attractive, pure bouquet and a beautiful, slightly earthy aftertaste. Guihoux lives in Mouzillon and owns a 62-acre vineyard.

Time and again at various wine tastings I have observed that the Muscadet de Sèvre et Maine Les Mesnils proves amazingly good, better even than many estate wines, although it is only a Muscadet brand — a credit to the maker, the firm of Barré Frères at Gorges. The wine is distinguished by its very pale colour and the almost succulent presence of fruit in the taste. It is supple, fresh and quite full. It makes no claims to grandeur, but is pleasant to drink.

In the Sèvre et Maine district the brothers Bernard, Michel and François Couillaud work 62 acres of adjoining vineyards around Château de la Ragotière near Vallet. Their Muscadet Sur Lie usually has a pleasant, fresh taste with some fruit and a good balance. Not one of the very top wines, but much above the average. The wine produced by their father, owner of Clos des Bourguignons, is simpler, less full-bodied, with more acid.

Other good Muscadet wines
Clos des Bois Gautier by Germain Luneau (Vallet); Clos de Beauregard and Château de Villarnoult by Antoine Guilbaud (Mouzillon); Domaine du Breil-Landon (also Domaine de Louveterie) by Joseph Landron (La Haie-Fouassière); Domaine des Montys, by Bernard Petiteau (Vallet); Château de la Bidière by Count de Camiran (Maisdon-sur-Sèvre, variable quality); Domaine de la Mainerie, a sandy vineyard rented from Château la Noë (Vallet); Domaine de Poissonais by Joseph Bahuaud (Le Pallet); Château de l'Oiselinière in Gorges.

Saint-Fiacre has the most expensive wine-growing land in the district.

Opposite page, below: Muscadet has its own wine fraternity, the Chevaliers Bretvins, the fourth oldest in France. The name refers to the Duchess Anne of Brittany, known as La Petite Brette. In the centre of the photo, with glass in hand, is Robert, 11th Marquis of Goulaine. The chapitres of the fraternity are held at his château.

Below: Château de Goulaine, declared a historic monument in 1913, is in Haute-Goulaine. When a new doctor arrived at the village he asked Robert de Goulaine when he could take a holiday. 'During the harvest,' was the reply, 'because no one is sick then!'

Since 1979 the Muscadet district has had its own bottle, called Le Muscadet.

Muscadet

be found to retain a little naturally produced carbon dioxide, which had kept it at maximum freshness. In the 1950s this old practice began to be applied on a wider scale: the wine was bottled direct from its first vat or tank, without transfer or *soutirage*, so that the wine remained in the same *fût* or *cuve* with the lees at the bottom. In this method, too, the minute amount of carbon dioxide present kept the Muscadet completely fresh. If the wine had first been pumped into a clean vat, this would have been lost through contact with oxygen.

Loopholes in the law

In principle, Muscadet Sur Lie is completely natural, untreated wine, fresh and almost fragile: in practice, however, perhaps only one in 50 Sur Lies has actually been produced by the method just described. There are loopholes in the legislation. Muscadet does not have to be bottled by the grower himself, which, in fact, ought to be essential. Many wine houses and growers are equipped with a gadget for introducing a minute amount of carbon dioxide bubbles into their wine: the initiated say that hundreds of them have been sold in Muscadet. Furthermore, Muscadet should be, but seldom is, an unfiltered wine. One of the rare producers who never filters his Muscadet is Louis Métaireau. When bottling *sur lie* he calls in a notary to guarantee to his customers that there has been no tampering. Yet even he has to admit that it is hard to distinguish a genuine Muscadet Sur Lie from the other kind. The genuine product is probably less *pétillant*, with barely visible bubbles, more delicate of bouquet and taste, and may contain less acid. Also it usually costs more: anyone who buys a distinctly cheap Muscadet Sur Lie is probably getting an imitation — perhaps even one of dubious quality.

Like his father, Robert, Marquis de Goulaine has long devoted himself to the Gros Plant du Pays Nantais. Naturally, he himself produces a good Gros Plant. The best quality is the Cuvée du Marquisat, an uncommonly pure, fresh wine that is not too acid or harsh, and even has some fruit. Every year the marquis also makes for private use 40 bottles of Eau-de-vie de Gros Plant. This distillation matures for five years in the barrel.

The house of Chéreau-Carré distributes the Gros Plant from the Domaine du Bois-Bruley. This belongs to Bernard Chéreau and lies in the hamlet of La Ramée, near Vertou. Its Gros Plant is characteristically tart and astringent; a Sur Lie with a good balance.

For his best quality Gros Plant du Pays Nantais, the grower Joseph Hallereau uses a remarkable method of maturing. He has bought vats of ash wood, which extracts acid from the wine, but, unlike oak, adds no tannin to it. The result is a good, not-too-assertive Gros Plant du Pays Nantais.

Other good wines
Gros Plant Sur Lie by Louis Métaireau (Maisdon-sur-Sèvre); Gros Plant by Georges Mercière (La Guillaudière near Courcoué-sur-Logne); Antoine Guilbaud (Mouzillon); Domaine des Bourdennes by Jean Dabin (Saint-Fiacre); Gaston Rolandeau (Tillières); Domaine du Fief de la Touche by Guilbaud Frères (Mouzillon); Jean de Chateclerc (subsidiary brand Sauvion/Château du Cléray, Le Vallet); Domaine de la Forchetière (Courcoué-sur-Logne).

Right:
The Gros Plant or Folle Blanche. This produces the Gros Plant du Pays Nantais in about 100 communes spread over the départements of Loire-Atlantique, Vendée and Maine-et-Loire.

Gros Plant du Pays Nantais has had VDQS status since 1954.

Long ago, it is said, Gros Plant used to be shipped to Bordeaux for adding to claret.

Below:
Vallet is the capital of Muscadet Sèvre et Maine, and is also the biggest producer of Gros Plant in the département.

Bottom:
Joseph Hallereau, wine grower in the Vallet area. Apart from good Muscadet, he usually makes an excellent Gros Plant.

Gros Plant du Pays Nantais

Like the Muscadet grape, the Folle Blanche was taken to the Nantes area by the Dutch in the 17th century, and with the same objective: a dry, light wine for distilling. The grape came from Cognac, where it is still widely present, and it has also been planted in the Armagnac and the district of Picpoul de Pinet in the Languedoc. Around Nantes the Gros Plant, as it is called there, produces the *vin délimité de qualité supérieure* Gros Plant du Nantais (the quality level of a VDQS wine is slightly lower than one with an *appellation contrôlée*). Today the Muscadet dominates the Loire estuary, but

for a long time the Folle Blanche was pre-eminent. In the 19th century, for example, no less than two-thirds of the vineyard area was planted with this variety. The saying, 'The Gros Plant is my bread, the Muscadet my wine', dates from this period. The growers, indeed, earned their livelihood mainly from Gros Plant, but preferred to drink their Muscadet — which they could seldom afford to do, for those were hard times. Until well into the present century it was usual to plant one Folle Blanche to every ten Muscadets.

Postwar restoration

In 1855 the parasite *Phylloxera vastatrix* began to devastate the region. Not a single vineyard was spared. Eventually four-fifths of the total Folle Blanche planting disappeared. Not until after World War II did a few growers start some modest replanting of the variety. The initiative here was taken by the Union des Producteurs de Gros Plant, set up by the Marquis de Goulaine (father of the present marquis). Nowadays, the Gros Plant covers about 5,930 acres, giving an average annual yield of 890,000 cases (the permitted yield per hectare is 50 hectolitres). Most of the vines are on the south of the Loire, notably around the Grand-Lieu lake. In general, Gros Plant vineyards are nearer the sea than the Muscadet, and the influence of the salt is more pronounced. However, there is also a lot of Folle Blanche in the Muscadet district of Sèvre et Maine. Vallet, for example, has the biggest Folle Blanche planting in the whole Loire-Atlantique *département*.

Good with fish

Gros Plant du Pays Nantais is not an outstanding wine: or, as the grower Pierre Guindon put it, 'The Gros Plant is only Muscadet's little brother.' The large Folle Blanche grape — which sometimes resembles a small plum — gives a pale wine of generally 11° alcohol (9° is the stipulated minimum). Its characteristics are high acidity, and a slightly bitter, and at the same time earthy, taste. In bouquet, longevity and refinement, the Gros Plant is obviously inferior to the Muscadet. Because of its acid, the wine would make a good basis for a *vin mousseux*. This fact has been recognized, but no more than a hesitant start has been made with production. I find that Gros Plant does especially well as an aperitif, and as an accompaniment to shellfish, crab and lobster. As with Muscadet, the best Gros Plant is often the Sur Lie. Gros Plant comes in slender green bottles with four ridges on the neck, the so-called Véronique.

The approximately 300 members of the Cave de la Noëlle work nearly 1,235 acres and produce an extensive list of wines, including a sparkling Crémant de Loire. The quality of their wines is usually quite adequate and very simple. These qualifications also apply to the red Coteaux d'Ancenis Gamay of Les Vignerons de la Noëlle, which I have tasted. La Noëlle is the name of the part of Ancenis where the cave is situated.

Jacques Guindon and his son Pierre own a 64-acre vineyard at Saint-Géreon, where production includes a good Coteaux d'Ancenis in rosé and red. The very fresh-coloured rosé has a hint of raspberries in fragrance and taste. The quality of their red depends greatly on the year. I remember that the 1979 was ordinarily pleasant; 1978 was amazingly good — rich in colour, bouquet and taste.

In the whole Coteaux d'Ancenis there are just three people who produce a mild, if not sweet, white wine from the Malvoisie grape. One of them is Jacques Guindon, together with his son Pierre. The wine generally has a light golden colour and a definitely sweet taste that is almost juicy. It is a very unusual white wine, especially in this region of dry whites. The Malvoisie has its charm for all that, and a place as an aperitif in France, where sweet wines for this purpose are fashionable.

Other good wines
Coteaux d'Ancenis Cabernet (red) by Auguste Athimon (Le Cellier); Vin de Pays des Marches de Bretagne Gamay by Pierre Landron (La Haie-Fouassière), one of the many wine growers in Muscadet Sèvre et Maine with a congenial rosé or light red table wine; Vin de Pays de Retz (rosé) from the Grolleau grape, by Aubert Frères (La Varenne) and Domaine de la Forchetière (Courcoué-sur-Logne) — the latter also producing a good red Cabernet; Vin de Pays des Fiefs Vendéens (rosé) by Guilbaud Frères (Mouzillon) and by Etienne Boureau (Rosnay).

Below:
Vineyard in the Coteaux d'Ancenis. A yield of 40 hectolitres per hectare is permitted.

Bottom left:
Jacques Guindon, a leading producer in the Coteaux d'Ancenis. He and his son Pierre process grapes from other estates apart from their own. Jacques' grandfather came from Sèvre et Maine, started here as a hairdresser and later bought his own vineyard.

Bottom right:
A few Guindon wines. The grape variety has to be stated on the label for Coteaux d'Ancenis.

Because the town of Ancenis is growing, the boundaries of the vineyard area are receding. In the village of Saint-Géreon the vineyard area has shrunk from up to 1,240 acres to less than 200 acres.

Ancenis is a former barony of the duchy of Brittany. The town is linked with the opposite bank of the Loire by a suspension bridge 1,640 feet long.

Coteaux d'Ancenis

For centuries the little town of Ancenis (present population 7,500) has been the key to the duchy of Brittany. Its fortification commanded the river. No doubt this is why in 1468 Duke Francis II of Brittany and King Louis XI of France signed a treaty here between the two states whereby Brittany lost its independence. Only the ruins of the castle where the treaty was signed remain, including a 15th-century tower, one 16th-century building and pavilions from the 17th century. At the end of the 18th century Ancenis became noted for the export of wine. It also produced sails for inland waterway craft. Nowadays, Ancenis is particularly famous for its pig market and also possesses a gigantic food-manufacturing concern, Cana, one of the biggest in the country. The huge grey buildings stand on the eastern side of the town. In addition to dairy and meat products, wine is produced. Since 1955, a cooperative of some 300 wine growers has operated under the Cana umbrella and the name of Les Vignerons de la Noëlle.

Rosé and red

Ancenis is the capital of the *appellation* Muscadet Coteaux de la Loire, but has closer connections with the VDQS wine Coteaux d'Ancenis. This *appellation* was created in 1954 chiefly, it is said, because of a gradually developing local interest in red and rosé. Coteaux d'Ancenis is mainly pink or red in colour. The Gamay grape predominates in the approximately 530 acres of vineyard, but some Cabernet also occurs. Only a small part of the 100,000-case production is white: here and there some Pineau de la Loire (or Chenin Blanc) is cultivated, as is the Malvoisie grape (practically identical with Pinot Beurot, Pinot Gris and Tokay d'Alsace). Rosé and red Coteaux d'Ancenis are both mostly fresh, pleasant, uncomplicated wines. The quality can sometimes be amazingly good — especially from the better growers in a good year. The Pineau de la Loire is austerely dry; the Malvoisie, on the other hand, produces both dry and really sweet wines.

Vin de pays

In *le pays Nantais*, besides Muscadet, Gros Plant du Pays Nantais and Coteaux d'Ancenis, there are a few *vins de pays,* usually of a very simple quality. The Loire-Atlantique *département* produces the Vin de Pays des Marches de Bretagne and Vin de Pays de Retz.

South of the Nantes district lies the Vendée with its Vin de Pays des Fiefs Vendéens. These are mainly rosé or red wines.

The Touchais family owns 420 acres, one-third planted with Chenin Blanc. The grapes are very carefully selected; only the best are used for Moulin Touchais. The wine is fermented slowly and little sulphur is employed. After bottling, the wine is left to mature for at least ten years in the extensive Touchais vaults. Touchais white wines keep their vitality for decades and are among the noblest products of Anjou. Touchais also produces rosé and red.

Domaine de Montchenin is the brand name under which the recently established Vignerons des Moulins de Vent market their dry white Anjou. It is made in a hyper-modern winery built in 1975 and has a basis of 90% Chenin Blanc and 10% Chardonnay. It usually has a bouquet with Chardonnay and fruit evident in it, and is lively, cool and rounded of taste — excellent of its kind. Les Vignerons des Moulins de Vent are located in Passavant on the southern boundary of Anjou.

Anjou

From Ancenis it is about 30 miles to Angers, capital of the old province of Anjou. This province — an 'earthly paradise' according to Ronsard — chiefly comprises the present *département* of Maine et Loire, together with parts of Vienne and Deux Sèvres. The landscape is as welcoming as the climate. Green fields, pastures and vineyards alternate with woods, flower nurseries and cherry orchards. Anjou has about 1,900 hours of sunshine a year and an average annual temperature one degree centigrade higher than Paris. Rainfall is relatively light — 600 mm (23.24 inches) per year. Autumn is always mild. In the villages people lead an unhurried existence, taking time to enjoy life — as I certainly found during my visits. Lunches lasting all afternoon were not exceptional. I recall enjoying the hospitality of the wine grower Gérard Chauvin. The meal began with Coteaux du Layon 1970 accompanying cucumber salad with radishes, French bread and lightly salted butter. This was followed by eels grilled over vine twigs — a dish that was passed round three times. The wine was a dry white Anjou. The main course was roast entrecôte, accompanied by two kinds of red Anjou. At this point I had to leave for appointments elsewhere, but I heard later that proceedings were concluded by cheese, a dessert, various wines, coffee, Cognac — and some lively songs from Madame Chauvin.

Centuries of wine-growing

Anjou is noted for various products: roses, orchids, tapestries (there is a world-famous collection in the castle at Angers), footwear, liqueur (Cointreau), the small black *guigne* cherry, and slate. This material was formerly much used in house-building, which is why Angers is known as 'the black town'. Finally, Anjou is famed for its wines. It is believed that the grape has been cultivated here since the 3rd century AD. At all events, Charlemagne is known to have given a vineyard to the abbey of Saint-Aubin-des-Vignes in 769. There is also a reference to viticulture in a document of 845. In 1154 Henry Plantagenet, Count of Anjou, came to the English throne. This resulted in an increasing export trade in Anjou wines to London. In due course legislation was introduced to protect quality; a law of 1331 stopped the import into Anjou of wine from anywhere outside the province in order to prevent dilution.

Dutch influence

The great leap forward that came in the 16th and 17th centuries was due to the Dutch. As mentioned, they had already stimulated wine-growing in Muscadet, in order to obtain wine for distillation. In Anjou they were looking for sweet white wines for the table —

good, but not the very top quality, and would pay reasonable prices. The Dutch presence in Anjou was so influential that for generations they monopolized the entire wine trade there. It was their agents who bought up the vintage, and their ships that transported the casks. So much wine was shipped from Anjou to Holland that the burgomaster of Rotterdam declared in 1681 that the wine trade was of absolutely vital importance to his city. Because of their dominating position, the Dutch could often even prescribe the grape varieties. Naturally they had the first pick of each vintage; what remained in France was usually of the poorest quality. A great difference in quality developed between the *vins pour la mer* and *vins pour Paris.* At the end of the 17th century Anjou's wine trade, and therefore its wine-growing activities, suffered a temporary collapse when war broke out between France and Holland. Peace restored Dutch influence, but in 1789 the French Revolution once again, and finally, put an end to it.

Many appellations

Today Anjou has over 69,000 acres of vineyards producing about one-quarter of all Loire wine — an annual average of roughly 11,000,000 cases. This large quantity of wine goes under a great variety of *appellations* —

Of his beautifully situated Domaine de la Soucherie, near Beaulieu-sur-Layon and the hamlet of Chaume, Pierre-Yves Tijou has devoted 12 acres to the production of dry white Anjou. He uses 90% Chenin Blanc and 10% Sauvignon. I find this an enchanting wine, fresh, clean, first-rate in balance, wonderful as a thirst quencher and as an accompaniment to crudités or fish of many kinds.

With their dry white Anjou Chauvigné, Henri Richou and his son Didier regularly win gold medals at the Paris agricultural show, and rightly so: the wine has a bouquet suggesting small flowers and, vaguely, spices. The taste is somewhat round, gently fresh and almost juicy. The Richou's estate, in Mozé-sur-Louet, covers 74 acres, 25 of which are for white Anjou.

Domaine des Rochettes is the name of a 50-acre estate where the owner, Gérard Chauvin of Mozé-sur-Louet, makes various wines, including dry white Anjou. This does not as a rule state its year, but normally comes from the latest vintage. The wine usually has a cool white colour and a rather distinct taste: not tart, but still fresh. Without being great, it measures up to requirements. It is made only from Chenin Blanc.

The craftsmanlike house of Aubert Frères (75% owned by Eschenauer) has 120 acres of its own, part of it in La Varenne itself. Here, in good years only, a red Cabernet d'Anjou is produced from three-quarters Cabernet Sauvignon and one-quarter Cabernet Franc. The wine is matured for two years in the vat. It has a dark red colour, a rather elusive bouquet and a robust taste, full of character, with a lingering aftertaste. A rather rustic Anjou Gamay is also made.

At Château de Chamboureau in Epiré, near Savennières, Yves Soulez makes a modest quantity of red Anjou from Cabernet Sauvignon. He has planted only 3¾ acres with this variety, but plans more. It is a wine with a lot of colour, some fruit in the bouquet and a distinct, somewhat idiosyncratic taste which you either like — or not. Exported mainly to Denmark.

Opposite page, above: The vineyards around Angers are called the vignoble angevin. The Cabernet d'Anjou on the sign was first made in 1905 by the wine grower Taveau of Saumur. Subsequently, the producer Daviau-Rozé of Brissac did much for the wine.

Both pages, below, left to right: A cooper's workshop in Anjou. In the Touchais vaults. Brightly coloured plastic picking-boxes being cleaned. Jean David of the Vignerons des Moulins de Vent in front of his Château de Passavant. Joseph Touchais with a bottle of his 1900.

A new superior appellation in the region, Anjou Villages, may soon be created.

Anjou

no Loire district has as many as Anjou. There are some 25 of them, including that of Saumur, which officially belongs to Anjou. The production is roughly divided into 30% white, 15% red and 55% rosé. Most of these *appellations* will be discussed in the following sections. Here we are concerned only with the regional wines, which include Anjou (white and red), Rosé d'Anjou, Cabernet d'Anjou and Rosé de la Loire.

White Anjou

Until well into the 19th century, white wine was predominant in Anjou. The wide-scale planting of black grapes, for rosé and later red wine, dates from this century. That white wine was always sweet or semi-sweet; even up to 10 or 20 years ago, hardly any dry white wine was produced in Anjou. A gradual change is now taking place: I have tried some very attractive dry whites in the district. The law prescribes that at least 80% of Anjou Blanc must come from Chenin Blanc (or Pineau de la Loire) grapes. To this may be added 20% of Chardonnay and/or Sauvignon. The addition of these two has a purpose. They help make the usually rather astringent Chenin Blanc wine more congenial. A white Anjou from 100% Chenin Blanc is of course possible, but this produces a wine that in its youth is often very acid and needs a long time to mature; and a white

Anjou can do just that. I have tasted the most remarkable examples in the cellar of Joseph Touchais, wine grower and merchant at Doué-la-Fontaine.
Joseph, a friendly, intelligent man, told me: 'Personally I sell no wine until it is 10 years old. The 1980 we are harvesting from our own estate this year will not be offered for sale until 1990. A good white Anjou only begins to indicate its qualities after 10 years, not until 20 years does it really taste right, and after 50 years still better. After that the wine has the strength to stay in condition.' Joseph Touchais then added that his white Anjou is usually not completely dry — at least the quality he sells under the name Moulin Touchais — because the grapes come partly from the *appellation* area of the generally (semi) sweet Coteaux du Layon. Nevertheless, it was interesting to taste.

The Touchais cellar

After this explanation, Joseph's son Jean-Marie, who is fully involved in the business, was sent to fetch the 1959, 1949, 1945, 1923 and 1900 from the well-stocked cellar. Here, in abbreviated form, are my notes on this tasting:
1959. Pale golden colour, ripe bouquet, perfect taste of grape, mild and sweet in character, a hint of *pourriture noble* (see page 25) in Sauternes style. M. Touchais opened

another 1959: this wine was fresher and drier, the bouquet stronger. Both gave an amazingly young impression.
1949. Beautifully ripe bouquet and taste, with a clear element of freshness alongside the sweetness. Could certainly go on for another half-century.
1945. Yellow-gold colour, riper and more concentrated than the 1949, as well as fuller and sweeter. A nice, lingering aftertaste. Not the broad luxuriance of a Sauternes, but nevertheless a splendid wine.
1923. Made from grapes with the stalks left on and therefore somewhat hard and woody, but lively. Hint of rosé in the colour.
1900. Made by Joseph's grandfather. More luxurious, sweeter, more rounded out than the 1923. A touch of apricots in the taste. Elegant, exciting — and still robust.
By chance, that same evening friends made me taste an 1870 Touchais, the oldest wine of the house. It was deep brown, with a bouquet that included mushrooms and molasses, combining in its taste a touch of sweetness and a touch of acid, and plenty of alcohol. The wine was still incredibly vital and drinking it was an experience. And remember, there are about a million bottles of white Anjou in the Touchais cellars....

The Domaine de la Bizolière at Savennières has about 19 acres planted with Cabernet grapes (mostly Cabernet Franc). The wine has tannin, fruit and at the same time a great suppleness. I found that the taste remained pleasantly in the mouth. Alcohol content is sometimes 12.5° — probably because people in Savennières are accustomed to making white wines of this strength.

Although in the past the red wines of Domaine des Rochettes were rather harsh and bitter, since 1978 Gérard Chauvin has made a totally different type: gentle, supple, genial and very clean. I have even tasted a Chauvin Anjou Rouge in which there was absolutely no sulphur. Chauvin makes his pleasant red wines principally from Cabernet Franc with a little Cabernet Sauvignon. Wines exclusively from one of the two varieties are sometimes produced.

Jean David, one of the owners of Les Vignerons des Moulins de Vent, lives in the ancient château in the village of Passavant (200 inhabitants). The red wine is not made at the château, but bears its name. It comes from 30 acres, mostly Cabernet Sauvignon. The wine does not mature in the wood, but is bottled within the year from stainless steel tanks. A good deep colour, pure Cabernet bouquet, supple but not too smooth taste. Astonishingly good of its kind.

The Richou family has planted about 12 acres with Gamay. A good, almost Beaujolais-like wine is produced; simple, pleasant, fruity and with a hint of terroir in the aftertaste. During my visit Henri Richou told me he hoped to experiment with the macération carbonique, a fermentation system that produces supple fragrant wines that are soon drinkable. The grapes are kept as intact as possible and go into a vat that is then hermetically sealed. The grape juice ferments of its own accord.

On his estate Domaine de la Motte at Rochefort-sur-Loire, André Sorin has planted 8¾ acres with Cabernet Franc and 3¾ acres with Cabernet Sauvignon. Besides giving a fairly rich, sweet Cabernet d'Anjou rosé, this also produces an interesting red Anjou, which is most successful in exceptional years, like 1976. At its best, Sorin's red Anjou is a wine with a fair amount of tannin, perhaps with no particularly overwhelming charms, but with personality and a suggestion of raspberries and cherries.

At a comparative tasting of eight kinds of Rosé d'Anjou, that of the firm of Henri Métaireau was one of the best. The wine is usually sold under its vintage year. Striking characteristics were a very pale pink colour with a tinge of orange, a pure bouquet and a lively, fruity taste; also a good balance.

Anjou

Classical versus modern

The classical, traditionally made wines of Touchais contrast sharply with the very up-to-date wine production of, say, the Vignerons des Moulins de Vent at Passavant. This young concern uses stainless steel and produces an Anjou Sec (10% Chardonnay) that tastes best when young.

Care is thus to be recommended when selecting a white Anjou, so as not to arrive home with one that is unexpectedly sweet or dry. Besides the ordinary white Anjou, there are the little-known *appellations d'origine* Anjou Mousseux (white and rosé) and Anjou Pétillant; but I have not tasted a memorable wine from either category.

An increase in red

As with dry white Anjou, hardly any red Anjou was made until a decade or two ago. Now, however, it is advancing steadily. Production has already passed 550,000 cases a year and is still on the increase. The declining demand for rosé certainly has had something to do with this. Two types of red Anjou are distinguished: Anjou Gamay, from the Beaujolais grape Gamay Noir à Jus Blanc only, and Anjou, mainly from Cabernet Franc and/or Cabernet Sauvignon, although the Pineau d'Aunis is also permitted. My impression is that many growers in Anjou still need to learn how to make a good red wine. They have long specialized in white wine, and later in rosé. Even so, there are quite a few good red Anjous around. The best kinds have a deep red colour, a pure Cabernet bouquet (usually with the fragrance of blackcurrant or raspberry) and a taste that is not too dour or full of tannin, at its best after two to five years. In Anjou I have tasted wines that were either too light, with sometimes a hint of oxidation, or too harsh, uncongenial and immature.

The 13th/14th-century Château de Tigné in the hamlet of the same name belongs to Georges Lalanne, brother-in-law of Jacques Lalanne, owner of Château de Belle Rive in Quarts de Chaume. M. Lalanne produces a Rosé d'Anjou (usually without vintage year) from his 74 acres. The wine has more colour than most and is fairly dry, rather astringent, fresh and full-bodied. The neighbouring Château de la Roche (37 acres) also makes a good rosé.

The large firm of Ackerman-Laurance at Saint-Hilaire-Saint-Florent, on the Saumur boundary, is mainly known for its sparkling wines. However, it sells a whole range of other Loire wines, including a most pleasant Cabernet d'Anjou — better than similar wines from many other houses. No vintage is stated. I have also tasted successful Cabernets d'Anjou from Aubert Frères (La Varenne) and Château de Beaulieu (Beaulieu-sur-Layon).

Henri Verdier is involved with a big wine concern in Montreuil-Bellay but also runs his own estate, Domaine de Champteloup in Brigné-sur-Layon. An immaculately maintained vineyard of 74 acres, 54 acres of this is planted half with Cabernet Franc, half with Cabernet Sauvignon. Verdier makes a light salmon-coloured Cabernet d'Anjou from these, quite elegant, fresh, and not too sweet. Much of it goes to Belgium.

There are many wine estates where a good, refreshing Rosé de Loire is made. One is the Château de la Roche in Rablay-sur-Layon, which uses the brand name Gris Fumé.
I have also tasted the following good Rosés de Loire: Domaine de la Gachère, St Pierre-à-Camp (whose owner, Claude Lemoine, also produces a delicious white Grolleau Gris, a Vin de Pays des Deux Sèvres); Les Moulins de Vent (Vignerons des Moulins de Vent); Aubert Frères; Gérard Chauvin.

Good Rosé d'Anjou can mature over a long period: one example was an outstandingly drinkable 1947 I was given to taste three decades after its vintage by Jean Douet in Concourson-sur-Layon.

Anjou boasts more lakes than any other French province, and more miles (342) of waterway.

Anjou has various wine fraternities, including the Confrérie des Fins Gousiers d'Anjou.

Opposite page:
Quiet afternoon in an Anjou town.

Below:
The tractor has replaced the horse nearly everywhere in Anjou, except on the steep slope of Coulée de Serrant in Savennières (see also page 22).

Most Anjou wine growers make various kinds of wine: rosé, red and white. Not all can support themselves by wine-making alone, and so there are many other forms of cultivation. There were far more vineyards at the beginning of the previous century than there are now: some 72,000 compared with 28,000.

Anjou also has a simple local wine, the Vin de Pays du Maine et Loire. Mostly produced from the Gamay, it is red or rosé.

Angers lies on the Sarthe, which flows into the Maine. The local castle has 17 round towers and was built by St Louis in the 13th century. A Festival d'Anjou is held every summer, mainly in Angers; events include concerts, films and theatre performances.

Anjou

Various types of rosé

The best-known Anjou wine is undoubtedly Rosé d'Anjou, a simple semi-sweet wine, of a pink or light salmon colour. The taste has not a great deal of character, but may be pleasantly fruity. In general, Rosé d'Anjou is a relatively cheap mass product that comes mainly from big wineries. The most important grape is called the Groslot, or Grolleau; an estimated 80% to 90% of the rosé vineyards are planted with it. The law also allows the use of Cabernet Franc, Cabernet Sauvignon, Gamay, Pineau d'Aunis and Cot or Malbec.
A rosé of slightly better quality is Cabernet d'Anjou. This is made from one or both of the Cabernet grapes. The yield per hectare is lower than for Rosé d'Anjou (40 instead of 50 hl) and the minimum alcohol content is higher at 10° instead of 9°. Remarkably enough, Cabernet d'Anjou can taste either drier or sweeter than Rosé d'Anjou. I have tasted examples of both variants.
Two other Anjou rosés are Rosé d'Anjou Pétillant and Rosé de Loire. I have not yet come across the former; the latter repeatedly. Rosé de Loire is a fairly recent *appellation* that extends also to Touraine. Created in 1974, it was designed to replace Rosé d'Anjou when the demand for semi-sweet rosé changed to dry rosé. This expectation, however, has hardly been fulfilled. People who have turned away from Rosé d'Anjou have usually gone over to a dry white wine rather than a dry rosé. Production of Rosé de Loire has therefore been restricted to 10% of that of Rosé d'Anjou. Rosé makers are facing difficult times, and this is why many of them have switched to red. There is a prescribed minimum of 30% Cabernet grapes for Rosé de Loire, and use of the Groslot, Pineau d'Aunis, Gamay and Pinot Noir is permitted. I find the Rosé de Loire the most appealing of all the pink-coloured wines of Anjou: fresh, light, refreshing and still reasonable in price.

Savennières

One of the smallest wine districts of Anjou is the almost legendary Savennières. It lies just west of Angers, untidily spread over hills and outcrops where slate predominates. The vineyards are so steep in places that they can only be worked with horses. Monks planted the first vines here in the 12th century. Savennières wine later caused a sensation at the French court: and Louis XIV is said to have set out on a journey to the district. One of the wine growers, owner of Château de la Roche-aux-Moines, added a second storey especially in honour of this royal visit, and built on new wings and towers. Unfortunately, Louis never actually arrived: his carriage stuck in the mud on a hill and an extremely irritated and frustrated Sun King had to turn back. Savennières was also served at court under Napoleon, having been introduced by the Countess of Serrant, lady-in-waiting to Josephine.

Legal handicap

There is nothing to see now of Savennières' glorious past. The village of the same name — many of whose houses are built of stone from a nearby castle dismantled at the end of the 16th century — lies slumbering around its 1,000-year-old church. The wine-growing area is less than 150 acres, although nearly 900 acres is available. Production fluctuates between about 6,000 and 14,000 cases a year — a drop in the Anjou ocean. There are 15 producers of Savennières, but only three make a living exclusively from their wine.

This difficult situation is partly explained by the microclimate. Because of bad weather, the Coulée de Serrant estate produced not a drop of Savennières in 1963, 1965 and 1972; 60% of the harvest was lost through frost in 1975, and 40% and 25% respectively in 1977 and 1978. An even greater handicap, however, is the relevant French wine law. When the *appellation* was created in 1952, Savennières was usually a sweet white wine, mostly made from grapes affected by *pourriture noble,* as in the Sauternes district of Bordeaux. Based on this, a yield of only 25 hectolitres per hectare was prescribed and a minimum alcohol content of 12°. But today Savennières is mainly a dry white, so that 25 hectolitres per hectare is impossibly low, and 12° alcohol impossibly high. The permitted yield has in the meantime been raised to 30 hectolitres, but this is still far below the 40 hectolitres of all the other dry white Anjous. The 12° minimum alcohol has been maintained. To achieve this the growers must either pick only very ripe grapes, so running the risk of bad weather and a rather watery end product, or they have to chaptalize (add sugar to the grape juice).

Coulée de Serrant

Given the additional difficulty of working much of the land, it is easy to understand why wine-making in Savennières is, as they say, a job for idiots. 'Running an estate in Savennières is as expensive as keeping a *danseuse* — only more moral,' is how one grower expressed it. Fortunately, however, there are still people who produce wine, even good wine, in Savennières. The best-known property is Clos de la Coulée de Serrant, which belongs to Madame Joly and her son Nicolas. This vineyard has its own *appellation contrôlée:* Savennières Coulée de

Since 1962 the Clos de la Coulée de Serrant, several other plots, and the Château de la Roche-aux-Moines have been in the possession of the Joly family. Their Savennières Coulée de Serrant ferments in wooden vats, is racked three times, clarified, lightly filtered, and bottled in May. It is the best-known — and one of the best — Savennières. The wine should be matured for at least five years, or better still for ten or more. It will happily last for 20-30 years. The ancient vines help give the wine its class.

The Domaine de la Bizolière covers 988 acres surrounding a beautiful country house. It is owned by the Brincard family and the estate is run by Baron Marc Brincard, who also works for Crédit Lyonnais. The 44 acres of vineyards produce Savennières La Roche-aux-Moines (about 9 acres — the best, most complex wine); Savennières (15 acres — another excellent wine); and several other wines, including a good red and a good white Anjou. The Savennières are fermented in wooden vats and bottled no later than early April.

The vineyard of Château d'Epiré dates from 1640 and the estate has been in the same family since 1749. The present owner, Armand Bizard, produces wine (25 acres) — and milk. His Savennières is fermented in wooden vats in a former church. Epiré's aromatic and distinctive Savennières 1974 was chosen out of all the 1973, 1974 and 1975 vintages as the most suitable Savennières to present to the French President. The 1979 has flowers, fruit and spices. A small amount of rosé and red is also produced.

Yves Soulez has rented Château de Chamboureau from his family since 1978. It is situated in Epiré and has a 25-acre vineyard, which Yves is hoping to extend by 17 acres. Twenty-one acres produce Savennières, which ferments at a cool temperature (17° to 18° C) for up to two months. Soulez does not allow his wines to come into contact with wood, saying; 'A woody flavour does not interest me; fruit does.' The result is a well-balanced wine of character, with much flavour and a certain suppleness.

Jean Baumard owns 28 acres in Savennières, making him the largest local wine grower. He is not over-fond of the old-style Savennières — a rather woody, dour wine needing a long time to mature. Jean deliberately produces a more supple type of Savennières, often with a soft, fruit and spicy flavour and bouquet. The aftertaste testifies to a wine of great quality. Part of Baumard's production comes from the Clos du Papillon, where he owns 4 acres; a distinguished wine with its own label.

Savennières

Serrant. It comprises 17 acres, divided into parcels of 10, 5 and 2 acres. As for all Savennières, the basis is the Chenin Blanc. The estate produces a yearly average of only 18,000 bottles. They are best not opened until they are five to ten years old. Prior to that the wine is too harsh, acid and woody. According to Nicolas Joly, the wine undergoes a great change between its second and fifth year. A mature Clos de la Coulée de Serrant is an exceptional white wine. Even after 15 years it often retains a remarkable *fraîcheur*, with a robust taste and a charming aroma reminiscent of a bunch of wild flowers. There is a tinge of green in the gold-yellow colour.

La Roche-aux-Moines

This vineyard also has its own Savennières *appellation*, but is shared by a number of growers. It is typical of the district that of the 70 acres available, only 17 are cultivated, and not all of them with the Chenin Blanc. Many growers can only keep their heads above water by making 'easier' wines alongside their Savennières: dry white, rosé and red Anjou. An estate that produces a very good, concentrated Savennières La Roche-aux-Moines is the Domaine de la Bizolière (988 acres, of which 44 acres is vineyard, including about 9 acres of La Roche-aux-Moines). I detected a blend of honey, flowers and vanilla in the wine, together with the rather stringy freshness so characteristic of Savennières, such as the often outstanding Château d'Epiré (the 1976) had an aroma of geraniums) and the Château de Chamboureau, full of taste. None of these wines were particularly remarkable for their charm or suppleness for Savennières is not basically an endearing wine. However, as you get to know it, you discover more and more nuances and qualities. Someone who does make a Savennières that is soon agreeably drinkable is Jean Baumard, chairman of the local *syndicat viticole*. Even in their early youth, his 1978 and 1979 were rounded, soft, supple wines with cultivated suggestions of soft fruit and spices in aroma and taste. Savennières may be small, but the differences in its wines are considerable.

D54

4 BEAULIEU
SUR-LAYON

ROUTE DU VIN

D125

ST-AUBIN-DE-LUIGNÉ 3
CHAUDEFONDS -SUR-
LAYON 7

ROUTE DU VIN

Left:
Coteaux du Layon has had its own wine route since 1865.

Below:
French customers buy much of their wine straight from the growers in 'cubitainers'. Filling up at Domaine de la Soucherie, which also sells wine in bottles.

Opposite page:
Some talented wine growers from the Coteaux du Layon. From top to bottom: Michel Doucet of the Château de la Guimonière; Pierre-Yves Tijou of Domaine de la Soucherie; Jean Baumard, who also produces excllent wines in Savennières and Quarts de Chaume; and André Sorin of the Domaine de la Motte.

Coteaux du Layon

Loire

The little Layon river rises in the lakes of Beaurepaire in the Deux Sèvres *département* and winds its way northwest for about 44 miles to join the Loire. A first view of this insignificant stream hardly suggests that through the ages it has carved out the often wide and sometimes impressive Layon valley. The northern slope of this valley rises regularly more than 300 feet above the river, with similar heights at intervals on the southern side. Wine-growing is practised almost the whole length of the Layon, and has been for centuries. Layon wine is mentioned in a manuscript of the 4th century A.D. It is small wonder that the Layon valley should have been planted with vines: most other types of cultivation on its one-in-four slopes would be impossible.

Taste for sweet wine

Dutch influence was considerable around the Layon. They were looking for the sweetest possible white wines from the ripest possible grapes — which was exactly what the valley could provide in generous measure. The growers, it should be admitted, treated their customers somewhat contemptuously when it came to quality, giving most of the wines a good dose of molasses to make them sweeter.

Trade with Holland reached its high point when the Layon canal was finished in 1779. Mainly intended for carrying coal from Saint-Georges-sur-Layon, it was gratefully used by Dutch ships for transporting wine.

An enormous family

Although sweet white wine has been made for centuries along the banks of the Layon, the *appellation* Coteaux du Layon dates only from 1950. Before that time the wine was sold as ordinary white Anjou. Most, and generally the best, Coteaux du Layon vineyards lie on the north bank. Altogether

Coteaux du Layon

the district has about 4,000 acres of vineyards, spread over 25 different communes. Now that sweet white wines have been out of favour for decades, the growers often have a hard time. Their hospitality, however, remains unchanged: few other Loire districts extend such a warm, hearty welcome to the visitor. Many of the wine growers are related to one another and sometimes seen to be a single enormous family. Pierre-Yves Tijou (Domaine de la Soucherie) is, for example, the brother of Jean-Paul Tijou (Château Bellevue), the nephew of Joseph Touchais (of the estate and wine house of that name), and the uncle of Jacques Boivin (Château de Fesles, Bonnezeaux), Jacques Lalanne (Château Belle Rive, Quarts de Chaume) and Michel Doucet (Château de la Guimonière).

Pourriture noble

The white wines of Coteaux du Layon are made exclusively from Chenin Blanc. Not more than 30 hectolitres per hectare may be harvested (5 hectolitres more than in Sauternes). The vintage varies from about 335,000 to 670,000 cases in a poor year like 1977 to almost double that figure in sunny years such as 1976. The wine growers endeavour to have the largest possible percentage of the grapes affected by *pourriture noble*; this 'noble rot' dries out the fruit and increases its sugar, also bringing about subtle changes in the flesh. *Pourriture noble* is a speciality of the Bordeaux district of Sauternes, but is also emulated in Coteaux du Layon. Ideally, only ripe fruit should be picked during the vintage — which means that the pickers have to go through the vineyards several times. This method of picking — the *tris* — is becoming rarer because the prices that can be asked for Coteaux du Layon are too low to offset rising labour costs. Usually there is only one picking nowadays, but as late as possible. Only growers aiming at very high quality still keep up the *tris* system, at least in good years when it is worth the trouble.

Blossoming lime trees

The French gastronome Curnonsky compared drinking Coteaux du Layon to 'a walk under blossoming lime trees in a beautiful sunset with a pretty fair-haired girl'. In less romantic vein, I would add my personal observation that a good Coteaux du Layon benefits greatly from maturing in the bottle, although the wine has charm even in the year of its vintage. A fully matured Coteaux du Layon — I have tasted wines from 1959 and 1964, two excellent years — is gold-green in colour (sometimes also pinkish-gold), teases the nose with a diversity of impressions (sweet fruit, nuts, and spices like nutmeg), and delights the tongue with a fresh, sometimes almost austere sweetness — distinctly less luxurious and heavy than Sauternes, but nevertheless present. In addition, many Coteaux du Layon have a gently bitter aftertaste and perfect balance. The sweet content of a good Coteaux du Layon is not as a rule high enough for it to be classified purely as a dessert wine, although it tastes marvellously with desserts that are themselves not too sweet. Locally, the wine is often served as an aperitif. Coteaux du Layon is an excellent adjunct to all kinds of poached, fried and baked fish, especially freshwater varieties, from eel to salmon. The wine also combines pleasantly with poultry and game (chicken, quail, duck, etc.) and veal, including sweetbreads, especially if these are prepared with a creamy or slightly sweet sauce.

The seven giants

Since 1955 French wine law has distinguished a superior kind of Coteaux du Layon, from seven communes. Six of them are grouped under the designation Coteaux du Layon Villages — their name can be stated on the labels. They are Beaulieu-sur-Layon, Faye-d'Anjou, Rablay-sur-Layon, Rochefort-sur-Loire, Saint-Aubin-de-Luigné and Saint-Lambert-du-Lattay. The wine from these villages must have at least 1° more alcohol than those of Coteaux du

Couteaux du Layon

Layon: 12° instead of 11°. The seventh commune is Chaume. Wine growers there may take only 25 hectolitres per hectare — the same as Sauternes, and one-fifth less than their colleagues in Coteaux du Layon and Coteaux du Layon Villages. Naturally this concentration can only do good. Coteaux du Layon Chaume is often an extremely good wine with a modest richness. Average annual production is around 14,500 cases. Whereas in Coteaux du Layon Villages clay, gravel and sometimes sand predominate, the clay content of the soil is appreciably higher in Chaume than it is in the surrounding communes.

Villages and their wines

The Club des Layon Villages (at the Mairie de Beaulieu-sur-Layon, 49490 Rochefort-sur-Loire) represents the interests of the seven communes. It undertakes publicity on behalf of its members and has issued a description of the wines from the different communes. I have already described the character of Chaume; for descriptions of the remaining six wines I have based myself on the material supplied by the Club des Layon Villages.

Beaulieu-sur-Layon: soft, faint aroma, lingering, sweet aftertaste, sometimes too firm (although there are also fine, elegant, velvety wines).

Faye-d'Anjou: somewhat reserved wines, with a scent sometimes reminiscent of brushwood.

Rablay-sur-Layon: bold, rounded, strong wines, 'as sound as one hundred-year-old oaks'.

Rochefort-sur-Loire: elegant, nervy, quite a lot of tannin; always full-bodied; matures well.

Saint-Aubin-de-Luigné: delicate nose that often opens up like a peacock's tail. I find the taste sometimes slightly drier than the other communes.

Saint-Lambert-du-Lattay: round, robust wines that can mature over a long period and also have a certain finesse. This commune has the largest area of vines in the whole Layon.

With its 57 acres, (42 acres carrying the appellation *Quarts de Chaume*), this estate is one of the two largest in the district. The owner Jacques Lalanne ferments his wine in wood and bottles it during the first spring after harvesting. Before he moved into the château, it had not been inhabited for a quarter of a century and he has completely renovated it. Jacques' Quarts de Chaume is a beautiful wine with a suggestion of quince in its elegant sweetness.

Wherever Jean Baumard owns land, he makes excellent wine, as at Quarts de Chaume (15 acres). In recent years he has been vinifying in such a manner that as much of the aroma of the grapes is retained as possible and oxidation is kept to a minimum, so that the wine ferments very slowly — the 1978 took about six months. I greatly liked the 1978, which is richer and more subtle than the wine of sunny 1976. I also remember a beautiful, golden 1959. Baumard exports to the United Kingdom, Belgium and the Netherlands.

Quarts de Chaume

Loire

The two most important *crus* from the Coteaux du Layon are Quarts de Chaume and Bonnezeaux. The former has the more northerly situation, three miles or so from Rochefort-sur-Loire. It consists of only 104 acres of vineyards, which stretch south from the hamlet of Chaume over four low, flat-topped ridges towards the Layon valley. The horseshoe-shaped plateau behind Chaume protects the vine-clad hills from all except the south wind. Quarts de Chaume therefore has a microclimate with higher temperatures than its immediate surroundings, and the grapes ripen better. The soil has a high iron content. Quarts de Chaume derives its name from the fact that the Seigneur de la Guerche used to demand a quarter of the vintage — and not, of course, the worst quarter.

Lowest yield in the Loire

Quarts de Chaume is also the name of the wine: white and exclusively made from Chenin Blanc. In Quarts de Chaume the lowest yield of the whole Loire valley is prescribed — 22 hectolitres per hectare. But sometimes even this is not attained and only 18 hectolitres are produced. In good years the nine owners of Quarts de Chaume attempt not only to ripen their grapes to perfection but also aim for *pourriture noble*, as in Sauternes. The pickers then go through the vineyards several times, gathering only the ripest grapes. In favourable circumstances there are always at least three pickings at, for example, Château de Belle Rive (the *tris* system). The low yield and the long harvest mean that Quarts de Chaume can never be a cheap wine.

Aftertaste of quince

The three most important owners of Quarts de Chaume are Jacques Lalanne (Château de Belle Rive, about 42 acres); The Laffourcade family (the Suronde and l'Echarderie estates, about 42 acres), and Jean Baumard (15 acres). I know the wines of Lalanne and Baumard, two growers who aim for high quality. A good Quarts de Chaume (always with a minimum 12° alcohol) is drunk either very young or very old — preferably the latter. The wine tastes best between its 10th and 15th year. By then it has a golden gleam and an astounding richness and complexity. It is never a heavy wine: Quarts de Chaume always possesses an unmistakable elegance. Another striking characteristic is its slightly bitter aftertaste, strongly reminiscent of quince. Quarts de Chaume makes a very pleasant aperitif but also combines most agreeably with items such as *foie-gras*, *poulet à la creme* and blue-veined cheese with unsalted butter. If chilled, a bottle once opened can usually be kept for days if not weeks.

For four generations the Boivin family have been making wine at Château de Fesles. The best, known as Bonnezeaux since 1951, has always been a sweet white. In the château cellars are bottles dating back to 1875. The present wine maker is Jacques Boivin. While young his wines have a tinge of green, a restrained bouquet and a sharply fresh flavour with elegant, sweet overtones. It takes about ten years for their true class to become apparent. On the label the 's' in Fesles has been left off by mistake.

Vincent Goizil took charge of the rather neglected property of his father-in-law in 1954 when it covered 15 acres; today there are 37 acres, of which four produce Bonnezeaux. Goizil, somewhat of a stickler for cleanliness, only produces Bonnezeaux in sunny years. The wine has a sharpish, almost spicy sweetness, perfect balance and pleasant nuances. Vincent has been joined by his son Denis. Another producer of good Bonnezeaux is René Renou, who owns 10 acres and is the sixth generation of a wine-growing family.

Bonnezeaux

Loire

Although much less well known than Quarts de Chaume, this little district received its own *appellation contrôlée* as an Anjou *premier cru* on 6 November 1961. Quarts de Chaume did not follow until four years later. Bonnezeaux takes its name from a hamlet in the commune of Thouarcé and forms an enclave in the much larger territory of Coteaux du Layon. Only the Chenin Blanc grape is permitted in Bonnezeaux. It is planted over a distance of nearly two miles, along a fairly broad band of gently sloping ground. The subsoil consists mainly of clay and limestone.

Fragmented holdings

The Bonnezeaux district extends over some 300 acres, of which only 100-135 acres are used for wine-growing: and this land is cut up into small properties. Jacques Boivin of Château de Fesles is by far the biggest local owner with his 32 acres (he also holds 260 acres in other *appellations*). The yield in Bonnezeaux is very low, not more than 15 to 25 hectolitres per hectare. The vintage fluctuates between 8,900 and 15,600 cases. Not all of this is of equally good quality: a lot of Bonnezeaux from small growers does not merit its *appellation*.

Fatness and grace

The grapes for Bonnezeaux have to be picked as ripe as possible; for preference they should, in fact, be over-ripe and affected to some degree by *pourriture noble*. The wine is usually fermented in conventional concrete vats. Sometimes, however, as at Château de Fesles, small wooden vats are used. On this estate the wine generally ferments very slowly until Christmas, sometimes until mid-January (Jean Boivin, Jacques' father, learned this technique during a period at Château d'Yquem in the Sauternes).

Bonnezeaux does not offer a great breadth of luxury, but an elegantly restrained sweetness: according to Jean Boivin, it is a perfect combination of fatness and grace. Often there is a discernible piquancy in the taste, which is sometimes even peppery. Bonnezeaux can, and should, age. It only starts to reveal its good qualities after about five years, and its true class after ten. Jacques Boivin convincingly demonstrated the ageing capacity of his wines by letting me taste examples that included a sublime 1947. This wine, from grapes of which about half had been affected by *pourriture noble*, was golden in colour with a reddish glint, a fine nose and a beautifully ripe, rich and at the same time amazingly fresh taste that lingered long in the mouth. I thought it a great, even unique, wine. Château de Fesles only produces Bonnezeaux in good years: wine from lesser vintages is sold as ordinary Coteaux du Layon. Other wine growers, too, maintain this laudable policy.

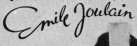

Toi qui jadis en diligence
En carrosse à pied à cheval
Allais du Layon vers l'Aubance
Tu t'arrêtais au "Petit Val"

Eternel passant le vin chante
Même au triste temps du grésil
Blanc ou rosé pour qu'il t'enchante
Fais halte chez Vincent Goizil
Emile Joulain

Left:
Gérard Chauvin. As well as a large wine estate he owns a flock of sheep.

Below left:
An aerial view of the Domaine des Rochettes. In the foreground is Gérard Chauvin's house. The extension contains a large dining room and kitchen.

Below right:
Henri Richou proudly displays some medals he won with Coteaux de l'Aubance and dry white Anjou.

Brissac in the Coteaux de l'Aubance is an important production centre for Rosé d'Anjou. There is also a large cooperative. Brissac and 10 other villages may be granted their own appellation: Brissac Villages.

Gérard Chauvin is one of the most important growers in the Coteaux de l'Aubance. He owns 82 acres in the district, although only a small part is for the production of Coteaux de l'Aubance — a plot in the village of Mozé-sur-Louet. Chauvin's Coteaux de l'Aubance is full of character with a hint of earthiness in its pure and restrained sweetness. The colour has a very slight tinge of green and the bouquet is mild, the balance excellent.

Henri Richou and his son Didier run the Richou-Rousseau estate (Richou's wife is a Rousseau). About one-fifth of their 74-acre vineyards produces Coteaux de l'Aubance. It is a wine that matures well but does not achieve great longevity. In 1980 I thought the 1967 (an average year) was just past its best, although I enjoyed tasting this mature and now golden-hued vintage. Richou's 1979 won a gold medal at the Concours Agricole in Paris.

Coteaux de l'Aubance

Coteaux de l'Aubance is one of the most nebulous of the Anjou *appellations*. The district of origin of this white wine is very big, yet the yield is modest. Ten wine communes produce (from less than 200 acres) only between 13,500 and 30,000 cases a year, the reason being that they grow much more of other wines than of Coteaux de l'Aubance, as for example, large quantities of Rosé d'Anjou and Cabernet d'Anjou, and also red Anjou and dry white Anjou. In my experience, if you go looking for Coteaux de l'Aubance hereabouts, you most frequently come across the other types; so much so that you may be left wondering why ever the *appellation* Coteaux de l'Aubance was created in 1950.

Tiny river

The district takes its name from the little Aubance river, which is so minute as to take some discovering. On the west the district is bordered by the Coteaux du Layon. It then stretches about 12½ miles eastward. Coteaux de l'Aubance lies directly south of Angers, on the left bank of the Loire. The wine is white, of varying sweetness, and can be made only from the Chenin Blanc. The maximum yield is 30 hectolitres per hectare — the same as for Coteaux du Layon and Coteaux du Layon Villages. The minimum alcohol content is 11°. That Coteaux de l'Aubance has its own *appellation contrôlée* might give the impression that, like Quarts de Chaume and Bonnezeaux, the district is a *cru* of Coteaux du Layon. This is not so: if a comparison were to be made, it would be with ordinary Coteaux du Layon.

Lively and fresh

Most wine growers in the district regard Coteaux de l'Aubance as their best wine. They mostly use the latest picked, ripest grapes and allow the must to ferment slowly. In general, Coteaux de l'Aubance is somewhat fresher and livelier than Coteaux du Layon ('plus nerveux,' as one grower said to me). Very sweet types hardly ever occur; some Coteaux de l'Aubance even tend towards medium dry. The better wines are pale in colour, with a hint of green when young. Their nose is usually genial and soft, their taste sweetish but not heavy or cloying. I have often detected a slight *terroir*. The wine matures well but is also good to drink young. Wines somewhat comparable to Coteaux de l'Aubance are grown west of Angers on the right bank of the Loire. These come from 11 communes, are also made from Chenin Blanc grapes, have an alcohol content of at least 11° and give virtually the same yield. They are termed Anjou Coteaux de la Loire.

Saumur

Saumur, 'pearl of Anjou', is a typical French provincial town with about 25,000 inhabitants, too many cars, a Saturday market and its own castle. This imposing structure, some six centuries old, towers high above the roofs and dominates the Loire valley for far around. In addition to a museum of fine arts, it has another devoted to the horse, for the Cadre Noir cavalry school has been established at Saumur since 1814. A further curiosity is a factory that makes carnival masks, the biggest of its kind in Europe.

Wine centre

In the Saumur district there are 51 châteaux, 61 historic churches, 22 prehistoric menhirs, two Roman amphitheatres and four Roman baths. The Romans also introduced wine-growing to the area. It declined after their departure, but the monks began to revive it in 1066. In 1194 the first wine was shipped

to England. At that time the price of land was higher in Saumur than in Champagne. As elsewhere along the Loire, the Dutch played an important role in the 17th and 18th centuries in the development of wine-growing and the wine trade. The annals record that two Dutch wine merchants set themselves up in the village of Souzay, near Saumur, in 1617. Today Saumur (including the adjoining Saint-Hilaire-Saint-Florent) is perhaps the most important wine centre of the whole Loire valley, with a number of very large concerns, among them Rémy-Pannier and the associated Ackerman-Laurance and Albert Besombes.

Caves in the tuff

The soil around Saumur, as in Champagne, is in general calcareous. The locality is also notable for tuff — a rock of volcanic origin formerly much used for building. It is said to have been used in rebuilding London after

Ackerman-Laurance is the largest producer of sparkling wine in Saumur (about 2.7 million bottles by the méthode champenoise). Many varieties are made. This Saumur d'Origine with its red neckband is full of sparkle and has a clean, pure, refreshing flavour. Simpler and less effervescent is the Brut Royal. The majority of shares are owned by the Rémy family of Rémy-Pannier.

One of my favourite sparkling Saumurs is the Blanc de Blancs of Langlois-Chateau (without an accent on the 'a'). The firm was founded in 1885 and was taken over in the 1970s by the champagne company of Bollinger. A wine with a civilized sparkle and a soft fresh flavour — delicious as an aperitif — is produced exclusively from the Chenin Blanc. Langlois-Chateau also produces a lot of sparkling wine for other houses who sell the bottles under their own labels.

The vineyards of Gratien, Meyer, Seydoux & Cie (the brand name is Gratien & Meyer) are high up on the hillside along the road between Saumur and Chinon. Not all the wines of this family firm, founded in 1864, appeal to me, but I like the dry sparkling Saumur which is a pleasant, pretty wine, of decent quality with a refreshing flavour. Each year 1.5 to 1.8 million bottles are produced by the méthode champenoise. The firm owns 50 acres of vineyards in Saumur, as well as the Alfred Gratien concern in the Champagne. A Saumur sous-marque is Henri d'Arlan.

The best sparkling wine of Ackerman-Laurance is the Cuvée Privée, a Crémant de Loire, sold in limited quantities with numbered labels. The firm's rosé also merits recommendation. It is a true rosé (from black grapes only — Cabernet in this case — not from white sparkling wine to which some still red has been added). The wine has a nice sparkle and tastes pure, is sound and amenably fresh. Another fine Crémant de Loire is the Cuvée Privilège.

The Cave Coopérative des Vignerons de Saumur, set up in 1957, has about 220 members who cultivate a total of 1,600 to 1,730 acres; half is planted with white, half with black varieties. One of the most pleasant wines is the Saumur Blanc, fresh and clear in taste, but not too severe. The cooperative produces about 89,000 cases (Chenin Blanc only). Altogether the company processes about 78,000 cases (including 39,000 cases of wine made by non-members). Nicolas buys its sparkling Saumur here.

Gilles Collé is a grower and merchant producing his own Saumur wines. He uses the Château de Parnay cellars. His 30-acre vineyard bears the name Clos du Château; 17 acres are planted with white grapes, 12 with red. I particularly remember Collé's white wine, which is pure and refreshing. It improves in quality if left to mature in the bottle for three to five years.

Saumur

the Great Fire of 1666, and the Dutch city of Maastricht has many old houses built of it. As a consequence of this chalk layer, from 65 to 260 feet thick, it is estimated that there are some 620 miles of underground chambers and passages in Saumur — perfect for maturing the wine — with a constant temperature of 13°C throughout the year.

An enterprising Belgian

Because of the geology of the area the white wines of Saumur, like those of Champagne, tend naturally to be sparkling. It is not surprising, therefore, that the man who first made a true sparkling Saumur had worked for years in Champagne. Jean Ackerman (1788-1866) was a Belgian who married a girl named Laurance, from Saumur. He produced his first sparkling Saumur in 1811, but, strangely, his example was not followed immediately: for 37 years he was the only

grower to apply the *méthode champenoise* to a local white wine. Today Ackerman-Laurance is still the biggest producer of this type of wine in the region, but the firm has, of course, acquired company in the meantime. The wine houses ran into difficulties when the name 'Champagne' was given legal protection, as prior to that time sparkling Saumur had often been sold as a type of champagne. In the office of Philippe Songy, director of Ackerman-Laurance, himself a Champenois, there is an old poster in English, proclaiming 'Dry Royal Champagne, Finest imported from Saumur'.

Reasonable prices

At present some ten houses produce ten million bottles of Saumur Mousseux a year, and this output is rising steadily (partly as a result of high champagne prices). The wine can have various grapes as its basis: white

Chenin Blanc, Chardonnay and Sauvignon (the last two not more than 20%), as well as black Cabernet Franc, Cabernet-Sauvignon, Malbec, Gamay, Groslot, Pineau d'Aunis and Pinot Noir (with a maximum of 60% for any of the black varieties in conjunction). The grapes come from any of 93 communes. Since 1977 many growers have contracted to sell all their grapes to the wine houses. Given a yield of 60 hectolitres per hectare and a very reasonable price for the grapes, it is not surprising that 540 growers, who jointly work about 35,000 acres, have signed such agreements. The wine houses prefer grapes to wine, and will even pay a premium for fruit.

For publicity purposes the name Saumur Mousseux has been replaced by the more stylish Saumur d'Origine. The quality of sparkling Saumur varies from firm to firm, but as a rule it is a good wine of reliable standard. It does not equal champagne — it

Château de Villeneuve is a 57-acre estate situated in Souzay-Champigny and owned by Robert Chevallier. It produces roughly equal quantities of Saumur Blanc and Saumur Champigny. Of the two, I prefer the Blanc: a dry, very fresh wine tasting of the chalk it was grown on. It also has fruit, and suppleness, making it a most agreeable drink.

André Fourrier in Distré owns 54 acres of vineyards — 36 acres with Cabernet Sauvignon, and 15 with Chenin Blanc. Some of the grapes produce a rather rare wine, Coteaux de Saumur. Fourrier makes only 335 to 390 cases of this a year. I found it an excellent wine of its kind: a rich bouquet (with a hint of spice), a balanced, mild flavour.

Visitors to the magnificent castle of Montreuil-Bellay can buy its wine. Besides some 1,240 acres of woodland the castle, still privately owned, has a small 22-acre vineyard where rosé, white and red wine is produced. Not great wines, but the rosé in particular is quite pleasant. I find it full of character if a little recalcitrant, a wine that needs to mature to become more tractable. Allow it at least four or five years.

Gabriel Pérols produces a fairly attractive, if rather bland Saumur Blanc, and also a good Saumur Rouge. It is made exclusively from the Cabernet Franc, planted in this case in mainly gravelly soil with some clay, near the hamlet of La Coudray-Macouard. The red wine is left for a year in great wooden vats. The 1976, which I tasted in 1980, was delicious; later years were equally rewarding. Pérols owns 59 acres, 27 for white and 32 for red wine.

Although André Fourrier owns old, rather mouldy underground cellars, above ground he uses the most modern equipment, including stainless-steel fermentation tanks. His red Saumur (grown on 35 acres) is fermented by the macération carbonique method and matured in wooden barrels. The result is an aromatic, supple yet firm wine. It is of excellent quality. If this is the new style Saumur, I am greatly attracted to it.

This is one of the labels under which the Saint-Cyr-en-Bourg cooperative sells its Saumur-Champigny — available in several qualities, with or without the vintage date. At its best it is of a deep colour, not exceptionally aromatic, but has a lively flavour, often with fruit, and is quite supple. The cooperative processes about 30% to 40% of all Saumur-Champigny. Some of the wine is fermented in super-modern stainless-steel 'vinimatic' tanks.

Saumur

is lighter, fresher, simpler — but it costs a good deal less; Saumur Mousseux offers an especially agreeable price-quality ratio. Some of the champagne houses have realized this too. Taittinger is the owner of Bouvet-Ladubay (via the firm of Monmousseau, also established in the Loire valley), and Bollinger has Longlois-Chateau.

Crémant de Loire

In 1975 a new *appellation* was created for another kind of sparkling wine, Crémant de Loire. Its area of production takes in not only Saumur, but also Anjou and Touraine. French wine laws governing the production of Crémant de Loire resemble those for the *méthode champenoise,* but are rather more stringent than the rules for Saumur Mousseux. Yield per hectare is thus set at 50 instead of 60 hectolitres, and 150 kilograms (331 lb) of grapes have to be used for one hectolitre of Crémant, compared with 130 kilograms (287 lb) for Saumur Mousseux. Furthermore, Crémant de Loire has to remain on its *lie* — the sediment formed during its second fermentation in the bottle — for 12 months and Saumur Mousseux for only 9 months. Normally, Crémant de Loire is a superior product, but few people know it, and this is one reason why the *appellation* has not so far been a great success. At the time of writing, production has not reached two million bottles — less than one-fifth of Saumur Mousseux.

Chalk-dry taste

Although sparkling wine is by far the most important product, Saumur also has a number of still varieties. The districts of Saumur Blanc and Saumur Rouge are both much smaller in extent than Saumur Mousseux: 38 communes compared to 93. With a yield of 45 hectolitres per hectare, white Saumur is made mainly from the Chenin Blanc. Up to 20% of Chardonnay and Sauvignon grapes is allowed and alcoholic content must be at least 10°.
Saumur Blanc is usually a chalk-dry white wine with a cool personality and an astringent, sometimes acid taste. It is often difficult to find a really successful white Saumur. I agree with Philippe Songé of Ackerman-Laurance, who said: 'Saumur Blanc can be compared with the Coteaux Champenois. Both taste best when transformed by bubbles.' Coteaux de Saumur, which I have occasionally tasted, is usually a semi-sweet white wine exclusively from Chenin Blanc grapes. It comes from 13 communes and must contain minimum 12° alcohol. The permitted yield is 30 hectolitres per hectare. Production ranges from only 220 to 1,230 cases a year. Apparently there are white and rosé Saumur Pétillant wines, but I have not yet been able to find them.

Alain Sanzay of Varrains is a young wine grower who tries to work in as craftsmanlike way as possible, in the tradition of his forefathers. So, naturally, the Saumur-Champigny is matured in wooden casks for a whole year. The wine tastes of both fruit and tannin, and the bouquet is good. Alain owns 12 acres of Les Poyeux vineyard, the best cru of Varrains and Chacé. The white grapes from his other 25 acres go to the cooperative.

Paul Filliatreau of Chaintres is one of the most renowned wine makers of the Saumur-Champigny appellation. He cultivates 67 acres — 5 acres being white grapes. Paul's Saumur-Champigny Vieilles Vignes is astonishingly good: deep in colour, intense, fruity, soft in flavour. He has been making this wine since 1978 (at that time only 7,000 bottles). His ordinary Saumur-Champigny, with its soft, supple, sometimes rather rich fruity taste, is also a pleasure to drink. He uses stainless-steel fermentation tanks.

The silent hamlet of Chaintres has its own château owned by Bernard de Tigny and his American wife. The generally attractive wines are produced from 49 acres (42 of Saumur-Champigny, 7 of Saumur Blanc). I greatly prefer the red, which has a strong colour, pleasant bouquet and a supple yet firm taste. The quality often varies quite widely from year to year; I thought the 1975 and 1976 were excellent, the 1979 just good, and the 1978 comparatively disappointing.

Claude Daheuiller produces some very fine red wines. I tasted a series of Saumur-Champignys going back to 1961: all were harmonious, full of character, supple and yet not without fruit or tannin. Daheuiller lives in Varrains and owns 45 acres (30 for Saumur-Champigny, 15 with white grapes for still and sparkling wines).

Jean-Pierre Charruau of Parnay produces a good rosé with the appellation d'origine Cabernet de Saumur. He makes it from half Cabernet Franc and half Cabernet Sauvignon. It is pale pink in colour and has a fresh but very slightly sweet taste. Charruau has other wines worthy of note. I have pleasant memories of both his Saumur Blanc and his Saumur-Champigny (with a slight preference for the former). His vineyard covers 35 acres.

Other good sparkling wines
Veuve Amiot (Saint-Hilaire-Saint-Florent owned by Martini & Rossi); Bouvet-Ladubay (Saint-Hilaire-Saint-Florent; Champagne Taittinger); De Neuville (Saint-Hilaire-Saint-Florent; Cointreau); Coopérative des Vignerons de Saumur (Saint Cyr-en-Bourg).

Opposite page:
The white castle of Saumur. Before its present use as a museum, it served as a fortress, a royal residence, a barracks and a prison.

Below:
Wine maker Claude Daheuiller and his wife Marie-Françoise.

Bottom:
In the Saint-Cyr-en-Bourg cooperative.

Saumur

Two types of red Saumur

Production of red Saumur has quadrupled in about 15 years and is still growing; justifiably so, for in quality it has more to recommend it than its white counterpart. The permitted yield for all red Saumur is 40 hectolitres per hectare and only Cabernet Franc, Cabernet Sauvignon and Pineau d'Aunis are allowed to be used (the two latter seldom, in fact, occurring). There are two kinds of red Saumur: Saumur Rouge, from 38 communes, and Saumur-Champigny, from the communes of Chacé, Dampierre, Montsoreau, Parnay, Saint-Cyr-en-Bourg, Saumur and Souzay-Champigny. Saumur-Champigny is generally the better proposition. Its vineyards are the best in the area, mostly on La Côte, the vine-clad chalk plateau immediately east of Saumur, a couple of hundred feet above the Loire. The villages lie mostly at the foot of this plateau, wedged between the cliffs and the Saumur-Chinon road. The roads up to the plateau are narrow, winding and mostly steep. There are few houses on the plateau itself, probably because for centuries the soil here has been regarded as so ideal for wine-growing that every square yard of it has been used for this purpose.

Cooperative initiative

The great French statesman Clemenceau drank Saumur-Champigny, but despite his enthusiasm the wine was little known and not produced in large quantities until the 1960s. It is principally due to the Saint-Cyr-en-Bourg cooperative that the *appellation* has expanded from less than 78,000 cases a year to between 245,000 and 340,000 cases. Its director, Marcel Neau, stated that the growers used to be uncertain whether to use their black grapes for sparkling white or for still red. The *cave coopérative* was the first Saumur concern to make a distinction. When selection was introduced to achieve the best possible quality for Saumur-Champigny, it resulted in a better wine, which led to increased demand and bigger production. The importance of this cooperative for the *appellation* is shown by the fact that its 220 members produce 30% to 40% of all Saumur-Champigny. Saumur-Champigny is generally fuller, more supple, and with more fruit than Saumur Rouge — although I have tasted Saumurs that come close in quality to Saumur-Champigny. Production of Saumur Rouge varies between 55,000 and 135,000 cases. A third Saumur wine from black grapes is Cabernet de Saumur, a rosé that is paler, lighter and drier than the better known Cabernet d'Anjou. Not more than 10,000 to 23,000 cases are produced annually.

The simplest Chinon marketed by Couly-Dutheil carries no indication of vineyard. The wine is sometimes good, sometimes disappointing. I prefer the Chinon from Domaine René Couly, better and more reliable quality. The soil of the 37-acre vineyard contains gravel and clay; the vines are on average about 20 years old. The lively wine with its bouquet of fruit matures in wood for six to nine months before bottling.

Domaine des Bouquerries is contracted to Couly-Dutheil. The 35 acres are on partly level, partly hilly ground in Cravant-les-Coteaux. Like all the Couly-Dutheil wines this Chinon remains in the fermentation vats for 30 to 40 days, all stalks and seeds having been previously removed. I find the Chinon from Domaine des Bouquerries particularly refined both in scent and taste. The colour is often a beautiful clear red.

Clos de l'Echo once belonged to the parents of Rabelais. Its 35 acres produce a sublime Chinon that is one of the very best red Loire wines. The vineyard is on a southern slope looking out over the castle of Chinon and some of the vines are 25 years old. The wine from these vines matures for 12 to 18 months in oak casks. It has a fuller taste than most Chinons, but is subtle at the same time. Bouquet and taste often suggest fruit and flowers. A privilege to drink.

Plouzeau & Fils is a Chinon firm on the south bank of the Vienne, opposite the old town. It owns 25 acres in Touraine, 5 in Chinon. The owner/manager Pierre Plouzeau considers his speciality to be his Chinon Bellamour, which he makes from good Chinons bought from various growers. I found it a delicious, sound wine, rather elegant with good fruit in the taste, which tends to be rather smooth.

In the village of Beaumont-en-Véron wine merchant Robert Allouin has rock cellars which look somewhat surrealistic, the fermentation vats and casks seeming to struggle vainly against the mustiness and grime. Allouin usually produces a not very refined, rather rustic Chinon, which is nevertheless quite attractive. It normally has some fruit and a certain roundness, filling the mouth.

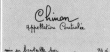

Time and again I have enjoyed Chinon bearing the Audebert & Fils label, a family firm run by Georges Audebert and son Jean-Claude. They are very quality conscious and have made the red wines of Bourgueil, Saint-Nicolas-de-Bourgueil and Chinon their speciality. The wines, including the Chinon, generally mature for a year in demi-muids, very large oak casks.

Chinon

Not far to the southeast of Saumur the river Vienne flows into the Loire. This is where you leave Anjou and enter Touraine, the next great wine district of the Loire valley. The first *appellation* is Chinon. This is one of the most renowned wine districts of the Loire, where you might expect the farmers to have no problem in marketing their product for themselves. Yet a Chinon grower once said to me: 'We make wine for our friends, and for the big firms.' The implication was that he and his colleagues bottled relatively little of their wine themselves, and that this modest quantity was sold only within a small area. Indeed, about three-quarters of all the wine produced in the Chinon district — and this is a vast quantity — is bought up by the *négociants*.

The fame of Chinon wine — which is mainly red — was established in no small degree by François Rabelais, whose statue stands on the bank of the local river Vienne. The famous writer was born near Chinon and the exploits of many of his great comic heroes took place in the neighbourhood.

Possessing a legendary thirst, Rabelais frequently drank Chinon and was enthusiastic in its praise. Local wine growers still quote the well known line from the fifth book of *Pantagruel*: 'Chinon, Chinon, little town, great renown.'

Castle ruins

Cardinal Richelieu, Count of Chinon, is said to have been responsible for the fact that Chinon wine is predominantly red. He despatched his steward, Abbé Breton, to Bordeaux in 1631 to bring back the noble Cabernet Franc grape. (Although in and around Chinon this grape is called the *breton*, this is not necessarily a reference to the Abbé: some French writers suggest that the name comes from 'Breton wine', i.e. wine intended for Brittany). Today, about 98% of the vineyard area is planted with Cabernet Franc. Apart from introducing red wine-growing, the cardinal dismantled Chinon's three castles. Their remains rise above the little town, covering a site of 1,300 by 230 feet. Chinon itself, at

the foot of the fortified hill, is one of the most delightful little towns of the Loire valley. It lies six miles south of the left bank of the Loire, on the river Vienne. The narrow streets offer many surprises, such as beautiful half-timbered houses of the 14th, 15th and 16th centuries. The English kings Henry II and Richard Lionheart were here, and this is where the 18-year-old peasant girl Joan of Arc persuaded Charles VII to have himself crowned at Reims.

Three types of terrain

Chinon wines come not only from the town itself but from a total of 17 communes spread over a large area. The *appellation* embraces about 2,986 acres of vineyard — not a vast area, but 20 years ago it was only 1,240 acres. The vineyards are dispersed over different kinds of terrain and therefore produce different types of Chinon. *Vins de sables* come from the sands and gravels of the flat land along the Vienne; light fruity

One of the most talented wine growers in Cravant-les-Coteaux is Jean-François Olek. He owns nearly 20 acres of vineyard, half of it on the slopes, and is a great advocate of maturation in wooden casks instead of tanks, 'for the wood helps to impart character and longevity to the wine'. So the wine which Olek bottles himself (as yet only part of his production) usually matures for a year or even longer in wood (the 1976 for two years). The final result is classic and outstanding.

The father of Gérard and Daniel Chauveau bought the Domaine de Pallus Beauséjour for his own enjoyment and planted fruit trees there. In 1969 the two brothers made it into a vineyard. Of approximately 62 acres, it could expand up to a maximum of 86 acres. Most of the land (44 acres) is in Cravant-les-Coteaux. Stainless-steel fermentation tanks ensure vinification in the modern way. The vineyard produces a soft type of Chinon; in 1978, for example, it was fleshy and fruity, but was somewhat lacking in character in 1979.

I had difficulty finding the home of Serge Sourdais because there are many families in Cravant-les-Coteaux of this surname — and the house was hidden among the hills, down a no-through road. Serge Soudais, who is assisted by his son Daniel, owns 54 acres of land, all in Cravant-les-Coteaux (two-thirds on the coteaux, one-third on the sables). First-class for keeping, dark red in colour, and with a strong, spicy taste, the wine regularly wins prizes.

When Jean Spelty died in 1978 his son Gérard took over the estate: 25 acres of vineyard (70% sables, 30% coteaux). The wine ferments in vats of wood and concrete, then remains for three months to a year in wooden casks. Only part of the vintage is bottled by Gérard himself, but this is continually increasing. Spelty's Chinon is usually rich in tannin and less fruity than many of its kind. It should therefore mature for up to four years.

Opposite page:
The impressive castle of Chinon, actually the adjacent ruins of three castles. Cardinal Richelieu had the fortifications dismantled and used the stone to create a village which was named after him. This still stands, a model of 17th-century town planning. The French author La Fontaine once described Richelieu as 'the most beautiful village in the whole universe'. A little steam train runs from Chinon to Richelieu from May to mid-October.

Below:
Panorama over Chinon and the Vienne valley.

Bottom:
Jean-François Olek, a modest wine grower producing excellent Chinons in Cravant-les-Coteaux.

Places of interest in Chinon include an attractive local museum, a wine museum and a church hewn entirely out of the rocks. In August each year the small town (approx. 8,500 inhabitants) puts on a medieval market. Chinon was a fortification as far back as Roman times.

There is a permitted yield of 40 hectolitres per hectare and a minimum alcohol content of 9.5° for all Chinon wines.

The Cabernet-Sauvignon has been planted in Chinon in addition to the Cabernet Franc, albeit on a very modest scale and with little success.

Chinon

wines that are soon drinkable, but short-lived. *Vins de plateaux*, also called *vins de graviers*, come mainly from plateaux, and sometimes from slopes, with a lot of clay and gravel. These wines have more depth, strength and refinement. The *vins de coteaux* come from the land most in demand — hill slopes and plateaux or terraces with clay and lime. They are colourful, generous wines for laying down that only show their true class after maturing for some years. But although the nature of the soil has a significant bearing on the character of the wine, the human factor is, of course, equally important. A good grower on the low-lying *sables* can produce a better Chinon than a less experienced grower on the slopes. Moreover, quite a few growers own plots on different types of land. Gérard Spelty, for example, grows 70% of his wine on the *sables*, and 30% on the *coteaux*.

High above Panzoult, along a narrow, winding road, is the house of Guy Lemaire, a wine wholesaler and grower. He owns 12 acres of land spread over a considerable number of plots. I found his Chinon to be an old-fashioned, deep-coloured, sometimes even opaque, wine for keeping, robust, with a lingering aftertaste. It is a Chinon of good quality, requiring a lot of patience.

Charles Joguet is considered one of the leading Chinon wine growers. He lives and works in Sazilly but also has land in Chinon. Charles cultivates about 27 acres, 9 acres with vines over 45 years old, 4 acres with vines over 20. Vinification and bottling of the wine from these old vines is carried out separately, as indicated on this label of the Cuvée du Clos de la Dioterie. Joguet wines usually have an interesting quality.

Among the green hills facing the little town of Chinon, beyond the Vienne, is Pierre Manzagol's Domaine de la Noblaie. He purchased it with its 20 acres of vineyard in 1953 and has been extremely successful with the wines. They are usually clear-coloured with a rather full, spicy-toned flavour and contain some fruit. Manzagol is one of the few wine growers who also makes some white Chinon. The wine comes from very chalky ground, has a splendid bouquet and a fresh, pure taste.

There are so many Raffaults in Chinon and the surrounding area that Raymond Raffault sells his wine under the name Domaine du Raifault. Raymond lives and works in Savigny-en-Véron, a commune on very sandy soil. His 30 acres (soon to be 42) are also partly on clay and limestone. He was kind enough to let me taste seven different types of Chinon from the cask. Once bottled, Raffault's Chinon is a firm, well-made wine that appears to benefit from some maturing.

Olga Raffault's 37 acres of vines are scattered over different plots of land in the district. Her best-quality red wine is often selected by the celebrated Barrier restaurant in Tours. I have sometimes found the wine very disappointing (e.g. 1978), and sometimes have been astonished at its class (e.g. 1973). I prefer her white Chinon, which comes from a plot known as Champ Chenin. This can be almost sweet and luxurious (like the aromatic, elegant 1976) but also very refreshing.

Chinon

Cravant-les-Coteaux

The largest wine commune of the Chinon *appellation* is Cravant-les-Coteaux, a little to the east of the town. Its 1,246 acres produce about 45% of all Chinon wine, because of its outstandingly suitable wine-growing soil. The name of the village indicates this: 'Cravant' comes from a Gaulish word meaning 'gravelly soil'. In fact it contains a lot of clay, with either gravel or lime, but the lime content is lower than in other parts of Chinon.

At the end of May the annual wine fair takes place in Cravant-les-Coteaux. The quiet village comes to life and attracts many visitors from far and wide. The growers put out their youngest wine for tasting — normally the fullest, meatiest type of Chinon. For about 80 of the farmers wine is the most important source of income. Cravant-les-Coteaux has another 40 growers who produce wine from a tiny plot as a supplementary activity. There are hardly any large estates: 25 acres is considered sizeable. This state of affairs is characteristic of Chinon as a whole. The fact that no cooperative has been set up is due to the important role played by the wine houses, and perhaps also to the individualistic attitude of the growers themselves.

The firm of Couly-Dutheil

It would not be fair to criticize all the *négociants* for their domination of the trade, and for their sometimes mediocre wine. A number of them have worked hard in recent years to make Chinon known and respected. Couly-Dutheil, in particular, deserves praise. Chinons from this house firm are served in many high-class French restaurants, and appear abroad on the lists of quality importers. It was not until I drank a bottle of Clos de l'Echo, a wine

Left:
Wine fair in Cravant-les-Coteaux. This is always held on Ascension Day. Chinon has its wine fair on the second Saturday in March, Panzoult on 1 May.

Opposite page, below left:
Jacques Couly, general manager of Couly-Dutheil. He lives at Clos de l'Echo (background).

Opposite page, below right:
Photograph taken in about 1920 above Clos de l'Echo. It includes Jacques Couly's grandparents and also his own parents as children.

Opposite page, above:
Raymond Raffault, who lives in Savigny-en-Véron, owns the estate called Domaine du Raifault.

Below:
The Clos de l'Echo, birthplace of a wonderful Chinon. This 35-acre vineyard faces south, and is on clay and limestone.

Chinon and Bourgueil have their own wineglasses, inscribed 'Buvez tousjours, ne mourrez jamais'.

The red wine of Chinon tastes best when served cool.

Chinon's wine fraternity is called Les Entonneurs Rabelaisiens de Chinon.

Chinon

from Couly-Dutheil, some years ago, that I realized Chinon could be so astonishingly good. Couly-Dutheil is a family firm, its day-to-day management in the hands of the brothers Jacques and Pierre Couly. The family owns or rents nearly 100 acres, and is the sole buyer of grapes from 160 acres. Wine from the latter sites is prepared under Couly-Dutheil supervision, then transferred in February to rock cellars in Chinon. Vineyards contracted to Couly-Dutheil are Domaine des Bouquerries (35 acres), Domaine du Puy (37 acres), Domaine de la Semellerie (47 acres), Domaine de Versailles (30 acres), and Domaine de la Haute Olive (12 acres). The last estate lies in Chinon itself, the rest in Cravant-les-Coteaux. The firm's own properties are Clos de l'Echo (35 acres, Chinon), Clos de l'Olive (5 acres, Chinon), and Domaine René Couly (37 acres on the plateau above Chinon); the Domaine de Turpenay (22 acres between Chinon and Cravant-les-Coteaux) is rented.

Violets and wild strawberries

In my opinion, a good Chinon is one of the best Loire red wines, with a style quite its own: glowing red in colour, with a seductive aroma sometimes of violets, wild strawberries, or other fruit, an elegant taste offering a lot of fruit, a pleasant *fraîcheur*, and a captivating refinement. Chinon is generally less robust than, for example, Bourgueil (which is often mentioned in the same breath). There is a saying that compares them: 'You look for roughness in Bourgueil, for finesse in Chinon.' Chinon can usually be drunk younger than Bourgueil, even wine from the *coteaux*. This does not imply, however, that Chinon cannot age. Wine from sunny years in particular often has tremendous potential. I have tasted various Chinons from the splendid vintage of 1964, all full of vitality after 15 or so years. At a wine tasting, a Clos de l'Echo 1964 was even rated higher than Château Batailley 1966, a *grand cru* from the Bordeaux commune of Pauillac.

In addition to red Chinon, a small quantity of rosé is produced, a dry wine that is certainly not without merit. The yield from the two types together varies between 330,000 and 418,000 cases a year. Finally, there is white Chinon, exclusively from the Chenin Blanc. It is rare (less than 1,600 cases a year), sometimes dry, sometimes softer, with a bouquet of spices, various flowers, and acacia blossom.

Audebert & Fils started to buy up its own wine-growing land in the 1960s. It now has 64 acres. One of its properties is the Domaine du Grand Clos with its 22 acres distributed over plateau and slopes. It produces a deep-coloured, full-bodied, spicy, tannin-rich, classic Bourgueil that requires many years maturing in the bottle. It is vinified in stainless steel but is then transferred to wooden casks.

Audebert's 4-acre Vignoble Les Marquises, near Benais; is not quite a coteau, but has clay and chalk in the soil. I consider the wine to be one of the best Bourgueils; particularly in its flavour: quite complex, a touch peppery, with a little fruit and a good dose of tannin. As a rule the bouquet only begins to get really attractive after about five years. Then is the time to start drinking the wine.

The Lamé-Delille-Boucard estate in Ingrandes-de-Touraine has 62 acres of vineyard, 49 of them in Bourgueil. The plots are spread over different types of terrain. In 1974 Lucien Lamé (whose wife is a Delille), with his son-in-law René Boucard, had a new vinification plant built. Here stand the big wooden casks for maturing the wine. Various qualities are marketed. The export quality has the most body (this wine often contains 25% Cabernet Sauvignon).

Since 1975 Jean-Baptiste Thouet and Michel Lorieux have managed 17 acres of Clos de l'Abbaye in return for part of the harvest. They make an extremely good wine with a rich fruit bouquet (e.g. raspberry), fairly robust with a lingering aftertaste. In 1979 the Clos de l'Abbaye was one of the few vineyards to produce a very good wine because the vines were not affected by the frost. The official name of the estate is G.A.E.C. de la Dime.

Bourgueil

The village of Bourgueil and its surroundings used to be administered from Saumur and was part of the province of Anjou. In 1790, when France was divided into *départements*, it was peacefully annexed by Indre-et-Loire. The village lies about three miles from the right bank of the Loire. Roman remains have been found in the district, but the village only became significant when a Benedictine abbey was established there in AD 990. This still exists and for centuries it served as a refuge in time of war and flood. In Bourgueil it is related with some pride that it was Baudry, who became abbot in 1089, who first planted the

Cabernet Franc, the grape that is the basis of all the well-known red wines of the Loire — a story somewhat at variance with Chinon's account of Cardinal Richelieu's importation of the grape from Bordeaux in 1631. Abbé Baudry wrote to his friends urging them to come to drink his wine at least once a year, 'for it brings joy to saddened hearts'.

Mild microclimate

Modern Bourgueil is a grey village with not a great deal to offer the visitor, apart from the abbey, and the church, dedicated to St Germain, which possesses, in addition to its 15th-century parts, a magnificent 12th-century choir. Only on Tuesday — market day — does life and colour come to Bourgueil. On the north side of the village a partly wooded plateau rises to about 400 feet, protecting the land in front of it from cold north winds. This perhaps explains Bourgueil's mild climate; it is called 'the little Vaucluse'. Rainfall is less than 24 inches a year. Thanks to this gentle climate, Mediterranean produce, such as liquorice, anise and Muscat grapes, was once grown here. Besides grapes, the district produces fruit, including strawberries, cherries, blackcurrants, pears and apples (among them the Pépin de Bourgueil), and vegetables such as asparagus, French beans, carrots, onions and leeks. Most Bourgueil wine growers could not earn a living from their wine alone and therefore cultivate other crops. Only a handful of wine growers have 35 or more acres of vineyard; the average property is not more than about 5 acres.

Three zones

The *appellation* Bourgueil is spread over eight communes: Bourgueil, Saint-Nicolas-de-Bourgueil, Restigné, Ingrandes-de-Touraine, Saint-Patrice, Benais, La Chapelle-sur-Loire and Chouzé-sur-Loire. Three wine-growing zones are distinguished, each producing its own type. The broadest zone is *la vallée*, a flat, very sandy stretch from the

Loire to the boundaries of Bourgueil, Restigné and Ingrandes-de-Touraine. Here wine-growing is only practised on a few gravelly enclaves, principally at La Chapelle-sur-Loire and Chouzé-sur-Loire. The wine, soon ready, has little body and is usually somewhat flat. The second zone is *la terrasse*. Most Bourgueil is produced on this three-mile-long plateau where the soil consists principally of a mixture of coarse sand and gravel. It yields fragrant wines with more power and depth than those from the valley. The third zone is called *les coteaux*. The ground rises steeply here and the soil changes radically. Sand and gravel give way to clay and tuff with a lot of lime. These are south-facing slopes and receive the maximum sunshine, and it is drier here than elsewhere in the district. This microclimate results in sound grapes that sometimes ripen two weeks earlier than their neighbours. The wine from *les coteaux* is firmer, stronger and less fruity than that from *la terrasse;* truly a wine for keeping. The best type of Bourgueil is often derived from a blend of *coteaux* and *terrasse* wine; and the most successful Bourgueils are most frequently produced by growers with land in both these zones.

Simple homes

Bourgueil has in all about 2,200 acres of vineyards, with an annual production of between 242,000 and 385,000 cases. Practically all of this is red wine, with only a modest amount of rosé. In contrast to Chinon, not a drop of white is made. Both the red and the rosé come mainly from the Cabernet Franc; although the law also allows the Cabernet Sauvignon, the latter occurs only here and there in Bourgueil. The permitted yield per hectare for red and rosé is 40 hectolitres.

Wine-growing in Bourgueil is mainly practised by hard-working small farmers. There may be châteaux and imposing country houses in Saumur, but not in this corner of the Loire valley. The Bourgueil growers often live in old, simply furnished dwellings, often with the wine cellar below or

Pierre Grégoire owns nearly 22 acres of vineyard, including a small plot on the coteaux. The wine matures for 8 to 18 months in large wooden casks and is never filtered. Grégoire's wine often has a subtle flavour and usually rather a lot of fruit for a Bourgueil. Here, as with the majority of Bourgueil growers, it makes sense to choose the best cuvées. Part of Grégoire's vineyard is in Saint-Nicolas-de-Bourgueil but he sells all his wine as Bourgueil.

Marc Mureau lives in the hamlet of Lossay near Restigné and owns 25 fragmented acres of vineyard. Eighty per cent is on volcanic tuff slopes. Mureau sells no wine before it has matured for a year in wood. After bottling, the wine is generally worth all the trouble: very deep in colour, powerful, with a lingering tannin-rich flavour, sometimes slightly peppery with the agreeable presence of some fruit. Mureau said of his 1976, 'C'est un maréchal!'

From the back of Paul Caslot's house, on one of the tuff slopes near the village of Restigné, his cellars run into the cliff. Helped by his son Pierre, he produces decent, and sometimes extremely good wines under the names Caslot-Jamet (his wife is a Jamet, of a Saint-Nicolas-de-Bourgueil family) and Domaine de la Chevalerie (25 acres). The 1977 was disappointing, the 1978 and 1979 were adequate, the 1969 tasted marvellous.

At a modest wine-tasting of some 1978 Bourgueils which I held in 1980 (including wines from firms from well outside the Bourgueil district), the wine of Raphaël Galteau won hands down. It had a deep, classic yet youthful purple colour, a pure fragrance and a pleasant, rather full flavour, more amenable than the average Bourgueil. The aftertaste had a fair amount of tannin which was not unpleasant. Galteau owns 25 acres, mainly on the coteaux.

Most of the 600,000 bottles the firm of Audebert & Fils sells each year — mainly to French restaurateurs — are red, from Bourgueil, Saint-Nicolas-de-Bourgueil and Chinon. Jean-Claude Audebert did, however, allow me to taste a rosé from Bourgueil. This was a clear orange-pink in colour with a soft bouquet, a pronounced refreshing taste, with a slight terroir. I found it a good, pleasant wine.

Other good Bourgueil wines
Paul Maître (Benais); Roland Fleury (Restigné); Jean Nau (Ingrandes-de-Touraine); Paul Gambier (Ingrandes-de-Touraine); Jean-Louis Richer (Restigné); Plouzeau & Fils Cuvée de la Chevalerie (Chinon); Aimé-Boucher (Huisseau-sur-Cosson).

Bourgueil

beside the house. Guests are received, not in an elegant *salle de réception,* but in the cellar (where there may be a simple tasting counter installed), in a small office or in the kitchen. The modest décor suggests that Bourgueil has brought its makers no great prosperity. This is probably due both to the relative unfamiliarity, and also the personality, of the wine.

A peasant quality

Bourgueil is not an easy wine that makes an instant appeal because of its charm. Indeed, it has a rather dour, peasant quality and is clearly less refined and elegant than Chinon, without the latter's fruit and flowery fragrance. The refractory, not very amenable character of Bourgueil might be compared to an unpolished semi-precious stone, the rough edges of which only begin to wear smooth after many years. The true class of this Loire wine takes time to become apparent, bearing out what the grower Paul Caslot said to me: 'Ten or so years are needed before my wines can be drunk.' I have frequently heard other growers express the same view. It is odd therefore, to find many wine books asserting that Bourgueil must be drunk young. This is one of many misunderstandings that exist about Loire wines. In Bourgueil the stalks and seeds are removed from all the grapes. If this were not done the wine would be even harsher, and perhaps unsaleable. Other characteristics of Bourgueil are an often rather sombre red colour, a bouquet that may suggest raspberries (the only element of any charm to be present initially) and a strong, sometimes almost peppery taste. The particular Bourgueil personality makes it an especially good partner for no-nonsense meat dishes from country cuisine, ranging from game to *charcuterie.* Even when mature, the wine tastes best at about 18°C.

Bourgueil Rosé is a completely dry wine, fresh of taste and often possessing a certain *terroir.* In contrast to its red namesake, it derives no benefit from long maturation.

Centre:
The village café in Saint-Nicolas-de-Bourgueil displays a map of the district (1,160-1,240 acres of vineyards) and a list of wine growers.

Below left:
Wine grower Pierre Jamet with his wine. He often shows his guests a little book kept by his father in the 19th century to record wine sales.

Below right:
Regulars drinking the local wine in the village café, glasses filled to the brim.

Asparagus is grown in Saint-Nicolas-de-Bourgueil as well as grapes.

The ground is very porous here: rainwater drains away almost at once.

With his sons Francis and Jean-Jacques, Pierre Jamet works 35 acres of sandy, gravelly land. Underneath the Jamet's house there is a vaulted cellar dating from 1890 (see label). Pierre Jamet makes very decent, albeit sometimes rather astringent wines, somewhat rustic, but honest. Before bottling they stay for 3 to 12 months in wooden casks, having been in lined fermentation vats for a year.

Anselme Jamet, Pierre's brother, is also a wine grower. He owns 44 acres, 9 on coteaux of tuff. The wine matures in oak casks for 12 to 18 months at his own house. Up to the time of bottling, Anselme's wine is often most agreeable, with a slightly fruity bouquet. However, once bottled it is often disappointing: evidently there is a problem which needs resolving with expert advice.

Audebert & Fils of Bourgueil has 12 acres in Saint-Nicolas-de-Bourgueil and also buys wine. The vintages I sampled were of good quality. There was a hint of the spicy peppery flavour of the Bourgueil and after about two years they were already drinkable, with a quite pleasant bouquet. The wine from the firm of Plouzeau & Fils (Chinon) also appealed to me, though I found it somewhat smoother with slightly less character.

The cellars of Jean-Paul Mabileau are situated next door to the church of Saint-Nicolas-de-Bourgueil, although there is also a cave in the cliffs. The 23-acre vineyard is planted partly with fairly young vines. Vinification and maturation of the wines from old and young vines is carried out separately. The best is from the old vines (Les Fosses): clear-coloured, a distinctive bouquet, a definite impression of both wood and fruit.

Joël Taluau lives in the hamlet of Chevrette on the boundaries of Saint-Nicolas-de-Bourgueil and Bourgueil. He owns 22 acres of wine land (Cave de l'Ormeau de Maures). I judge his wine to be the best in the district: always very sound and agreeable in flavour. The 1980, for example, had an almost buttery, pleasant softness and within a year of its vintage was marvellous to drink. The old-fashioned rustic wine from Daniel Moreau (about 12 acres) was a complete contrast.

Saint-Nicolas-de-Bourgueil

This is the only individual commune in Bourgueil with its own *appellation contrôlée*. Bourgueil, Vouvray, Montlouis and others are named after communes, but various other villages are included in their territories. Saint-Nicolas-de-Bourgueil lies about a mile due west of Bourgueil. It makes no memorable impressions, for outwardly it resembles countless other French villages. It is bisected by a fairly wide, busy road, there is a church with a high steeple, and the café opposite is a meeting place for the men of the village. There is a map on one wall of the café showing where the local wine growers are to be found.

Poorer soil

The vineyards of Saint-Nicolas-de-Bourgueil cover an area of 1,235 acres (about half that of Bourgueil) and yield between 154,000 and 204,000 cases a year. The actual soil content does not differ greatly from Bourgueil, but the commune has no land in Bourgueil's *vallée* zone by the river. It does have plateaux with sand and gravel, and slopes with clay and lime; and in Saint-Nicolas-de-Bourgueil, too, the *coteaux* produce the strongest wines with the most tannin. In general, however, the soil here is sandier and poorer than in Bourgueil. In fact, in all the communes of the Bourgueil *appellation*, 80% of the land is cultivable, but in Saint-Nicolas-de-Bourgueil the figure is under 50%. It is undoubtedly because of its somewhat different soil composition that Saint-Nicolas has been given its own *appellation*.

Lighter and friendlier

The most important legal distinction between Bourgueil and Saint-Nicolas is in yield per hectare: in the former it is 40 hectolitres, in the latter 35. Other stipulations — grape varieties, minimum alcohol content, etc. — are identical. The poorer soil of Saint-Nicolas-de-Bourgueil results in a rather lighter, friendlier wine, with less colour and body than the related Bourgueil. A Saint-Nicolas-de-Bourgueil can normally be drunk younger, but cannot be kept for so long. The commune also produces a modest amount of dry rosé.

This is one of the labels under which the Confrérie des Vignerons de Oisly et Thésée sells its usually excellent Sauvignon. It is often one of the best wines in the whole of Touraine: honest, with a bouquet of spring flowers, fresh and pure in flavour. The wine is shipped to Britain, Belgium, Germany and the Netherlands among other countries. The Pineau de la Loire (Chenin Blanc) also merits commendation.

Maurice Barbou cultivates 42 acres in Oisly and makes a splendid range of wines from the Chardonnay, Gamay, Cabernet Sauvignon, Pinot Noir and Pineau d'Aunis (for rosé). I have enjoyed them all, but I think Maurice's best wine is his Sauvignon, which usually has an alluring bouquet of flowers and fruit and a soft, refreshing, pure taste.

I remember with pleasure the fresh asparagus served to me by Henri Marionnet (a grower in Soigns) accompanied by his Sauvignon de Touraine — a sublime combination. The wine was distinctive because the hint of vegetable in the flavour, something to which many Sauvignons are prone, was absent. It tasted fruity, supple and fairly full-bodied. Henri has planted 22 of his 91 acres, in the highest part of Loir-et-Cher, with the Sauvignon. He presses the grapes very delicately after de-stalking.

Patrick de Ladoucette is fast acquiring a reputation in all the main white wine areas of France. He has marketed wine from the district of Pouilly-Fumé, Sancerre, Chablis, Vouvray and also Touraine with great success. His Baron Briare is a Sauvignon de Touraine made up of clear wine and must, bought up and then fermented in the firm's cellars. These are close to Château du Breuil in Saint-Paterne-Racon. The wine has a handsome quality.

At the time when Patrick de Ladoucette brought out a superior Pouilly-Fumé under the name Baron de L, he was also launching a superior white Touraine, called Baron Philippe de La Bouillerie after the gérant of the Touraine wine firm at Château du Breuil in Saint-Paterne. The 1978 was the first vintage. It was only offered to a few of the best restaurants in the Loire valley. I found it to be a very elegant wine, subtle, well-balanced, very pure — almost a less substantial Pouilly-Fumé.

Touraine

'Shame on anyone who does not admire my joyous, my beautiful, my brave Touraine, with its seven valleys where wine and water flow.' So wrote Balzac of his beloved native Touraine, the region that takes its name from the city of Tours. Balzac is not the only great writer that Touraine has produced. Descartes, Ronsard, Rabelais and Alfred de Vigny were all born here, and often referred to Touraine in their work. The region is indeed inspiring. The green valleys of the Loire, Cher, Indre and Vienne, and of streams like the Cisse and Brenne, give romantic accents to a somewhat melancholy landscape of low hills, wide woods and a rich variety of vineyards, orchards, fields and gardens. The climate reinforces the almost proverbial *douceur* of this 'garden of France'; winters are seldom really severe, the summers hardly ever too hot, and less rain falls hereabouts than, for example, in Reims with its more northerly situation. It is hardly surprising that the wealthy French aristocracy chose Touraine for building splendid residences for themselves, or sometimes for their mistresses. So it is that Touraine can be likened to a vast open-air museum assembling the world's most elegant collection of châteaux, with such gems as Amboise, Azay-le-Rideau, Chaumont, Chenonceaux, Chinon, Cinq-Mars, Langeais, Loches, Luynes, Ussé and Villandry.

The saint and the donkey

Touraine was formerly a province, mainly comprising the present *département* of Indre-et-Loire, an area of 2,364 square miles. Added to this are the 772 square miles of the Loir-et-Cher *département*, and a scrap of Indre territory. It is believed that grapes were already grown here in the 2nd century AD. According to the familiar old legend of St Martin, his donkey broke off and ate some vine shoots — and it was later discovered that the remaining branches bore even better fruit. This is how pruning is said to have been started. Touraine still has many reminders of St Martin, such as the

The Domaine du Grand Moulin is a 12-acre estate in Châteauvieux. The ground is very chalky and so the Sauvignon grape thrives there. This often gives the wine an intense, fruity, flowery bouquet. The taste, too, is generally slightly fruity, with sometimes a vague hint of vegetable. This agreeable Touraine wine is made by Yves Seneau and handled by the firm of Pierre Chainier. Another pleasant Chainier Sauvignon is Domaine des Roussières (17 acres).

In 1972 Plouzeau & Fils (Chinon) bought the Domaine de la Garrelière, at present comprising 25 acres of vineyard. The estate is near Richelieu and was once owned by the Duke of Richelieu. The vines are still young: 1980 produced the first Sauvignon harvest. Earlier Plouzeau produced a refreshing, light little wine from the black Cabernet Franc. As time passes, both the white and red wines from this estate will gain depth.

The village of Huisseau, near the imposing castle of Chambord, is where Aimé Boucher is established. This is the only firm in the Loire valley with the right to collect distillates from the growers, so it has excellent contacts. Aimé Boucher thus carries an extremely good range of Loire wines, which naturally includes the Sauvignon de Touraine: generally very aromatic and pure in flavour.

Jean-Claude Bougrier is in Saint-Georges-sur-Cher, a pleasant village with an old river harbour and an interesting Romanesque church. The firm is known for its honest wines. I have been drinking Bougrier's Sauvignon de Touraine for many years and have always been completely satisfied. The vintage date is not usually stated. The wine is of a wholly decent quality, with a spring-like bouquet.

As Chablis prices are extremely high and the market for this wine is therefore limited, J. Moreau & Fils offers more reasonable dry white wines from other areas of France — including a very adequate Sauvignon de Touraine. Brands that Moreau handles are Héritiers du Marquis de Bieville and André Meunier. Another house with generally acceptable Touraine wines is Buisse in the Loire district of Montrichard. It also trades under the name Caves de Boule Blanche.

Confrérie des Vignerons de Oisly et Thésée produces a remarkable red wine from thermo-regulated fermentation tanks called Baronnie d'Aignan. It is made from the Gamay and the Malbec and usually has a rather deep, almost dark colour and sometimes a strong bouquet of strawberries and a fruity, extremely supple, full flavour. I prefer it to the other Confrérie red wines such as the Gamay and the Cabernet.

Touraine

magnificent basilica dedicated to him at Tours and the ancient church of Azay-le-Rideau. Despite the destruction wrought by *Phylloxera*, the parasite that afflicted all the French vineyards at the end of the 19th century, in 1900 wine-growing remained the most important source of income in Touraine. At that time 156,900 acres were planted with vines, producing the annual equivalent of approximately 9,700,000 cases. Today there are some 19,800 acres yielding about 3,700,000 cases.

Travelling across Touraine

Type of soil, microclimate and tradition are the reasons for Touraine's great diversity of wines and *appellations*. Chinon, Bourgueil

and Saint-Nicolas-de-Bourgueil have already been discussed; Touraine Azay-le-Rideau, Touraine-Amboise, Touraine-Mesland, Vouvray and Montlouis will be examined in the following sections. We are concerned here with the everyday wines, those sold under the general name of Touraine. Their native soil is the whole, 60 mile-wide district of Touraine; in no other part of the Loire have I had to travel such long distances to keep my appointments. This general *appellation d'origine* of Touraine refers to about one-third of the vineyard area here, about 7,400 acres. In a poor year like 1977 this produced nearly 518,000 cases of rosé and red wine, as well as almost 422,300 cases of white. For an abundant year such as 1979, the vintage figures were in the region of 1,290,000 and 1,580,000 cases respectively.

Rich variety of grapes

In the district where Touraine wines originate, grape varieties from many regions of France are encountered; it is, so to speak, a vinous melting pot. Grapes for red wines are the Gamay from Beaujolais, the Cabernet Franc, the Cabernet Sauvignon and Malbec from Bordeaux; the Pinot Gris from Alsace; the Pinot Meunier from Champagne; and the Pinot Noir from Burgundy. In addition, the Pineau d'Aunis and the Groslot can be used for rosé, both originating in the Loire valley itself. Varieties for white are the Chenin Blanc, Pineau Menu and Sauvignon, all three apparently from the Loire; and the Burgundian Chardonnay (up to a maximum of 20% of the total planting). Red and rosé have a minimum alcohol content of 9°, with 9.5° for white. Leading roles are reserved for two varieties: the Gamay and the Sauvignon. The former grape provides an estimated two-thirds of all red wine, the latter about one-quarter of all the white.
Because Touraine is so large an area, many different types of soil occur, resulting in a wide spectrum of wines. There are few large estates. Big wine firms and cooperatives to a great extent determine the 'image' of the *appellation*, although this situation is undergoing gradual change. As the growers acquire increased vineyard area, they gain in independence and are more inclined not only to make their own wine, but also to bottle and sell it. By the same token, mixed cultivation will also gradually disappear. Maurice Barbou, a grower of Oisly, confided to me that until 1979 he had to earn his livelihood partly from asparagus, and only

TOURAINE
GAMAY
APPELLATION TOURAINE CONTRÔLÉE

Henri Marionnet has been making a Gamay at his Domaine de la Charmoise by macération carbonique since 1973. This method produces aromatic, supple wines which are soon ready to drink. Marionnet's wines are no exception to the rule. His Gamays generally have a good deep colour, mild fresh nose, rather full, sometimes almost racy flavour with fruit and a great purity. I find them delicious. Marionnet has 91 acres, 64 planted with Gamay, 2½ with Cabernet, 2½ with Malbec and 22 with Sauvignon.

Domaine des Sablons
Touraine
Appellation Touraine Contrôlée
CABERNET

Pouillé is a village on the left bank of the Cher, nearly opposite Thésée on the right bank. One of the most important local wine producers is Jacques Delaunay, owner of 30 acres of vineyard. A quarter is planted with white grapes, the remainder with black, I think the Cabernet is one of Jacques' most attractive wines and in good years this has a deep, clear red colour and a racy, rather firm flavour. The Gamay, too, is often worthwhile.

PINEAU D'AUNIS
TOURAINE GRIS
APPELLATION TOURAINE CONTRÔLÉE
Cuvée Prestige
37cl

An interesting but seldom cited speciality of Touraine is the rosé Pineau d'Aunis. This can be rather thin. The Confrérie des Vignerons de Oisly et Thésée does, however, select its Pineau d'Aunis with great care, which means a pale pink colour, rather subtle, refined fragrance and a pure, elegant, lovely flavour: a really excellent rosé deserving more attention. Another good Confrérie wine is the white Baronnie d'Aignan (Sauvignon, Chenin Blanc, Menu Pineau).

BLANC FOUSSY
Vin Vif
TOURAINE

Blanc Foussy is by far the most widely sold sparkling Touraine wine. Every year about 3 million of the rotund bottles with their effervescent contents are sold. The grapes for the Blanc Foussy come partly from vineyards owned by the Société Foltz, partly from hundreds of growers who supply them. Only the Chenin Blanc is used. The méthode champenoise is used to produce a wine that is well made and serves as a pleasant aperitif.

Opposite page:
The firm of Foltz produces various types of wine in Rochecorbon (near Vouvray), including the Blanc Foussy, a successful Touraine Mousseux. The appellation Touraine Mousseux has existed since 1974. The wine may be white, rosé or even red. The appellation Touraine Pétillant was known much earlier — from 1959 — but is nowadays hardly ever made.

Below:
Maurice Barbou and his wife.

Centre:
A small café in Azay-le-Rideau.

Bottom:
On the way home in the neighbourhood of Oisly.

Touraine wine has three fraternities: the Chevalier des Cuers du Baril, the Tire-Douzils de la Grande Brosse and the Maîtres de Chais. Wine fairs include: Tours-Fondettes (the second Saturday in February), Saint-Georges-sur-Cher (Easter), Meusnes (Whitsun) and Thésée (the first Saturday in July).

Other good Touraine wines
The splendid Sauvignon of Jean-Marie Penet, brother-in-law of Henri Marionnet (Oisly). His Gamay, Cabernet-Sauvignon and Pineau de la Loire are also very interesting; the Sauvignon of Domaine de Châteauvieux (Châteauvieux); the Sauvignon and the Cot from Jean-Claude Barbeillon (Oisly).

Touraine

since 1980 had he been able to specialize in wine-growing. He owns a vineyard of 42 acres. I was surprised to find that there were jars of preserved asparagus stored in his cellar. The reason? Some of his private customers insisted on placing their asparagus orders with him despite the fact that he no longer officially grew it.

A shop full of spring flowers

It was Maurice Barbou's grandfather who first planted the Sauvignon in Touraine. In the neighbourhood of Oisly, Thésée, Contres and Soigns — on land with a sandy topsoil and a clay subsoil — this variety proved ideal. A good Touraine Sauvignon from these parts gives a dry wine with an enchanting bouquet — it is like walking into a shop full of spring flowers. In few other French districts does the Sauvignon grape, which probably originated from around Bourges, flourish so successfully as here. With its aroma and fresh taste, the wine goes better with poached or fried fish than with salty shellfish such as oysters. One of the wine workers of Oisly told me that Sauvignon tasted different according to the weather. It seems an interesting proposition to research; is the difference really in the wine or in the taster? In general I find the white wines of the Touraine *appellation*, especially the Sauvignon, more successful than the reds. The red wines, principally made from the Gamay, too often lack colour, strength, character — and charm. I have had to struggle through a lot of rather meagre, sometimes even 'green'-tasting red wines to find just a few really good ones. Many growers apparently do not know enough about the vinification of red wine.

An exemplary firm

One concern that might serve as an example to many others is the Confrérie des Vignerons de Oisly et Thésée. It was set up in 1961 by nine growers who were tired of taking their grapes to a cooperative, or their

Touraine

wine to a *négociant.* They decided to
establish a collective enterprise in Oisly that
would care for, bottle and market the wines
they made. The number of members has now
grown to 60, working a total of 740 acres.
They always make 90% of their own white
wine, but only 25% of their red: as already
mentioned, in Touraine they seem to have
some difficulty making red wine. Not all the
wine produced by the members is bought by
the Confrérie. Under the direction of Jacques
Choquet, only the best qualities are selected.
The equivalent of about 130,000 cases
remains after selection. The Confrérie is
equipped for the vinification of red wine,
with stainless-steel tanks in which
temperature can be precisely controlled
during fermentation. That selection is no
mere formality for the Confrérie is clear from
the following examples. Normally the
collective sells 120,000 to 130,000 bottles of
Pineau d'Aunis rosé. In 1979, however, so
much of the members' wine was rejected,

that only 35,000 bottles were left. The great
respect that wines from the Confrérie have
won far beyond the borders of France makes
it clear that the quality standards upheld by
this group of growers are worthwhile. Of
course there are other people and firms
producing good Touraine wines. Henri
Marionnet, Maurice Barbou and others offer
particularly attractive products. It is to be
hoped that Touraine continues to aim at
quality.

Sparkling wines

Sparkling wines form a separate chapter in
the Touraine story. The creation of an
appellation for them in 1974 was welcomed
by a number of growers. Those who had
hitherto been scarcely able to dispose of their
white wine now had the opportunity of
selling at least a part, and sometimes even
the whole, of their vintage of Chenin Blanc
grapes at reasonable prices. The quantities

involved are revealed by statistics from
Blanc Foussy, the great specialist in
sparkling Touraine wines. This firm alone
processes a quarter of all the white grapes
harvested in the Touraine *appellation.* It
sells some three million bottles of its Vin Vif
de Touraine and, in addition to cellars at
Rochecorbon, near Vouvray, owns an ultra-
modern pressing and vinification centre in
Bléré. There are three variants of Blanc
Foussy, all made by the *méthode
champenoise*: dry white, semi-dry white and
rosé. The company, owned by the Société
Foltz and belonging to the group Société des
Vins de France, carries two other brands:
Veuve Oudinot, also a sparkling Touraine,
mainly for the French market; and Château
Moncontour — various types of Vouvray.
The firm of Monmousseau, owned by
Champagne Taittinger, is also very active in
the sparkling Touraine market with its Brut
de Mosny and other brands.

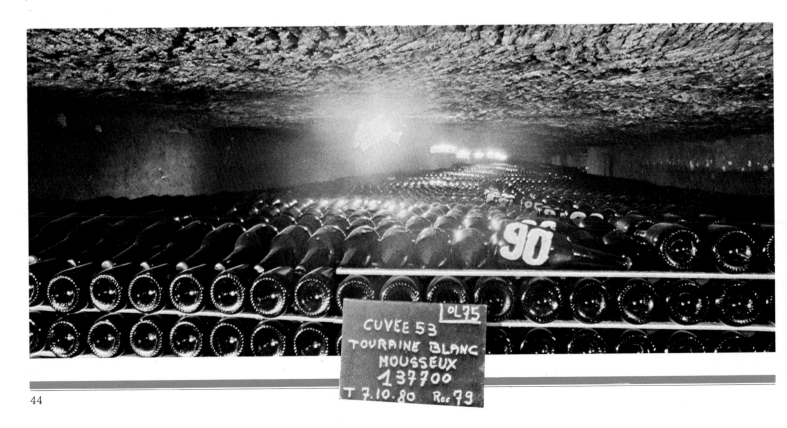

Touraine Azay-le-Rideau

Loire

The village of Azay-le-Rideau derives its name from a feudal lord of Azay named Ridel, who ruled his domain from a small castle. This was destroyed in 1418 on the orders of Charles VII. A later minister of finance built a gem of a château on the same spot. Completed in 1529, it remains a perfect example of a Renaissance castle. The French state, which has owned it since 1905, has established it as a museum, with a collection including period tapestries and furniture.

Azay-le-Rideau attracts thousands of visitors each year, but most of them see only this 'most feminine' of the Loire châteaux and ignore the village itself. This is a pity, for the little place is full of atmosphere and there are pleasant discoveries to be made, such as a historical exhibition, an old corner house from 1442, a friendly café and the 11th-century church of St Symphorien.

Small vineyard area

The flood of visitors to Azay-le-Rideau might suggest that the villagers could easily dispose of their local wine. This is not the case, however: the growers have great difficulty selling it, and then only at a low price. Before World War II, Azay-le-Rideau's wine-growing area was much bigger than it is today — almost as large as Vouvray's; but around 1955 the wine was selling so badly that many growers went over to fruit. The village's *vignoble* now amounts to only some 245 acres cut up into small plots. The wine growers' association has 45 members, which indicates the tiny size of these properties. The largest local vineyard, that of Château de l'Aulée, is not locally owned but belongs to a Champagne firm.

White and rosé only

The vineyards of Azay-le-Rideau are located in eight communes; Azay-le-Rideau; Artannes; Cheillé, where a Romano-Gallic wine press was discovered in 1950; Lignières; Rivarennes; Saché, where Balzac wrote his famous *Le Lys dans la Vallee*; Thiliouze and Vallères. They produce only white and rosé wine. The white has the Chenin Blanc as its basis and is produced almost bitingly fresh and also semi-sweet. The latter type is of incredible longevity. The grower Gaston Pavy made me try a gold-coloured, still absolutely fresh, Azay-le-Rideau 1911.
It was not until 1976 that the rosé of this district was given its own *appellation contrôlée*, 23 years after the white. It is made mainly from the Groslot — an obligatory minimum of 60%; Gamay, Malbec, Cabernet Franc and Cabernet Sauvignon are permitted, the maximum for the two Cabernets being 10%. The rosé is pale pink, astringently dry and refreshing. Rosé production varies between 6,700 and 16,700 cases a year; white between 5,000 and 16,700 cases.

Hubert Denay and his son
Thierry cultivate about 22 acres
just east of Amboise: 5 acres
Chenin, 11 Gamay, 3½ Cabernet
and 2½ acres Malbec.
Vinification and bottling of the
three black grape varieties is
carried out separately. I find the
Denays' range to be of a very
high quality. The dry white and
the dry rosé (half Gamay, half
Cabernet) and the red Gamay
are very good of their type.
However, the Cot (or Malbec) is
the most impressive: fruity,
powerful, rich in colour and full
of character.

The Château de Pocé is on the
north bank of the Loire in Pocé-
sur-Cisse. The clayey, chalky
vineyard is planted with Gamay
(37 acres) and Chenin Blanc (37
acres). The castle, surrounded by
a glorious park, produces wine
of various qualities including
the light, pleasant red Touraine-
Amboise from the Gamay grape,
bottled by the firm of Pierre
Chainier in Amboise.

Centre:
Limeray is one of the communes
of the Touraine-Amboise
appellation. There are about 120
wine growers in the whole
district.

Bottom:
Hubert Denay and his son
Thierry in front of the rock cellar
where they make good wines.

Below:
This drawing of the castle in
Amboise adorns many labels.
The town holds a wine fair at
Easter and on 15 August.

A 45 hectolitre per hectare yield
is applicable for Amboise wines.
In practice the Malbec often
does not exceed 25-30
hectolitres.

Commanderie des Grands Vins
d'Amboise is a wine fraternity
founded in 1966.

Dutertre & Fils of Limeray (on
the north bank of the Loire) is a
large, well-known producer of
Touraine-Amboise. Gabriël
Dutertre and his son Jacques
work 67 acres of vineyard, 15 of
white grapes and 52 of black
(Gamay, Cabernets, Pinot Noir
and Malbec). About a third of
the black grapes are used to
make rosé. The impressive rock
cellars contain good wines of the
Touraine-Amboise appellation,
and still and sparkling white
wines of the Touraine
appellation.

Touraine-Amboise

The town of Amboise is dominated by the
castle towering high above its roofs. If you
look down from its heights at the houses
below, they resemble, in Flaubert's words, 'a
heap of pebbles at the foot of a rock'. The
fine, partly 15th-century château has had
various royal residents, including Charles
VIII, Francis I and Francis II. It was
Francis I who in 1515 invited Leonardo da
Vinci to Amboise. Four years later the
Italian genius died on his nearby estate
which today houses a museum that includes
scale models of Leonardo's inventions. A
more sinister episode occurred in 1560 when
a group of Protestants were hanged from the
balustrades after an unsuccessful attempt to
dethrone the young Francis II.

Vines on both banks

Amboise and the immediate surroundings
have their own wine: Touraine-Amboise.
This *appellation* was created in 1954 thanks
to the efforts of the mayor, Michel Debré. It
covers Amboise, Cangey, Chargé, Limeray,
Mosnes, Nazelles, Pocé-sur-Cisse and Saint-
Ouen-les-Vignes. Some of these communes,
including Amboise itself, are on the south
bank of the Loire, others on the north. Wine
from Nazelles and Pocé-sur-Cisse was
formerly sold as Vouvray, which is also on
the north bank. Roughly 370 acres are
planted with vines and this area is gradually
being increased. The average holding in
Touraine-Amboise is 17 to 20 acres.

Amazingly good Malbecs

Touraine-Amboise produces mostly red and
rosé wines (35,500 to 58,500 cases). The red
must contain at least 9.5° alcohol, the rosé
10°. Black grape planting consists of
Gamay, Malbec (known locally as Cot, as
elsewhere in the Loire), Cabernet Franc and
Cabernet Sauvignon. The Malbec can give
amazingly good wines around Amboise. The
local *collège viticole* particularly
recommended this grape after extensive
tests. Whereas the Malbec produces
striking, robust, durable wines, those from

the Gamay are generally lighter, more
supple, and drinkable earlier. Much
Cabernet is used, together with the
Gamay, for making thirst-quenching
dry rosés.
White Touraine-Amboise (11,000 to
40,000 cases a year) comes exclusively
from the Chenin Blanc and at its best is
a fresh, dry, clean wine that must
contain a minimum 10.5° alcohol.

François Girault (married to an Artois) is a busy grower who produces a range of perfect wines in the modern manner (e.g. harvesting machines, stainless-steel fermentation tanks). The Gamay is one of the best from both the 49-acre Domaine d'Artois and the 30-acre Château Gaillard; the latter is a somewhat firmer wine. I like the taste of the fresh rosé Gris de Touraine and the dry white Pineau de la Loire. The Girault-Artois vineyards and cellars are in Mesland, the office in Amboise.

Philippe Brossillon lives in Mesland and owns 86 acres of vineyard, approximately 74 planted with the Gamay. His red is usually a good-quality, supple wine, fairly light on the palate and of an affable nature. Philippe produces a first-class rosé from the same grape with a nice fruity bouquet and taste; delicious on a summer's day.

Gilbert Breuzin of Onzain works 20 acres of vineyard, 15 planted with Gamay, from which he makes an interesting red wine: the 1978, for example, had an opaque colour and, after two years, still had a certain reserve and full, spirited flavour which, with some tannin, lingered nicely on the palate. Strangely, however, the same wine was very disappointing a year later. Another cuve? Faulty bottling? Whatever it was, the quality is evidently variable.

José Chollet and his father Rolland own 49 acres, three-quarters of which are planted with Gamay. They make a racy sort of Gamay, none too fruity or fragrant, but nevertheless pleasing. Rolland is one of the leading growers of Touraine-Mesland, President of the appellation and of the community in Onzain.

André Rediguère has acquired 7 acres of wine land through sheer effort and hard work. The plots — often on difficult terrain are very scattered but André — working towards a bigger, more homogeneous vineyard for himself and his sons through exchange and further purchases. André does not yet make any red wine. He does produce a nice Gamay rosé (with some terroir in the taste) and a good Pineau de la Loire (from the Chenin) which retains its soft freshness for 10 to 15 years.

Touraine-Mesland

To reach the district of Touraine-Mesland you leave the *département* of Indre-et-Loire and travel east into Loir-et-Cher. The vineyards all lie on the north bank of the Loire, mainly in and around the village of Mesland. The 550 inhabitants are nearly all engaged in wine-growing; or, as the mayor, Paul Roger, put it to me: 'If all goes well with the wine, all goes well with Mesland.' The other communes included in the *appellation* are Chambon-sur-Cisse, Chouzy-sur-Cisse, Molineuf, Monteaux and Onzain. In Onzain there is an important cooperative that produces roughly one-third of all Touraine-Mesland. Unfortunately this concern and its members have experienced some difficulties because of management problems. The Touraine-Mesland district covers 3,460 to 3,700 acres, but only 620 are actually utilized for the *appellation*. The rest of the growers find it too complicated to make wine under an *appellation contrôlée* and prefer the easier task of producing a simple table wine.

Large and small holdings

Touraine-Mesland has both small plots and big estates. Among the latter are the holdings of Philippe Brossillon (86 acres), Girault-Artois (79 acres), and Paul Roger (74 acres, whose wines I found disappointing). The soil is very clayey in many places and lends itself particularly to the production of red wine, and also of rosé. Mesland white wines are usually not so successful, although there are exceptions to this rule. The whites may only be made from the Chenin Blanc, but four varieties are permitted for the red: Gamay, by far the most commonly planted; Cabernet Franc; Cabernet Sauvignon; and Malbec (Cot). Production of white Touraine-Mesland does not exceed 5,500 to 24,500 cases a year; that of red varies from 52,000 to 113,500 cases.

Splendid red wines

I always taste and drink red Touraine-Mesland wines with pleasure. They often possess more colour and strength than any other wine bearing the name of Touraine. In this district even the Gamay can be a pleasantly full-bodied wine that benefits from a few years' maturing in the bottle, but nevertheless in early youth already has enough fruit and suppleness to be fully drinkable. I refer of course to Gamays that are vinified with true craftsmanship, such as those of the Domaine Girault-Artois. French wine legislation implicitly acknowledges that Touraine-Mesland wines are the strongest of the four kinds of Touraine. In Mesland the minimum alcoholic content for red and rosé is 10° and 10.5° respectively (both the highest in their category), and 10.5° for white, the highest with Azay-le-Rideau. In my opinion Touraine-Mesland is a district with great potential, especially in its red wines. Whether it is exploited depends in the first instance on its 66 or so wine growers.

Vouvray

Loire

In the village of Vouvray, six miles east of Tours on the north bank of the Loire, wine-growing has been practised since early times. The first vines were probably planted in the 4th century AD, after St Martin had become abbot of Marmoutier, later to become a very powerful house. The clergy continued to put their stamp on Vouvray for a considerable period. We read that Charlemagne gave the village to the abbey of Saint Martin at Tours in the 8th century. The abbey lost the village of Vouvray in 887, but it returned to the abbey in 1364, this time for another four centuries. The industrious monks contributed much to the further development of viticulture, not only by clearing new land, but also by planting the right grapes in the right soil. Abbot Baudoin, who became a vineyard owner in Vouvray in 1704, was especially active in the selection of grape varieties. However, the wine of Vouvray had enjoyed renown much earlier than this, Rabelais describing it in the 15th century as being 'like taffeta'.

Unknown Vouvray

Rabelais knew Vouvray because he lived and worked in the neighbourhood, at Chinon. Few other Frenchmen were familiar with the wine, because from the 15th century until the end of the 19th century, almost the whole vintage was shipped each year to the Low Countries. Once there, it was given a dose of sweet Spanish wine — so the foreigners were not acquainted with real Vouvray either. After this once-important export market had declined, the wine growers of Vouvray were faced with another problem. There was as yet no law governing the naming of wine, so that for decades all Touraine white wine was sold as Vouvray. This situation lasted until the granting of an *appellation contrôlée* in 1936. Since then Vouvray has been restricted to eight communes: Vouvray, Rochecorbon, Vernou-sur-Brenne, Sainte-Ragonde, Chançay, Moizay, Reugny and a part of Parçay Meslay. One of the eight, Sainte-Ragonde, is no longer included as it has been absorbed by

Tours. A total of 3,950 acres is planted, exclusively with Chenin Blanc (Pineau de la Loire).

Cave dwellings

On the road from Tours to Vouvray you see the broad Loire on your right, and on your left a long row of houses behind which rises a steep cliff. From the tuff have been hollowed out not only cellars but complete dwellings, some of them three storeys high, and some still inhabited. The deep stratum of tuff, which contains chalk, forms the subsoil for Vouvray wines. Clay and gravel are common in the topsoil. The vineyards themselves are situated up on the plateau, the houses down below. Many of the homes are set in narrow sheltered valleys, where even an occasional banana plant or lemon tree grows.
Vouvray itself is the most charming of the district's villages. Although rather tourist-orientated, it has retained its intimate character. Most of its 2,800 inhabitants are involved in wine-growing; locally they talk of 'Vouvray-les-Vins'. Apart from the many cellars, the 13th-century church is certainly worth visiting. Here and there in Vouvray they still celebrate *la bernache* — the vintage festival at which the fermenting wine is served with roast chestnuts.

Long fermentation

The vintage is late in Vouvray. It is exceptional for the grapes to be picked before 15 October. Usually the harvesting takes place between 10 October and 10 November, and sometimes the *vendangeurs* are busy until 20 November. The most classic Vouvray is made from over-ripe grapes, a soft wine with some degree of sweetness. This type of wine made Vouvray's reputation in the first half of this century; and rightly so, for it can be truly magnificent. I have tasted sublime *demi-sec* Vouvrays, or *moelleux* (slightly sweeter), with a perfect balance between acidity and sweetness, with impressions in both bouquet and taste of ripe fruit, pear, quince, cooked

plums, apple, honey, flowers and anise, and with extraordinary longevity. A good Vouvray can be kept, without problems, for decades. Locally they say: 'Our wine doesn't get old, it just matures.' Even a Vouvray from a moderate vintage will retain its vitality for five to ten years. One from a great vintage will reach 50 years. The potential class of a medium-sweet old Vouvray is indicated by a *Wine & Food* entry of 1954. A celebrated Sauternes Château d'Yquem 1921 was served during a dinner, followed by a Vouvray Clos le Mont 1921. The comment was: 'The Vouvray can be considered a viticultural curiosity, in that it possessed a fullness and richness of body superior to the Yquem, a more delicate bouquet and was amazingly sound, considering its age.' In other words, the Vouvray was regarded as the better wine.

High acidity

Unfortunately, this old original type of Vouvray has become quite rare. The white Vouvray table wine now marketed consists mainly of medium-sweet, characterless little wines, often bearing the label of a wine firm from far outside the district. Vouvray has therefore acquired the reputation of a cheap white wine. Only a few individual growers, like Gaston Huet, Prince Poniatowski and others, who are very conscious of quality, still make a classic Vouvray, and then usually only in sunny years. There is also, of course, dry Vouvray. This is often labelled as Vouvray *sec* (an otherwise rather loosely used term, since less astringent wines are also offered as *sec*; if there is no indication at all on the label, uncertainty as to sugar content remains until the first sip). I often experience difficulty with a really dry Vouvray because of the high degree of acidity. Many young dry Vouvrays I have tasted have made my tongue curl. They have proved as undrinkable as young Bordeaux drawn from the vat. Maturing is essential for dry Vouvray; only after four or five years in the bottle does it begin to become attractive. The best dry Vouvrays are made by growers

Vouvray

who leave the grapes on the vine for as long as they can, so that as much of the acid as possible is converted to sugar. Here, too, names such as Huet and Poniatowski crop up. Huet's conscientiousness is demonstrated by the fact that in 1979 he ordered his pickers to leave the green bunches on the vine, 'because that was a better way of ridding the wine of acid than later by chemical means'.

Bubbles mean business

As mentioned, the accent in the first half of the present century was on the classic, sweet kind of Vouvray. In the 1950s, this situation began to change, as increasing interest was shown both in dry white wines and sparkling varieties. Consequently, a very active, and, initially, extremely successful sparkling wine industry grew up in Vouvray. The dry, acid basic wine lent itself perfectly to a good Vouvray Mousseux, made by the *méthode champenoise.* For almost 20 years about 70% of all Vouvray wine was treated in this way. In the 1970s, however, demand for this type of Vouvray fell off, mainly through competition from similar wines from other areas. This dwindling demand was also associated with a series of small vintages:

Gaston Huet, who works with his son-in-law Noël Pinguet, is Vouvray's mayor and also one of the best growers. He owns 79 acres, including the 20 acres of Le Haut-Lieu vineyard. In sunny years such as 1976 and 1959, fabulous wines were produced here with a fine sweetness yet a perfect balance. 'They are wines you can eat,' says Huet. He harvests late and vinification is carried out in the traditional manner. He never uses weedkiller in his vineyards.

Le Mont belongs to the Domaine Huet and comprises 17 acres. I tasted an extremely successful 1969 demi-sec from this vineyard — ripe fruit in the pure, mild bouquet and a harmonious, elegant taste, and noted down: 'You've just learned how to appreciate a semi-dry wine!' Gaston Huet keeps a 5-year stock, or approximately 600,000 bottles. He has enormous rock cellars on different levels linked by a flight of 62 steps which he built in 1968.

The Clos du Bourg appears to be Vouvray's oldest cru, already in existence in the 5th century AD. Nowadays the 15-acre vineyard belongs to Gaston Huet. In 1979 it produced a surprisingly soft dry Vouvray with a bouquet reminiscent of a juicy pear. Many of Huet's wines ripen in very large oak barrels, the so-called demi-muids. Huet also produces sparkling and pétillant Vouvrays.

Clos Baudoin derives its name from Abbot Baudoin who experimented with grape selection there in the 18th century. Since 1918 the estate has belonged to the family of the present owner, Prince Poniatowski. He lives in Paris but travels regularly to Vouvray. The vineyard covers 44 acres. The vineyard and the wine are handled in a very traditional way. The Clos Baudoin Vouvrays have a distinctive flavour. The sweetness varies according to the vintage. They will mature over a long period.

The firm of Marc Brédif, dating from 1893, is in Rochecorbon. It has an extensive complex of rock cellars. In 1980 Jacques Cartier, who took over the firm in 1965 from his father-in-law Marc Brédif, sold it to Patrick de Ladoucette whose Pouilly-Fumé is famous throughout the world. Cartier stayed on at Marc Brédif as technical adviser. The firm's wines include an excellent Vouvray Pétillant (sec and demi-sec). The label may vary slightly.

André Freslier works about 20 acres with his son Jean-Pierre. They produce mainly dry wines. They ferment in wooden demi-muids and sometimes have a perceptible hint of apple in the flavour. At the start this dry Vouvray is very acid so it must be allowed to mature, preferably for at least four to five years. Their Vouvray Pétillant is often very successful, but the Fresliers do not carbonate it.

Vouvray

where Vouvray was lacking another sparkling wine often replaced it for good. The shortage of the basic wine also forced a number of local wine firms to close. Some vintage figures illustrate the trend: 1975 produced 438,000 cases of still Vouvray and 127,000 cases of sparkling; for 1976 it was 605,000 and 236,000 cases respectively; for 1977 it was 236,000 and 147,000; and for 1978 it was 438,000 and 189,000. The ample vintage of 1979 enabled the wine makers to replenish shrunken stocks as the equivalent of 460,000 cases of still wine and 528,000 cases of sparkling was produced.

The permitted yield is the same for all types of Vouvray at 45 hectolitres per hectare. In principle, however, the law allows a higher yield for wine intended for Vouvray Mousseux; in 1979, at the request of the growers, 60 hectolitres per hectare was permitted (with a further ceiling set 20% higher), while a 40-hectolitre maximum was maintained for still Vouvray.

Vouvray Pétillant

This type comprises approximately half of all sparkling Vouvray. Only a slight effervescence is allowed to develop. Often it is only visible when the wine is poured out; the tiny bubbles mostly disappear if it is left for a while in the glass. Vouvray Pétillant was created in about 1920 by Marc Brédif; and today the firm of Marc Brédif, owned by the de Ladoucette group, still produces one of the best *pétillants*. It takes more professional skill to make a Vouvray Pétillant than a Vouvray Mousseux. The wine requires just a sufficient amount of effervescence, but not too much. Only a very few are able to make a really successful Vouvray Pétillant. As one local expert put it: 'Eight out of ten *pétillants* are failed *mousseux*.' A good Vouvray Pétillant is better than a good Vouvray Mousseux, for less can be concealed by the bubbles: the basic wine has to be of a better standard. Remarkably enough, few people know this. In addition, Vouvray Pétillant should acquire its effervescence via secondary

Domaine Allias is managed by Daniel Allias and his sister Denise. They own 25 acres and a still Vouvray is their speciality. I have pleasant memories of their demi-secs (sometimes so dry that they almost tasted sec — like the 1975). Semi-dry wines were made here in, for example, 1975, 1976 (very good with a rather concentrated taste and agreeable subtlety), 1978 and 1979. The wine ferments mainly in large wooden casks.

The 37-acre Domaine des Barguins has been in the hands of the same family since 1710. About 40% of the vintage is made into sparkling wine. The owner, Pierre-Jean Mathias, also let me taste his still Vouvrays, including a dry 1978, full of character but still far too young, and a 1970 that imparted an impression of honey and fruit and was still wholly vital. Even better than the still Vouvray, in my opinion, is the sparkling one, a truly excellent wine. It is one of the best Vouvray has to offer.

Bernard Courson is chairman of one of the two Vouvray cooperatives — Vallée Coquette; 60% of the grapes he harvests from his 25 acres are taken there. His own still, dry Vouvray occasionally wins medals at fairs. I recall a very pure 1978 — not lacking in personality, but after two years still rather reserved in bouquet and sourish in taste. This type of Vouvray requires at least four to five years' maturation.

The largest vineyard property of Vouvray is the 160-acre Château Moncontour. The 15th-century castle with its vineyards and cellars was purchased in 1961 by the firm of Foltz, which also owns the Blanc Foussy brand (Touraine Mousseux). A lot of Moncontour wine is shipped to America. The wines usually seem well made. I prefer the dry sparkling wines (the Crémant and the Pétillant) to the still wines. Veuve Oudinot is another sparkling Vouvray from Foltz.

Other good Vouvray wines
Domaine de Monclos (Roger Pineau of Vouvray); the Chablis firm of J. Moreau & Fils (Les Héritiers de Biéville brand); Daniel Jarry (Vouvray); Lucien Pinet (Chançay).

Vouvray's motto is: 'Je rejouis les coeurs' (I gladden the hearts).

*Opposite page, centre left:
Local café.*

*Opposite page, centre right:
These old bottles, forerunners of the Champagne type, stand in a little corner of Marc Brédif's cellar.*

*Opposite page, below:
Gaston Huet, a talented wine grower, fervent promoter of Vouvray and mayor of his village. In front of him — from left to right — a Vouvray Sec, a Demi-Sec and a Moelleux. Notice the difference in colour. Huet uses ordinary tasting glasses and not the peculiar Vouvray glass which, against all the rules, is wider at the top.*

*Below:
Scarecrows to keep the birds off the ripening grapes. The growers of Vouvray own, on average, 17-20 acres.*

*Bottom:
A quiet morning in Vouvray. One of the signposts indicates the district wine route.*

Vouvray

fermentation in the bottle — a kind of controlled *méthode champenoise*. Both sparkling and *pétillant* Vouvrays must contain a minimum 9.5° alcohol, compared with 11° for the still.

All out for quality

Vouvray's wine spectrum is broad and subtly shaded. There are still, *pétillant* and sparkling wines in various measures of sweetness, and in a wide range of qualities. The image of Vouvray has been badly tarnished by too many cheap, middling wines, yet Vouvray is still one of the best-known Loire *appellations*. It is to be hoped that the wine growers of the district will choose high standards instead of bulk — and that their efforts will be recognized by the public. I take an optimistic view of this. In my opinion, the take-over of the firm of Marc Brédif by Patrick de Ladoucette will within a few years restore quality Vouvrays to the catalogue of high-class importers, the wine lists of leading restaurants, and the stocks of good retailers. If this happens, it will encourage others — individual wine growers as well as Vouvray's two cooperatives — to go all out for quality.

One of the best wine makers in Montlouis — specializing in a dry still wine — is Dominique Moyer with about 27 acres of appellation *Montlouis*. Only organic fertilizer is used. At Moyer's vineyard the pickers often go two or three times through the vineyard so as to harvest only the ripest bunches. Moyer bottles any wine he deems good enough; the rest is sold in bulk. I have always enjoyed drinking the Montlouis *sec*, a generally fresh, soft wine, pure and quite fruity.

The brothers Jean and Michel Berger have cellars in Saint-Martin-le-Beau. They own about 30 acres entitled to the appellation *Montlouis*. I thought their Montlouis *sec* was very good — not too aggressive and with cool, mineral-like undertones and the suggestion of slightly tart apples. The Bergers also make a good sparkling Montlouis. They export their wine to Britain, Belgium and Germany.

Below:
Montlouis calls itself a 'capital of wine'.

Bottom:
Montlouis and Vouvray are linked across the Loire only by a railway bridge.

Right:
The square in Montlouis. The wine fairs take place at the same time as Vouvray.

Montlouis wines must contain at least 9.5° alcohol.

The local fraternity is the Cotérie des Closiers de Montlouis.

Good Montlouis is also grown by the Déletangs on 35 acres in Saint-Martin-le-Beau. Like many of their colleagues, they produce some rosé and red wines under the *Touraine* appellation.

Montlouis

The wines of Montlouis and Vouvray are sufficiently alike for them to have been sold for generations under the same name. The wine growers of Montlouis even lodged a legal protest in 1936 when it appeared that their district was not to be included in the Vouvray *appellation contrôlée*. Their protest was in vain, however, being rejected by the court of appeal. On 6 December 1938 Montlouis was given its own *appellation*. This was, in fact, a major setback for the growers — no one had ever heard of Montlouis. Vouvray was then a renowned wine for which good prices were paid, but who could be expected to pay as much for a completely unknown one? Despite difficult times, the Montlouis growers struggled on and survived the crisis. Nevertheless, in familiarity and reputation, Montlouis has always remained in Vouvray's shadow.

Sandier soil

The villages of Vouvray and Montlouis-sur-Loire are about two miles apart as the crow flies. Vouvray is on the north bank of the Loire, Montlouis on the south, on a spit of land between Loire and Cher. The distance by road is much greater because motor traffic has to go via Amboise or Tours — only the railway crosses the river at this point. The district consists of three communes: Montlouis-sur-Loire, Lussault and Saint-Martin-le-Beau. Most of the vineyards are on a gently rolling plateau 200 feet and more above the level of the river. Here too there is a chalky subsoil in many places, although, unlike Vouvray, it is largely covered by a rather sandy topsoil in which clay and gravel also occur. This somewhat different soil accounts for the slight variations between Montlouis and Vouvray wines.

Need for sun

Because of the sandier soil of Montlouis's 740 acres, the wine is generally quicker-maturing than Vouvray and at the same time not so full-bodied. I also get the impression that a Montlouis *sec* usually has less acid than the average Vouvray *sec*. The Montlouis possesses a more mineral, cooler and 'stonier' character. It can mature well in the bottle. The Chenin Blanc totally dominates the scene here and, as in Vouvray, a varied range of wines is made from it: still, *pétillant*, and sparkling, dry, semi-dry and *moelleux*. The last two kinds are only made in sunny years. Indeed, in Montlouis they seem to need much more sun than in Vouvray for successful results. Whereas in a moderate year the Vouvray wines are still acceptable, those of Montlouis are often too meagre. Perhaps this is one of the reasons why the district is continually increasing its sparkling wine production. In 1976, a year of plenty, some 117,500 cases of still wine were produced compared with 23,500 cases of sparkling, but in 1978 the respective figures were 69,500 and 56,500 cases, and in 1979 58,000 and 44,500 cases.

I first became acquainted with the fresh, cool Jasnières of the young wine grower Joël Gigou in the André Paul restaurant in Coëmont. Gigou owns nearly 20 acres: about 7½ acres of Jasnières (this acreage is being increased) and about 12½ of Coteaux du Loir. He lives in La Chartre-sur-le-Loir. I have tasted other good Jasnières from André Fresneau (Marçon) and Jean-Baptiste Pinon (Lhomme).

André Fresneau and his son François cultivate 20 acres: 17 Coteaux du Loir and 3 Jasnières. Their red Coteaux du Loir is made exclusively from the Pineau d'Aunis and matures for at least 18 months in wooden casks. It is a distinctive wine that gains a certain roundness in sunny years and there is a slightly bitter element in the taste and some tannin. The Fresneaus advise drinking it fresh like Beaujolais.

It was no easy task to find Robert Minier, a grower in the Coteaux du Vendômois, because his house and cellars lie high up on a slope at the end of an unmade, no-through road. With his son Claude he works a 15-acre vineyard. Their wines are simple, light and refreshing. The rosé from the Pineau d'Aunis is to be recommended with charcuterie or with small grilled sausages. The white and the red both tasted very nice with goat's cheese, which the Miniers also make themselves. The red matures in wood for some time.

Below left:
There are many rock-hewn cellars in Jasnières such as this one belonging to André and François Fresneau.

Below right:
Robert Minier. He is one of about 30 people producing Coteaux du Vendômois. Permitted yield is 50 hectolitres per hectare. The district is made up of 35 communes in Loir-et-Cher.

Right:
Vineyard in the Jasnières district.

There is a permitted yield of 30 hectolitres per hectare for Coteaux du Loir red and rosé, and 25 for the white.

Coteaux du Vendômois must contain at least 9° alcohol; Coteaux du Loir 9.5° and Jasnières 10°.

Jasnières and its neighbours

About 25 miles north of Tours and the Loire lies another river valley, that of the Loir, where wine is also produced. Officially the wine counts as Val de Loire. The vineyards lie on either side of the river, mostly on chalky slopes, sometimes up on the plateaux. The best-known district is Jasnières, whose wine was mentioned centuries ago by French authors such as Ronsard and Rabelais. Jasnières received its *appellation contrôlée* in 1937. What is immediately striking is the low yield per hectare — only 25 hectolitres, or exactly the same as the very sweet Sauternes. But anyone who expects a sweet wine will soon be disillusioned; Jasnières (exclusively white) tastes extraordinarily dry. The Chenin Blanc grape and the subsoil of tuff produce a really chalk-dry, austere and initially tart wine that should be matured for at least five years. Very occasionally, as in 1964, 1959 and the 'year of the century' 1947, semi-sweet wines are also produced. The Jasnières *appellation* comes within the boundaries of Lhomme and Ruillé-sur-Loir. Near Lhomme is the hamlet of Jasnières itself — just a few houses. Whereas in the past a possible 988 acres of vines were cultivated, the total is now about 49 acres. The production varies from about 1,450 to 2,800 cases a year.

Coteaux du Loir

The originating district of the Coteaux du Loir wines — red, rosé and white — is closely linked with that of Jasnières, but is nominally bigger. It consists of 22 communes, including the Jasnières villages of Lhomme and Ruillé-sur-Loir, where many growers produce both white Jasnières and red or rosé Coteaux du Loir. Red and rosé are in the majority in the Coteaux. The yield varies from approximately 1,900 to 3,350 cases a year, whereas white does not exceed about 1,050 to 1,450 cases. White Coteaux du Loir is scarcely distinguishable from Jasnières: it comes exclusively from the Chenin Blanc and the yield is 25 hectolitres per hectare. The red wines (30 hectolitres per hectare) come principally from the Pineau d'Aunis; Cabernet, Gamay and Malbec are also permitted. The wines have quite a distinctive, slightly bitter taste. They are usually light, rather lacking in depth. I prefer those from sunny years such as 1976. The rosés, in which a maximum of 25% of Groslot may supplement the aforementioned black grapes, have a fairly astringent, fresh character. The Coteaux de Loir district may be potentially bigger than Jansières, but the present vineyard area is not much larger at 74 acres.

Coteaux du Vendômois

This district lies some 30 miles east of the Loir valley, near the town of Vendôme. Its wine has been classed as *vin délimité de qualité supérieure* (VDQS) since 1968. The wines are white (Chenin Blanc with a maximum of 20% Chardonnay), rosé (Pineau d'Aunis with no more than 20% Gamay) and red (a minimum 30% of Pineau d'Aunis, with Gamay, Pinot Noir, Cabernet Franc and Cabernet Sauvignon). The district covers 618 acres, distributed over 35 communes. Only about 100 acres of this area produces Coteaux du Vendômois. In good years the vintage reaches the equivalent of some 16,700 cases, consisting mainly of light wines, but of quality.

Bottom:
The château of Cheverny. It was completed in 1634.

In Cheverny 50 hectolitres per hectare is permitted, and there is a minimum alcohol content of 9° for red, and 9.5° for white and rosé, just as in Valençay.

Below:
Bust of Talleyrand in Valençay. He lived in the château.

Valençay's fraternity is the Confrérie Gastronomique des Grands Escuyers de Valençay en Gastine.

Romorantin is one of the specialities of the Chai des Vignerons, a collective enterprise consisting of about 20 growers. It is generally a pale, bone dry, rather thin wine with an unusual bouquet. The Sauvignon is usually a little more supple. I also tasted an agreeable rosé Pineau d'Aunis and red wines with 90% Gamay and 10% Pinot Noir. The latter has slightly more roundness and fullness than the wine from the Gamay only: a creditable attempt to make the red Cheverny wines more attractive.

The Domaine Gendrier (about 50 acres) is the joint property of Marcel Gendrier, his son Michel and his son-in-law Michel Cadoux. They have planted about a quarter of their vineyard with the Romorantin. In scent and taste their Romorantin is milder than most of its kind, though it remains fresh, and rather harsh. I discovered an enjoyable little white Cheverny, pure, lively and fairly mild, at the firm of Pierre Chainier in Amboise (brand: Ph. de Guerois).

Hubert Sinson, frequent medal-winner, owns 37 acres, 17 with the Valençay appellation. His land is planted mainly with the Gamay, but I consider Sinson's best wine to be Cot (another name for Malbec). In good years this has a deep colour, soft, with a firm fragrance and an equally firm, rather hearty, flavour. Not a great wine, but much better than many lightweight Valençays from the Gamay. Hubert Sinson, who also makes a successful rosé Pineau d'Aunis, lives near Meusnes.

Julienne Beschon runs a typical smallholding in the district of Valençay (near Faverolles). The yard is like a typical small farm with chickens, rabbits, geese, a goat and kittens. She also makes wine from 11 acres, more than half of this planted with the Gamay. The Gamay wine tastes light, pure, simple and agreeable; delicious for everyday drinking. I thought the white Sauvignon and the Cabernet rosé were not quite on the same level, but well made.

Cherverny and Valençay

Loire

The vineyards of Cheverny occupy a fairly extensive district on the south bank of the Loire, southwest of Blois. It takes in 22 communes, including Cheverny and Cour-Cheverny. At present 1,236 acres are cultivated, an area that could be doubled. Cheverny has been a VDQS wine since 1973; but the *appellation* has not been an unqualified success. In trying to make Cheverny known, the 230 wine growers have to contend with all kinds of problems, among them too small a vintage (approximately 156,000 cases in a good year). Moreover, their wines to some extent resemble those of the adjoining *appellation* of Touraine. The Cheverny growers do not make a great deal of money. Most of them sell their wine in bulk to the *négociants* or take their grapes to the cooperative. A serious attempt to change this situation is being made, however, by the Chai des Vignerons at Chitenay. This enterprise, set up in 1976, is owned by 20 or so growers who cultivate a total of 370 acres. They vinify their own wine and the best of it is then selected, bottled and sold by the Chai des Vignerons.

An unusual grape

Cheverny possesses an uncommon type of white grape, the Romorantin. Francis I introduced it in 1519 to his château near Romorantin from somewhere in Burgundy (80,000 vines according to the records). It has disappeared from around the locality itself, but retains the name. In Cheverny it produces a white wine that the French describe as very dry and very bracing, with a distinctive bouquet. It could be related to the Gros Plant du Pays Nantais (page 16). Other white wines are made from the Chenin Blanc, Sauvignon, Chardonnay and Pineau Menu (Arbois). The Sauvignon is the most commonly planted variety. Most of the red and rosé wines come from the Gamay Noir à Jus Blanc, although other varieties, such as the Cabernet Sauvignon, Cabernet Franc, Pinot Noir and Malbec, are permitted. Some sparkling wine is also produced by the *méthode champenoise*. The château of Cheverny may be impressively luxurious, but the same cannot be said of its local wines. The average Cheverny is usually rather meagre and austere, without much fruit or roundness. Nevertheless, some growers are doing their best to make the wines more agreeable — with encouraging results here and there.

Valençay

This is a small wine district that borders on Touraine in the southeast. Although it comprises 15 communes, the vineyard area of the *vin délimité de qualité supérieure* is only 272 acres. The 35 wine growers produce at most 33,500 cases a year. The wine is mainly red from the Gamay grape, although wines from the Cabernet Sauvignon, Cabernet Franc, Malbec (Cot) and Pinot Noir are also made. All red or rosé Valençay must have a minimum 75% of the grapes mentioned; no more than 25% from four other types is permitted. Red Valençay is a pleasant, uncomplicated, usually light wine that is drunk young and fresh; the same is true of the rosé. The Valençay white is light and not unappetizing. It must be made from at least 60% Pineau Menu (Arbois), Chardonnay or Sauvignon; a maximum of 40% Chenin Blanc and Romorantin is permitted.

The best-known figure in Reuilly is Robert Cordier, a genial character who is chairman of the syndicat viticole, chairman of the land redistribution board, and member of the Institut National des Appellations d'Origine. Some 10 of his 15 acres are planted with Sauvignon. This gives a fresh, pure wine, with a racy and vaguely vegetable bouquet. This white Reuilly can easily mature for six to seven years without losing freshness.

Robert Cordier, assisted by his son Gérard, makes his rosé only from the Pinot Gris. He has 5 acres planted with this. The wine is bottled in March after first remaining in large wooden casks or concrete or metal vats for some months. Cordier's Pinot Rosé tastes delicious. Despite the limited production these and other Cordier wines (including a pleasant red Vin de Pays de l'Indre) are exported to various countries in small amounts. •

The young wine grower Claude Lafond is held in great local esteem because he has been appointed vice-chairman of the syndicat viticole. He owns about 21 acres: 10 planted with Sauvignon, 3½ with Pinot Gris, 1½ with Pinot Noir and about 6 with Gamay (for the Vin de Pays de l'Indre). I thought his pale, beige-pink rosé was excellent. The astringently dry Sauvignon, with just a hint of grass or vegetable in the taste, was rather pleasant.

Henri Beurdin lives in the hamlet of Preuilly near Reuilly and owns 17 acres of wine land, 15 acres being entitled to the Reuilly appellation. Some 12 acres are planted with Sauvignon, the rest with Pinot Noir. Beurdin's white Reuilly often has a rather austere, clean taste, unusually fresh. The bouquet often lacks depth but is not unpleasant.

Right:
Robert Cordier, a leading wine grower.

Below:
A weather-beaten town map in Reuilly; on the left is a list of a dozen growers.

Bottom left:
Village café in Reuilly. A sign mentions the white Sauvignon yet the rosé is actually Reuilly's best wine.

Bottom right:
Reuilly is not only a district and a wine but also a village.

Reuilly

About halfway between the district of Valençay and the city of Bourges are two small, isolated wine districts, Reuilly and Quincy. Their wines are regarded as belonging to the Loire valley, although that river is 44 miles away at its nearest point. Both districts derive their name from villages, and Reuilly is the more westerly of the pair. This little place, built on a hill, creates rather a worn impression, like some cyclist who once won the Tour de France but is now old and forgotten, left alone with his memories. That Reuilly once knew better times is shown by some surprisingly spacious squares and a large old church. The village only comes to life once a year, during the wine fair at Easter.

Soil like Chablis

Reuilly received its *appellation contrôlée* in 1937, about a year after Quincy. The district consists officially of seven communes, two, including Reuilly, in the Indre *département* and five, like Quincy, in Cher. Most of the vineyards are around Reuilly itself, on the left bank of the little river Arnon. The soil contains a lot of lime and in composition is very reminiscent of Chablis. Only 148 acres produce the *appellation* wine. From a further 245 acres comes a simple table wine (usually a red Gamay sold as Vin de Pays de l'Indre).

Too little wine

The modest vineyard area of Reuilly is in the hands of a few dozen growers, so, obviously, most of their plots are very small. Twelve acres puts a man among the big landowners here. Few of the growers can make a living from wine alone. Even Robert Cordier, who with 13 acres of vines is the second largest owner, also grows cereals on 124 acres.
It is not easy to find the wine growers of Reuilly. Their houses and cellars are usually hidden away in small hamlets and not always provided with clear nameplates (things are quite different in Quincy). The Reuilly growers, however, have no need to sell to casual passers by: they are always short of their wine.

The white wine of Reuilly differs from that of Quincy due to the different nature of the soil: it is somewhat drier, less round.

Even Reuilly has its own fraternity: the Echansonnerie de Reuilly.

Reuilly is unremarkable apart from an old church. Outside the village is the small castle of Ormeteau with its three round towers.

On sunny days the inhabitants of Reuilly relax on the banks of the Cher where there is a small sandy beach.

Below:
The hamlet of La Ferté — where Robert Cordier lives — is on the Reuilly-Issoudon road. It is a quiet, rather secluded collection of houses, one of which accommodates the Café de la Gaieté.

Right:
Two essential ingredients of any wine tasting, a corkscrew and glasses.

Reuilly

Excellent with oysters

When I first visited Reuilly I knew the district only through its white wine. This is made from the Sauvignon grape and should contain a minimum 10.5° alcohol. The coolness of the underlying chalk is unmistakable in the taste, and there is often a discernible element of green vegetable or of asparagus, as in many wines from Sancerre and Pouilly-Fumé. The wine is somewhat lean and austere, but could not be described as meagre or thin. The bouquet is not, as a rule, very pronounced. Reuilly partners shellfish extremely well; no doubt this is why Reuilly and Marennes (famous for its oysters) have 'adopted' each other. During this first visit my image of white Reuilly was wholly confirmed. However, I did discover another type there — Reuilly rosé.

A Reuilly speciality

This rosé used to be known as *vin gris* and Reuilly was especially noted for it. Robert Cordier told me that his father used to take a big barrel of *vin gris* to Bourges and Vierzon to sell to cafés and restaurants. The customers there would order a *chopine* (half a litre) and drink it from beakers. Robert added that his father did not earn much money that way. Rosé is still a speciality of Reuilly. If wine growers from Sancerre come to visit their colleagues here, this is the wine they drink. Robert Cordier confided, with some pride, that the local fire brigade had ordered a hundred bottles of his rosé for a party.

An attractive rosé

Reuilly rosé was a revelation: it is undoubtedly one of the most attractive rosés of the entire Loire region. It is usually made from the Pinot Gris, which in Alsace gives Tokay d'Alsace. The Pinot Noir can also be used, but this variety produces a different kind of rosé. A really good Reuilly rosé, i.e. from the Pinot Gris, is distinguished by a soft, beige-pink colour, a pure, agreeable bouquet and light taste, refreshing and gentle at the same time. It is a cheerful thirst-quencher, suitable for summer picnics and prestigious restaurants alike. The wine

must contain at least 10° alcohol, which also applies to red Reuilly (hardly any of which is produced). Permitted yield for all the wines of this district is 40 hectolitres per hectare. It is a pity that Reuilly makes so little wine, especially this delightful rosé: production of it varies between about 1,900 and 4,450 cases a year. White fluctuates between roughly 3,900 and 12,000 cases annually. It is to be hoped, however, that eventually there will be so much interest in Reuilly rosé that production will be greatly increased.

Below:
Wine grower Raymond Pipet.

Bottom:
Scene in Quincy where you can enjoy a refreshing glass of local wine with some goat's cheese in the village café.

The grape harvest in Quincy normally takes place one week before Sancerre and Pouilly-sur-Loire.

Quincy wine must contain at least 10.5° alcohol.

On Quincy wine labels you often find the words Vin noble. A local tradition?

After the death of Gilbert Surtel, his vineyard was taken over by his daughter and her husband Gérard Brisset. The Brisset-Surtel estate has 11 acres mainly planted with Sauvignon. There is also a little Pinot Noir for some simple rosé and red wine. The Quincy from the Sauvignon is normally a pure, tasty wine with a considerable, but not intrusive, freshness.

There are about 30 growers making their living solely from wine in the Quincy district. One of the most important — and quality conscious — is Raymond Pipet. He owns 35 acres, 32 planted with the Sauvignon. Pipet de-stalks all his white grapes and then presses them firmly 'to get all the finesse out of the pulp'. The only treatment the wine gets after fermentation is filtration. This Quincy is very pure and smooth in taste and quite supple from the start.

Like Raymond Pipet, Claude Houssier occasionally ships wine to Britain, among other countries. He cultivates 15 acres of vineyard. I was impressed by his wine, which often had an almost juicy scent and a clean, refreshing, slightly spicy taste.

The 62-acre Domaine de Maison Blanche has by far the most wine-growing land in Quincy; it represents nearly a quarter of the entire appellation. The vineyard is scattered over various plots in Quincy. The wine — very pleasant, with a flowery bouquet and a good taste — is processed and bottled by the firm of Albert Besombes of Saint-Hilaire-Saint-Florent, near Saumur.

Maurice Rapin's cellars are in the middle of Quincy. He makes a successful wine with a pleasant aftertaste. There are 7 acres of vineyard.

Pierre Mardon also makes a good wine. He owns 17 acres. His 1980 was fresh and lively; the 1979 rather disappointing.

I have tasted Quincys which, if not world-shaking, were wholly adequate, from the firms of Alphonse Mellot (Sancerre) and Nicolas (near Paris).

Quincy

The district of Quincy lies six miles east of Reuilly and is almost twice the size. The vineyards — about 272 acres — are on the left bank of the Cher valley. Mainly because of its location close to a waterway, Quincy wines were being drunk in Paris centuries ago. The monks of Cîteaux were the first to stimulate wine-growing in the district, in the 14th century. It was the long tradition of wine here that undoubtedly helped Quincy in 1936 to become the second district in France (after Châteauneuf-du-Pape) to receive an *appellation d'origine contrôlée*.

A genuine wine village

Apart from a few plots in Brinay, all the vineyards of this little district are within the boundaries of Quincy itself. The village is completely agrarian in character. That most of the inhabitants are involved in wine-growing is abundantly clear from signboards, wall paintings and even a few window displays: the visitor is emphatically pointed towards *caves* and *dégustations*. Compared with Reuilly, for example, Quincy has a very small church, with the most modest of towers. Probably the villagers were never rich enough to afford a large building. Even today, things are not always easy. On 9 April 1977, for example, 90% of the vintage was affected by frost and only the equivalent of 5,400 cases was produced that year. In 1978 too the vintage was small — this time it was a violent storm that did the damage. It started at eight o'clock in the evening of 29 July and a few hours later half the fruit had been destroyed. Fortunately 1979 brought some consolation with an abundant yield of 54,000 cases.

Exclusively white

The *appellation* Quincy applies solely to white wine from the Sauvignon grape, and it differs from Reuilly because the soil here contains less lime and more gravel. Quincy is somewhat rounder than Reuilly, with less evidence of the chalk, and more genial. The soil difference is also obvious from a higher yield per hectare: 40 hectolitres in Reuilly, 45 in Quincy. The grower Raymond Pipet told me that the vineyards of his district are mainly situated on what was once the bed of the river Cher. According to him, they closely resemble certain sites in the Pouilly-Fumé district, especially Les Loges. He also made an interesting observation: 'If I were a young grower and could choose, I would have land in Reuilly for growing rosé wine, in Menetou-Salon for red, and in Quincy for white.' He himself cultivates vines only in Quincy, but is quite content.

Wines from the Bailly-Reverdy estate are served in many good French restaurants. With his sons Jean-François and Phillipe, Bernard Baily cultivates about 25 acres — 15 of these being in Bué, including 2½ in the Clos du Chêne Marchand. This produces a distinctive, fruity and appealing wine. At Bailly-Reverdy (Bernard's wife is a Reverdy) I also tasted one of the few good red Sancerres.

One of Bué's best-known growers is Lucien Picard. He has 12¾ acres planted with Sauvignon (including 5 acres in Clos du Chêne Marchand and 3 acres in Clos du Roy) and 4¼ with Pinot Noir. His white wines are of immaculate quality, have a pure bouquet and lingering aftertaste. My favourite is the Clos du Chêne Marchand; distinctive in flavour, full in the mouth and usually capable of maturing for three to four years.

Sancerre

In the lovely green valley of the Loire with its meadows and willow trees, Sancerre comes as something of a shock. Quite unexpectedly, a steep hill rises to 1,000 feet above the peaceful landscape; and clearly visible on its slopes are the irregular outlines of a village. Sancerre dominates its surroundings, like a silent sentinel high above the neighbouring villages and the nearby Loire. The strategic value of this position was recognized long ago. Some historians maintain that Julius Caesar started a settlement here (there is a Porte César in the village); others say that Sancerre came into being when a group of Saxons established themselves here in the time of Charlemagne. At all events, Sancerre has its origins in the remote past. It grew from probably a few dwellings into a sizeable village in the 10th century when Count Thibault of Champagne built an impressive castle on this formidable height.

Starved into surrender

One of Thibault's descendants, Stephen I, called himself Comte de Sancerre and adopted for himself and his troops the motto: 'The best comes first'. The imposing castle, of which there are old engravings extant, brought trouble to Sancerre during the fierce French religious wars. Early in the 16th century it became a refuge for Protestants, which resulted in a calamitous siege under

SANCERRE
APPELLATION SANCERRE CONTROLEE
Clos du Chêne Marchand
1976   75 d
PRODUCE OF FRANCE
LUCIEN CROCHET - BUÉ (CHER) FRANCE
MISE EN BOUTEILLE A LA PROPRIETE

SANCERRE
"LE GRAND CHEMARIN"
1979
Jean-Max ROGER
à BUÉ (Cher)
75 d

SANCERRE
BLANC DE BLANCS
Clos de la Poussie
1977
CORDIER

SANCERRE
APPELLATION SANCERRE CONTROLEE
Le Grand Chemarin
Mis en bouteille à la Propriété par
Pierre GIBAULT
Fougeuilhon-Villoublon, BUÉ (Cher) France
• 75 cl

Lucien Crochet's cellars are near to Lucien Picard's. They are large, modern and tiled. Lucien Crochet is a shipper as well as a grower, buying grapes from other growers. He himself owns about 25 acres of land in Clos du Chêne Marchand and in Clos du Roy. The former produces the best wine, substantial rather than refined, with some terroir in the taste. It is an outstanding Sancerre of high quality.

Wine maker Jean-Max Roger (Bué) has a long family tradition and a thorough grounding in Burgundy wine. About 75% of his 17 acres are in Le Grand Chemarin, the rest mainly in Clos du Chêne Marchand. Some 3¾ acres have been planted with Pinot Noir and Jean-Max makes the better red wines from these. My favourite white is the rather astringent, very clean, well-balanced Le Grand Chemarin. Jean-Max is also a wine merchant and uses a special label for the wines he sells.

The whole of the amphitheatre-like Clos de la Poussie in Bué (25 acres exclusively planted with Sauvignon) is owned by the Bordeaux firm of Cordier. There it produces a fairly supple type of Sancerre, rather flat but often with some fruit and terroir. It is a good, well-made wine but not of top quality. From 50 acres elsewhere (Domaine de l'Orme aux Loups near Sancerre and 17 acres in Ménétréol) a not-too-brilliant rosé and a red are made.

Le Grand Chemarin from Pierre Girault is generally a nice, decently full wine with a tinge of green, a characteristic vegetable bouquet and a compatible taste in which juice, a touch of fruit and a pleasant freshness are discernible. Pierre Girault lives in Bué and owns 10 acres.

Opposite page, above: The Sauvignon grape, basis of all Sancerres. There is a minimum alcohol content for this wine of 10.5°; 10° for red and rosé Sancerres. Permitted yield for all three wines is 40 hectolitres per hectare.

Below: The village of Sancerre from the south. From the village church you can clearly see the 12th-century Tour des Fiefs. This is all that remains of the fortifications here. The tower is classed as an ancient monument.

Sancerre holds its wine fair at Whitsun and this always attracts many visitors.

At the entrance to the village, about half-way up the hill, are the Caves de la Mignonne, which are used as wine cellars and have been open to the public since 1972.

Château de Boucard is 6 miles from Sancerre in the commune of Noyer. It is a feudal building that was rebuilt in the 16th and 17th centuries. Concerts and exhibitions are held here in the summer.

Sancerre

Charles IX in 1573. An earlier attempt had been made to reduce Sancerre — 5,915 cannonballs had been fired at the castle in 1572 — but this time hunger was the cause of its downfall. The siege lasted for seven long months. In the archives we read: 'After the horses, asses and mules had been eaten, in May it was the turn of the rats, mice and moles, and even the surviving cows for feeding the children. In June there was no more bread . . .' On 19 August, Sancerre fell:

the toll was 585 dead (about one-quarter of the population), 139 wounded and some 200 sick. Part of the castle was laid waste and a heavy annual tax was imposed on the inhabitants. It is no wonder that many families fled to Switzerland and Holland. In 1621 Sancerre was again attacked, this time for purely political reasons. The ensuing defeat resulted in the total destruction of the castle, except for the 12th-century Tour des Fiefs.

Family names

Not everyone fled Sancerre in these grim times: many remained faithful to their village and their land. The Mellot family, for example, has lived in Sancerre since 1531 and now runs the house of Alphonse Mellot, the biggest wine business here. One ancestor was César Mellot, *conseiller viticole* to Louis XIV. It is noticeable how particular names appear repeatedly among the Sancerrois —

I have pleasant recollections of the Sancerre from the Domaine des Garennes, a fairly full, quite distinctive wine with an elegant perfume. Its makers are the brothers Michel and Jacques Fleuriet, of a family that for generations has produced wine in the hamlet of Chaudoux near Verdigny. Their father cultivated only 7½ acres and tended a few goats. The brothers have extended the vineyard to 25 acres and invested heavily in cellars and modern equipment. Clos du Carroy Maréchaux is their other wine.

In the Sancerre restaurant La Tasse d'Argent, I came across Sancerre from Michel Girard, grower at Chaudoux, near Verdigny. The 1979 was fresh and crisp, in which I tasted the coolness of the chalk soil and some fruit from the grape: an excellent wine from a 12-acre vineyard.

The Verdigny vineyard of La Perrière is on the caillottes: dry soil with limestone and gravel. This gives a fine, quite fruity Sancerre that can be drunk young. A good example is Bernard Reverdy's Sancerre Vignoble de la Perrière, a characterful wine of refined bouquet and taste with abundant freshness. Reverdy owns about 17 acres of wine estate.

Jean Reverdy in Verdigny makes an excellent Sancerre, called Domaine des Villots. It has fruit, a lot of breeding, a lively taste, a cool tone from the chalk and perfect balance. What struck me about the 1979 was the absence of the usual 'vegetable' element in bouquet and taste, which gave the wine added charm. Jean Reverdy cultivates 15 acres.

Many medals underline the exquisite quality of Pierre Prieur's wines. In good years they have a pure Sauvignon bouquet with a hint of spices, and a beautiful taste with fruit and a suggestion of asparagus. They are sold under the name Domaine de Saint-Pierre. Prieur's 15-acre vineyard is in Verdigny.

Pierre Archambault, whose Verdigny cellars attract many visitors, has quite a large range of wines, not all of equal quality. However, his best, Comte de la Perrière, has considerable class. This usually has a subtly nuanced bouquet in which asparagus is clearly discernible, and an almost juicy, elegant taste without assertive acidity. This wine has been selected by Count Xavier de la Perrière. Archambault's vineyard covers 62 acres, 90% used for white wine.

Sancerre

names such as Bailly, Crochet and Reverdy, Fleuriet, Raimbault and certain others. In Sancerre it is usually essential to know a particular grower's first name, otherwise it is almost impossible to track him down.

An attractive market square

Despite the fact that in the past armies have occupied Sancerre with a vengeance, the place still exudes the genuine charm of an ancient village. There are many old houses and other buildings of the 11th, 12th and 15th centuries, separated from each other by narrow, winding, steep little streets. In the centre of Sancerre is the market square, surrounded by a few cafés and restaurants, a pottery, some art shops, and a pâtisserie selling the local delicacy, Croquets de Sancerre (a sweet, crisp, nougat concoction). Sancerre has about 2,600 inhabitants. In good times the figure used to be around 3,500.

Monks and kings

As in many other wine districts, it was the monks, particularly those from the nearby village of Saint-Satur, who encouraged grape-growing here. French kings were most appreciative of Sancerre wines. Henry IV, planting an elm in the little village of Chavignol, remarked: 'Chavignol is the best wine I have drunk. If all the people of my kingdom were to drink it, there would be no more religious wars.' His tree still stands in Chavignol, which belongs to the Sancerre *appellation*, and nailed to it is a board bearing the king's words. Louis XVI too is said to have described Sancerre wines as the finest in the kingdom.

A range of vegetation

In the Sancerre district the vegetation is quite varied, a result of the hilly terrain. From the restaurant *La Tasse d'Argent* in the village of Sancerre, there is an excellent panoramic view of the landscape, consisting mainly of several valleys separated by ridges

of high ground. Vines predominate on south-facing slopes, with cereals on the north slopes and plateaux, and woods on the highest hilltops. The other villages nestle deep in the valleys. The vineyards of Sancerre certainly testify to the courage and persistence of the growers who work this land. Some slopes are so steep that neither horse nor tractor can get up them. Cultivation here has always been done by hand — and that includes carrying up any soil that has been washed down the slopes. For this reason some of the vineyard names have an ominous ring, like Les Monts Damnés. One random example of a difficult vineyard is Clos de la Poussie in Bué. In many places the slopes of this imposing amphitheatre rise at an angle of 60 degrees. The only mechanical aid is a system of ropes for hauling objects up or down. There is an old French saying:

'Money lost, nothing lost,
Honour lost, much lost,
Courage lost, all lost.'

How apt this is in Sancerre, additionally so because of the district's traditionally fickle weather. In the 18th century alone, there was the devastating storm of 20 July 1723, the eight months' rain of 1763, and the unremitting drought of 1778.

Revival of the vineyards

Sancerre is known today mainly as a white wine made exclusively from the Sauvignon grape. However, there used to be much more red wine produced in the district, from the Pinot Noir, while the white wine came from the Chasselas. The Chasselas has totally disappeared, and the importance of the Pinot Noir has been drastically reduced. The production of white Sancerre varies from the equivalent of about 378,000 cases to 500,000 cases. For red and rosé the figures are roughly 83,500 and 109,000 cases respectively.
At the beginning of the century Sancerre had approximately 4,200 acres of vines, an area

that declined slowly to about 1,480 acres in 1960. At that point the world discovered Sancerre, with the result that nowadays some 3,700 acres are cultivated; and this area is expected to grow to about 5,000 acres.

Fourteen communes

The *appellation* Sancerre, created in 1936, takes in 14 communes. In alphabetical order they are: Bannay, Bué, Crézancy, Menetou-Ratel, Ménétréol, Montigny, Saint-Satur, Sainte-Gemme, Sancerre, Sury-en-Vaux, Thauvenay, Veaugues, Verdigny and Vinon. Some of these villages (Vinon and Montigny for example) have only a few acres of vines and are of minor importance. Four communes — Crézancy, Sancerre, Verdigny and Sury-en-Vaux — have more than 250 acres of vines; one, Bué, has more than 500. I have spent a relatively longer time in Bué because its vintage is not only large but often of outstanding quality.

Poor man's cow

Bué, whose name probably derives from a Celtic word for 'spring', is an out-and-out wine village. At least 350 of its 400 inhabitants are involved in wine. The place consists of a few meandering streets in a valley surrounded on all sides by vine-clad slopes. Visitors are always welcome at the *Caveau des Vignerons*, a simple, friendly establishment where, with a glass or two of the local wine, you can eat a *coudré* (a goat's milk cheese, at a stage between fresh and blue), an omelet, a *grillade* and some *crudités*. The *Caveau* is owned by some 20 of the 60 growers of Bué.
Until ten years or so ago there were more goats in Bué than people — estimated at 1,000 to 1,500. All the growers kept them. As elsewhere in Sancerre, changes in the scale of wine-growing have caused them largely to disappear. Nowadays, the 'poor man's cow' is seldom encountered in the true wine villages. A little way out of the village of Sancerre, however, there is a large

I have frequently tasted wine of various vintages from the Cave des Chanvrières — a 30-acre property of Paul and Claude Fournier in Verdigny. It is a good Sancerre, not too full nor too meagre, pleasant of bouquet, often rather flowery, and somewhat astringent in taste. There is also often a little terroir. In 1950 the Fournier land only amounted to 5 acres.

Pierre and Etienne Riffault own about 12 acres of land in Verdigny. In good years their Sancerre has a rather refined bouquet and a mildly fresh flavour with sometimes an almost sweet aftertaste. I found it a harmonious wine — not top class, but it left a wholly agreeable impression.

Vincent Delaporte is a grower with about 25 acres in Chavignol. His best wine comes from the Clos Beaujeu, a vineyard next to the well-known Monts Damnés. It is an aromatic Sancerre with flowers in the scent and a mouth-filling, pleasant flavour which has freshness without being disturbingly tart. Even in such a difficult year as 1977 Vincent Delaporte managed to make a thoroughly acceptable wine.

From documents dated 1782, it appears that the Neveu family were already producing wine in Verdigny at that time. The present generation is represented by Roger Neveu who manages 25 acres: 20 of Sauvignon and 5 of Pinot Noir. The wine is served in a number of leading French restaurants. The first white Sancerre Clos des Boufants I tasted was the 1979. It had a very fine bouquet with fruit and flowers. The charming, delicious taste complemented the bouquet.

The low cellars of Denis Père & Fils, a firm founded in 1953 by the restaurateur Paul Denis, are in Chavignol. Paul's son Didier — who composes music in his spare time — is the present owner and director. Denis's wine is served in a number of Parisian and other good restaurants. Didier mainly buys his Sancerres from growers in Chavignol, Bué and Verdigny. The white Sancerre is particularly noteworthy: an honest wine nurtured by craftsmen.

Below left: The village of Chavignol enjoys a reputation both for its wine and its goat's cheese — the famous Chavignol crottin.

Bottom left: This sign is next to a baker's in the village square in Sancerre. The croquets are a crisp, local nougat speciality.

Below right: Alphonse Mellot, owner and director of the most important wine firm in Sancerre and of the largest wine estate. Alphonse has been working since 1970 in the family firm that bears the same name, having first studied in Dijon. His late father did much to promote Sancerre, and opened Le Sancerre, a wine-tasting establishment, in the Avenue Rapp, Paris.

Sancerre

goat's-milk cheese cooperative that keeps about 300 of the animals.

Soft porous tuff

The most famous of Bué's vineyards is Clos du Chêne Marchand, shared by a large number of growers. Its soil type is described locally as *caillottes,* a combination of fine gravel with porous, dry calciferous tuff. This volcanic rock is much softer here than in Vouvray, for example, and so no cellars have been carved out of it. The soil produces a fine type of Sancerre, usually fruity, with *fraîcheur* and a considerable bouquet, that can be drunk fairly young. The favourable, south-facing situation of Clos du Chêne Marchand accentuates and strengthens these features. Beyond the 74 acres of Clos du Chêne Marchand lies the 37-acre Clos du Roy, most of which has the same soil structure and lies mainly within the boundaries of Crézancy. Another Bué vineyard area with this soil type is the 50-acre Grand Chemarin, and part of Clos du la Poussie (about 15 acres). *Caillottes* soil is also found in parts of Chavignol, Ménétréol, Sancerre and Verdigny.

Marl and flint

A second type of soil is called *marne argileuse* or *terres blanches*, clayey marl, usually with some gravel. Bué's Clos de la Poussie in part exemplifies this, as does Mont Damnés in Verdigny and Chavignol, Clos Beaujeu in Chavignol, and much of the vineyard area of Sury-en-Vaux. This soil gives a firmer kind of wine that takes longer to develop its bouquet and taste. A third type is *silex*, or flint. On this soil, wines that are usually austere and almost steely are grown in Sancerre, Ménétréol, Saint-Satur and elsewhere. It is often said locally that the best Sancerres are made from the products of more than one soil type. This is only half true, as there are a good number of splendid Sancerres grown in one vineyard, certainly in Bué, where many growers of the Clos du Chêne Marchand produce beautiful,

The Château de Maimbray in the commune of Sury-en-Vaux is owned by the Roblin family. The vineyard covers 27 acres. it is a very appealing wine: pure in bouquet with hints of fruit, wild flowers and vegetables, also pure in taste, supple, racy and adequately full. The Roblins make red and rosé wines (25% of their production) in addition to their white.

Alphonse Mellot is the owner and manager of the firm that bears his name and has about 104 acres of vineyard. Both the firm and the estate are Sancerre's largest. Alphonse's most famous wine is his Domaine la Moussière (82 acres). It is a clean, somewhat astringent Sancerre and it usually has an agreeable amount of fruit; the bouquet is not over-emphasized. As a rule all the elements of ths wine, which is full of character, are excellently balanced. Mellot supervises the vinification of all his wines.

The label illustrated is one of the many under which the Sancerre cooperative, founded 1963, sells its wines. It has around 180 members, and a good reputation; it also has stainless-steel tanks — a rarity in Sancerre. The best wines from the Cave des Vins de Sancerre may not have a particularly distinct personality, but they are far ahead of many Sancerres from individual growers. Eugène Renaud is the manager.

With his sons Jean-Louis and Denis, Jean Vacheron works 44 acres and runs the tasting booth Grenier au Sel in the market square in Sancerre. The Vacherons produce a really good wine from their 12 acres of Pinot Noir — the best I have encountered in the district. The 1978 — deep in colour, full of taste, tannin — was an excellent wine of its type, granted that this was the best year for red Sancerres since 1921; but wine from lesser years also appeared to be very successful. The Vacheron white wines are also worthwhile.

The only remaining Château in Sancerre dates from 1874 and since 1920 has belonged to the Marnier-Lapostolle family (of Grand Marnier fame). The large cellars, where they make their own wine from their 35-acre vineyard, are near the château. Clarifying, cold treatment and filtering produce a very civilized, fairly light Sancerre, pleasing without being really great. Gérard Cherrier is the very capable régisseur.

Marcel Gitton and his son Pascal make some superior wines in Sancerre and in Pouilly-sur-Loire. Vinification of about three-quarters of their wines is in very large wooden vats, the remainder in stainless-steel tanks. In Sancerre the Gittons own land in Les Montachins vineyard (22 acres: aromatic wine with a lot of terroir); Les Belles Dames (17 acres: more sultry, smoother, not my style); and Les Romains (5 acres: delightful wine and the slowest developer of the three.)

Sancerre

---

mouth-filling wines, and Le Grand Chemarin too, from which come some high-class Sancerres. There is much justification for Bué's motto: 'Des vins du Sancerrois, celui de Bué est roi'.

The Sancerre cooperative

Sancerre's 3,700 acres are in the hands of about 600 growers, so the average plot is small. By no means all of them can make a living from their vineyards. Three to four acres used to be enough for a comfortable existence, but at least twice this is necessary today. Some 180 of the smaller growers belong to the Sancerre cooperative. Its excellent equipment includes stainless-steel tanks and it makes a good, reliable range of wines. This *cave coopérative* produces approximately one-tenth of all Sancerre — it could be much more, as many members are contracted to supply only a minimum 20% of their vintage to the enterprise. The *cave* takes grapes (about one-fifth), must (two-fifths) and wine (about two-fifths). Under various labels it supplies the French wine giant Nicolas, and also many foreign importers and certain airlines.

Bouquet of asparagus

As is obvious from the growth of the vineyard area, interest in Sancerre has greatly increased since the 1960s. The increasingly 'dry' taste of the wine-drinking public has contributed much to this; so has Sancerre's location — a convenient drive (125 miles) from Paris. Sancerre white wines can nowadays be reckoned among the best-

SANCERRE
COTE DE CHAMPTIN

Paul Millérioux lives in Crézancy where he cultivates 27 acres. His white wines, from 22 acres, are mainly distinguished by a very clear colour, by the asparagus and fruit in the bouquet, and a rather light taste that is fresh without being really acid. There is a little terroir in the aftertaste. This wine leaves no overwhelming impression but can be drunk with much enjoyment.

'Until 1970 Domaine du Nozay was a blessed haven of idleness,' says the owner Philippe de Benoist. He planted the first vines on the land. At present they cover 11 acres and will expand. From this new vineyard de Benoist produces a particularly agreeable Sancerre, full and soft in the mouth with an impression of ripe fruits in the bouquet and a slightly nutty aftertaste. It is an almost atypical Sancerre — with no chalkiness — but very pleasant.

The Paris-based firm of Patrick de Ladoucette offers its Sancerre under the brand name Comte Lafond. Patrick owns no land in Sancerre but he buys must (25%) and ready wine there after the latter has been racked (75%). Further treatment, bottling, etc. is carried out in the cellars of Pouilly's Château du Nozet. The Comte Lafond is one of the better-quality Sancerres: pure, lively, supple and only slightly chalky or vegetable-like in taste.

Other good Sancerre wines
Jean Delaporte (Chavignol: particularly his Les Monts-Damnés); Pierre-Millet Roger (Bué: notably his delicious Le Grand Chemarin); Jean Vatan (Verdigny); Alain Dezat (Maimbray near Sury-en-Vaux); Château de Thauvenay (Thauvenay); Gérard Millet (Bué); Maurice Raimbault-Pineau (Domaine des Godons, Sury-en-Vaux); Côte des Chante-Merles from Michel Thomas (Sury-en-Vaux); Grande Réserve from Bourgeois (Chavignol); Cave de la Petite Fontaine (F. Fleuriet, Verdigny); Domaine de Sarry (M. Brock, Le Briou-de-Veaygues); Les Baronnes of H. Bourgeois & Fils (Chavignol).

*Opposite page, left:
Baskets of newly picked grapes ready for pressing, from Alphonse Mellot's own vineyards.*

*Opposite page, right:
The Château de Sancerre from its beautifully kept gardens. It was built in 1874 and bought in 1919 by Louis-Alexandre Marnier-Lapostolle. At present it is owned by the Société Marnier-Lapostolle (of Grand Marnier liqueur fame), which belongs to the heirs of Louis-Alexandre. The château is usually only occupied at weekends. A carefully made, refined and elegant Sancerre is produced here.*

*Below:
Two generations of talented growers, Jean-Max Roger of Bué (left) and Jean Vacheron of Sancerre.*

Sancerre has its own wine fraternity, the Chevaliers de Sancerre.

There is a record — Arion 33359, distributed by CBS — of 'Danses du Pays de Sancerre' by La Sabotée Sancerroise.

Sancerre

---

known in France. They possess more strength and class than Muscadet, and are rather more congenial than Chablis — in price as well. There is usually a tinge of green in the colour, and the bouquet is often strongly reminiscent of asparagus. There is also a discernible hint of grass, or greens, while the better wines also have fruit. The taste of a really good Sancerre is very dry and refreshing without being harsh or thin. It combines pleasantly with all kinds of fish and shellfish, and with pâtés and other cold hors d'oeuvres. Also, anyone in the district who has had 'elevenses' consisting of a glass of cold Sancerre with a piece of fresh French bread and some goat's cheese will know how delightfully they combine. One of the most famous of these cheeses, from the wine village, is Crottin de Chavignol.

Unpredictable quality

For some years Sancerre has been fetching good prices without difficulty. This has led a number of growers to make as much wine as possible, regardless of quality. The younger generation, too often lacking either the sense of vocation or the qualities necessary to make a good wine grower, tend to stay on the land merely to make money. The results are passed on to the consumer in a large number of mediocre Sancerres. This was strikingly shown by two large comparative tastings — each of 15 wines — that I organized for the present work. Half of the wines tasted were either unsatisfactory or barely passed muster. It is, therefore, advisable to choose Sancerre with great care.

Sancerre red and rosé

What is true for white Sancerre is even truer for red and rosé, which received their *appellation* in 1959, 23 years after that for the white. Both Sancerre *rouge* and *rosé* are very much in fashion, especially in Paris. I find this strange, for in quality neither of them are up to the standard of sound examples of their white conterpart. Their popularity must be due to a combination of novelty and rarity. Some French restaurants obviously succeed by offering their clients unusual (but certainly not cheap) *petit vin*. Still Champagne or Coteaux Champenois is another such example (see pages 190-1). That red and rosé Sancerres leave much to be desired in the way of quality has been demonstrated for me not only by tastings, but also by the comment of the Bué grower Jean-Max Roger, who said that you would be lucky to find 10 good red wines in the whole of the district — and he was right. This is partly due to the fact that most growers plant their best land with the Sauvignon grape, and the Pinot Noir is often grown on rather unsuitable soil. Many 'red' vineyards are wholly or partly north-facing. One man who has deliberately not done this is Jean Vacheron in Sancerre itself. His Pinot Noir vines face south — and give very good wine.

Because supply of red and rosé Sancerre falls far short of demand, quite a few growers tend to give priority to the Pinot Noir when planting new land, or replanting. It is to be hoped that this is a temporary trend: firstly because white Sancerre is the better wine, and secondly because no one knows how long the current fashion for the red and rosé will last. It would be a pity if Sancerre produced a surplus of middling rosé and red wines, while the white became scarce and priced out of reach.

Menetou-Salon

While Sancerre continues to bathe, star-like, in the limelight centre stage, Menetou-Salon lurks somewhere in the semi-darkness of the wings. For despite the fact that some of the Menetou-Salon wines greatly resemble those of Sancerre, and the two districts are only half an hour's drive apart, Sancerre is well known, and Menetou hardly at all. The main reason may be their respective locations. Sancerre is close to the Loire, so that for centuries it was always easy to ship the wine out. Menetou-Salon lies inland from the river, which used to be a definite handicap. Sancerre is also just a little nearer Paris and the motorways. Why, once having found the right sort of wine, should anyone travel farther?

Unpromising introduction

As you drive from Sancerre towards Menetou-Salon, the landscape characterized in the former district by chalky hills, once more becomes typically French. The road runs over gently rolling hills with pasture and arable land, an occasional wood, and silent, weathered hamlets. Grapes are no longer to be seen. Not until a few miles from the village of Menetou-Salon do a few vineyards appear, mostly small plots lost in the landscape. The first important wine estate you see on the narrow, winding D25 is the Caves Gilbert. It does not constitute the most cheerful of introductions to the district as its wines are generally of moderate quality. You find them again in the village itself, where the estate has a tasting booth.

Splendid château

As a village, Menetou-Salon is not especially memorable. The centre consists of a large square with trees, around which stand the most important buildings, including the church, some cafés and a few restaurants.

Near this square, however, is Menetou-Salon's magnificent château. It belonged to Jacques Coeur, minister of finance under Charles XII. His motto was: 'For the brave of heart nothing is impossible' ('À vaillants coeurs riens impossible' — coeurs, of course, being a pun). This maxim perhaps helped Coeur to become the richest man in France. In the 19th century the château was completely renovated by Prince Auguste d'Arenberg, president of the Suez Canal Company. He was responsible for assembling the castle's collection of paintings, antique furniture and Flemish tapestries. Today the château is Menetou-Salon's most important attraction; tomorrow perhaps it will be the wine.

Expanding vineyards

This is not yet the case. The Menetou-Salon vineyards are only just reaching the 250-acre mark; Sancerre has 15 times this area. Yet expansion has begun. When I first visited the village in 1977, I was told that someone had planted a further 17 acres in Saint-Céols, which for this district represented a respectable gain. Henry Pellé, wine grower and mayor of Morogues, informed me in that same year that he hoped to double his 27-acre vineyard within five years. Bernard Clément wanted to increase his 37 acres to about 60 in a similar period. On a later visit I met Georges Chavet, who with his two sons was busy building a modern cellar with the capacity to handle an increase of 2½ acres a year on his original 27 acres.

The appellation Menetou-Salon, created only in 1959, comprises ten communes. These are, apart from Menetou-Salon itself, Morogues, Parassy (the three most important), Vignoux-sous-les-Aux, Saint-Céols, Humbligny, Aubinges, Pigny, Quantilly and Soulangis.

Similar to Sancerre

Two varieties of grape thrive in the district: the Sauvignon for white wines (8,900 to 23,500 cases a year) and the Pinot Noir for

Henry Pellé is the mayor of Morogues. His house faces the 13th-century church; his cellars are just outside the village. Pellé works about 37 acres at present and hopes gradually to expand this to 54 (it was 27 acres in 1977). The business is in excellent technical order. His wines, white, red and rosé, usually come near to perfection. The reds are often matured for a year in wooden casks.

The Domaine de Chatenoy comprises 235 acres of which 62 will ultimately be planted with vines. The owner Bernard Clément cultivates under 50 acres at present. I only know Clément's white Menetou-Salon which usually has a very fruity bouquet (the 1978 reminded me of peaches) and a fresh, pleasant, not too light taste.

I tasted a beautiful Menetou-Salon rosé from Georges Chavet. The Chavets (Georges is assisted by his sons Michel and Jean-Philippe) own about 25 acres of vineyard and hope to expand steadily by 2½ acres a year. Their red Menetou-Salon was very agreeable and the white smelled and tasted absolutely delicious. Half of the vineyard is planted with Pinot Noir.

The small firm of Denis Père & Fils in Chavignol (Sancerre) buys red and white Menetou-Salons, often from four growers — provided the wines are of acceptable quality. They are personally selected by the director, Didier Denis (who also supplies the master chef Michel Guérard). Both the red and the white Menetou-Salons I tasted at Denis's establishment were, if not first-rate, of very decent quality.

Other good Menetou-Salon wines
Jean Teiller (Menetou-Salon); Paul and Jean-Paul Gilbert (Menetou-Salon); Alphonse Mellot (Sancerre); Joseph Mellot (Sancerre).

Menetou-Salon village names may be given on the label.

The local fraternity is the Confrérie du Paissian.

The local wine cooperative makes about 11,000 cases a year. All the growers bring in part of their vintage.

White Menetou-Salon must contain at least 10.5° alcohol, the red and the rosé 10°.

Opposite page, above left: Henry Pellé in his office in Morogues. He is assisted by his son.

Opposite page, above right: Wine growers Georges Chavet and son Philippe.

Opposite page, below: The château of Menetou-Salon.

Below: Menetou-Salon is built on a hillside.

Bottom: The vineyards of Menetou-Salon with the village church in the background. These could be expanded to about 740 acres.

Menetou-Salon

reds and rosés (7,600 to 13,300 cases). Permitted yield for both varieties is 40 hectolitres per hectare. On the north the vineyards are sheltered by extensive woods with many oak trees. The soil on which the vines grow is mostly calcareous. Probably the best soil is in Morogues, and it is noticeably similar to that of Sancerre. Henry Pellé asserts that there is often more difference between two Sancerres than between a Sancerre and a Menetou-Salon, especially when the latter comes from Morogues. It may be significant that part of Pellé's wine is bottled for the grower and *négociant* Jean-Max Roger of Bué in Sancerre district, and that my first contact with Pellé was made through the Sancerre firm of Alphonse Mellot. The Sancerrois have always known that they make a good wine in Menetou-Salon. When will the rest of the world discover this?

Delicious thirst-quenchers

Although there may be a great resemblance between white Menetou-Salon and white Sancerre, they are not identical wines. The scent and taste of Menetou-Salon can have more charm than its better-known neighbour. It often has a seductive bouquet, strongly evocative of wild flowers and fruit, and the taste is vital and fresh, but without the chalky dryness or the weight of some Sancerres. Menetou-Salon sometimes possesses rather less depth than Sancerre, but for me this is more than adequately compensated by sheer drinking pleasure afforded. Although the white wines of Menetou-Salon are not quite of the standard of good Sancerres, this is not the case with the reds and rosés. In Sancerre these may just pass muster, but in Menetou-Salon, if the season has been sunny enough, the reds are gently full-flavoured, often fruity and even capable of maturing; the rosés are delicious thirst-quenchers, usually of an amenable freshness, light of taste and transparent pink in colour.

Pouilly-Fumé

As you drive back from Menetou-Salon to the Loire, Sancerre lies on the left bank of the river, Pouilly-sur-Loire on the right. The two communes are barely six miles apart and both produce a fresh, dry white wine, mainly from the Sauvignon grape; hence the saying in Pouilly: 'Water divides us, wine unites us'. There are, nevertheless, clear differences between the villages and their wines. Sancerre is a charming place, sparkling with vitality, and visited by thousands of tourists every year. Pouilly-sur-Loire, in contrast, seems rather subdued. For years the busy N7 highway, the *Route Bleue*, ran through the centre of the village. Although the ceaseless traffic was cursed by the inhabitants, some earned a good living from it, for there were many flourishing hotels and restaurants there. All this came to an end on 21 October 1973, the day the N7 bypass was opened. Peace and quiet suddenly returned to Pouilly, and the place does not yet seem to have recovered from the shock. The passing tourist trade has dwindled almost to nothing and only the unnecessarily large car parks at the entrance to the village are a reminder of former bustling times.

A monastic possession

Pouilly-sur-Loire, however, is by no means a poor commune. The local wine created something of a sensation in the 1970s, and increasingly high prices were demanded by the growers, many of whom are prosperous folk with comfortable homes, well-equipped cellars and big cars.

Pouilly is of Roman origin: the name derives from Pauliaca Villa, 'the villa of Paulus'. The Romans also stimulated wine-growing, probably already established in embryo here. There are the remains of a Roman road near the village. In the annals of Pouilly we read that in AD 680 the Archbishop of Auxerre honoured the local vineyards with a visit. These were totally laid waste in a war in 840, but in 859 wine-growing was again flourishing. In the 11th century the village was held by Baron Humbault, but when he failed to return from a crusade, his lands appear to have been bequeathed to the Benedictine monastery at La Charité-sur-Loire (still a beautiful old village with an imposing basilica). The monks of this Romanesque abbey steadily and diligently extended Pouilly's vineyard area. They had time enough to do this, for the village

Opposite page, above:
Wine harvest at Les Loges.

Opposite page, below:
Château de Tracy in the well-wooded commune of Tracy.

Below:
Saint-Andelain church.

De Ladoucette, the most famous and most widely sold Pouilly-Fumé, is frequently encountered in the best restaurants. Although 1 to 2 million bottles are sold annually, the quality leaves nothing to be desired. In fact it has more class than almost all the other Pouilly-Fumés. There is often some fruit and spices in the perfume and in the taste, which is lively, balanced, complete and noble.

In good years Patrick de Ladoucette, with his cellar master and two independent négociants, selects the very best wine from his vineyard. it is usually an utterly civilized and, for a Pouilly-Fumé, rather soft wine of great distinction. It comes in a heavy, old-fashioned bulbous bottle, with a crowned 'L' on the shoulders. Despite the extremely high price, there is no problem selling it.

Château de Tracy is one of the oldest Pouilly wine estates. An ancient deed shows that wine has been made there since 1396. Just under 50 of the 247 acres are planted with vines. The cellars struck me as traditional, and somewhat grimy. The wine from Château de Tracy — owned by Count Alain d'Estutt d'Assay — is a rather hard Pouilly-Fumé with a good body and a modest amount of fruit. It matures extremely well. At its best in sunny years.

Marcel Gitton and his son Pascal live in Sancerre, where they vinify their Pouilly-Fumés from their 22 acres. The Gittons produce various qualities of wine, all to a high standard. I greatly preferred their Les Chantalouettes (also sold as Clos Joanne d'Orion), one of the very few wines that approach the class of the De Ladoucette. The wine — from a 10-acre plot — has an unassuming elegance, a lot of style and a pure freshness.

Maurice Bailly's house is in a street running parallel to the main thoroughfare in the hamlet of Les Loges. With his sons Jean-Pierre and Michel, Maurice cultivates 30 acres (approx. 5 planted with the Chasselas). The Baillys make a really good Pouilly-Fumé that is much exported and regularly wins medals. Their cellar is in Les Loges and the wine is bottled in Tracy.

Pouilly-Fumé

remained the property of the monastery until the French Revolution at the end of the 18th century.

Dessert grapes for Paris

The 19th century proved remarkable for Pouilly. Although the local wine had already acquired a good reputation, an increasing number of growers began producing dessert grapes in response to a heavy demand for the fruit in Paris. Pouilly was then planted principally with Chasselas, a variety that can be made into wine but also tastes well as a dessert grape. Tons of these grapes were shipped from tiny Loire ports such as Pouilly and neighbouring Tracy via Orléans to Paris.

This trade was curtailed with the arrival of the railways, when Pouilly's grapes could no longer compete with the much cheaper fruit from the south of France. How far the Chasselas dominated the scene is clear from the fact that at the beginning of the 18th century, 2,470 out of 2,720 acres were planted with this variety. Only after 1920 did the Chasselas lose its predominance. It is still grown today, but to a far lesser extent: about 80% of Pouilly's area is nowadays planted with the Sauvignon.
Whereas before 1914 the district still had 2,470 acres under vines, postwar lack of interest in the wine, plus a variety of other difficulties, led to a marked decline. During the early 1970s, however, Pouilly's wine — Pouilly Fumé or Blanc Fumé de Pouilly — became very fashionable, so that there are now about 1,480 acres of vineyard.

Seven communes

The wine district of Pouilly-sur-Loire, with its surroundings, embraces the land of seven communes: Pouilly-sur-Loire itself (including the hamlet of Les Loges), Saint-Andelain (including the hamlet of Les Berthiers), Tracy-sur-Loire, Saint-Laurent, Saint-Martin-sur-Nohain, Garchy and Mesves-sur-Loire. The first three of these villages are the most important; and the best vineyards are situated within a fan-shaped, four-mile-wide area north of Pouilly-sur-Loire. Farther north, the terrain becomes flatter and therefore more vulnerable to night frost, and

Pouilly-Fumé

many vineyards have been abandoned over the years as their exploitation has become unprofitable. In the entire Pouilly district, the risk of frost looms larger than in Sancerre, simply because the landscape is more open and uninterrupted, although the problem is as nothing compared to that of Chablis. Much of the soil of Pouilly-sur-Loire and the surrounding villages is of the same type as in Chablis and parts of Sancerre — *terres blanches* or *marne argileuse*, calciferous with varying amounts of clay. Areas with a lot of limestone occur, for example, near the hamlet of Les Loges, where many comma-shaped fossils of tiny oysters have been found.

Les Loges

Les Loges is, too, the only place in the district where the vineyards rise steeply, far above the roofs of the houses. The name of one of the vineyards, La Loge aux Moines, indicates that the first vines here were planted by monks. The hamlet lies close to

the Loire and was once the home of river boatmen. Today it is inhabited by about 15 wine-growing families and a number of elderly people. Les Loges is little more than a couple of streets without shops, church, or even a café; but on nearly all the house fronts there are signs of *vente directe, dégustation,* or similar inscriptions, for wine is all-important here. On my first visit to Les Loges I met Maurice Bailly, who with his two sons produces a good Pouilly-Fumé. It was about seven o'clock in the evening, the day's work was done, and the whole family, together with a few neighbours, sat in the spotless Bailly kitchen drinking the still very young wine, with French bread and goat's milk cheese.

The hamlet of Les Berthiers

Les Loges occupies a somewhat isolated position on the *route du vin* that meanders through the district. The hamlet of Les Berthiers — equally well-known in wine circles — is a bottle's throw from the N7,

situated at the foot of a 900-foot hill on which lies the village of Saint-Andelain. Its tall-steepled church, built on behalf of the great-grandmother of the local grower Patrick de Ladoucette in gratitude for the safe return of her son from World War I, can be seen from afar. Les Berthiers lies between the larger Saint-Andelain and a *Route Nationale,* yet it is even smaller and quieter than Les Loges. Only wine growers live here, folk like André Chatelain and his son Jean-Claude. Together they work 25 acres, enough to allow their two families to live in comparative prosperity. The Chatelains would like to plant more vines but can find no one to assist them — for the Pouilly district has a severe labour shortage. Only a few very large estates can afford hired help, offering their workers free board and lodging and other facilities. With their 25 acres the Chatelains have already reached their limit: one man can normally maintain 10 acres a year.

Opposite page, above left:
Château du Nozet is owned by
the de Ladoucette family. The
winery buildings are at the side
and rear. The château dates
from around 1850 and is used
mainly for business receptions
and dinners.

Opposite page, above right:
The smart bottle for Baron de L,
Patrick de Ladoucette's very
best wine.

Opposite page, below:
Landscape near Les Loges. The
Pouilly-Fumé district has its
own rather confused wine route.

Centre:
In the Château du Nozet cellars.

Bottom:
The hamlet of Les Loges.

Jean-Claude Chatelain and his father own a 25-acre vineyard. Their houses, cellars and a tasting room are in Les Berthiers. Around 90% of their wine is exported. I usually find their ordinary Pouilly-Fumé (see label illustrated) to be up to standard: noticeably fragrant and with a fruity taste. A slightly more rustic wine, with a different label, comes from the 7-acre Domaine de Saint-Laurent-l'Abbaye, on a hill near Saint-Laurent.

Landrat and Guyollot are neighbours of the Chatelains in Les Berthiers and cultivate about 20 acres. One of their wines is sold with the label illustrated above and the name Les Chaudoux. It is usually a very decent, rather firm wine with a hint of grass, vegetable or asparagus in the aroma and taste. The quality is not always equally immaculate: two different versions of the 1979 tasted very good, but the almost pomade-like 1978 was very disappointing.

Robert Pesson is a quality-conscious grower with 12 acres of land in Saint-Andelain. The wine ferments in concrete cuves and wooden casks of approx. 600 litres. His Pouilly-Fumé definitely appealed to me: sometimes a slight spiciness in the aroma, supple, with breeding and a first-class flavour. It does not have much depth or nuance, but is a pleasure to drink. Robert also produces a pleasant Pouilly-sur-Loire (3 acres).

Marcel Langoux lives on the Domaine du Petit Soumard near Saint-Andelain. From his 20-acre vineyard (17 acres of Sauvignon) he makes a decent wine, rather austere perhaps, but fruity and with breeding. Marcel bottles less than half his own wine because he sells a lot 'to the trade'. However, he does expect this situation to change gradually.

Pouilly-Fumé

High alcohol content

Pouilly-Fumé wine received its *appellation contrôlée* in 1937. It may only be made from the Sauvignon grape; permitted yield per acre is 45 hectolitres; the minimum alcohol content is 11° (white Sancerre is 10.5°). In practice this percentage is often exceeded: most good Pouilly-Fumés have 12.5° to 13° alcohol, and in really good sunny years more than 14° is common. The wine should never, of course, be confused with Pouilly-Fuissé from Burgundy, which is made from the luxurious Chardonnay grape and grown on quite different soil.

Best of the Loire

I consider Pouilly-Fumé the best dry white wine of the whole Loire valley, and this opinion has long been shared by others. In 1857 Victor Rendu wrote in his *Ampélographie française*: 'Of all the wines

Pouilly-Fumé

of the Centre, the most renowned is incontestably the white wine of Pouilly (Nièvre), a dry wine enriched by a fairly pronounced taste of flint, and which matures excellently.' About a quarter of a century earlier, the writer Jullien noted in his *Topographie de tous les Vignobles connus*: 'Pouilly-sur-Loire produces white wines that are firm and spirituous, with a light scent of flint and a very pleasant taste.' It is not clear whether the two gentlemen were referring to wine made from the Sauvignon, or from the Chasselas, then much more prevalent; but since they praised the quality and specifically mentioned the flint (technically 'gun flint'), they were presumably alluding to the Sauvignon, forerunner of the present Pouilly-Fumé. Pouilly-Fumé has rather more quality than its nearest neighbour Sancerre, and this is due to the slightly different composition of the soil. In general, Pouilly has somewhat more clay, producing a wine that is normally heavier than Sancerre and with a higher minimum alcohol content.

Time to mature

Pouilly-Fumé requires a longer period to develop. A Sancerre can often be drunk in its first year, but a good Pouilly-Fumé usually only begins to show its true quality after two to four years. Furthermore, Pouilly-Fumé, although somewhat more astringent and less amenable than Sancerre, possesses more breeding and refinement. It has more to offer: the colour of a good Pouilly-Fumé is usually green-tinged, and in the bouquet a very slight hint of musk, together with impressions of asparagus, fennel, grass and spices, can be detected. The flinty coolness of the limestone is often discernible as well; and this also occurs in the taste, which is sometimes extremely dry, sometimes almost metallic, although in a good wine never thin or obtrusive. Pouilly-Fumé has enough natural glycerine to make it supple and of a decent fullness. Patrick de Ladoucette, the biggest local grower and *négociant*, describes his wine as 'a good bouquet with a maximum of body'. Finally, experience proves that Pouilly-Fumé seems better able to tolerate a bad or mediocre year than Sancerre. Most Pouilly-Fumés of 1977, for example, were more drinkable than their very poor Sancerre contemporaries.

Pouilly-Fumé's versatility

The popular local maxim of 'Qui Pouilly boit, femme ne deçoit' may or may not have something to do with the success of Pouilly-Fumé. I believe that Pouilly-Fumé and Sancerre probably owe much of their popularity in the first instance to the high price and limited availability of the better-known Chablis at a time when there was increasing interest in dry white wines. Here, as acceptable alternatives to Chablis — and not too far from Paris — were two good dry, fresh wines, and still at agreeably low prices. Nowadays, of course, Pouilly-Fumé and Sancerre have won a share of the market on their own account. Since Pouilly-Fumé tastes rather firmer than Sancerre, its uses are more extensive. It combines excellently with many kinds of fish from sea, river or lake, with shellfish (in 1958 at the Château du Nozet *le grand mariage* was celebrated between Pouilly-Fumé and the Marennes oyster); and also with poultry, veal, pork and even lamb. The versatility of the wine was eminently demonstrated during a lunch at the Amsterdam Hilton where Patrick de Ladoucette served his wine as an accompaniment to *poulet de Bresse* with chicory, finely chopped calf's liver on creamed leeks, and spring lamb with mint. Contrary to what is often asserted, the *fumé* of Pouilly-Fumé does not imply a smoky taste but applies to the grey, smoky bloom that covers ripening Sauvignon grapes.

An obsession with wine

Until the beginning of the 1970s, production of Pouilly-Fumé was controlled by the local *cave coopérative*. Today, however, the 30-year-old cooperative processes, at most, 15% to 20% of the 100,000 to 245,000 cases of Pouilly-Fumé harvested each year; and as a rule its production is unmemorable. In both capacity and quality the cooperative has been surpassed by another local firm, that of the de Ladoucette family. The enterprise is based at the Château du Nozet, dating from 1850, which belongs to Baron Patrick de Ladoucette and his two married sisters. Patrick is a dynamic individual, with no hobbies; wine is his entire life. He lives in Paris, drives enormous distances every year and flies his own plane all over Europe. From 1973 he set about reviving the somewhat somnolent family business, with the result that it now sells an estimated 60% to 70% of all Pouilly-Fumé. Patrick has also acquired interests in Touraine (the Baron Briare brand), produces Sancerre (Comte Lafon), has taken over the Vouvray firm of Marc Brédif, makes a Chablis, and has obtained 44 acres for grapes in the Napa Valley, California, currently processed there by Robert Mondavi.

'Good wine is never too dear'

Behind the graceful, stylish Château du Nozet there is an extremely efficient system of cellars. In stainless-steel tanks, at an average temperature of 15°C, must from the château's own vineyard (about 136 acres and increasing steadily) and from other producers is fermented.
Patrick de Ladoucette buys mainly grape juice from the growers so that he can make the wine as he wants. He also buys wine after its first racking. A third of the production comes from his own estate, the rest from other vineyards (in the proportion of about 70% must and 30% wine). Not all the wine is bottled in May. Part is kept in glazed tanks where it remains perfectly fresh. Pouilly-Fumé de Ladoucette, despite the large volume, has great class: complete, very balanced, pure, indeed a noble wine. At various tastings that I have attended or organized, this Pouilly-Fumé nearly always beats the rest. Besides his usual Pouilly-Fumé, Patrick de Ladoucette also sells small quantities of his Baron de L, which comes

The greatest years for Pouilly-Fumé were 1934, 1945 and 1959, when some wines reached a natural 15° alcohol.

The foundation for the family fortunes of the de Ladoucettes was laid by Patrick's great-great-grandfather, Count Lafon, a governor of the Banque de France. Patrick is a dynamic wine entrepreneur whose maxim is: 'I work with the growers and not against them.' This may well account for his success.

It is said that Louis XIV, Marie-Antoinette and Napoleon loved drinking Pouilly wine. There is a letter extant in which the emperor complains that his barrels have still not arrived in Russia.

The small firm of Denis Père & Fils, with cellars in Chavignol near Sancerre, deliberately processes no more than 60,000 bottles a year divided among the appellations Sancerre, Menetou-Salon, Pouilly-sur-Loire and Pouilly-Fumé: quality wins here over quantity. The Pouilly-Fumé is usually a good wine, racy, fairly full in the mouth and with a long aftertaste. If possible it ought to mature for 2 to 3 years. A different label than the one illustrated also occurs.

Near the castle and park of Chambord lies Huisseau and the firm of Aimé Boucher. Under the management of its owner Aimé Boucher and his son-in-law Claude Kisner it sells 800,000 to 1,000,000 bottles annually. They collect marc from the growers and so they know the numerous cellars and wines in the Loire valley. No doubt that is why their Pouilly-Fumé is of such good quality. It often has around 13° alcohol, a mouth-filling taste and a subtle fragrance.

The Domaine Saint-Michel is a wine estate of about 21 acres in Les Berthiers. It is rented by the Bourgogne firm of Prosper Maufoux, established in Santenay, which also supervises vinification and bottling. The Pouilly-Fumé is usually a fine, tasty wine, soft and fairly lively. I also found the Pouilly-sur-Loire (from 3 acres) a very pleasant wine of its type. Domaine Saint-Michel was previously called Domaine de Riaux.

Pouilly-Fumé

from his own vineyard, and then only the best *cuvées*. The selection is made by Patrick himself, his cellar master and two independent *négociants*. The quality, needless to say, is excellent. Baron de L is bottled in an especially attractive heavy bottle and is a very expensive wine. Nor is de Ladoucette's 'ordinary' Pouilly-Fumé exactly cheap. I once heard Patrick remark, wisely, that 'Good wine is never too dear — the bad always is.'

'Less serious' wine

The second wine of the district, Pouilly-sur-Loire, from the Chasselas grape, comes from the same seven communes and has the identical permitted yield of 45 hectolitres per hectare. The minimum alcohol content is lower than for Pouilly-Fumé — 9° instead of 11°. Production is gradually diminishing. At present it varies between 15,500 and 55,500 cases a year. Pouilly-sur-Loire is distinctly a lesser wine than Pouilly-Fumé in bouquet, taste, aftertaste, character and class. Nevertheless, this wine, which the growers describe as 'less serious', is a pleasant, fairly neutral, inexpensive thirst-quencher for drinking young.

One of the most surprising visits of my Loire journey was to the Montigny family (Roger and his son Daniel) who own 21 acres of vineyard in Mareau-aux-Prés. I had no very high hopes following my other experiences with Orléans wines. However, one good wine followed another: a supple, juicy Auvernat Blanc, an extremely charming Gris Meunier, an uncommonly fruity, light Pinot Noir and a very pleasant Cabernet. They work under the name G.A.E.C. Clos Saint Fiacre.

Arnold Javoy works 25 acres in the Orléanais with his sons Jean-Claude and Michel. Their premises are in Mezières-les-Cléry, where thir wines mature in large wooden casks. Of the wines I tasted I was most enthusiastic about the light, delicious Cabernet Rosé. The Pinot Noir and the Cabernet also had a very decent flavour. The Javoys are experimenting with the Cot (or Malbec) grape.

Paul Paulat has long been the president of the growers' association in the Coteaux du Giennois. He and his son Alain cultivate 15 acres on chalk and clay near the hamlet of Ville-Moison, not far from Cosne-sur-Loire. The Paulats are well equipped. Although I had problems with their Gamay and Pinot Noir, I quite liked the rosé (supple, not too light, 85% Gamay, 15% Pinot Noir) and their white Sauvignon from young vines.

Right:
Daniel Montigny from Mareau-aux-Prés. I tasted delicious wines at his house.

Centre left:
Invitation to a tasting in the Giennois.

Centre right:
This metal bottle stands in front of wine growers Roger and Daniel Montigny's door.

Bottom:
Vintage still life at the Paulat estate (Giennois).

In Orléanais and Giennois there is a minimum alcohol content of 10° for white and rosé, 9° for red. Yield is 45 hectolitres per hectare.

In the Orléanais approx. 170 acres are planted with Gris Meunier, 148 with Cabernet, 17 with Pinot Noir and 32 with Chardonnay plus Pinot Gris.

Orléanais, Giennois & southern districts

Loire

In the preceding pages we have made the acquaintance of many Loire wines. The journey along this wine river now concludes with a few small districts whose products belong to the VDQS category (*vins délimités de qualité supérieure*). At the point where the Loire makes its most northerly bend is the city of Orléans. Wines have been made in the surrounding area for centuries, once on a large scale, now only in small measure. A good year here produces no more than 39,000 cases of Vin de l'Orléanais. About 370 of the permitted 1,000 acres are planted and worked by some 50 growers. The vineyards are on both banks of the river, spread over 24 communes. The most characteristic wine of the district is the Gris Meunier, usually a fresh, congenial, light red wine with a distinct *terroir*. It is made from the Pinot Meunier grape, which thrives best on limestone and clay. In the Orléanais, however, I have also tasted quite pleasant wines from the Auvernat Rouge (Pinot Noir) and the Cabernet, refreshing rosés, also from the Cabernet, and surprisingly good white wines from the Auvernat Blanc (Chardonnay).

Coteaux du Giennois

In the 1920s Gien and its surroundings claimed about 4,950 acres and 800 or so growers. Things, however, are different today. A search for the Coteaux du Giennois vineyards nowadays reveals only two or three growers, for Giennois wines are found 25 miles upstream in a southeasterly direction, at Cosne-sur-Loire. Formerly, Cosne had its own *appellation d'origine simple*. When this was rescinded, the growers did not opt for a new VDQS name but for the existing 'Coteaux du Giennois' (with the right to put Cosne-sur-Loire on the label). Altogether the district produces an annual 16,700 cases from about 125 acres, out of a potential 500 acres. The Gamay is the most commonly planted grape here, followed by the Pinot Noir and the white Sauvignon. I am not very fond of the Giennois wines. Most of them have a curious, almost muddy bouquet and are of mediocre quality. A lot of Coteaux du Giennois is vinified by the Pouilly-sur-Loire cooperative.

The far south

The wines of the Orléanais and Giennois are locally consumed and hardly ever exported. This also applies to the red and rosé wines of the Côtes Roannaise. These minor wines, based on the Gamay grape, are made on either side of the Loire around Roanne. Production is around 22,000 cases annually and 70 or so growers cultivate almost 1,500 acres, but only some 250 of these produce wine with an *appellation d'origine*.
The Gamay also predominates in the most southerly district of the Loire, Côtes du Forez. Production here is controlled by a cooperative and a handful of growers who exploit a total of 500 acres. In good years the vintage is in the region of 110,000 cases.

Alsace

Left:
A sign in the centre of Colmar by the Alsace artist Hansi. The charcuterie referred to is opposite the Maison des Têtes, where there is a restaurant.

Below:
Pickers' meal time near Eguisheim. In Alsace the harvest usually takes place between 15 October and 15 November. They hardly ever start picking before 10 October.

There are 7,000 vineyards in the Haut-Rhin département compared with rather more than 4,000 in Bas-Rhin.

Documents show that there were still bison, elk and aurochs in the woods of Alsace around the 10th century AD. Wild horses are mentioned up to the 16th century.

As well as wine (about 25% of agricultural production), Alsace also grows cereals, vegetables, fruit, tobacco and hops.

Hansi, or Uncle Hansi, was the pseudonym of Jean-Jacques Waltz (1875—1951), a superlative artist and satirist who illustrated the genial, happy-go-lucky ways of the people of Alsace during and after World War I.

Alsace, on the linguistic boundaries of French and German, has its own dialect.

The name Alsace was probably derived from the river Ill, formerly also called the Ell.

In addition to its decorative signboards, Alsace is noted for its storks' nests. The stork was supposed to bring good fortune. Unfortunately most of the nests are now empty; the stork has all but vanished from the region. For this reason stork colonies are being created in Kintzheim and Hunawihr.

Between Rhine and Vosges

In northeast France the Vosges mountains run for more than 100 miles parallel to the Rhine. Here, between the river and the mountain peaks, lies Alsace, comprising the *départements* of Bas-Rhin and Haut-Rhin. Much of the region consists of a fertile plain 16 to 20 miles wide, but there is a good deal of hilly terrain as well. Most vineyards, for example, are on the foothills of the Vosges, 650 to 1,300 feet above sea level.

Because of its strategic position between France and Germany, Alsace has been the focal point of many international disputes and conflicts; as wine maker Jean Hugel expressed it: 'We are specialists in wars and white wine.' In early times the Celts in this region succumbed to the Romans, the Romans in turn to the barbarians, and the various barbarians to the Franks. The Frankish king Clovis gained a decisive victory near Wissembourg in AD 496. His followers founded many settlements: numerous Alsace wine villages have names of Frankish origin, and in some places Frankish burials have been found.

Feudal times

After the Frankish and Merovingian kings, Alsace was ruled by dukes, among them the brutal Etichon, father of St Odile (see page 95). In the 10th century the region came under German rule — and was to remain so for 700 years. However, the power of the German emperors was limited. The fortunes of the population, for good or ill, were determined by dukes and other feudal lords, as well as by the mighty archbishops of Strasbourg and the numerous monasteries. In the early 6th century Alsace had 40 abbeys; in the 13th century they numbered 300. Most of them have wholly disappeared, and little is left of the castles of the secular lords. The majority of the existing 45 castles, often crowning a hill or mountain top, are in ruins. In the 14th century the Décapole, a federation of ten Alsace towns, was formed in protest against feudal excesses. A century later the region was ravaged by the Armagnacs, who invaded Alsace in 1439. Another black year was 1525, when 20,000 peasants rose in revolt against their masters: all were killed.

The Thirty Years' War

The second half of the 16th and the beginning of the 17th century brought peace and great prosperity to the region. Alsace became the richest, most populous part of the Holy Roman Empire. The Renaissance, with its more secular attitudes and innovations in all fields of art, made an

Right:
Place de la République in
Rouffach with the Corn
Exchange (end of 15th,
beginning of 16th century) and
the Witches' Tower (13th and
15th centuries).

Below:
A dairy farm in the Vosges, near
Munster. The cows that supply
the milk for Munster cheese,
probably made here since the
8th century, graze on mountain
meadows like these. In Alsace
the custom (of Jewish origin) is
to dip the Munster in kümmel or
to sprinkle some over it. The
custom is also found in Leiden
(Holland) and Mainz (Germany).

Between Rhine and Vosges

impact here much later than elsewhere in
France. Many splendid, perfectly preserved
buildings date from this time, as in the wine
village of Riquewihr. This prosperous
interlude was shattered by the outbreak of
the Thirty Years' War in 1618. Alsace was
invaded several times. The Swedes caused
great devastation in 1633; plague and
famine, too, exacted a heavy toll. When the

peace of Westphalia was signed in 1648,
Alsace passed to France. King Louis XIV —
who on seeing the region is supposed to have
exclaimed 'l'Alsace . . . quel beau jardin!' —
organized its repopulation. Catholics, in
particular, were encouraged to settle here
and many of them were Swiss. This explains
why the traditional costumes of Alsace are
so similar to those of Switzerland.

The Marseillaise

In 1674 the German emperor attempted to
win back Alsace and invaded with 60,000
men. At Turckheim, however, this army was
defeated by a much smaller force led by
Maréchal Turenne (see page 126). In 1681
Strasbourg. hitherto independent, was
attached to France. It was in this city, in

Between Rhine and Vosges

1792, that the *Marseillaise* was sung for the first time. The French Revolution had erupted in all its violence and patriots were concerned by the fact that the revolutionaries lacked an inspiring marching song. In a single day, Rouget d l'Isle composed such a song, based on contemporary slogans and calls to arms. He himself sang his 'war song of the Army of the Rhine' on the evening of 26 April at the house of the mayor, Baron Frédéric de Dietrich. A modest plaque on number 4, Place Broglie, now a bank, commemorates the house that occupied this site.

German, French, German, French

In 1870 Napoleon III declared war on Prussia, with the result that the Germans invaded and annexed Alsace. Under their harsh regime, with German the mandatory language of communication, one out of every eight inhabitants fled Alsace. Later, during World War I, Alsace was in the main battle zone. In 1918 the French flag was hoisted again, but 22 years later, in World War II, the Germans returned with a reign of terror. Many young Alsatians were forced into the German army and sent to the Russian front. About 43,000 of these men perished and thousands more ended up in Russian camps. The last of the survivors did not return until 1955. In the final winter of the war, 1944-45, there was heavy fighting around Colmar. Villages such as Mitttelwihr, Bennwihr, Sigolsheim, Ammerschwihr and Katzenthal were almost totally destroyed.

Proud bon vivants

Despite generations of suffering, the Alsatians are by nature optimistic *bon vivants*, with a keen sense of humour. An acquaintance from Ammerschwihr told me of a wartime episode concerning the great statue of Christ with outstretched arms that stands near Les Trois-Epis. As it had been paid for by wealthy Jews, the Germans wanted to destroy it. One villager who had heard of their intention is reputed to have

remarked to the German commander: 'Why are you doing this? He is the only man in Alsace to have received you with open arms!' The statue is still there.

Joie de vivre is also apparent in the wealth of flowers that bloom continuously from spring to autumn in window boxes, on balconies, and in gardens, parks and squares. The Alsatians are very proud of their region. Old buildings are lovingly maintained or restored (some of the castle ruins even by volunteers), and there are innumerable books and periodicals wholly devoted to Alsace. Apart from French and German, there is also a local dialect that is quite incomprehensible to outsiders.

Architectural styles

Alsace has a great deal to offer the visitor. In summer you can walk in the Vosges through great forests of pine, fir and beech, beside beautiful, tranquil lakes (Lac Noir is 236 feet deep), or across upland meadows, where the cows that give the milk for Munster cheese graze from May to October. In the winter you can ski in the mountains.

On and around the foothills of the Vosges are the wine villages, often marvellous fairy-tale places full of atmosphere, with half-timbered houses, old churches and picturesque fountains. Down on the plain lie cities such as Strasbourg, Colmar and Mulhouse, and scattered here and there are more tiny, peaceful villages with orchards full of blossom. Architecture is widely varied in Alsace. The Romanesque style (11th and 12th century) produced solid churches with thick walls and small windows, as in the church of Saint-Léger at Guebwiller and the church tower at Gueberschwihr. The Gothic style (12th to 15th centuries), with its pointed arches, ornamentation, statuary, slender towers and large windows is exemplified by the beautiful Strasbourg cathedral and the church at Thann. The Renaissance period (in Alsace, as at Riquewihr, for example, late 16th and early 17th century) introduced stone houses with pointed gables and steep roofs, often

stylishly ornamented and with projecting windows, galleries and outside staircases. The Classical style is also represented as, for instance, by soberly rebuilt monasteries dating from after the Thirty Years' War.

Sheltered vineyards

Alsace offers gastronomic as well as visual pleasure. Its cuisine — German quantity, French refinement — and its wines are renowned. Wine-growing has been practised here since Roman times. In a document of AD 785 there is the first reference to a good vintage: and more than 160 wine-producing localities are recorded before the year 900. It is hardly surprising that Alsace is a good area for wine-making. The region is protected by the Vosges from damp, oceanic influences. Rainfall is relatively light. In Colmar, for example, it amounts to only 19 inches a year (which makes it the driest town in France after Perpignan). In the Vosges mountains, however, more than 79 inches falls annually. The soil, too, lends itself to the cultivation of grapes; it is very varied and thus produces a wide spectrum of wines, further diversified by local microclimates, some ten varieties of grape and thousands of wine growers.

Most Alsace wine, about 95%, is white and dry. Only a little rosé and red is made. Alsace produces an annual average of some 115 million bottles. This is roughly one-fifth of all French white wine with an *appellation contrôlée*. The region itself received its *appellation contrôlée* on 3 October 1962. Ten years later it was stipulated that all Alsace wine had to be bottled in the region itself. No other French wineland has suffered so much disruption in this century, yet the manner in which it has revived, preserving its high reputation for quality, is quite remarkable.

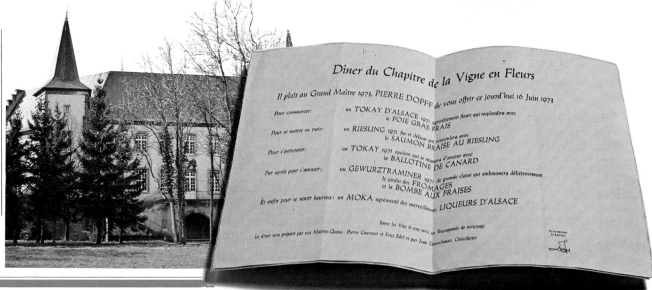

The Confrérie Saint-Etienne

Alsace

The Alsace wine fraternity of La Confrérie Saint-Etienne originated in the 14th century when a so-called *Herrenstubengesellschaft*, a kind of association of important citizens, was set up in the wine village of Ammerschwihr. In 1561 this was officially authorized to control the quality of the local wine. In time the society came to be called La Confrérie Saint-Etienne, because every year on 26 December — St Stephen's Day — the president gave the members a banquet in the best Alsace tradition. Between 1848 and 1947 the activities of the fraternity lapsed because of wars, German occupations and other tribulations. In 1947 it was revived, again at Ammerschwihr. Four years later it graduated from a local to a regional association.

Blue, red and green

Today the Confrérie Saint-Etienne is a very flourishing society with thousands of members in dozens of countries. It endeavours to 'unite all friends of Alsace, its wines, its gastronomy and its ambiance' — and in this it succeeds. The fraternity organizes at least four *grands chapitres* in Alsace and holds many smaller meetings elsewhere in France and abroad. Unlike most other wine fraternities, the Confrérie imposes certain requirements on those wishing to join. Anyone attending a *chapitre* for the first time is asked to distinguish between a fine wine, a simple wine, and an intermediate wine. On the second occasion the task is to recognize Riesling, Muscat, Tokay and Gewürztraminer. On the third visit the candidate must identify three out of a whole range of Alsace wines. The reward is a scroll bearing a blue, red and green ribbon respectively for the three tests. At least one year must elapse between these tests of proficiency. Success in earning the three ribbons is generally assured by a great deal of friendly prompting, although most candidates do their level best to pass the test themselves — and therein lies the purpose of the Confrérie.

Château de Kientzheim

Saturday 7 May 1977 was a memorable day for the Confrérie: the Château de Kientzheim was opened as its new headquarters. This enterprise cost the fraternity 3.2 million francs, most of the money being collected by the members themselves. Two hundred people can sit down to dinner in the four great halls of the fully restored château. The sumptuous banquets that the Confrérie holds there, after each *grand chapitre*, consist of at least four courses and last many hours.
The château contains a wine museum and an oenothèque, a 'bottle library' that includes sample bottles of all the wines to which the fraternity has given its seal of approval. Every year, at a double tasting, the Confrérie chooses the best wines from the region, taking particular account of purity and character. The wines in question have to exemplify their grape variety and vintage.

They are judged only in their second year, when they have been able to develop fully. A wine producer may submit no more than five different wines for approval. The *sigille de qualité* awarded is valid for two years only; after that the wine has to be judged again.

Alsace cuisine

The visitor to Alsace can expect to enjoy regional food as well as regional wines. Alsace has its own honoured cuisine with many interesting specialities. Most local restaurants are small, simple *winstub*, to use the local name, but there are also eminent establishments with Michelin stars. As early as 1580, after a visit to the region, Michel de Montaigne wrote: 'The smallest meals last three or four hours because they take so long to serve; and truly they eat with much less haste than we and much more soundly.' Yet it was another hundred years before the Alsace cuisine really began to take shape — for then the region became French. At the end of the Thirty Years' War, in 1648, Alsace passed to the French crown and came under the influence of French cuisine. The chefs had their work cut out if we are to believe the words of a French doctor writing in the second half of the 17th century: 'Their meats are badly prepared, their ragoûts without refinement, their roasts dry.' This contrasts strongly with Montaigne's remarks, though it is only fair to note that three decades of war must undoubtedly have left their mark.

Pâté de foie gras

In Strasbourg, around 1780, *pâté de foie gras*, a delicacy that eventually reached the court of Louis XVI, was made for the first time by Jean-Pierre Clause. Its quality was improved when a Bordeaux chef suggested adding truffles. This goose-liver pâté is still one of the finest dishes served in Alsace (although the livers now come mainly from Israel and some of the Eastern bloc countries). Two of my favourite places for *pâté de foie gras* are the restaurants *Aux Armes de France* in Ammerschwir and *Moulin du Kaegy* in Steinbrunn-le-Bas — at both, of course, the pâté is made on the premises. Goose liver is not necessarily the only ingredient; in restaurants and private homes you come across many variations. One of the best examples of a hot pâté is the *pâte vigneron* at the *Winstub Gilg* at Mittelbergheim.

Famous specialities

Alsace cooking, of course, has much more to offer than pâtés. The region is rich in all kinds of natural produce. The Rhine valley produces potatoes, grain, cattle, vegetables, a rich range of fruit from the many orchards, and even hops and tobacco. The foothills of the Vosges produce wine. There is game and fruit from the mountain forests, and fish from the few as yet unpolluted rivers and streams. Much has been written about Alsace specialities, but among the best are: *tarte à l'oignon*; *tarte flambée* or *flammekeuche* (a kind of pizza); soups, including potato, lentil, onion and beer; dishes that contain frog's legs (seldom of local origin nowadays); *truite au bleu*, pike and pike-perch; *baekeoffe* (also written *baekoffa*, *bäckeofe*, *baekenoffa* or *baeckaoffa*), a stew with beef, pork and mutton; *schiefala* (smoked shoulder of pork,

Alsace cuisine

often served with horseradish sauce); *coq au Riesling*; game, including venison, hare, pheasant and partridge; *Kugelhopf* (a kind of raisin cake); tarts with apple, plum or whortleberry (blueberry or bilberry); and *sorbet au Marc de Gewürztraminer*.

A formidable sauerkraut recipe

A particularly impressive dish is the *choucroute à l'Alsacienne*, consisting always of sauerkraut, potatoes and often five or six kinds of meat (sausages, bacon, smoked shoulder of veal, pork chops, etc.). The sauerkraut tastes at its best in September, when the new crop of cabbages has arrived. Cultivation is concentrated in the flat country southwest of Strasbourg, where nearly 2,500 acres are planted with cabbages. There is even a *route du choucroute* running through the most important villages. That most aptly named village of Krautergersheim alone produces about one-seventh of all French sauerkraut.

Munster cheese

Special mention must of course be made of Munster, the renowned, full-flavoured cheese that has been produced around the town of Munster for many centuries. The best-tasting Munster is to be had along the *route du fromage*, which encircles 28 cheese farms. They lie near mountain meadows high above Munster. Nearly all have a taproom where their own speciality can be enjoyed with bread and wine. The Alsatians themselves sprinkle it with kümmel or cummin, for taste and easy digestion. Gewürztraminer is regarded as the ideal accompaniment to this exquisite cheese.

Classic and contemporary

Although the Alsace cuisine is of very traditional origins, time does not stand still in the restaurants of the region. The dishes prepared by a new generation of chefs are inventive and often refreshingly light-hearted. Sometimes they use purely local ingredients, sometimes not. Just as most countries of western Europe are represented politically in Strasbourg, so a cosmopolitan range of food appears in the ovens and on the tables of Alsace. Classical and modern cuisine flourish side by side. On the same day you can eat a nourishing *baekeoffe* at *Winstub Arnold* in Itterswiller and an ultra-light *blanc de Saint-Pierre aux huîtres de pleine mer et beurre de basilic* at the *Auberge de l'Ill* in Illhaeusern. The contrast could hardly be greater. However, the old and the new Alsace cuisine have one thing in common: the regional wines taste excellent with either.

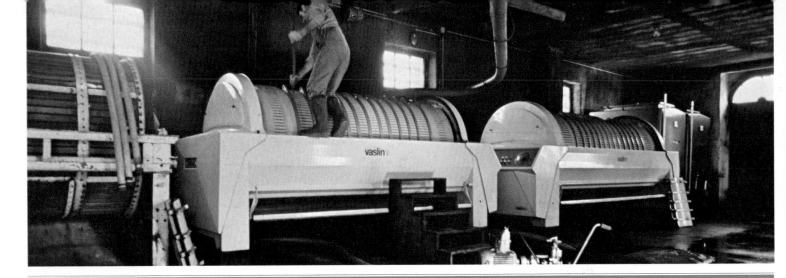

Wine production

There are few French districts where the wine-growing land is so broken up as in Alsace. Approximately 31,000 acres are owned by very nearly 9,000 different growers and it is these, not merely a few large producers, who dominate the wine-making scene. The great majority cannot make a living from wine alone. As already mentioned, 10 acres is the minimum required nowadays for a comfortable existence. More than 6,000 growers here own less than 2½ acres. Of the remaining growers, there are 1,000 with 2½ to 5 acres; 1,450 with 5 to 12½ acres; 405 with 12½ to 25 acres; and only 45 with more than 25 acres. These figures may, of course, have altered slightly since the time of writing, but the fact remains that only a minority of the region's growers derive their income solely from wine, and that is why so many other crops are grown.

The rise of the cooperatives

This socio-economic situation explains why the *négociants* and cooperatives are in such a strong position. Most of the growers possess too little land and facilities to process the grapes, let alone nurture, bottle and sell the wine. The majority — about 5,000 — sell their grapes to a *négociant* or take them to a cooperative. At present roughly 40% of all Alsace wine is produced by wine firms, 30% by cooperatives. This latter percentage is rather surprising considering that the cooperatives have been important only since 1950. Before then, and after the departure of

Opposite page, above:
Modern Vaslin presses at the Weinbach estate, Kaysersberg.

Opposite page, below:
Wooden vats in Marcel Deiss's cellar in Bergheim.

Alsatian growers who make their own wine, bottle and sell it, have as their symbol a yellow stylized vineleaf with the words 'Alsace Propriété Véritas'.

Alsatian producers seldom have a vineyard all in one piece. An estate is usually distributed over various plots of ground. It has been calculated that in Alsace the total vineyard area is divided into some 120,000 such plots, of an average 2 acres.

Right:
Presses and metal fermentation tanks at the Zind-Humbrecht estate, Wintzenheim.

Below right:
By joint effort the grapes are tipped into the fouloir-égrappoir, an apparatus that bruises and de-stalks them.

There are wine cooperatives in the following villages: Andlau, Beblenheim, Bennwihr, Cléebourg, Dambach-la-Ville, Eguisheim, Hunawihr, Ingersheim, Kientzheim, Obernai, Orschwiller, Pfaffenheim, Ribeauvillé, Traenheim, Sigolsheim, Soultz, Turckheim and Westhalten. Some of these cooperatives have branches in other communes.

Wine production

the Germans in 1918, it was almost exclusively the *négociants* who marketed the wine. For many decades this was beneficial to all; new markets were created for Alsace wines and many other positive developments were stimulated.

Reluctant competitors

The cooperative concept made a very cautious beginning in Alsace. The first such enterprises, founded just after 1900, were in fact merely central, collective cellars in which a surplus of wine could be stored. They were used as a means of regulating supply. It was only after World War II that true *caves coopératives* came into being for vinification as well as storage. The initiative came from the growers of Bennwihr and Sigolsheim, two villages that were totally devastated in the winter of 1944-5. At the start these growers did not plan to market their own wine, but simply hoped to sell it collectively to their traditional customers, the wine houses. The *négociants*, however, mistrusted these two new, strong groups and either bought little or nothing at all from them. As a result, the new cooperatives, rather reluctantly, had to start bottling and marketing. Instead of being suppliers to the *négociants*, they now became their competitors. At present Alsace has 17 wine cooperatives with about 2,600 members. Some of these enterprises collaborate in various ways. It is possible that the cooperatives' position will become even stronger. They can sell their wines more cheaply than the *négociants* because they have no transport costs for the grapes; they obtain better credit terms; and they pay no profit tax. If Alsace wine prices in general were ever to rise steeply, their lower price levels would make a considerable impact. Nowadays the cooperatives sell about 26% of all wine, the *négociants* 44%.

Expansion by the growers

While the *négociants* have been facing effective competition from the cooperatives, they have also had to cope with more and more *propriétaires-viticulteurs* or *manipulants* — growers who make, bottle and sell their own wine from their own grapes. These now claim almost 30% of the market. The ever-increasing number of tourists visiting Alsace are also a factor. All over France, in fact, direct selling by the grower is very much in vogue. Greater self-sufficiency not merely puts pressure on the *négociants*, with predominantly regional sales, but also means fewer grapes and less wine. The wine firms own only 3.5% of the land. I get the impression from conversations that they believe they can only maintain their turnover if the total vineyard area is significantly enlarged. Legally this is quite feasible, but in practice permission for new planting often rests with existing growers — and they are in no hurry to expand for fear that too much wine would depress the price. The *négociants*, on the other hand, argue that a larger area planted with vines would lead to bigger sales and more stable prices, which would be better for everyone. It remains to be seen how effective the persuasive powers of the *négociants* are likely to be.

Making the wine

Many of the Alsace cooperatives, wine houses and growers who vinify their own wine regularly use a centrifuge to remove impurities left after pressing. There are, nevertheless, exceptions. Some establishments are unable to afford this rather expensive apparatus, others employ it more cautiously. The Zind-Humbrecht estate at Wintzenheim, for example, maintains that centrifuging the must deprives the wine of

fruit, and applies it only when there is an exceptional amount of impurities in the pressed juice. If no centrifuge is used, the impurities are simply left to settle (*débourbage statique*). Fermentation takes place in barrels, tanks or casks. The first, alcoholic fermentation is often, though not always, followed by a further process producing lactic acid. This has to be decided by the individual producer. As a rule the wine is initially filtered in January by passing it through kieselguhr, a siliceous medium composed of microscopic fossils; there is often further filtration before bottling later in the year. Some producers also apply a 'cold treatment' to avoid tartaric acid. One thing, however, is certain: the more treatment a wine undergoes, the more character it loses. Vinification methods, whether practised by a large or small producer, contribute a great deal to the ultimate quality of the wine.

Following the Schlossberg (Kientzheim and Kaysersberg), the following vineyards were granted grand cru status in 1981:
Brand (Turckheim), Furstentum (Kientzheim and Sigolsheim), Geisberg (Ribeauvillé), Gloeckelberg (Rodern), Goldert (Gueberschwihr), Hatschbourg (Voegtlinshoffen and Hattstatt), Hengst (Wintzenheim), Kanzlerberg (Bergheim), Kastelberg (Andlau), Moenchberg (Eichhoffen), Ollwiller (Wuenheim), Sommerberg (Niedermorschwihr), Spiegel (Guebwiller) and Wibelsberg (Andlau).
These vineyards are expected to follow in due course: Altenberg (Bergheim), Kessler (Guebwiller), Kirchberg (Barr), Kirchberg (Ribeauvillé), Kitterlé (Guebwiller), Rosacker (Hunawihr), Saering (Guebwiller) and Sonnenglanz (Beblenheim).

The fact that use of the term grand cru is restricted in no way prevents names of individual vineyards appearing on labels. Districts of origin may also be stated.

Probably no French wine region participates so wholeheartedly in fairs and shows as Alsace. The illustration shows some of the distinctions that can be seen worn on the necks of bottles in Alsace. Experience has shown that those awarded at Colmar and by the Confrérie Saint-Etienne (the local wine fraternity, see page 77) are worth most. The Paris Show comes too early for Alsatian wines; they are still developing then. Judging here is almost a game of chance. Producers have repeatedly told me that the judging and subsequent checking was often less than serious at Mâcon and other fairs. 'In Mâcon one in three wines usually wins a prize,' said one

grower. The Colmar fair takes place in August when the wine has been bottled for some months — and the tasting is taken very seriously here. In 1980 500 different wines were submitted to the Colmar jury.

Right:
Harvesting near Katzenthal.

Below:
This sign indicates growers who sell their own wines.

Bottom:
Grapes arriving at the Ribeauvillé firm of Trimbach.

Grapes and wines

Alsace

For centuries, Alsace distinguished only between wines from ordinary grapes and those from superior varieties (*unedlen und edlen Stöckh*); and almost all its wines were blended. Not until the beginning of the present century did the region start to produce wines from single grape varieties. After World War I, when Alsace again became French, this practice came increasingly into fashion. Today the overwhelming majority of Alsace wines are made from a single grape variety, from which they take their names. There are Chasselas, Sylvaner, Pinot Blanc (or Klevner), Muscat, Riesling, Tokay d'Alsace (or Pinot Gris), Gewürztraminer and Pinot Noir (the only grape yielding rosé or red wine in Alsace). There is also the Edelzwicker, a blended wine that can be made from one or more of these wines or their grapes.

Edelzwicker and Chasselas

It would appear, judging from old menus of about 1890 and from other sources, that Edelzwicker was once regarded as second only in quality to Tokay. The latter was generally the last, and best, wine served with a meal and Edelzwicker (then known as Gentil) the last but one. Then made principally from superior varieties, Edelzwicker is considered nowadays as the simplest of the Alsace wines. It almost always contains a generous percentage of Pinot Blanc, and if Chasselas is available, this goes in as well. Many Edelzwickers are sold as brand wines under the *appellation* Vin d'Alsace or Alsace: often the word 'Edelzwicker' does not appear on the label. Obviously the quality varies greatly from one producer to another.

Protected labelling terms

Alsace wines normally have a permitted yield of 100 hectolitres per hectare and an alcohol content of at least 8.5° before the almost universal application of chaptalization. These limits are different for

the *grand cru* quality. Yield is then 70 hectolitres per hectare; Muscat and Riesling have to contain at least 10° alcohol, Gewürztraminer, Tokay and Pinot Noir 11°. Other grape varieties are not permitted in this category.

The first vineyard to be declared a *grand cru* was Schlossberg at Kientzheim-Kaysersberg. Others followed, and more will do so in the future — but not necessarily all the better vineyards. Many owners of vineyards that might be eligible have problems with the restrictions of grape varieties and low yield, plus the fact that all *grand cru* wines have to be subjected to stringent testing; and if the majority of owners with land in a particular vineyard do not want it raised to the status of *grand cru*, then this does not happen.

In 1981 there was quite widespread use of the epithet *grand cru* for wines that did not come from vineyards entitled to the term. French legislation will probably prevent this unauthorized use in the future. Other protected terms such as *vendange tardive* and *sélection de grains nobles* may only be used for Riesling, Tokay and Gewürztraminer, and refer to wines from late-picked grapes which are therefore high in sugar content. For the Riesling there has to be sufficient sugar for a potential alcohol content of 12.9° (*vendange tardive*) or 15.1° (*sélection de grains nobles*); for Tokay and Gewürztraminer the figures are 14.3° and 16.4°. Both categories give generally heavy, fairly sweet wines that are justly regarded as remarkable in this northerly wine area, but are not typical of the region as a whole. Alsace bottles are also adorned with terms like 'Réserve', 'Réserve Personelle' and 'Cuvée Exceptionelle', but these are not protected. Each producer interprets them in his own way.

Right:
The Sylvaner — about 20% of the area is planted with this grape. Fresh Sylvaner grapes and Munster cheese are a traditional delicacy during the vintage.

Centre:
Chasselas Blanc. About 4% of the vineyard area is planted with the Chasselas. Not so long ago it was 20%.

Far right:
Chasselas Rose.

Centre:
Vineyard between Westhalten and Orschwihr.

Bottom:
Picker at work near Kaysersberg.

Sylvaner and Chasselas

The Sylvaner grape very probably came from Transylvania, a plateau in Romania surrounded by mountains. Nevertheless, some researchers maintain that its homeland was Austria; others suggest France, or claim that the Sylvaner was originally a wild woodland grape from the banks of the German Rhine. Whatever its origins, the Sylvaner has been recorded in Alsace since 1870. It is a grape that gives a high yield even in cool regions and is also resistant to rot resulting from rain, which undoubtedly explains why one-fifth of the vineyard area is planted with this variety. The Sylvaner is particularly prevalent in the Bas-Rhin *département*; it gives very good results in Barr, Mittelbergheim, Epfig and Dambach-la-Ville.

A refreshing wine

Sylvaner is a wine with few pretensions, intended as an uncomplicated thirst-quencher, best for picnics, salads and simple dishes with seafood, white meat, chicken, etc. Locally it is often served by the glass. Along with Riesling, the Sylvaner has the most acid taste of all Alsace wines. The *fraîcheur* is often accentuated by a very slight effervescence, or the impression of it: in the better kinds there is also a discreet hint of fruit and a certain juiciness. Pierre Seltz of Mittelbergheim proved to me that a final glass of chilled Sylvaner has a very refreshing effect taken after a large meal that has been rounded off with a full Gewürztraminer.

The vanishing Chasselas

The Chasselas is grown elsewhere in France as a dessert grape — but in Alsace it is cultivated for wine. However, this grape is gradually disappearing from the scene. In 1969, 20% of the vineyard area was planted with Chasselas, but only 4.3% ten years later. Nearly all the wine from the Chasselas goes into Edelzwicker. Only very

occasionally is a wine made exclusively from it (for example, at the Keintzler estate in Ribeauvillé). Yet in Switzerland, remarkably enough, some extremely pleasant wines of obvious class are produced on a large scale from the Chasselas, such as the Fendant of the Valais district. The Swiss explained to me that the Chasselas demands the most

careful vinification; the least mistake is heavily penalized. Has the true potential of the Chasselas never been appreciated in Alsace? Or does the reason for a lower quality lie in differences of soil or climate? These are hypothetical questions: within a generation there will be hardly any Chasselas vines left in Alsace.

Pinot Blanc

The wine discussed on this page is sold under three names in Alsace: Pinot Blanc, Klevner and Clevner. This complicates matters, as does the fact that it can be made from five different grape varieties. It is perhaps not surprising that the Pinot Blanc is one of the most frequently undervalued and least understood of Alsace wines. The two most important grape varieties are the Pinot Blanc and the Pinot-Auxerrois. The former originates from Burgundy, the latter either from Lorraine, on the other side of the Vosges, or from the Auxerrois, the ancient earldom near Chablis. The two grapes are closely related but produce somewhat different wine. What they have in common is their comparatively high resistance to frost — the Pinot-Auxerrois being the better in this respect — and their regular yield, even in years that are difficult for other varieties.

Best blended

The Pinot Blanc is the more productive of the two and gives pure and somewhat harsh wine ('square' as an Alsace grower once described it). The Pinot-Auxerrois ripens a little quicker, produces rather fewer grapes and forms the basis of a softer wine with perhaps a dash more spice. The wines from both varieties have little acid. Some growers — such as Louis Hauller in Dambach-la-Ville — vinify the two types separately and sell the wines individually as well. Wine from the Pinot Blanc is always known by this name; by tradition, that from the Pinot-Auxerrois is Klevner or Clevner. The latter almost always seems to be the better wine. Most producers, however, blend the two grapes and/or the two wines, and rightly so, for the whole proves to be more than the sum of the parts. The resulting blend — which may bear any of the three names — can sometimes come remarkably close to a Riesling, one example being the elegant Pinot Blanc from the house of Kuehn in Ammerschwihr.

There are also many Pinot Blancs with a striking softness complemented by an attractive bouquet and a lively, not too light,

very supple taste. As this is not a well-known wine it offers good value for money. Its production could easily be increased for at present much Pinot Blanc disappears anonymously into Edelzwicker. About one-sixth of the wine-growing area in Alsace is planted with Pinot Blanc and Pinot-Auxerrois, with much success at Cléebourg, Wintzenheim, Pfaffenheim and Westhalten and elsewhere.

The three other permitted varieties are the Pinot Noir (vinified as white wine, just as in Champagne), the Pinot Gris or Tokay d'Alsace, and the Chardonnay. An example of the Pinot Noir comes from Marcel Rentz in Zellenberg — a wine I found astonishingly good. I have not come across a Pinot Blanc from the Pinot Gris grape. A little Chardonnay, worthy of consideration, is sold as Pinot Blanc by the firm of Boeckel at Mittelbergheim.

The Klevner de Heiligenstein (see page 96) is a special case: it does not come from any of the afore-mentioned grape varieties, but from the Savagnin Rose, related to the Gewürztraminer.

Muscat

Alsace

The parish records of Wolxheim record the Muscat from the first half of the 16th century; that is how long the white and bluish-pink Muscat à Petits Grains has been cultivated in Alsace. Some scientists have traced the origin of this grape to the *vitis apiana* of the Romans, 'the grape that attracts bees'. The Muscat thrives in the sun and is mainly found around the Mediterranean. In France itself, the Muscat de Frontignan is identical to the white Muscat à Petits Grains. Basking in the Mediterranean sun, the grape supplies emphatically sweet, usually heavy wines; but in Alsace it produces a wine so fresh and light that it is regarded as the perfect aperitif, nicknamed the 'crown prince'. Unfortunately, the grape has to contend with problems in this northerly region. There are generally more bad than good harvests, so vulnerable is it to mildew and rot. This is why in the mid-19th century a second type of Muscat was introduced into Alsace, the Muscat Ottonel — faster-ripening and therefore less troubled by autumn rains.

Best combination

The Muscat Ottonel gives a somewhat finer wine, which is why it is increasingly replacing the Muscat à Petits Grains (or Muscat d'Alsace). Yet the latter variety still has its advantages, for it imparts body to the wine, some extra fullness, which a Muscat made from the Ottonel alone often lacks: and it also adds fruit. It is generally agreed that the best Muscat consists of two-thirds wine from the Muscat Ottonel, one-third from the Muscat à Petits Grains; and in some communities the older variety is making a modest comeback. At the Westhalten cooperative I was told that the growers had been persuaded to plant Muscat à Petits Grains again to give the wine more strength and fruit. Percentages there are now 70% Ottonel and 30% à Petits Grains — to everyone's satisfaction.

Search for a new Muscat

Despite its advantages, the Muscat Ottonel too is a sensitive variety, and only about two out of five harvests are fully successful. The other three years either yield mediocre wine, or hardly any at all, as in 1980. With good reason the Institut National des Recherches Agronomiques at Colmar has for some time been engaged in developing a less vulnerable Muscat grape. Until that happens, the two existing types of grape will yield Muscat that currently amounts to a mere 3.6% or 3.7% of total production. As things stand, a good Muscat from a good year remains quite rare, and certainly not cheap. But such a wine is well worth acquiring, for it is delightful in bouquet and savour, with an aroma of newly picked sweet grapes, and a mild yet dry, fresh taste not unlike that of the grape itself. This splendid and charming Alsace wine deserves to be drunk not just as an aperitif, but with asparagus, fresh shrimps, fish accompanied by sauces that are not too rich and preferably mild, and with pastries. It is excellent in the evening after dinner. Among communes with a good reputation for their Muscat are Mittelwihr, Wettolsheim, Voegtlinshoffen and Gueberschwihr.

Riesling

Alsace

The Riesling is the 'king' of the Alsace wines, produced from the grape of the same name. The origin of this superior variety is obscure. It could be derived from the grape described by the Roman Pliny (AD 23-79), but it might also have originated along the Rhine; it probably began to be cultivated along the banks of this river around the 9th century. In 1430, too, there is mention of a *Rusling* vineyard near Worms. The earliest mention of the grape in Alsace dates from 1477 — in the form *Rissling*. Three centuries later the variety had apparently spread all over the region. From 1756 it is recorded at Guebwiller, Sélestat, Colmar, Molsheim, Riquewihr and elsewhere. Yet the Riesling's real breakthrough came only after World War II. With more acreage available, planting of Riesling gradually increased and today represents approximately 18% of the total. Not surprisingly, the reputation of the wine grew as well: in France and abroad the image of Alsace has been largely moulded by the Riesling and the Gewürztraminer. There is a local saying: 'Whoever knows the Riesling, knows Alsace, and whoever loves Alsace, loves the Riesling.'

Breeding and refinement

That the Riesling should thrive in Alsace is something of a miracle. It requires a long ripening period, not too much rain and plenty of sunshine, all of which are problems so far north; but these handicaps are offset by the sheltered position of the Alsatian vineyards and the nature of the soil. In contrast to its German namesake, the Alsace Riesling, as a rule, has no trace of sugar. It is a dry, fresh-tasting wine of characteristic breed and refinement.

A good Riesling offers elegance and vitality, and in bouquet and taste fruit and flowers are both discernible, with sometimes the merest hint of spices. It is an honest, clean wine with subtle nuances and a sound balance between acid and suppleness.

Of course, not all Alsace Rieslings are alike. Minor differences of soil and vinification give each producer his own style of Riesling. Wines from light soils, for example, can be drunk young; those from the limestone develop perceptibly more slowly.

Someone once wrote: 'Du Riesling dans le verre, c'est le ciel sur la terre.' This is even truer if the wine is drunk as an accompaniment to *truite au bleu* or other kinds of freshwater or sea fish, plain or with a sauce. When it comes to choosing a Riesling, the following communes usually produce wine of good quality: Wolxheim, Dambach-la-Ville, Scherwiller, Ribeauvillé, Hunawihr, Mittelwihr, Kaysersberg, Ammerschwihr, Husseren-les-Châteaux, Orschwihr and Thann.

Tokay d'Alsace

Lazare de Schwendi, born in 1522, who lived and died in the village of Kientzheim, had a remarkable military career, culminating in Hungary, where between 1564 and 1568 he commanded an expedition to drive out the Turks. On 11 February 1565 he attacked the fortress of Tokaj. He won the battle — and took over 4,000 vats of Tokay wine. Tradition has it that the general liked the wines so much that on his return to Alsace he bought in Tokay vines from Hungary, which is how Tokay d'Alsace or Pinot Gris arrived in the region. Fact or fiction? No one really knows. What is certain is that Tokay d'Alsace has no connection at all with the Hungarian wine, except in name. Hungarian Tokay is made from the Furmint, a wholly different type of grape. The Pinot Gris, however, is to be found elsewhere in Hungary, around Lake Balaton, where it is known as the Szürkebarat, or 'grey monk'. Did Schwendi's quartermaster get hold of the wrong variety? Or was the Pinot Gris brought to Hungary by Alsatian soldiers, as the Hungarians themselves maintain? Again, there is no knowing.

An absurd ban

Some researchers believe it quite possible that Hungary received the Pinot Gris from France, and not the other way around. They claim that the Pinot Gris is simply a mutation of the Burgundian Pinot Noir — which would explain the name. Initially the grape was also called the Grauklevner, as in a document of 1644 from Riquewihr. Why then did the grape and its wine acquire a Hungarian name? There is a certain piquancy in the fact that for decades the Hungarians have been attempting to have the use of the name Tokay for Alsace wines banned; and not without success, for in 1980 the EEC suddenly introduced legislation prohibiting the use of 'Tokay d'Alsace' on labels, etc., at a time when the Brussels bureaucrats had not even heard the case put forward by the Alsace wine growers. Protests from France were so fierce that although the regulation still stands it has no effect in practice. In this book, therefore, the name Tokay d'Alsace is used unless the producer himself prefers Pinot Gris.

A question of taste

Tokay d'Alsace is one of the most robust wines of the region — fuller, richer and also softer of taste than, for example, the Riesling, and with more alcohol. It sometimes seems almost fat in structure. In good types you can detect a slight smoky overtone in the aroma, and I have also come across hints of nuts and honey. The wine — nicknamed 'the sultan' — benefits greatly from a few years' maturing and can be laid down for a decade or more if from a good vintage.

In Alsace the producers consider Tokay d'Alsace and *foie gras* an ideal combination; but suppliers of goose livers often prefer a Riesling with their product. Bernard Heydt-Trimbach once remarked: 'It is a question of taste. The wine growers want their wine to take precedence, the *foie gras* producers their goose liver.' Other recommended dishes with Tokay d'Alsace are poultry, white meat, small game, the regional speciality *baekeoffe*, and salad. Rather less than 5% the vineyard area is planted with Pinot Gris because it is such a delicate grape. Among the wine communes producing successful Tokays are Cléebourg, Obernai, Beblenheim, Mittelwihr and Kientzheim.

Gewürztraminer

For generations the Gewürztraminer has been the ambassador of Alsace. Many people only knew of the region from the wine, and this still holds true today. The Gewürztraminer shares pride of place with the Riesling, but of the two wines the former certainly makes the stronger impression. To drink this wine is never to forget it; indeed, in France the Gewürztraminer is a unique wine, comparable with no other. the *Gewürz* part of the name indicates a certain spiciness. In addition there are in bouquet and taste impressions of fruit, and in some kinds a slight overtone of muscat. The typical Gewürztraminer has a soft, if not mild taste that opens out in the mouth. It is generally strong in alcohol. The later the grapes are picked, the stronger and sweeter the end product. I have tasted more Gewürztraminer designated *vendange tardive* than of any other Alsace wines, and even 20-year-old examples have been in perfect condition.

Heavy and perfumed

Not all examples conform to this description of a typical Gewürztraminer, for character and quality vary greatly in Alsace. There are Gewürztraminers that are light and fresh, wines that can readily be served during a meal. There are also heavy Gewürztraminers, so sultry that they seem over-perfumed, almost pomaded: growers in fact refer to these as *pommadé*. A director of a wine firm once said to me: 'If the Alsatians made their Gewürztraminer for themselves rather than for the Parisians, it would be much less like pomade.' I am not too fond of the mild, over-perfumed, usually rather heavy Gewürztraminer type; I prefer either the light kinds, or the fuller, more classical variety that retains a certain elegance. Such a wine goes excellently with Munster cheese, even after drinking red wine with the main course. It also partners smoked salmon, grilled sardines, curries or other spiced foods, *homard à l'Américaine* and other fairly strongly flavoured dishes.

The Traminer

Alsace used to distinguish between Traminer and Gewürztraminer, the latter being stronger, spicier and more perfumed. Both were based on the Traminer, a grape that was present in Alsace at least from 1551. Possibly it came from the village of Tramin (or Termeno) in the Italian region of Trentino Alto Adige. Today this grape — or a gradually improved version of it — is called the Gewürztraminer, and is a small, reddish coloured variety, best in deep heavy soil, preferably with clay or limestone. Communes in which superior Gewürztraminers are made are Barr, Rorschwihr, Bergheim, Beblenheim, Mittelwihr, Sigolsheim, Kientzheim, Kaysersberg, Ammerschwihr, Ingersheim, Turckheim, Wintzenheim, Eguisheim, Westhalten and Orschwihr.

Pinot Noir

The Pinot grapes are well represented in Alsace: besides the Pinot Blanc and the Pinot Gris (Tokay d'Alsace), the Pinot Noir is also cultivated, albeit on a modest scale, and this grape is used for all regional rosé and red wines. The word *pinot* is derived from *pin*, 'pine tree': the bunches of this variety are very compact, something like a big pine cone in shape. The Pinot Noir, known to the ancient Gauls, is very common in Burgundy, where it produces all the great red wines, and in Champagne. Pale champagne can be made from a black grape because the juice of this variety is almost colourless, although the skins, which impart colour, are of course separated from the must. In Alsace the skins are left in contact with the juice for several hours to produce rosé, and for several days in the case of red wine. Many Alsace producers heat the incoming grapes to about 20°C. There are two reasons for this: firstly, the grapes often arrive too cold (4°-10°C) for fermentation to start; secondly, the heating process gives the wine extra colour.

Adequate rosés and reds

I have the impression that the Pinot Noir is only grown in Alsace because people there occasionally want a change from white wine. The majority of the rosés and reds made from this grape are far inferior in quality to the Alsace white wines. They are pleasant in taste, agreeable and adequate, but usually that is all. Only exceptionally do you come across really good examples — rosés with fruit and vitality and reds with subtlety, depth and some tannin. I have tasted some superior Pinot Noir rosés and reds from Cléebourg, Marlenheim, Ottrott, Saint-Hippolyte, Rodern and Turckheim. The fact that a lot of Bordeaux is drunk in Alsace shows that the Pinot Noir is regarded, as a rule, as rather ordinary. Bordeaux is splendidly represented on the wine lists of such restaurants as the *Auberge de l'Ill* at Illhaeusern, the *Aux Armes de France*,, Ammerschwihr, and *Schillinger* at Colmar; and when I inspected the private cellar of Charles Sparr, a *négociant* at Sigolsheim, I saw 15 or so cases that included marvellous Médocs and Pomerols. Despite the modest quality of the Pinot Noir (90% or more of it vinified as rosé) there is, strangely, a lot of interest in it. This is no doubt why between 1969 and 1979 the percentage of Pinot Noir planting increased from 2.1% to 4.5%. It is to be hoped that this trend does not continue, for the future of Alsace lies in its white wine.

The firm of Dopff au Moulin in Riquewihr produces around 200,000 bottles of sparkling wine every year by the méthode champenoise. Mainly Pinot Blanc and Pinot-Auxerrois from 12 acres in the Harth vineyard near Colmar are used to make Crémant d'Alsace Cuvée Julien (the best wine). Some white wine from the Pinot Noir is usually added. Cuvée Julien is lightly sparkling and has an unassuming fragrance and a mature, pleasant taste with a hint of terroir.

In 1972 the Eguisheim cooperative produced 1,000 bottles of sparkling wine; in 1980 over 500,000. Two types are made with the brand name Wolfberger, both Crémant d'Alsace. The simpler type has the Pinot Blanc and Pinot-Auxerrois as a basis; the better one contains only Riesling. I found it a pure, delicious wine, firm and yet with a soft taste. It has little subtlety or depth, but is perfectly adequate as an aperitif. It is a bit too effervescent.

The Westhalten cooperative started to produce sparkling wine in 1974. The present annual output is around 150,000 bottles of Crémant d'Alsace, sold under the curious brand name of Producteur. Only the Pinot Blanc (not the Auxerrois) is used. The farmers receive instructions to pick the grapes for the Crémant d'Alsace a little earlier than the rest, so they are still a bit acid and do not produce too much alcohol. The wine is vinous, fresh and pure. It has a rather soft taste with fairly large bubbles.

Brut Réal is a fairly fruity, gently effervescent, attractive sparkling wine from the Bennwihr cooperative; not a Crémant d'Alsace but a vin mousseux. The cooperative has developed its own method which is not divulged. I only know that Pinot Blanc is the base.

Patrick Schaller, son of grower Edgard Schaller of Mittelwihr, completed his wine studies in the Champagne in 1973. Little wonder then that the Schaller estate has been making its own Crémant d'Alsace since that time. It produces around 12,000 bottles a year. There is often a hint of green in the colour, a liberal amount of small bubbles, a good, slightly rustic taste and a short aftertaste. Patrick makes it from Pinot grapes.

Lucien Albrecht has been producing his own Cremant d'Alsace from the Pinot Blanc in Orschwihr since 1977. This generally has a very decent quality — apart from the one bad bottle I happened to come across. The taste and aroma are pure and not too intrusive. The wine is fairly soft. Annual production: around 25,000 bottles.

In 1981 Dopff & Irion launched its Crémant d'Alsace, made exclusively from Pinot Blanc. It is a very pleasant, slightly fruity wine.

Other wines and drinks

Crémant d'Alsace is a rising star in the Alsace firmament, a sparkling wine that since 24 August 1976 has had its own *appellation contrôlée*. Production has been increasing rapidly: it already passed the five million bottle mark in 1981. Crémant d'Alsace is made by the *méthode champenoise*, described in detail on pages 142-5. The notable features of this method are secondary fermentation in the bottle and the procedures arising from this. Other specifications governing the making of Crémant d'Alsace concern the starting date of the picking, the transport of the grapes in non-watertight boxes, the pressing, and the quantity of juice that may be vinified (100 litres per 150 kilograms of grapes). Permitted grape varieties are the Pinot Blanc, Pinot-Auxerrois, Pinot Noir, Pinot Gris, Riesling and Chardonnay. The great majority of Crémants d'Alsace are made from those two widely planted varieties, the Pinot Blanc and the Pinot-Auxerrois.

Dopff au Moulin — pioneer

The firm of Dopff au Moulin at Riquewihr was a pioneer of sparkling Alsace wines; it began making these according to the Champagne method in 1900. Other houses were similarly active, but Dopff au Moulin is the only survivor from those early days. The present director, Pierre-Etienne Dopff, told me that his firm had often used its sparkling wine as an introduction or 'visiting card', since for a long time no other firm carried it. However, other concerns, especially wine cooperatives, now produce sparkling wine, and a few individual growers have also started making Crémant d'Alsace. Not all the sparkling wine made in the region, however, is Crémant d'Alsace. Dopff, for example, makes a *vin mousseux*, also by the Champagne method, but of simpler quality than Crémant. The Bennwihr cooperative produces no Crémant, only a *vin mousseux*. These simpler sparkling wines are not allowed to be labelled as 'Alsace'.

Beer and mineral waters

Alsace produces a considerable range of beers, including Kronenbourg, a brand of the powerful BSN-Bières group, which controls about half of the French market; Mutzig, a Heineken brand; Météor; Schutzenburger; Fischer; Adelshoffen; and Rheingold. The region also has mineral waters, such as the Carola springs at Ribeauvillé. On the other side of the Vosges, just outside Alsace itself, lie Vittel and Contrexéville, both large suppliers of mineral water. Finally, there are the distilled drinks, the *eau-de-vie* or *alcools blancs*. Alsace produces an incredible variety of these, made from fruit, flowers, buds and shoots, and roots.

Alcools blancs

In the 16th and 17th centuries there were many small distilleries, especially in Colmar, turning the regional wine into potent spirits. They disappeared as a result of war and shortage of wine. After a lengthy interval, distilling was started again, this time not from wine but from produce such as cereals and beer. These hesitant efforts met with little success, but in the 18th century the idea developed of making strong drinks from the many available kinds of fruit. Now, two centuries later, Alsace distillates enjoy a considerable, ever-growing reputation. A striking feature here is that, in contrast to Cognac, production and marketing have remained largely in the same hands.

An aroma of almonds

Kirsch is by far the greatest of these distillations. As with other drinks of this type, quality is determined in the first instance by the fruit used. After being picked, the fruit is taken as quickly as possible to the distillery, where it is fermented. When fermentation is complete, the resulting 'cherry wine' is left in contact with the skins and stones: the latter give Kirsch its characteristic aroma of almonds. The liquid is distilled and then matured, usually in earthenware or glass jars, sometimes in ashwood barrels. Just before bottling, distilled water is added to reduce *the alcohol content to 45°-50°. In roughly the same manner as Kirsch, but without using the stones or seeds, eaux-de-vie are made* from other naturally sweet fruits: Mirabelle, from the golden plum of that name; Quetsch; Reine Claude; Poire William, from the pear; Coign, from the quince; and Prune Sauvage, from the wild plum.
plum.

Other wines and drinks

Thirty varieties

All the other fruits, nuts and so forth that are used are first soaked either in alcohol or a sugar solution. Raspberries, for example — cultivated for Framboise, or wild for Framboise Sauvage — are soaked for up to a month in as neutral as possible a distillate of fruit or wine before they are distilled. For every four kilograms the law allows the addition of one litre of *eau-de-vie*. Holly berries, for Houx, have first to be soaked in sugar as they have so little of their own, then fermented and subsequently distilled. Some 30 different *alcools blancs* are made in Alsace. Other examples, besides those already mentioned, are Fraise (strawberry), Fraise des Bois (wild strawberry), Abricot, Pêche (peach), Prunelle (sloe), Pomme Golden, Mûre (blackberry), Cassis (blackcurrant), Alisier (serviceberry), Sorbier (rowanberry), Groseille (redcurrant), Airelle and Myrtille (whortleberry), Sureau (elderberry), Gratte-Cul or Eglantine (rosehip), Gentiane (gentian root), Fleur d'Acacia (acacia blossom) and Bourgeon de Sapin (pine shoots). Even this assortment does not exhaust the list. A thin wine is made from the skins, seeds and stalks left after Gewürztraminer grapes have been pressed and this is then distilled as 45° proof Marc de Gewürztraminer. There is plenty of choice if you want to finish off a typically sumptuous meal with an Alsace *digestif*.

The wine route

The following 46 pages will take you in word
and picture from north to south down the
Alsace *route du vin*. All the important wine-
producing communes, with their major
vineyards and growers, are described.
Names of good individual wines from the
villages are given, building up a picture that
is reasonably representative, although by no
means complete. The wine route was
ceremonially inaugurated on 30 May 1953. It
runs through almost 100 wine villages
between Marlenheim in the north, west of
Strasbourg, to Thann in the south, west of
Mulhouse. The length of the route varies
from about 75 to 110 miles, depending on
how many side roads you take.
The extreme north of Alsace is separated
from the main wine-producing area and has
its own, much shorter wine route.

Contrasts in wine

In terms of history, architecture, traditions
and wines, the *route du vin* offers a
succession of surprises. Anyone willing to
spend a little time in the villages will
discover a wealth of beauty and fascinating
detail. The people are generally hospitable,
but do not be too surprised if two local
growers suddenly start conversing in their
own incomprehensible dialect when the topic
is not meant for your ears. There are great
contrasts among the wines, as, for instance,
between the austere freshness of a Riesling
Rangen from the Zind-Humbrecht estate and
the broad, spicy sultriness of a
Gewürztraminer from the Eguisheim
cooperative; and the contrasts not only
apply to taste but also extend to scale and
approach.
The maps on this page will help to locate the
various communes. All the villages and
towns described in the text are marked, as
well as a few others. Obviously there is no
substitute for the real thing, but I hope the
ensuing text and illustrations will whet the
appetite and serve as a helpful prelude to
your own drive along the Alsace *route du
vin*.

The land in the villages of Cléebourg and Steinseltz is eminently suited to the cultivation of the Pinos Gris or Tokay d'Alsace. The Tokay from the local cooperative is thus an extremely good, rather spicy wine, and usually very agreeable even in the poorer years. The Tokay d'Alsace is sold under various brand names, like all the wines from the cooperative.

The Pinot d'Alsace from Cléebourg's cooperative is made exclusively from the Pinot-Auxerrois: a tasty, fairly full wine, possibly a little smooth but still very pleasant. The enterprise also produces a nice sparkling wine, the Duc Casimir, from the same Pinot-Auxerrois.

In the usually orange-pink Pinot Noir from the Coopérative Viticole de Cléebourg et Environs there is generally a distinct terroir in taste and aftertaste, a characteristic of most of the wines from this district. An attractive, vinous aroma and taste complete the picture. The Pinot Noir is above average, but not in my opinion the Sylvaner, Riesling and Gewürztraminer.

Vineyard acreages
Rott: 84
Oberhoffen: 59
Steinseltz: 82
Cléebourg: 74

Below:
A great many tourists, particularly Germans, visit the cooperative in Cléebourg. Production is 89,000 to 110,000 cases a year.

Bottom left:
The village of Cléebourg, where some of the half-timbered houses date from the period 1750-1840. Nearby Rott has a rare fortified church.

Bottom right:
Georges Rupp, manager of the Cléebourg cooperative, whose father helped found the enterprise.

This small north French wine district was the first to reallocate its vineyards in 1945 and 1946.

Cléebourg was in Swedish hands for many years in the 17th century.

The extreme north

The most northerly vines of Alsace grow in a small, isolated district close to the German frontier. If you drive from the German Rheinpfalz, or Rhine Palatinate, into Alsace at Wissembourg, it is only a mile or two to the first vineyards.

As you follow the road from Wissembourg to the wine villages of Rott and Cléebourg, the terrain becomes hillier and the first vines appear, and there is an inn called the *Relais de la Route du Vin*; small the district may be, but it still has its own wine route. In a place like Cléebourg, with its long, straight village street and its pretty, half-timbered houses, the atmosphere is more German than French. Only the aroma of garlic in the restaurant next to the local cooperative makes you realize that you are actually in France, as does the white wine, which is fresh and dry, not sweet.

A new start

Wine-growing in Cléebourg and its neighbourhood goes back some 12 centuries. Soon after the foundation of the Benedictine abbey of Wissembourg in AD 630, the monks began to plant their first vines. Yet despite these ancient origins, it was only after World War II that wine-growing really became important. In 1941 all 740 acres of vineyard were cleared on the initiative of Georges Rupp, whose son now manages the cooperative. This was done to allow a completely fresh start: about two-thirds of the plants then consisted of poor hybrids, or vines on slopes that could be reached neither by horse nor tractor. Soon after this, reallocation of vineyard land commenced,

the process being completed after the Liberation; and this time care was taken that the right vines should be planted in the right type of soil — on sunny hillsides that could be worked by tractor. In 1946 the local cooperative was set up.

Specializing in Tokay

All the 230 or so growers of the district are associated with the *cave coopérative*. They cultivate a total of 300 acres in the communes of Cléebourg, Rott, Steinseltz and Oberhoffen. Only one of the members lives entirely from his grapes; the others grow other crops as well. In this northern zone there are no Muscat grapes: they are too tender for the local microclimate. The Pinot varieties, however, do extremely well here; the Pinot Gris or Tokay d'Alsace is even a speciality ('There is no better Tokay than ours in Alsace,' according to Georges Rupp). It is, in fact, very good, but I have also enjoyed tasting the Pinot-Auxerrois and Pinot Noir in Cléebourg. I found the other wines disappointing. The cooperative sells its products principally to French retail chains and to Germans, importers as well as individuals — who often come over by the busload. Different brand names and labels are used for the various customers.

Vineyard acreages
Marlenheim: 141
Nordheim: 94
Wangen: 173
Kirchheim: 40

The Mosbachs are the most famous wine-growing family in Marlenheim. They live in the main street. Their cellars (with a large pink bottle in the front) are in a side street. Their 44-acre estate is in Marlenheim itself, representing practically one-third of the vineyard area. I have good recollections of the Mosbach Vorlauf: an orange-brown rosé, delicious and rather spicy in flavour with some terroir. Equally successful are the Tokay and Gewürztraminer.

The firm of Laugel owns around 25 acres in Marlenheim. Half of this is planted with Pinot Noir, producing a wine sold as Rosé de Marlenheim, a registered trademark. It is a satisfactory wine, decently firm in good years with a distinct terroir in the taste. The best of the other Laugel wines usually carry the badge of the Unidal, the growers from whom the firm buys grapes. Internal grading is in 'gold', 'silver' and 'bronze' qualities.

Right:
A few hundred yards separate the Mosbach and Laugel premises in Marlenheim.

Below:
The village of Marlenheim viewed from one of the vineyards.

The firm of Laugel was founded in 1889 by Michel Laugel who was also a wine-broker and lived in Wangen, near Marlenheim. In 1919 his son Paul took over the business and transferred it to Marlenheim. Present storage capacity is around 60,000 hectolitres, in glazed concrete vats and large oak barrels.

Laugel produces its own distillates after taking over the Ganter distillery in Mulhouse.

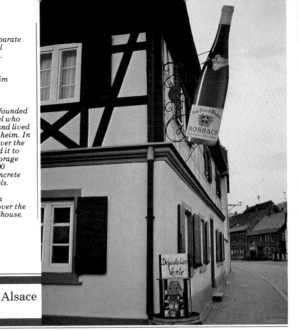

Marlenheim

For 30 miles south of Cléebourg there are no vines to be seen until you come to Marlenheim, the start of the long Alsace *route du vin*. Marlenheim, in fact, marks the real beginning of Alsace as a wine region historically as well as geographically.

The earliest mention of wine-growing in Alsace dates from AD 589. In that year the historian Gregory of Tours records that the Merovingian monarch Childebert II sentenced a rebellious lord to forced labour in the royal vineyards at Marlenheim. At that time there was a palace near Marlenheim, described by Dom Ruinart (see page 170) as 'one of the most magnificent' of the day.

Commuters and festivals

Today the village of Marlenheim is bisected by the busy N4 Strasbourg—Paris road. Many Strasbourg commuters have settled here, swelling the population from 1,800 to about 2,500 in five or six years. The village is well provided with shops and health and recreation facilities. Nevertheless, the old Marlenheim has not vanished altogether. It is preserved in the half-timbered houses near the *hôtel de ville* and along the main street. Moreover, in the autumn the traditional three-day vintage festival is celebrated, and in August there is the very carnival-like 'Wedding feast of friend Fritz'.

The Pinot Noir has long been cultivated in Marlenheim, under the local name of Vorlauf (wine from the first, and so the best, pressing). According to legend, in 1632 the plundering Swedes suddenly turned friendly after the Marlenheimers had given them liberal amounts of Vorlauf to drink. The wine has been recorded since 1582 and in 1748 a doctor named Behr wrote: 'The Vorlauf of Marlenheim is certainly a famous drink, wholesome and pleasant, which is got from noble black grapes and excels above many Burgundies.' The Pinot Noir thrives here due to the sheltered, dry position of the vineyards and the calciferous soil, kept moist by underground springs. The Vorlauf nearly always used to be a light-coloured red wine; today, as a rule, it is a rosé. Provided it comes from a good wine maker, it is one of the better Alsace rosés. The well-known family firm of Laugel (approximately four million bottles a year) is established in Marlenheim. This shipper has set up the Union des Producteurs de Raisins d'Alsace, comprising 500-600 growers from whom the firm buys its grapes. The Laugel wines generally have a fairly subdued bouquet, a smooth, almost metallic coolness of taste, and, at the least, a satisfactory quality.

The Traenheim cooperative helps its members with a planting plan for each commune, in order to get the most suitable type of grape into each of the many different types of soil. Glazed concrete vats and modern stainless-steel tanks are used for fermentation. One wine that appealed to me was the Sylvaner; very successful of its type. I found the Klevner and the generally non-vintage light red, supple Pinot very pleasant and also some of the selections from the Riesling. Pierre Goefft is the capable manager.

When the Bugatti drivers and enthusiasts have made their pilgrimage to Molsheim in mid-September, the municipality serves them with a Gewürztraminer with a special Bugatti label. The wine is made by the local grower Antoine Klingenfus. His vineyards lie next to the Rue Ettore Bugatti. Bugatti cars had many triumphs between 1925 and 1935, but today the factory only makes aircraft parts.

Obernai's Clos Sainte-Odile was created in 1920 and measures about 25 acres. There are three owners, the largest part being owned by Michel Weiss, general manager of the wine firm and distillery Sainte-Odile. Up until 1981 the estate produced only a Tokay: aromatic, robust, soft, harmonious — very fine. In 1981 production of a Riesling and a Gewürztraminer was started. Of the other ordinary Sainte-Odile wines (not from the Clos, differently labelled), I would pick out the Gewürztraminer; of the eaux-de-vie the Kirsch.

Charles Wantz, who founded the wine firm in Barr of the same name, was one of the first in Alsace to reintroduce the red Pinot Noir after World War II. For years Wantz bought all the Pinot Noir grapes in the village that was renowned for them — Ottrott. He still buys a lot there. His Rouge d'Ottrott is a fairly light red wine, clear in colour and with a juicy, grapy, delicious taste and a judicious amount of tannin remaining in the mouth.

Vineyard acreages
Furdenheim: 37
Westhoffen: 267
Scharragbergheim/Irmstett: 173
Dahlenheim: 68
Osthoffen: 32
Traenheim: 188
Soultz-les-Bains: 62
Balbronn: 225
Bergbieten: 114
Dangolsheim: 101
Wolxheim: 284
Ergersheim: 168
Avolsheim: 72
Mutzig: 25
Molsheim: 129
Dorlisheim: 336
Rosheim: 217
Rosenwiller: 173
Bisschoffsheim: 94
Obernai: 163
Boersch: 79
Ottrott: 96
Bernardswiller: 205

Below:
Barr church and churchyard. On the second Sunday in October there is usually a vintage festival in the town.

Near Ottrott — which has a feast of 'the wild boar on the spit' — there are two castles dating from the 12th and 13th centuries.

Odile died in 720. The convent she founded owned Obernai until the 12th century.

Clos Sainte-Odile produces 1,670 to 5,000 cases annually. The wine is served regularly at the Elysée Palace.

The Muscat was first mentioned in 1523 in Wolxheim.

In and around Obernai

Obernai lies about 12 miles south of Marlenheim. Although the vine more or less dominates the scene farther into Alsace, vineyards here often alternate with arable, pasture and woodland. Near medieval Westhoffen, for example, there is a forest consisting almost entirely of oaks. Just outside Traenheim — where according to tradition heroes of the *Nibelungenlied* were born — there is quite an important cooperative, founded in 1951. Some 240 growers who cultivate 740 acres in 14 villages bring their grapes here. The cooperative uses the brand name Roi Dagobert, after the Merovingian king who had lands in this district. Of all the wines I tasted from this cooperative, the Sylvaner, Klevner and Pinot Noir were the best.

Bonaparte, beer and Bugatti

After Soultz-les-Bains, where salts-rich mineral water is a more important source of income than wine, and Dangolsheim, where cider rules supreme, comes the wine commune of Wolxheim. The local vineyard of Altenberg apparently provided Napoleon's favourite white wine — although this is scarcely a compliment, for the Emperor had abominable eating and drinking habits, diluting his Chambertin with water. A part of Wolxheim soil contains red sandstone. In Avolsheim there is a lot of Sylvaner, whereas Mutzig is famous mainly for its beer. In Molsheim there is the splendid *Metzig*, a slaughterhouse dating from 1554, now a museum; and Molsheim is also the site of the Bugatti works, where every year enthusiasts of this legendary marque hold a nostalgic rally. There is even a special Bugatti Gewürztraminer.

St Odile

The rest of the route to Obernai is marked by vines and by sights such as the prehistoric menhir at Dorlisheim, the 12th-century house at Rosheim, the oldest dwelling in Alsace, and the three medieval gates of Boersch. Obernai itself has many visitors at weekends and holidays — and with reason. The many half-timbered houses, the 16th-century Corn Exchange, the market square, the 13th-century Kappelturn tower, the splendid carving around the 'Well of the Six Springs', and the walk around the town walls afford much visual pleasure. The little town is also famous for St Odile. She was born blind and mentally defective in the second half of the 7th century. Her father, who had wanted a son, gave orders for her to be killed, but a nurse managed to save her. When Odile was baptized she was suddenly endowed with sight, mental powers and beauty. After much domestic unhappiness, she founded her own convent, on the 2,500-foot Mont Sainte-Odile. It stands high above Obernai and draws thousands of visitors every year. In Obernai there is a Clos Sainte-Odile, a vineyard distributed over five terraces that produces very interesting wines. By far the biggest wine business in Obernai is Divinal, which has its own pressing centres and also markets wines from the cooperatives at Andlau, Barr and Traenheim. Mass production and quality here go hand in hand. Near Obernai is the village of Ottrott, noted for the rosé it makes from Pinot Noir.

The firm of A. Willm generally buys the rare Klevener de Heiligenstein grape from just one grower. This ancestor of the Gewürztraminer gives a very remarkable wine, distinctive in taste with an earthy bouquet. It does not usually contain much acid but still matures splendidly; Willm's 1976 and 1973 — tasted in 1980 — were still perfectly fresh.

The man who brought the Klevener from Italy to Heiligenstein was Ehrhardt (called Ehret) Wantz, a distant ancestor of the négociant Charles Wantz: hardly surprising then that the latter has a Klevener de Heiligenstein in his collection. It is usually an aromatic wine with a mild bouquet and fresh aftertaste.

Willm's Sylvaner (the Cordon d'Alsace brand) is served as a white house wine in some famous restaurants. The wine, in 1-litre bottles, has an honest, appealing simplicity, a touch of terroir, a hint of juiciness and also some fruit. Delicious to drink.

Willm has a 10-acre plot in Barr's Kirchberg planted with Riesling. The character of the wine is difficult to describe: a distinctive, quite pronounced bouquet and taste, supple and almost soft in the mouth, yet seeming to have a fresh, cool core and a hint of spiciness. Not a classic Riesling with breeding and refinement, but still very enjoyable. Willm's ordinary Riesling from its own estate is labelled as Réserve.

Klipfel's 37 acres of the Freiberg vineyard mainly produces Gewürztraminer. As in all Klipfel's estate wines it matures for at least three months in wood. However, manager André Lorentz will leave a great Gewürztraminer for at least a year in the cask; the quality of the vintage dictates the period of maturation. The Freiberg Gewürztraminer is generally a robust wine, rich in alcohol and full of scent and flavour. The Tokay from the Freiberg often has great merit.

The 12-acre Clos Zisser in Barr is the exclusive property of Klipfel. It can produce Gewürztraminers of greater strength and richness than those from the Freiberg. I recall the 1976 sélection de grains nobles, a wine made from over-ripe grapes picked on 28 November. In a perfectly natural way, it had achieved considerable sweetness, a sultry bouquet and taste and 15° alcohol. In poor years such as 1972, no Clos Zisser is marketed.

Heiligenstein and Barr

The hillside village of Heiligenstein lies on the road from Obernai to Barr. The narrow Rue Principale winds through its very old centre, but the outskirts date from the present century. Apart from its heart-shaped spiced loaves, the village is noted for its own grape variety, the Klevener de Heiligenstein. This is assumed to have come from Chiavenna in North Italy (Cleven in German), and was brought to Heiligenstein in 1742 by Ehrhardt Wantz, whose sculpted portrait adorns the front of the *hôtel de ville* over the inscription 'Knowledge brings Progress'. Unlike the Pinot Blanc, which is often referred to as the Klevner, this Italian grape is black. Its official French name is the Savagnin Rose, and it is regarded as the ancestor of the Gewürztraminer. It is, however, smaller and its wine less aromatic and drier in taste. Apparently only 32 acres in the whole of Alsace are planted with this grape, exclusively in the communes of Heiligenstein, Barr, Goxwiller and Gertwiller. Klevener de Heiligenstein is not a great wine, but still fairly aromatic and quite unlike any other Alsace type.

A maze of streets

Barr lies not far from Heiligenstein in the valley of the little river Kirneck. It has 4,500 inhabitants (1,000 more in summer) and the central area, with its tangle of small, winding streets, is attractive, especially around the *hôtel de ville*, built in 1640. The name Barr is probably derived from the Celtic *barra*, which may have meant 'barrier'. It is thought that local wine-growing started with the Romans.

Barr has an air of prosperity, partly due to its lovely gardens, especially on the south side of the town. Evidently the wealth of many families was based on the town's 19th-century leather industry, now greatly reduced, as well as wine-growing.

Good Gewürztraminers

Barr's vineyards extend over nearly 220 acres, three-quarters of this area being cultivated by people from the district itself. Two-thirds of the vineyard area is situated on the Kirchberg and the Freiberg slopes. On clear days there is a magnificent view from the Kirchberg, extending as far as Strasbourg. Other well-known but smaller vineyards are Clos Zisser and Clos Gaensbrœnnel, the latter being named after the Goose Fountain opposite the 18th-century museum of La Folie Marco. Various soils are encountered in Barr, but clay and limestone predominate. The Gewürztraminer is very successfully grown, on about 35% of the area; the second most important variety is the Sylvaner, on 25%, the Riesling on 17%. There is not much Pinot Blanc and Pinot Noir, but Pinot Gris (Tokay d'Alsace) and Muscat are more common, accounting for 8% and 6% respectively of the total area.

The house of Klipfel

The biggest shipper in Barr is Klipfel, which trades under two names: Louis Klipfel for wines from its own estate, and Eugène Klipfel for the rest (about a million bottles a year). André Lorentz, the director, who admits to a passion for wine, has had a fine reception area built for the 20,000 visitors who come to look and taste every year. In the Klipfel tasting room-cum-restaurant 300 people can sit down at a time to taste, dine and see a slide show. Antique wine objects adorn the area and 15 old winepresses stand in front of the building. The great Klipfel speciality — as might be expected — is the Gewürztraminer.

Although the 'trade' wines, the Eugène Klipfels, are of decent quality, I definitely prefer the Louis Klipfels from the firm's own estate. This comprises about 75 acres, including 17 on the Freiberg and the whole of the 12-acre Clos Zisser. Both vineyards grow a splendid Gewürztraminer, but I have also come across a good Tokay from the Freiberg.

Alsace-Willm

Another, much smaller firm is Alsace-Willm (about 500,000 bottles annually). Visitors who pass through its gate enter a charming inner courtyard, bright with flowers in summer. Willm's most attractive cellar, with wood panelling, lies under the house; the more functional rooms are farther up the hill. Edy Willm and his son Christian sold their firm in 1980 to Roger Bahl, the Alsace wine and spirits merchants, but stayed on as directors and retained their own 54 acres of wine-growing land. I consider the best-quality wine to be their Riesling from the Kirchberg (10 acres) and Gewürztraminer from Clos Gaensbrœnnel (17 acres, also with

The 17-acre Clos Gaensbrœnnel is a triangular-shaped vineyard immediately behind the Willm cellars and owned by the firm. Gewürztraminer Clos Gaensbrœnnel is sold only from really good years. It is normally properly concentrated, mildly spicy in taste and has just sufficient acid for it to be kept for an exceptionally long time — easily 10 to 20 years: even longer if from a great year.

The Gewürztraminer is one of the attractive specialities from Charles Wantz. The Reserve offers the best quality. It is less sultry and heavy than other Gewürztraminers from Barr, as I discovered with an example from sunny 1976. Other characteristics are a spicy tone to the taste and a good balance. At the tasting the commercial manager Frédéric Dock confided: 'This wine is my aperitif maison'. Wantz's Tokay 1975 is first class.

Vineyard acreages
*Heiligenstein: 319
Goxwiller: 178
Bourgheim: 82
Gertwiller: 208
Barr: 220
Zellwiller: 62*

*Opposite page, below:
Edy Willm (right) and his son Christian of the firm of the same name.*

*Below:
These large tasting premises are on the south side of Barr. The firm's name appears as Lorentz-Klipfel because it is managed by André Lorentz who is married to a Klipfel. André is assisted by his son Jean-Louis who studied in Beaune. André's brother Charles runs two wine firms in Bergheim: Gustave Lorentz and Jerôme Lorentz (see page 103). A number of old presses can be seen in and near the tasting hall. In front of Klipfel's office elsewhere in Barr is a fine antique press of 1708.*

One of the Klipfel brands is 'André Lorentz', named after the present owner/manager.

The first wine fair in Alsace took place in Barr on 14 March 1906. Nowadays it is held on 14 July, France's national holiday.

Barr has been almost wholly destroyed by fire on two occasions: in 1592 and 1678.

The firm of Charles Wantz uses the name Stein for its supermarket brand.

Heiligenstein and Barr

some Riesling and Sylvaner). Willm also sells some pleasant Sylvaner and a very successful Klevener de Heiligenstein. Although Willm wines do not in general have a very marked personality, or any captivating finesse or subtlety, I have often drunk the better types with great pleasure.

Charles Wantz

A third wine shipper at Barr is Charles Wantz, which started as a wholesale concern supplying the restaurant trade with wines from other parts of France. For their Alsace wines Charles Wantz and his son-in-law Frédéric Dock take grapes (and wine) from some 300 growers. The fruit is vinified along with that from their own 12 acres. The marked increase in the number of growers bottling their own wine, and the strong position of the cooperatives and of more notable shippers means that a medium-sized, little-known firm like Charles Wantz is going through a difficult period. Nevertheless, Wantz hopes to interest the largely untapped export market in a few good specialities such as Rouge d'Ottrott, Klevener de Heiligenstein, Sylvaner Zotzenberg and Gewürztraminer of the Réserve quality.

One firm that carries a Zotzenberg Sylvaner as a speciality is Charles Wantz of Barr. I noted its very pale colour, a taste that was elegant yet full of character, with some terroir in the pleasant aftertaste. Information on Wantz's other wines is given on the two preceding pages.

The Zotzenberg Réserve is a truly sublime Sylvaner from the house of Seltz. More rounded than other Sylvaners, it is rather racy and fruity and you can smell and taste the freshness of the limestone soil. This Sylvaner also matures splendidly. The Seltz family originally came from Andlau but has been active in the wine industry in Mittelbergheim since 1575. The firm also trades as Pierre Seltz.

Another excellent wine from A. Seltz & Fils is the often underrated Clevner or Pinot Blanc: very supple, harmonious and pure (at least the wine sold with its year of vintage). I also enjoyed a thoroughbred Riesling Réserve, perfectly made from grapes grown on the limestone and sand. Seltz's Gewürztraminer can also be very good (elegant, and not pomade-like), as can the Muscat. The best selections are always sold as Réserve and Réserve Particulière.

Brandluft — formerly called Brandloch — is a small vineyard on a site in Mittelbergheim where distillation waste used to be dumped; Boeckel with 4 acres owns the biggest plot. Boeckel produces a Riesling with a distinct, almost smoky bouquet and an often virile, spicy taste that seems to profit from a few years' maturation.

Boeckel owns 12 acres of the approx. 35-acre Wibelsberg in Andlau, all planted with Riesling. Compared to the Brandluft-Riesling, the Wibelsberg is smoother, friendlier and softer. Of the other Boeckel Rieslings I prefer the Riesling Réserve, which can have a very fruity taste and perfume. Another of Boeckel's brands is Les Héritiers André Schmidt.

In addition to its usual, fully adequate Pinot Blanc, Boeckel carries a Réserve that comes from the Chardonnay. This well-known grape from Burgundy and Champagne is planted on a 1¼-acre piece of land. I find the wine very distinctive, with impressions of spices, smoke, earth and juice in the bouquet and taste. This rare Alsace wine should mature for 3 to 4 years so that its initial acids are converted into an agreeable freshness.

Mittelbergheim and its neighbours

Mittelbergheim, whose vineyards border on those of Barr, came into being at the beginning of the 6th century AD. Unlike many other Alsace villages, it has never directly experienced violence and devastation. For centuries it enjoyed the threefold protection of the city and archbishopric of Strasbourg, and of the abbey of Andlau. Mittelbergheim has, in consequence, always been a fairly prosperous community — even more so when in the 16th century a number of hard-working Protestant families from Andlau settled here. Among them were some familiar names: such as Seltz, borne by a local wine firm, and Gilg, represented by the best local restaurant, the *Winstub Gilg*. The result of this early peace and prosperity is to be seen in present-day Mittelbergheim, which is a beautifully preserved wine village with many large 16th- and 17th-century houses, a 12th-century tower, ornamented gables, and much else. Mittelbergheim lies on a slope and consists essentially of two long intersecting streets. It is a village to be explored on foot: too much of the atmosphere and the detail is missed from a car.

Superior Sylvaner

At one time every Alsace village used to fix the selling price of its wine annually, by means of the *Weinschlag*. The prices, with remarks on the current vintage, were entered in the *Weinschlagbuch*. Some of these books still exist, but nowhere is the record so complete as at Mittelbergheim, where harvest results are recorded from the year 785 to the present day (prices are no longer noted, but details of the quantity and quality of the vintage are recorded). A unique picture of Mittelbergheim's ups and downs as a wine commune is thus documented. We read, for example, that the 1313 vintage was worse than any in the preceding 100 years. Today Mittelbergheim has nearly 430 acres of vineyards, about half the acreage of 50 years ago. The great speciality is the Sylvaner from the Zotzenberg vineyard, a 175-acre limestone area almost entirely planted with this variety. The ground here is shaped like a basin and traps the heat of the

Although Jean Beyer's name appears on the label, the wine is now made by his son Patrick, who runs the 15-acre estate at Epfig. Patrick Beyer is one of about 10 Epfig growers who bottle their own wines. The other 90 or so work through a shipper or a cooperative. The Sylvaner predominates in Epfig and from it Patrick makes a very good wine: soft, fresh, fruity and balanced. There is also some Gewürztraminer; the Riesling is good but somewhat lacking in real breed and refinement.

Vineyard acreages
Mittelbergheim: 427
Andlau: 237
Eichhoffen: 62
Saint-Pierre: 42
Stotzheim: 205
Itterswiller: 299
Bernardvillé: 126
Epfig: 660
Nothalten: 472
Blienschwiller: 447

Opposite page, left:
Pierre Seltz and his American wife Dolly. On the table are Californian manzanilla olives which Pierre imports: as I discovered, they taste delicious with wine, being juicy and not at all sharp.

Below:
Mittelbergheim, which has about 650 inhabitants. The little church bell used to ring when foreign wine buyers arrived.

Right:
This sign welcomes visitors to Mittelbergheim. The village celebrates its wine festival in the last weekend of July.

Bienvenue dans la Cité du Vin

---

sun, producing Sylvaner grapes with more sugar than elsewhere in Alsace.

Quality from A. Seltz et Fils

Some 25 growers live and work in Mittelbergheim, three of whom are also shippers. The firm of A. Seltz et Fils produces one of the best Zotzenberg Sylvaners, a wine of exceptional quality. I have also tasted excellent Clevner, Riesling and Gewürztraminer at the home of owner-manager Pierre Seltz and his American wife; and I drank a memorable Muscat from Seltz at the three-star *Auberge de l'Ill* restaurant. The firm owns 5 acres on the Zotzenberg and another 2 acres elsewhere in Mittelbergheim. Pierre Seltz, who studied oenology in California, prefers grapes picked as late as is practicable and then fermented as slowly as possible. Anyone who wants to sample the wines of A. Seltz et Fils would do well to order the Réserve and Réserve Particulière qualities, with year of vintage. I find the remaining, simpler wines much less

interesting. Production is about 200,000 bottles a year.

Boeckel, an individualistic firm

Mittelbergheim's biggest wine firm is E. Boeckel, which owns about 50 acres of land, mainly in Mittelbergheim, but also in Andlau, Barr and Heiligenstein, and which sells some 700,000 bottles a year. The Boeckel premises, with various small courtyards and dwellings, is virtually a village within a village. Boeckel is an individualistic firm, exemplified by the fact that it takes only Riesling and Gewürztraminer, but no Sylvaner, from the Zotzenberg. I also came across a Boeckel wine made from the Chardonnay, the Burgundy variety, but disguised as 'Pinot d'Alsace Réservé': this is from 1¼ acres of the firm's own land. Riesling wines are the speciality of this house, the best being from the Brandluft vineyard in Mittelbergheim and the Wibelsberg in Andlau.

South of Mittelbergheim

There are a few wine communes between Mittelbergheim and Dambach-la-Ville. Andlau, with its monastery, church and, in the surrounding valley, three ruined castles, has a cooperative that is part of the Divinal group in Obernai. Villages such as Eichhoffen, Saint-Pierre, Stotzheim, Bernardvillé and Nothalten may have little of note to offer, but Itterswiller, high up on a slope, has much charm — and an agreeable restaurant; Epfig has a large area of vineyard and a beautiful 11th-century chapel near the churchyard; and Blienswiller puts out a striking number of inviting signs, bottles, barrels and slogans along the road.

Willy Gisselbrecht's Pinot Blanc has always earned good marks from me — individually and also in comparative tastings. It is a juicy, genial, top-quality wine, very characteristic of its type. I have also made favourable notes on some vintages of Sylvaner, Riesling and Gewürztraminer Réserve. In the narrow modern cellars (with glazed concrete vats and stainless steel tanks) are bottles labelled Heinrich, a Gisselbrecht brand.

Louis Gisselbrecht wines are not as a rule markedly fruity or refined in type, but they are not too expensive and represent good value for money. The Sylvaner is a prime example, also the Pinot Blanc and the Edelzwicker. I find the Riesling usually very satisfactory.

The Riesling Réserve from Jean Hauller & Fils is usually a really good, fresh wine with finesse. The Sylvaner Réserve also deserves attention. Its grapes come from the granite rather than a heavy soil and so the wine tastes quite light and distinguished. Those who like a heavy, seductive, clinging and even sweet Gewürztraminer are referred to the Hauller Cuvée Saint-Sébastien of the vendange tardive quality, such as the memorable 1973. Other Hauller brands are Roth and Hellmuth.

Grower Louis Hauller is from the same family of coopers as the Jean Hauller people. His label depicts the tools of this trade. Louis works 16 acres (to be increased) planted with eight types of grape. Two of these, the Pinot Blanc and the Pinot-Auxerrois, are on 1 acre in Dambach-la-Ville. Contrary to the norm Louis does not mix the grapes. I found his Klevner (from the Pinot-Auxerrois) delightful and the better of the two: distinctive, supple and smooth.

Dambach-la-Ville

The biggest wine commune of the Bas-Rhin *département*, the northern part of Alsace, is Dambach-la-Ville. The vineyards, including those with recently planted vines, cover some 1,235 acres. The name Dambach — at that time still called Tannenbach, after the fir tree — first occurs in the archives in 1125. With the surrounding hamlets it belonged to the lords of Bernstein, or rather *Bären*stein, a form that explains why there is a bear as well as a conifer on the coat-of-arms. In 1333, after passing into the possession of the archbishopric of Strasbourg, it was fortified; and since this left the adjoining hamlets exposed, the entire local population settled within the protecting walls. The fine Saint-Sébastien chapel, which now stands surrounded by vineyards, was until the beginning of the 14th century the parish church of Oberkirch. The inhabitants of medieval Dambach may have been safe from armies and brigands, but not from the plague, which decimated the population later that century. In the following centuries the place was intermittently subjected to the miseries of war, and not until about 1650 was there a long period of peace, when much new wine-growing land was opened up.

Wine festival

In the second half of the 19th century and up to World War I, wine-growing was Dambach's sole source of income. In 1920 the place became Dambach-la-Vigne, later corrupted to the present form of the name; 'la Vigne' was added as a means of avoiding confusion with another Dambach in the Moselle *département*. In 1924 Dambach's mono-economy ended when a large shoe factory was opened. Apart from this decidedly ugly building (fortunately outside the walls), where some 750 people are presently employed, Dambach-la-Ville has remained a true Alsace wine village. Of the 500-600 families only about 100 gain a livelihood from their own wine, while about as many again look on wine-growing as a subsidiary source of income; and in many other households the breadwinner works for a shipper or a wine estate. Dambach-la-Ville has since 1964 held a wine festival during the first half of August, when a Wine King is chosen and given the name of Bacchus. The title is conferred on the person who has answered a list of questions correctly,

Vineyard acreage	Right:
Dambach-la-Ville: 961	*View of Dambach-la-Ville (Dambach is pronounced 'Dambak').*
Opposite page, above:	
René Hauller (of Jean Hauller & Fils) in his vineyard near the Saint-Sébastien chapel.	*Below:* *Saint-Sébastien chapel. The choir has 14-century Gothic windows. There is a wooden*
Opposite page, below:	*altar of splendid workmanship*
The square in Dambach-la-Ville with (from left to right) the hôtel de ville (1547), the Hôtel de la Couronne (1569) and the Bear Fountain.	*on which is depicted the Virgin Mary in Alsace costume. Since 1796 the chapel has been maintained by the volunteer Société Saint-Sébastien.*
	Dambach's folklore group 'Les Joyeux Vignerons' appeared at the Elysée in 1975.

Dambach-la-Ville

managed to identify three grape varieties at a wine-tasting, and who in addition is the fastest drinker of a litre of wine. For this final test the candidates stand on a table surrounded by a throng of onlookers. The winner — who at that stage of the proceedings probably cannot bear even to see another drop — is awarded his own weight in bottles of wine.

Village of flowers

Dambach-la-Ville takes great pride in its appearance. Most of the half-timbered houses — largely from the end of the 17th and the beginning of the 18th centuries — that you see as you drive in through one of the three medieval gateways are very well preserved. So are older buildings such as the *hôtel de ville* (1547) and the Hôtel de la Couronne (1569) next door. In the summer many windows are hung with flowers; the annual *villes et villages fleuris* competition has on several occasions been won by Dambach.

The most important wine firms lie just outside the old centre. Dambach-la-Ville has its own cooperative whose 90 members cultivate about 370 acres. Wine from this cooperative is not bottled here, however, but at Eguisheim. The latter establishment also sells most of the bottled wine. About three-quarters of the Dambach cooperative's wine is Sylvaner or Riesling as these are the principal local grape varieties. The Pinot Blanc also thrives here.

Willy Gisselbrecht & Fils

The biggest shipper in Dambach is Willy Gisselbrecht, established in 1936 by the father of the present directors, Léon and Jean Gisselbrecht. The business is situated south of the village, alongside the wine route. In addition to its modern cellars, the firm has the largest old *cave* in Dambach, complete with wooden casks. The Willy Gisselbrecht method is notable for the speedy bottling of its wines whereby, it is

said, relatively little sulphur needs to be used. In my opinion the Pinot Blanc is one of the most attractive wines from this firm, and I have also enjoyed the Sylvaner, Riesling and Gewürztraminer Réserve of various vintages. Grapes from the firm's own 25 acres are vinified separately. Annual production is from 1 to 1.6 million bottles.

Louis Gisselbrecht

This firm is located about 100 yards from Willy Gisselbrecht and was established in the same year. Louis Gisselbrecht, run by André Gisselbrecht and his son Gilbert, is the smaller of the two concerns. Its range of wine seems simpler — and cheaper. The house regards the Riesling as its speciality but, in the same class, I was most charmed by the Sylvaner. The firm owns 15 acres of vineyard, the grapes from which are processed along with those bought from other growers. About 600,000 to 750,000 bottles are handled each year.

The house of Hauller

The Haullers were originally a family of coopers. Gradually, however, in addition to making barrels, they became technical advisers to many of the growers. From this they progressed to being shippers, under the

name Jean Hauller & Fils, and finally stopped manufacturing barrels and casks in 1950. Only some beautifully worked casks in the attractive little reception area now remain from the cooperage period. The firm — midway in size between the two Gisselbrechts — has 44 acres of vineyard up to 7½ miles around Dambach-la-Ville. Hauller's own Riesling and Gewürztraminer grapes come from the Scherwiller and other sites, and Gewürztraminers only from the Hahnenberg and Châtenois. As a rule, the firm's own grapes are not separately vinified and bottled. Jean Hauller and his son René allow their best-quality grapes to ferment very slowly in unheated pressing tanks. I always like drinking the Hauller Riesling and Sylvaner, especially the Réserve quality. A couple of exceptional wines come from about 4 acres of vineyard near the Saint-Sébastien chapel, which is harvested late almost every year, resulting in a potent Riesling and a usually broad, rich and mild Gewürztraminer. Both are sold as Cuvée Saint-Sébastien.

The 17-acre estate of Louis Siffert & Fils in Orschwiller is managed by Maurice Siffert. The Siffert family live near the church and also have tasting rooms there. The Gewürztraminer and the Pinot Noir are of good quality, but I was most impressed by the Riesling: agreeable and not too acid, with a pleasant fruitiness.

In 1966 the Huber and Bléger families founded one of the first French groupements viticoles under the name G.A.E.C. Saint-Fulrade. The jointly run estate totals about 25 acres, in Saint-Hippolyte. Specialities are Clevner (full, spicy, soft) and the Pinot Noir, traditional for Saint-Hippolyte (a soft, vinous rosé, quite broad in taste, very successful of its type).

Roughly 80%-90% of all Pinot Noir grapes produced by the village of Rodern are processed by the cooperative in Ribeauvillé. The grapes are heated slightly so as to give more colour to the wine. I thought this Pinot Noir rosé came nearer in taste and colour to an Alsace red. It had the aroma of the grape and a fair amount of flavour for its type.

Fernand Engel's cellars are along the busy route du vin. On a summer's day he sells 1,200-1,500 bottles of wine to passing travellers. His wines usually are satisfactory but not distinctive in quality. I thought the best was the Muscat Réserve: aromatic and with a distinctly dry taste. Fernand Engel plans to increase his 45 acres by a further 12 acres.

Louis Gassmann and his wife Marie-Thérèse (née Rolly) cultivate 37 acres in Rorschwihr (where they live), Bergheim and Rodern. The quality of their wines is generally excellent: the full-flavoured, light-pink Pinot Noir from Rodern; the Tokay; the ordinary Riesling; and the often fantastic 'Réserve', more powerful, richer, and more subtle. The Gewürztraminer is also very impressive, a powerful wine with spices and often a mild tone to the taste and a great purity.

Vineyard acreages
Dieffenthal: 96
Scherwiller: 556
Châtenois: 146
Albé: 35
Ohrschwiller: 272
Saint-Hippolyte: 546
Rodern: 282
Rorschwihr: 274

Below, left:
Marie-Thérèse and Louis Gassmann of the Rolly-Gassmann estate in Rorschwihr.

Below, right:
Queueing to visit Haut-Koeningsbourg.

The fête du vin nouveau in Saint-Hippolyte is usually held on the third Sunday in September.

Above the Scherwiller vineyards are the unique granite ruins of Ortenbourg castle.

At the foot of Haut-Koeningsbourg

Alsace

One of the most important tourist attractions in Alsace is the citadel of Haut-Koeningsbourg. This crowns a hill, 2,500-foot high, providing a view across a smiling landscape of vineyards and wine villages, and over the Rhine valley. After a history of devastation — including one onslaught by the Swedes back in 1633 — the town council of Sélestat donated the ruins to Kaiser Wilhelm II. Between 1901 and 1908 his architect built a new castle on the remains of the old — not an architectural beauty, but impressive. It is now a French national monument. At the foot of Haut-Koeningsbourg, between Dambach-la-Ville and Bergheim, there are some pretty wine villages.

Riesling, zoos and springs

The most northerly of these villages is Dieffenthal, where the grapes ripen rather earlier than elsewhere because of a warmer microclimate. There is a lot of Pinot Blanc here. Farther on is the large wine district of Scherwiller, where 90% of the vines are Rieslings, justifying the name of Rieslinger for the local wine fraternity founded in 1980. The wine route takes a right-angled turn through Scherwiller. It is well worth visiting the old centre, with its ancient houses and a little stream that here and there runs beneath the buildings. Châtenois, of Roman origin, has a main street so wide that it seems like a market square. Other features are a 12th century watchtower and mineral springs containing salt, iron and iodine that were exploited until 1904. The Hahneberg is a noted vineyard here. Nine miles west of Châtenois, deep in a mountain valley, is the little wine village of Albé, producing mainly fruit brandies. After Châtenois comes Kientzheim, with one animal park containing eagles, buzzards, vultures and falcons, and another accommodating hundreds of monkeys. Ohrswiller, with its baroque-fronted church, is the most southerly village of the Bas-Rhin *département*. Wine has been made here since the 8th century AD. The products of the local cooperative (140 members cultivating about 245 acres) are unfortunately only of simple quality.

Into the Haut-Rhin département

Haut-Rhin begins with Saint-Hippolyte. The actual village lies within a rectangle of 13th-century walls. It takes its name from the Roman martyr Hippolytus (d. 235), whose relics were brought here from Rome in the 8th century by an individual named Fulrade, said also to have introduced the Pinot Noir from Italy. The Rouge de Saint-Hippolyte was once quite famous. Neighbouring Rodern is also noted for its Pinot Noir; in this remote little hamlet there is even a Fête de Pinot Noir, celebrated in July. In Rorschwihr, a village with 270 inhabitants, the favourite wine is the Gewürztraminer; wine-growing here dates from at least before the year 742. The name of the village was originally Chrodoldesvillare and it boasts archaeological finds from the Bronze Age and the Roman period.

Marcel Deiss's modern, beautifully maintained and splendidly equipped cellars are just outside old Bergheim on the Ribeauvillé road. With his son Jean-Michel, he cultivates 32 acres, one-third planted with Gewürztraminer, one-third with Riesling, the remainder with other grapes. The Gewürztraminer from the Altenberg vineyard is excellent: the 1979 was selected as the best from Bergheim. The Riesling from the Altenberg (elegant, fresh, fruity) also usually has a lot of class. The Pinot Blanc is full-bodied.

Gewürztraminers were the best wines I tasted from Gustave Lorentz: the Cuvée Particulière and the Cuvée Réservée Altenberg. The former was a classic, broad type of Gewürztraminer. The Altenberg seemed to have more finesse, and a full, mouth-filling flavour and long aftertaste. In sunny years it has a distinctly mild flavour. The Riesling Altenberg was not on the same level, but not at all bad.

Gustave Lorentz set up his own wine firm in 1836 and it was not long before his nephew Jerôme followed suit. Gustave and Jerôme Lorentz are now under the same management. However, both firms have their own land: Gustave in the Altenberg, Jerôme in Kanzlerberg. I did not think the Kanzlerberg Riesling was outstanding, but the Gewürztraminer can be a very full, robust wine with subtleties of taste.

Vineyard acreages
Bergheim: 608

Below left:
Market in Bergheim with the early 14th-century Porte-Haute in the background. Frescoes from the same period have been found in some of the houses.

Below right:
Charles Lorentz, general manager and owner of the firms of Gustave Lorentz and Jerôme Lorentz, tastes the former's fine Gewürztraminer 1971. Most Bergheim wines can — and should — mature. Two years is considered the minimum. This is on account of Bergheim's heavy soil.

Bottom right:
Freshly picked grapes arriving at Marcel Deiss's estate. The cellars and tasting hall are on the outskirts of Bergheim towards Ribeauvillé. Marcel Deiss (wearing hat) is on the left.

Criminals, but not sorcerers, were once welcome in Bergheim. One of the three towers in the wall on the northern side of the village is the Tour des Sorciers — The Sorcerers' Tower. People suspected of carrying out occult practices were locked up and tortured there.

Bergheim

The hamlet of Perchaim, as it was then known, was fortified at the beginning of the 14th century and thereafter developed into the village now called Bergheim. Of these fortifications there remains the encircling wall on the north with its three towers, including the Porte-Haute that gives access to the village. Even older than these walls is the lime tree that stands just outside and apparently dates from the 13th century. Bergheim once enjoyed a remarkable privilege: anyone who had committed a murder, or who was unable to satisfy his creditors, could claim sanctuary within the walls and was then immune from prosecution. This privilege, which remained in force for about 100 years, was symbolized by a little statue near the Porte-Haute — a man presenting his backside in a gesture of defiance. A prudish mayor eventually removed this rude piece of sculpture.

Heavy soil with clay and limestone

Probably no Alsace village has seen so many different owners as Bergheim. It was once calculated that between AD 700 and the Revolution in 1789 the place had no fewer than 32 different landlords. Bergheim has largely managed to preserve its medieval character. It is a peaceful, small wine village with a number of fine old houses, a partly 14th-century sandstone church, and masses of summer flowers in gardens, on balconies and on windowsills. Many of its 1,700 inhabitants are involved in wine-growing. The soil on Bergheim's slopes is heavy and contains clay and limestone, ideal for the Gewürztraminer. The Riesling too produces good results, but Sylvaner is rare, except perhaps on lower-lying ground. The village's best-known vineyards are the Kanzlerberg and Altenberg.

Lorentz and Lorentz

There are about 15 wine producers in Bergheim, including a number of shippers. The Bordeaux firm of Eschenauer has a branch here, called Jules Muller. Regrettably, I found its wines disappointing, even those from the Domaine d'Engelgarten. I was more favourably impressed by two other firms, Gustave Lorentz (50 acres of its own and about 2 million bottles a year) and Jerôme Lorentz (25 acres and about 1 million bottles). Although the two concerns often operate separately and in different markets, with different wines, they have been amalgamated since 1975. Their director is Charles Lorentz Jnr. Not all the wines from Gustave and Jerôme Lorentz are equally appealing, but the Gewürztraminers, in particular from the top of the range, and also some of the Rieslings can be very good.

The careful way in which Bott Frères works was typified in 1978: the Muscat Ottonel did not put in an appearance, but the firm still managed to make a particularly fine Muscat with the pure scent of the grape and a soft, lively taste with just enough freshness. It was a Cuvée Exceptionnelle; Muscats with this title from other years also merit attention. Bott Frères uses no other brand names. The firm of Bott-Geyl in Beblenheim is managed by a brother of Pierre Bott.

Réserve Personnelle is the supreme quality at Bott Frères. The ripest grapes are selected, with the highest sugar content; and often only the first juice from the press is used. The Riesling of this quality is aromatic, elegant and usually has a certain softness alongside its fraîcheur. I thought the wine was of a higher quality than the Cuvée Exceptionnelle or the Réserve categories. The Réserve Pinot Noir is usually delightful, light-coloured, fresh yet soft.

Trimbach's Riesling Cuvée Frédéric Emile (named after the firm's founder) nearly always comes from its own land in the Osterberg vineyard. The wine will mature and generally ought not to be drunk before its third or fourth year. It is a Riesling with a distinct personality: aromatic, complete, with a long aftertaste. Not an easy wine but very captivating.

The Kirchberg, where Louis Sipp has 3 acres, has clay and limestone in its soil. You can taste the coolness of the latter in the Riesling from this vineyard. It can also have true finesse and some fruit in its discreet fragrance. I thought the 1978 was delicious but the 1971 and 1976 — both sunny years — disappointing. They seemed to lack breeding and so tasted rather flat. This Riesling Kirchberg is perhaps better from ordinarily good years than from exceptional ones.

Jean Sipp lives in the big old family house and works his own estate of 50 acres (40 acres in Ribeauvillé). Jean is a perfectionist. He had a soil analysis carried out to determine the optimum vine planting and fertilization. About 15 acres is planted with Riesling. Riesling from the Kirchberg gives the best result: mildly fresh, supple and sound with a slight terroir.

Clos du Schlossberg is a 2-acre vineyard owned by Jean Sipp. He grows mainly Riesling with some Gewürztraminer and Muscat. The three types are made into a wine that in a sunny year such as 1976 has a mild bouquet, a light golden-yellow colour and a powerful, quite rich, slightly spicy taste somewhere between a Tokay and a Gewürztraminer. Jean Sipp's Cuvée Particulière Gewürztraminer is a wine with balance and allure.

Ribeauvillé

Ribeauvillé was first mentioned — as Ratboldovilare, 'Ratbold's villa' — around the middle of the 8th century. After being the property successively of the Dukes of Alsace, the Counts of Eguisheim and the Archbishops of Basle, the village finally came into the possession of the Counts of Ribeaupierre, who did not live in Ribeauvillé itself but in castles set high on neighbouring hills. Their ruins still stand: Saint-Ulrich, the largest and most beautiful, Girsberg and Haut-Ribeaupierre. From 1715 onward, minstrels made their way every year to Ribeauvillé, playing before the counts and the public, and staying at the *Auberge du Soleil* — still intact, though no longer an inn. The Counts of Ribeaupierre disappeared with the French Revolution, but the minstrel tradition survived. On the first Sunday of September, Ribeauvillé celebrates its Pfifferdaj or Fête des Ménétriers. Street musicians, singers and storytellers gather in the village and on the following Monday, when the rest of Alsace is at work, Ribeauvillé enjoys an official holiday.

Prosperous citizens

Ribeauvillé, with its 4,700 inhabitants, is well worth visiting. The centre, roughly rectangular in shape, nestles in a valley. There are many beautiful houses, especially in picturesque streets like the long Grand-Rue and Rue de la Fraternité. The style and size of these buildings indicate that the citizens of Ribeauvillé were once very prosperous. Parts of the 13th-century walls, as well as the great Tour des Bouchers of the same period, have been preserved. Many of the vineyards rise above the rooftops. The three most noted names are Geisberg, Kirchberg and Zahnacker, producing wine drunk by Louis XIV. The soil around Ribeauvillé is quite varied so that all the superior grape varieties can be grown. The Riesling, however, does best of all, and very good results are obtained with the Gewürztraminer.

The wine firms

Although the Steiner textile factory is established within the boundaries, along with printers who specialize in bank cheques and securities, the Carola mineral waters concern, and a model farm with 200 cows, the economic scene is still largely dominated by wine. In terms of vineyard area Ribeauvillé comes seventh in the Haut-Rhin *département* and in addition it has a number of shippers: Bott Frères, Robert Faller & Fils, Metz Frères, Louis Sipp and F. E. Trimbach. These firms buy grapes, and sometimes wine, from Ribeauvillé growers and also from villages far away. In addition, Ribeauvillé has its own wine cooperative, the oldest enterprise of its kind in France. Founded in 1895, it has kept going even in difficult times.

Zahn's field

Ribeauvillé has some 80 wine growers, 30 of them members of the cooperative; another 50 or so members come from surrounding villages. The cooperative processes 80% to 90% of all the Pinot Noir grapes from Rodern, a commune noted for this variety (see page 102). The cooperative members work a total of more than 400 acres. In 1950 things were going so badly that the enterprise was threatened with liquidation; but Emile Traber, who was appointed to wind up the business, instead restored it to prosperity. The cooperative is nowadays well equipped and produces some very decent wines. Examples I have tasted include the afore-mentioned Pinot Noir, a Riesling, a Tokay d'Alsace and a Gewürztraminer. The great speciality, however, is Clos du Zahnacker. The grapes for this — Riesling, Gewürztraminer and Tokay — come from 3 acres of land on which the monks planted vines in the 9th century. This little vineyard takes its name from one Martin Zahn: a document of 1419 mentions 'Martin Zans Acker' (Martin Zahn's field).

Jean-Baptiste Faller is the owner and manager of the small firm of Robert Faller & Fils, which has 25 acres in Ribeauvillé, sufficient for half its wine production. The speciality is the Riesling-Geisberg: Faller has 3 acres of the Geisberg. This vineyard often gives a rather aromatic wine that matures well. In 1980, the 1973 was very pleasant and well-defined — still perfectly fresh. The 1978 tasted sour and rather thin, the 1977, from a more moderate year, quite rightly attracted attention by its taste; the 1979 was elegant and firm.

The François Kientzler & Fils estate is one of the better ones in Ribeauvillé and district. Manager André Kientzler runs the 25 acres of vineyard, 3 of them in the Geisberg. The Riesling from here usually has a lot of flavour, a good dose of fruit and a pleasing freshness. Other recommended wines from Kientzler are the gracious, refreshing Muscat-Kirchberg and the simple but exceedingly pleasant Chasselas from approx. 1½ acres of the Osterberg. Kientzler is situated on the Bergheim side of Ribeauvillé.

The 3-acre Clos du Zahnacker is planted with Riesling, Gewürztraminer and Tokay. The three varieties are vinified together and produce 15,000–20,000 bottles a year. The Zahnacker has heavy soil and the wine must therefore mature for some years before it can be drunk: five years is not unusual. Initially the wine has a fair amount of acid, certain subtleties and an elusive personality. It is exclusive to Ribeauvillé's cooperative. Martin Zahn is a subsidiary brand.

In addition to a remarkably good Pinot Blanc and Muscats and Tokays of great class, I also tasted the Gewürztraminer Cuvée des Seigneurs de Ribeaupierre at Trimbach. It is not one of those broadly sultry and luxurious wines, even from sunny years. It usually has fruit and subtleties of taste, and a certain freshness. Wine from a good year will easily mature for 10 years or more. The firm produces it only from its own land in Ribeauvillé's Trottacker vineyard.

Vineyard acreage
Ribeauvillé: 638

Opposite page:
Ribeauvillé's Place du Bouc at dusk. The castle of Saint-Ulrich is in the background.

Below:
The imposing residence of grower Jean Sipp. The cellars are below the house.

Bottom:
The brothers Bernard (left) and Hubert Heydt-Trimbach from the firm of Trimbach. The vintage is in full swing.

Ribeauvillé celebrates the Fête du Kugelhopf in June and holds its wine fair in July. Ribeauvillé was formerly the wine capital of the Alsace. Now it is Colmar.

The Kirchberg is a famous vineyard in Ribeauvillé. There is another with the same name in Barr.

Heydt is another Trimbach brand name, mainly for sales to private individuals.

When I visited Bott Frères there were four generations under one roof: Paul Bott, his son Pierre, his son Laurent and Laurent's little son. The Bott family has been producing wine since 1835. See also page 112.

The Auberge du Zahnacker restaurant has been owned by the local cooperative since 1966.

Another way of spelling Pfifferdaj, the minstrels' day, is Pfiffertag. There is a statue of a minstrel in Ribeauvillé park.

Quality from Trimbach

Towards Bergheim, at the foot of Ribeauvillé's Osterberg, are the buildings of my favourite Alsace shipper, F. E. Trimbach. This is a very quality-conscious family business run by the Heydt-Trimbach brothers, Bernard, supervising vinification, and Hubert, who handles sales. Although the firm has stainless-steel fermentation tanks, all the better wines go into oak casks for one to two months. Then, after bottling, the wines are usually given at least six months' rest; in relation to turnover, Trimbach has one of the biggest stocks of bottles in the whole of Alsace. The firm itself owns 27 acres of land, half in Ribeauvillé, the rest in Hunawihr and Bergheim. In my opinion, Trimbach excels in the more potent kinds of wine, such as Gewürztraminer, Tokay and Muscat, particularly in the Réserve and Réserve Personnelle qualities. However, alongside these the house produces some magnificent Rieslings, such as the Cuvée Frédéric Emile and the Clos Saint Hune (see page 106). I also have pleasant recollections of the Pinot Blanc.

Louis Sipp

Another well-known firm from Ribeauvillé is Louis Sipp. This house, energetically run by Pierre Sipp and his wife Simone, has 74 acres of land in Ribeauvillé and the immediate surroundings. Riesling and Gewürztraminer account for more than half the vines (30% and 25% respectively). Only the grapes from the Kirchberg, where Louis Sipp owns 3 acres, are vinified separately. The rest are mixed with grapes bought from about 100 mainly small growers. In the large cellars of Louis Sipp are many wooden casks which are still in use. Wines from this house can be said to be no more than adequate; I have discovered no especially good qualities or striking personalities in the range offered. The best wine tends to be the Riesling Kirchberg (although not all years), and the Gewürztraminer can sometimes be termed successful.

Bott Frères: an elegant style

A third shipper of importance is Bott Frères, owning 30 acres of vineyard, mainly in Ribeauvillé itself, with some in Hunawihr and Beblenheim. Grapes from these sites are vinified separately, but the resulting wines are later blended with others. Where Trimbach sells about 800,000 bottles a year, and Louis Sipp a million, the figure for Bott Frères varies around 300,000 bottles. This firm principally uses wooden vats for vinification and storage, some of them dating from 1890. Pierre Bott, the director, told me that he regarded Riesling as the speciality of the house. This confirms my impression that Bott Frères makes rather elegant wines, quite different in style, for instance, from those of Trimbach. Apart from good Riesling, I have drunk an excellent Muscat, a not very substantial but pleasant Tokay, and a very good Pinot Noir. The best qualities are sold as Cuvée Exceptionnelle and Réserve Personelle.

. Vineyard acreage
Hunawihr: 554

OWNED BY
TRIMBACH

The fountain where in the 7th
century St Huna is said to have
washed the clothing of the sick
still exists. Once, after a poor
harvest, the water from this
fountain is supposed to have
turned into wine.

The village of Hunawihr was
first recorded by name in 1114.
Its attractive hôtel de ville dates
from 1517.

Below:
The famous fortified church of
Hunawihr, partly surrounded by
vines. Since 1929 the building
has been classed as a historic
monument.

I sorted through a range of
wines from various years on the
counter in the reception hall of
the Hunawihr cooperative. The
Sylvaner was very pleasant of
its sort and fairly broad in
flavour. The Rieslings tasted
soft and fresh without being of
impressive depth or refinement.
The Gewürztraminers tasted
good, but, like the other wines,
they seemed to lack substance.
The Pinot Noir was acceptable
in all respects and had a fairly
strong colour.

The brothers Louis and André
Mittnacht married two sisters
from another Mittnacht family,
also from Hunawihr, and started
up a vineyard in 1963. This
comprises 25 acres (16½ in
Hunawihr itself). I tasted a good
Riesling with little acid but still
adequately fresh, supple, fleshy,
fruity and with sufficient
terroir. I found the Tokay
d'Alsace Réserve Particulière
excellent, and the mildly spicy
Klevner also appealed to me.

Hunawihr's 3-acre Clos Sainte
Hune is owned by the firm of
Trimbach. Production averages
only 7,000 bottles annually,
excluding Riesling. The wine is
very special: fresh, elegant, with
nuances of flavour and a long
aftertaste. It has a gracious and
memorable personality, but it is
much less aromatic than
Rieslings from neighbouring
Ribeauvillé. Riesling Clos Saint
Hune has been served regularly
at the Elysée. It matures
perfectly.

Hunawihr

Alsace

Hunawihr, with 520 inhabitants, lies just
south of Ribeauvillé and about half a mile off
the wine route. Hidden among the trees
beside the road to the village is a park, where
since 1976 naturalists have been engaged in
reintroducing storks to Alsace. Hunawihr
takes its name from Huna, wife of Hunon.
She lived in the 7th century and performed
many acts of charity. According to tradition,
she washed the clothes of the sick in a
fountain. This legendary wash-place is still
there, and is decorated with flowers in spring
and summer. Hunon and Huna also built the
first local church. The foundations may have
served for Hunawihr's present church, one of
the most remarkable sights in Alsace.

Fortified church

Hunawihr's church dates largely from the
14th and 15th centuries, although some
parts, such as the Gothic door, are 16th-
century. The church is surrounded by a
thick, hexagonal wall with semi-circular
towers. It stands like a small fortress on a
vine-clad hill above the little village. The
villagers used to shelter here in times of war
or disaster. The building was, and still is,
used for worship both by Catholics and
Protestants. There are some fine wall
paintings inside. The hands on the church
clock are ornamented with bunches of grapes
— which shows that Hunawihr has long been
a wine village.

The Hunawihr cooperative

The vine-growing soil of Hunawihr is rather
heavy, with clay and limestone in which not
only the Riesling and Gewürztraminer, but
also the Sylvaner, Pinot Blanc and Pinot
Noir grow very well. The best-known
vineyard is Rosacker, increasingly used by
the local cooperative. This collective
enterprise, with 120 members, mostly from
Hunawihr itself, and formed in 1955,
processes grapes from about 445 acres. The
director, Jacques Ruhlmann and his team,
produce the full range of Alsace table wines
— of decent and sometimes good quality.
Depending on the vintage year, the
Sylvaner, Riesling, Gewürztraminer and
Pinot tend to be among the better kinds.

Zellenberg

Alsace

Most Alsace wine villages lie in a valley, some half-way up a slope. Zellenberg, however, is built on a hilltop and looks down from 400 feet in one direction on the Rhine valley and, in the other, on its own vineyards and those of Riquewihr. For centuries the little place (300 inhabitants) had its own castle, but all that remains are two towers. The rest was sold stone by stone by the heirs of Christian Bott, *bourgeois* of Ribeauvillé, who bought the decayed citadel in 1782; by about 1820 the building had almost completely disappeared. Only these two towers and the vineyard of Schlossberg perpetuate the memory of the castle. The Zellenbergers were once nicknamed donkeys — for reasons I have been unable to discover. Maybe Zellenberg once provided cheap labour — you paid less for a donkey than for a horse. Alternatively, it may have had something to do with Zellenberg's steep slopes: perhaps folk thought you must be an ass to start a vineyard there. Or it may just have been the fact that rain washed soil down the slopes, which the growers then had to haul back up. Judging by the special sled-like trays I saw at the local wine firm of Becker, this still happens.

Varied soil

Zellenberg has both heavy clay soil, for the Gewürztraminer, and the somewhat lighter, calciferous type, for the Riesling. The commune has about 20 growers, most of them associated with a cooperative (those of Beblenheim, Bennwihr or Hunawihr). There is also a shipper in the village, namely J. Becker. The Becker family is one of the oldest here. With the Rentz, Roeckel and Stinnes families, it has been traced back to the beginning of the 17th century. This medium-sized firm (0.8 to 1 million bottles annually) is run by Jean-Jacques Becker, his son Jean-Philippe (vinification) and his daughter Martine (sales). The firm's own estate covers 25 acres, in the vineyards of Hagenschlauf, Riemelsberg and other sites. The intention is that estate wines from these vineyards should be separately vinified and bottled under Jean-Philippe's supervision, and to some extent this is already happening. I have frequently detected a slightly bitter element in the taste of Rieslings from Becker, and in some of the other wines. For that reason they do not greatly appeal to me. I was most impressed by the Gewürztraminer (various vintages) and a Muscat 1973, seven years old at the time. Perhaps in the future the increasing number of estate-bottled wines will raise the general level of quality.

Riquewihr

There is an apt old saying: 'Anyone who has not seen Riquewihr has not seen Alsace.' No other village in the region draws so many visitors. On summer weekends the parking places along the length of the outer wall are filled with cars, and coach after coach unloads its passengers next to the entrance gate under the *hôtel de ville*. At such times Riquewihr has an influx of up to 20,000 people, more than a dozen times its own population. The reason for the village's appeal is obvious. From the viewpoint of architecture, character and atmosphere, Riquewihr represents Alsace at its most beautiful. It is one big museum, a medieval fairy-tale spot that has preserved its charm for hundreds of years. There are innumerable things to see: half-timbered houses, Renaissance buildings, fountains and wells, courtyards, cellars, defensive walls, gateways, dungeons and towers, signboards, wood carvings, pictures and decorated motifs — all taking the visitor back in time to the 16th and 17th centuries.

A rich community

Although burials from the Merovingian period (5th-8th centuries) have been found near Riquewihr, little is known of its origin. It probably derives its name from a Frankish lord called Richo: it is recorded as Richovilare in a document of 1094. In 1291, Riquewihr was given permission to build fortifications. The earliest monuments, the north wall and the Dolder, a high tower on the west side of the village, date from that year. This was later strengthened, in the 15th and 16th centuries, and during the latter period Riquewihr built a second wall outside the first. By the 14th century the place was known as Reichenweier, 'rich village' — a clear reference to the prosperity of the inhabitants, who profited from their wine. For 472 years, from 1324 until the French Revolution, the village belonged to the Dukes of Württemberg. In those early times it was besieged by the Archbishop of Strasbourg; after it surrendered in 1333, the prelate ordered all the vats of local wine (which was already famed) to be taken to Strasbourg. Three centuries later the village went through difficult times during the Thirty Years' War.

Early wine laws

Riquewihr is surrounded on all sides by vineyards, most of which extend over gently rising hills, only the Schoenenberg vineyard lying on a rather steep slope. Because of these gradual slopes, the vineyards enjoy maximum exposure to the sun, from early morning to late afternoon. The subsoil is very varied so that most types of grapes grow extremely well. There is little sandy soil, which no one regrets. According to a local saying: 'Three sandy plots and three girls can ruin the best wine grower.' The pursuit of quality was evident from the start. In 1575 a decree was issued that distinguished between superior ('noble') and other grapes. Fines were imposed on unauthorized vines. In 1589, for example, a grower had to uproot his Elbling vines.

Decrees in 1644 and 1674 further strengthened local wine legislation. The influence of the wine growers' own association should not be underestimated. Founded in 1520, it was responsible for correct planting and every year it decided exactly when the harvest should begin — preferably quite late, in order to have the ripest possible grapes.

Noted vineyards

The best-known Riquewihr vineyard is the steep Schoenenberg (also called the Schoenenburg or Schoenenbourg), on the north side of the village. It stretches over some 50 acres and receives so much sun that formerly it was also called the Sonnenberg. The soil is rich, with clay and limestone and random patches of gypsum. It is almost exclusively planted with Riesling. Another famous vineyard is the Sporen, on the southeast of the village. Of its 25 acres, 16 belong to the firm of Hugel. On this high-quality soil, Hugel grows 50% Tokay, 25% Riesling, 20% Gewürztraminer and 5% Muscat. These grapes are picked and fermented together to produce a very delicious wine.

The Dopff & Irion giant

The Riquewihr district not only accommodates many growers but also a number of important wine houses, such as Dopff & Irion, Dopff au Moulin, and Hugel et Fils; and here too the smaller firm of Jean Preiss-Zimmer has its headquarters. Unseen by the tourist, there is a sea of wine under the streets and behind the walls of Riquewihr, in tanks, barrels, casks and bottles. By far the biggest quantity is to be found in the establishments of Dopff & Irion, that with more than 4 million bottles a year leaves all other Alsace shippers far behind. It is a firm with modern equipment; half its vast storage capacity, for example, consists of stainless-steel tanks. Yet in spite of its size, Dopff & Irion has remained a family concern. It is run most efficiently by Guy

The 7-acre Amandiers vineyard is near the Schoenenberg and has gypsum in places, and almond trees that give it its name. It is owned by Dopff & Irion. This firm produces a soft Muscat here that is usually able to mature for up to five years. The fragrance of the grapes, which is typical of a Muscat, is not overpoweringly strong but is present. Dopff & Irion's largest export markets are Germany, America, Belgium, Canada and the Netherlands.

Les Murailles is a 25-acre vineyard near the Schoenenberg. The land belongs to Dopff & Irion, which has planted Riesling. The Riesling Les Murailles has not much depth of perfume and taste. However, the taste is fresh without being too acid, adequately full and reliable. Its freshness remains for a long time. Dopff & Irion's other, better Riesling is the velvety, but definitely not sweet, vendange tardive quality, rounded yet discreet.

The site where witches used to be burned is called Les Sorcières. It is now a 27-acre vineyard owned by Dopff & Irion. The heavy soil lends itself to growing the Gewürztraminer. However, I find the Gewürztraminer Les Sorcières just a little too modest in bouquet and taste. I prefer the more pronounced, mildly fresh vendange tardive, a wine also from the firm's own land (Domaines du Château de Riquewihr, named after the Dopff & Irion building).

Riquewihr

Dopff, and the equally capable Jean-Louis Irion supervises production.

Dry, agreeable wines

The firm itself cultivates 310 acres, including the 210 acres of the Domaine Charles Jux (which it took over) near Colmar. Charles Jux is now one of Dopff & Irion's subsidiary brands, along with Ernest Preiss and Kugler. In addition, about 600 growers are contracted to sell Dopff & Irion their grapes. Guy Dopff described the style of his firm as 'vins secs, agréables à boire'. A fairly dry, not too fruity, type of wine is produced, and is widely popular. Dopff & Irion's concern to make a range of dry wines is obvious from the qualities of its late-picked grapes (vendange tardive), which do not taste really sweet, unlike those of other producers. The massive scale on which this firm works precludes its wines showing great refinement or strong personality. However, they taste pure and are made with craftsmanlike skill. The best qualities are to be found among the Dopff & Irion estate wines, labelled as Domaines du Château de Riquewihr. I recommend the vendange tardive Riesling and Gewürztraminer, the Muscat Les Amandiers, the Riesling Les Murailles and the Gewürztraminer Les Sorcières. My impression from various tastings is that the average quality of the subsidiary brands is slightly inferior to that of the main Dopff & Irion lines.

Dopff au Moulin

The premises of this firm lie on either side of the road just before you reach the centre of Riquewihr from the direction of Zellenberg. The 'au Moulin' was added to the firm's name and appears on all its labels and brochures in order to avoid confusion with Dopff & Irion. The concern is directed by Pierre Etienne Dopff, whose father, Julien Pierre, is still active in the business. The Dopff families in the two firms are related to each other (the first Dopff settled in Riquewihr in 1574), but have no business connections. Dopff au Moulin has 185 acres of vineyard and sells well over 2 million bottles annually, including a good quantity of sparkling wine (see page 90). The style of working — and of wine — is very different from Dopff & Irion. At Dopff au Moulin, for example, efforts are made to avoid malolactic fermentation, whereas the other firm seeks to achieve it — especially with Riesling and Sylvaner — except in very sunny years. The Dopff au Moulin range has many more undated 'standard' wines. In general I am not too fond of this company's wines — they are not always equally sound and often lack character. However, I must except a number of its estate wines, including the Muscat, Riesling Schoenenburg, Gewürztraminer Eichberg (see Turckheim, page 126), the rare Gewürztraminer Cuvée Exceptionnelle and the sparkling Crémant d'Alsace. Among the firm's subsidiary brands are P. E. Dopff & Fils, Mergy and Caves Dolder.

Hugel: three centuries of wine

In terms of reputation rather than scale, pride of place in Riquewihr indisputably

Dopff au Moulin — where the son is always given his father's second name as a first name — makes a pleasant Muscat from its own land, exclusively from the Muscat Ottonel grape. At its best the wine has a sound, soft bouquet with hints of spices and ripe fruit. The taste is also soft, perhaps a little flat but still a great pleasure to drink on a summer day. Dopff au Moulin prints its own labels.

Dopff au Moulin owns 10 acres of the Schoenenberg vineyard (called Schoenenburg by this firm), distributed over various plots. Initially the Riesling has a fair amount of acidity in the taste, while the bouquet is still undeveloped. Often the wine only begins to reveal its charms and class after four to five years. It is usually rather broad and substantial in the mouth. Dopff au Moulin generally harvests the Schoenenberg grapes late; récolte tardive frequently appears on the label.

Dopff au Moulin produces a small quantity of Gewürztraminer Cuvée Exceptionnelle, only in good years and from its own vineyards in Riquewihr. This late-picked 1973 had the same pourriture noble scent as, for example, Sauternes, a full, fairly sweet and at the same time refreshing taste and a suggestion of toast in the long aftertaste. I thought it was a splendid wine, full of style and fortunately not too sweet or too heavy.

The quality of a firm is not proved solely by a few great wines but also — and perhaps mainly — by a bigger range of small wines of a good, or very good, level. Thus Hugel's Edelzwicker is, of its type, a very successful wine (brands include the Couronne d'Or, Fleur d'Alsace and Flambeau d'Alsace), as is the Pinot Blanc. This is a more rounded wine, an agreeable thirst-quencher. Hugel exports 80% of its wines, Britain being the largest market.

Hugel's 16 acres in the Sporen vineyard are planted with 50% Tokay, 25% Riesling, 20% Gewürztraminer, and 5% Muscat. The grapes are fermented together and give a good, rather firm wine without many acids. I enjoyed it once with asparagus. According to the letter of the law, the Sporen is an Edelzwicker. Jean Hugel refuses to put this on the label, although he is prepared to use the old term 'Gentil'. This used to indicate blended wine from superior grape varieties. However, this is no longer allowed.

Hugel's ordinary Riesling is too flat for me, although it is generally pure and elegant. The level distinctly rises with the Cuvée Tradition which has more to offer by way of bouquet and taste. Even in the moderate year of 1977 Hugel made this a very acceptable wine. The Réserve Personnelle is still better, mouth-filling and distinguished. The vendange tardive category usually has too much alcohol and is too sweet in my opinion: the true Riesling character seems to have been lost.

Riquewihr

VIN D'ALSACE
APPELLATION ALSACE CONTROLÉE

belongs to Hugel et Fils. For quality, this is one of the leading houses in the whole of Alsace. It is run by Jean Hugel, whose family has been active in the wine industry here since 1639. Jean once remarked: 'Our firm is now about 300 years old. That shows three things. Firstly, that wine is less unhealthy than is often alleged. Secondly, that this wine business is not very profitable, for after three centuries we are still the owners. Thirdly, that a wine firm like ours has a considerable future, otherwise we would have gone out of business long ago.' Hugel obtains its grapes from 51 acres in Riquewihr and from about 300 growers with whom long-term contracts have been signed. Quality control of the grapes is always strict, 'because the wine is never better than its grapes'. The firm maintains the principle that it is much better to treat grapes than wine. Therefore the must is clarified (after centrifuging) rather than the wine. It is characteristic of Hugel that the whole wine-making process is supervised by one man, with nature allowed to take its course. As lactic acid bacteria are present in the cellar, the *fermentation malolactique* takes place automatically, especially in the Riesling and Sylvaner.

During a simple lunch at the home of Jean and Simone Hugel, it was demonstrated yet again that Hugel's Tokay has great class. A Tokay Réserve Personnelle 1976, very distinctive in taste, agreeable and full of style, was served with the hors d'oeuvre — stuffed eggs and radishes from their own garden. A 1976 Tokay of vendange tardive followed with the chicken and salad. This had a sweeter taste and was also of a very high standard.

Hugel's own vineyards — all in Riquewihr — are planted with 47% Riesling, 46% Gewürztraminer, the remaining 7% with Tokay and Muscat. The best Gewürztraminer (Réserve Personnelle quality) often comes exclusively from the Hugel estate. It is a rather robust wine, rich, sometimes slightly sweet. There is still sweetness in the vendange tardive, a truly great wine that can only be made in one year out of five. Hugel uses no other names for any of its wines.

Preiss-Zimmer sells three qualities of wine: non-vintage, Réserve and Réserve Particulière. For the Gewürztraminer only there is the further quality Réserve Comte Jean de Beaumont. The two top categories of Gewürztraminer are the best wines from Preiss-Zimmer. They are rich and soft, but have the marked freshness in their taste so typical of this firm. Do not expect any heavy, sultry spiciness. The Riesling Cuvée Particulière also has plenty of fraîcheur. The Sylvaner is pleasant.

Robert Schmidt is the third generation of owners of the René Schmidt estate (immediately on the right as you enter the centre of Riquewihr). He works 22 acres of vineyard, 5 in the Schoenenberg. The top wine from the Schoenenberg range, the Cuvée Exceptionnelle, usually lacks depth but there is compensation in a pleasing amount of fruit in the bouquet and taste. This wine is best not drunk until two or three years after vintage because of its acidity.

Vineyard acreage
Riquewihr: 679

Opposite page, centre:
The Preiss-Zimmer coat-of-arms, as on the labels. It hangs as a signboard on the front of the premises. Preiss-Zimmer sells about 10% of its wines locally to tourists through a shop, a caveau and a winstub, Le Tire Bouchon.

Opposite page, below:
Riquewihr by night, seen from the Schoenenberg.

Below:
Grape harvest in Riquewihr. In the background you can just see the roofs of some of Dopff au Moulin's buildings.

Jean-Frédéric Hugel, (known by many in England as Johnny), is manager of the firm of Hugel and was born in 1924. He is one of the great characters and promoters of Alsace, like his late father Jean.

Dopff & Irion is the biggest wine firm in Alsace and the largest producer of Pinot Noir. Guy Dopff thinks this wine is 'one of the most original, agreeable rosés in France'. The firm has planted a lot of Pinot Noir (including in the Domaine Jux, which it has taken over) and buys black grapes in Ottrott and Rodern.

Double stock of bottles

Another feature of the Hugel method is that the majority of the wines are encouraged to mature. The stock of bottles represents about twice the annual production (between 1 and 1.4 million bottles). Each bottle is held up to the light and checked, because, according to Jean Hugel, 'we would rather lose a bottle than a customer'. Almost everywhere else the wine is filtered twice, but at Hugel only once, just before bottling. The so-called cold treatment is taboo here because, according to Hugel, it kills the wine. In short, this house aims at the highest possible quality consistent with a considerable volume of production; and it often attains its target. The simple wines — Edelzwicker, Pinot Blanc — are of exceptional merit in their category. The Cuvée Tradition and Réserve Personnelle qualities of the Riesling, Tokay and Gewürztraminer are quite simply excellent, as are the wines designated *vendange tardive*. The afore-mentioned Sporen wine is also particularly agreeable.

Jean Preiss-Zimmer

The best-known, and undoubtedly most photographed, sign in Riquewihr shows a smiling man with glass and bottle in hand and the words 'Jan Preiss, Sccr. J.J. Zimmer, gourmet-viticulteur'. It adorns the front of the handsome premises of Jean Preiss-Zimmer in the main street. This fairly small concern, owned and run by Jean-Jacques Zimmer, produces about 300,000 bottles a year, and has 30 acres of vineyard, all in Riquewihr, including some in the Schoenenberg. Zimmer says that his firm aims at 'dry, dry wines, with a minimum of sugar, but not acid; light, agreeable and as natural as possible'. My own tastings suggest that Zimmer succeeds best in this with the Gewürztraminers, and I have also relished the clear-tasting Riesling Réserve Particulière. Subsidiary brands include Clos du Vigneron.

Although the walls in the tasting room at Beblenheim's cooperative are covered in all kinds of certificates, even the top wines of the range offer very little in the way of depth, class or character. Nevertheless, the cooperative's wines are nice to drink and usually correctly made; just good thirst-quenchers and reasonable in price. I have a slight preference for the simpler types such as the Sylvaner and Pinot Blanc, although the Riesling and Tokay are not bad.

After a good Riesling Réserve and a fresh and fruity Muscat, Edouard Bott from the firm Bott-Geyl let me taste his Tokay. He remarked: 'Tokay turns out well here in Beblenheim'. It was indeed a very successful wine, mildly broad, and with the almost smoky bouquet that you sometimes get in a really good Tokay.

Bott-Geyl owns about 5 acres in the Sonnenglanz vineyard, producing a Gewürztraminer with a broad, rather powerful but not sultry taste. I have discovered more finesse, freshness and subtleties in different years of this Gewürztraminer than in the ordinary Beblenheim Gewürztraminer, including that from Bott-Geyl. Eaux de vie that you distil yourself are one of the by-products of this firm.

Vineyard acreages
Beblenheim: 493
Ostheim: 63

Below:
The village street in Beblenheim. The name of the village was first mentioned in 1249.

Beblenheim has not had a wine festival for over 10 years because on one occasion people were injured during the festivities.

In 1898 the village had 260 acres of vineyard, compared with the present 493.

The Beblenheim cooperative also uses the brand name Caves de Hoen.

In 1944 Beblenheim escaped the fate of nearby Mittelwihr, which was completely destroyed. Ostheim, a neighbouring village, was also flattened. After the winter of 1944-5 only a church wall was still standing.

Until 1947 Bott-Geyl was called Edouard et Jules Geyl after the two brothers who founded it around 1910. Jules remained a bachelor; Edouard married and had two daughters, one of whom married Paul Bott from Ribeauvillé (of the Bott Frères firm). Eduard Bott — the present owner/manager of Bott-Geyl — is the son of that marriage. He has worked here since 1954.

Beblenheim

Alsace

Fewer tourists come to Beblenheim than to other wine villages, because it lies a little off the wine route, at the foot of its Sonnenglanz vineyard. The village street winds downhill beside 16th- and 17th-century half-timbered houses and past Beblenheim's only notable feature, the rather dilapidated 15th-century Bawla fountain. Some famous men were born in Beblenheim. Christian Oberlin was one of the pioneers of Alsace viticulture. At the end of the 19th century he made systematic studies of many grape varieties and founded the oenological institute at Colmar. Another local personality was Christian Pfister, a talented historian who published many works on Alsace. Beblenheim also has reminders of Jean Macé who established the first French village library here.

The Sonnenglanz

Beblenheim is a genuine wine village. Out of a population of 920, there are about 250 wine growers, most of whom take their grapes to a cooperative, usually the one at Beblenheim itself. Only 12 growers make, bottle and sell their own wine. The villagers boast that their Sonnenglanz, together with the Kaefferkopf at Ammerschwihr, was the first individual Alsace vineyard to be recognized, on 24 February 1932, by the tribunal at Colmar. Strangely, they have hardly made full use of the Sonnenglanz *appellation*. Whereas the Kaefferkopf enjoys a solid reputation, Sonnenglanz is virtually ignored, as is illustrated by the fact that the Beblenheim cooperative normally sells only one wine with the Sonnenglanz name. That wine is the Edelzwicker — whereas this 86-acre vineyard, largely on limestone, is eminently suited to growing Gewürztraminer and Tokay d'Alsace.

One cooperative and one shipper

I have found that the fairly cheap wines from the Beblenheim cooperative are of adequate quality but no more. Even the top wines seem to lack depth and character. The cooperative — 220 members who work about 545 acres — supplies ordinary, pleasant thirst-quenchers at reasonable prices. It is possible, however, that the standard of quality will improve, because a new and expert manager, Pierre Wagner, arrived there in 1980 from the Pfaffenheim cooperative.

The only local shipper is Bott-Geyl, run by Beblenheim's mayor, Edouard Bott. The firm produces only about 65,000 bottles a year. About 95% of the grapes come from its own 20 acres of vineyard in Beblenheim, Zellenberg, Mittelwihr, Riquewihr and Ribeauvillé. In this shipper's colourful reception cellar, between an old winepress and big wooden casks, I have tasted excellent wines, among them a Riesling Réserve, a Muscat, a Tokay and a Gewürztraminer Sonnenglanz.

Right: Flowers and a large wine bottle mark the northern entrance to the village.

Below left: Hubert Preiss in his working clothes during the vinification period. He has headed Preiss-Henny since 1978.

Below right: A photo of pre-war Mittelwihr in the office of grower Edgar Schaller.

I held a great many comparative tastings, including Alsace wines, for the purposes of this book. Preiss-Henny's always ended up among the best — the non-vintage, light, pure Sylvaner as well as the Muscat. The latter had a wonderful fragrance and a delicious, elegant, extraordinarily clean taste with the very slightest sparkle of carbon dioxide. The wine retains its freshness for up to five years. About 5% of the Preiss-Henny land is planted with Muscat.

For economic reasons, the firm of Preiss-Henny has since 1981 practically closed down its offices in Mittelwihr, and has moved in with Léon Beyer of Eguisheim. The Preiss and Beyer families are related to each other since Hubert Preiss married a Beyer girl. Hubert told me that cooperation with Léon Beyer is purely a matter of viticulture and administration: Hubert still handles the making of the wine. Unfortunately, Preiss-Henny sold off its small holding — about 10 acres — of

the Mandelberg, from which a delicious Gewürztraminer and Riesling were made, among the very best in the whole of Alsace. To find these wines, one would probably have to visit one of the region's better restaurants, which might still feature some rare bottles on its lists. The Gewürztraminer Mandelberg from Preiss-Henny had particularly good keeping qualities. The Riesling Mandelberg was brought out under the 'Réserve Hennij' label.

Mittelwihr

The distance from Beblenheim to Mittelheim is short, but the difference between the two villages is vast. Beblenheim was largely spared during World War II, but Mittelwihr was completely devastated. Fighting between the Germans and the Allies in the 'Colmar pocket' began on 5 December 1944 and continued with incredible violence until February 1945. All the villages in the combat zone — including Mittelwihr, Bennwihr, Sigolsheim and Ammerschwihr — were flattened. In Mittelwihr only parts of the church were left standing along with the 'wall of the martyrs' flowers', which runs along the village street and belongs to the firm of Preiss-Henny. It received its name because during the war it was three times planted with red geraniums, white petunias and blue convolvulus (the French colours); and three times the Gestapo cut down the offending flowers.

The demolished castle

Mittelwihr's origins have been traced back to Roman times. When the old village church was demolished in 1867, the remains of a Roman aqueduct were found with an inscription from AD 254, now in the Unterlinden Museum in Colmar. Under the Romans the place was called Flaviacum; the name Mittenwihre first occurs in 974. For centuries the village had a large castle, of which Preiss-Henny was the last owner. This too was destroyed in 1944 and survives only in old engravings and in Château de Mittelwihr, one of Preiss-Henny's brands.

Separate identities

Mittelwihr consists of little more than a long main street with a few side turnings. Its houses virtually adjoin those of Bennwihr (see page 115) and the two communities share the same post office. They do, however, have separate administrations. There is also a religious difference: Mittelwihr is mainly Protestant, Bennwihr

Catholic. Nor do the two villages mirror each other in wine-making. Many independent wine growers are active in Mittelwihr, but in Bennwihr practically everyone delivers his grapes to the local cooperative. In my opinion, Mittelwihr definitely makes the better wines. I have tasted some sublime wines here that are quite simply among the best anywhere in Alsace.

The Midi of Alsace

The quality of these wines is due in no small measure to Mittelwihr's microclimate. On the west of the village lie wine slopes that are sheltered on three sides by high hills. It is warmer here than elsewhere in Alsace, which is why people talk of 'le Midi de l'Alsace'. The best local vineyard is the Mandelberg, or Côte des Amandiers, so called because almond trees blossom there every year (and *mandeltartes* — almond tarts — are the local delicacy). The Mandelberg measures about 74 acres and is mainly planted with Gewürztraminer, with some Riesling and Muscat. The underlying rock includes granite.

The firm of Preiss-Henny

The best-quality Mittelwihr wines are to be found at the house of Preiss-Henny. The Preiss family, growers since 1535, came originally from Riquewihr, where they still rent land from the local commune. This produces a superior Pinot Gris. Altogether, Preiss-Henny works 85 acres, which naturally includes land in Mittelwihr itself. The firm's own acreage supplies more than three-quarters of the grapes required. Hubert Preiss, the general manager,

Whereas some 30% of Preiss-Henny's 111 acres are planted with Riesling, there is only 5% of Pinot Gris (Tokay d'Alsace). However, this does not affect the quality; that is exemplary, particularly the Réserve Henny — fruity, elegant, fresh — a not too exaggerated Pinot Gris/Tokay. The Preiss-Henny Pinot Gris, the Riesling and the Muscat appear on the wine list of the 3-star Auberge de l'Ill restaurant.

Edgard Schaller (born 1922) lives in Mittelwihr and with his son Patrick (born 1953) cultivates about 20 acres, distributed over various communes, including Mittelwihr, Zellenberg and Riquewihr. Edgard's father — Charles-Frédéric — was nicknamed 'The Muscat King'. Edgard also produces a usually delicious Muscat with an effect almost of fresh grapes.

Edgard and Patrick Schaller's Riesling has much elegance and finesse without being too light; a very good wine skilfully made. The Schallers have glazed concrete and enamel fermentation vats, stainless-steel fermentation tanks and also traditional wooden casks. Besides tables wines they produce a good sparkling Crémant d'Alsace (see page 90).

There is a particularly good caveau in Mittelwihr where the young owner cooks delicious food and serves a lavish range of local wines. There I discovered the Mandelberger-Riesling from Alfred Burghoffer Père & Fils. It was an extremely refreshing wine with pleasing nuances. The Burghoffer family has a 15-acre vineyard, ¾ acres in the Mandelberg. The wines ferment in wood. A nice reception cellar.

Vineyard acreage
Mittelwihr: 505

Below:
Mittelwihr's famous wall of flowers. During the last war it was planted three times with blue, white and red flowers, the French national colours.

Bottom:
This typically Alsatian drawing adorns the labels of Alfred Burghoffer's wines.

Mittelwihr has no wine festival, but it does celebrate its almond trees, usually in August.

The village has about 670 inhabitants, 130 of them growers.

After World War II Hubert Preiss's parents rebuilt the Preiss-Henny cellars first, and then their own house. Until 1952 the family lived in huts. Preiss-Henny use mainly wooden vats for vinification, always the same vat for the same wines from the same site. 'In this way the scent of the wine stays in the wood,' says Hubert Preiss. In France he only supplies his wines exclusively to private individuals, restaurants and a few shops (like Fauchon in Paris). Preiss-Henny also has its own distillery (see photo on page 90).

Mittelwihr

deliberately limits production, so that the firm's own grapes remain the dominating factor. Only in this way can the entire wine-making process be controlled from start to finish. Quality is apparent in everything Preiss-Henny does. The wines are vinified according to the sites they come from, in medium-sized vats. Clarifying is not done by chemical means: in the winter the cellar doors are simply opened, the cold air comes in and the wine clarifies itself.

Maximum freshness

Another very characteristic aspect of the Preiss-Henny method is the bottling *sur lie* — the sediment produced in fermentation and deposited in the vats. The wine is therefore not transferred to clean vats, but goes directly from its first vat into the bottle. Contact with oxygen is thus minimal and the wine retains maximum freshness, often with a slight carbonation. Preiss-Henny practises *sur lie* bottling with all

wines except Gewürztraminer, Tokay and Pinot Noir, which cannot tolerate carbon dioxide. The *sur lie* method is seldom used in Alsace (but often in Muscadet in the Loire: see pages 12-15). The extraordinary care taken by Hubert Preiss and his staff can be tasted in their wines. In my experience the Preiss-Henny range is astonishingly good, whether it is a simple Sylvaner, or superior wines such as Muscat, Riesling, Pinot Gris or Gewürztraminer.

Having tasted various wines from the Bennwihr cooperative, on the premises and elsewhere under a number of labels, I rated the Sylvaner Pinot Blanc, Muscat, Tokay, Pinot Noir and Rieslings of various categories as adequate — amply so in some instances. The best Riesling was from the Rebgarten in Bennwihr: fuller than the ordinary sorts; a distinct *terroir* in the taste.

The best Gewürztraminers from the Bennwihr cooperative were designated Sélection or Réserve, often with a medal. This type of wine is usually rather strong in alcohol and robust, sultry, lightly spiced, and in sunny years distinctly a little too sweet. There are few subtleties of taste and bouquet. You need to like this style of Gewürztraminer. Another product of the cooperative is the sparkling Brut Réal (see page 90).

Vineyard acreages
Bennwihr: 684
Houssen: 114

Bennwihr's wine festival takes place at the beginning of August, but other wine festivities are usually organized in May and October.

Right:
Wine is transferred from one vat to another by hoses of various dimensions.

Below:
The cooperative of Bennwihr. There are six automatic Willmes presses here that can process up to 600 metric tons of grapes a day. In the Relais Hansi — *the cooperative's restaurant — there is an older type of press dating from 1948.*

Bennwihr

Alsace

In the winter of 1944-5 Bennwihr suffered the same fate as its immediate neighbour Mittelwihr and was completely destroyed. All that was spared, ironically, was the monument to the fallen of World War I. Between 1947 and 1959 Bennwihr was rebuilt, unfortunately with less loving care than, for example, Ammerschwihr. Modern Bennwihr is rather colourless, lacking in character; the links with the old village have gone for ever. The most striking building is the church. Bennwihr's first church was built in AD 777, when the village was called Benonisvilare. The outside of the present church is fairly austere, but the interior glows with a wealth of warm colours from the tall stained-glass windows.

A powerful cooperative

The vineyards of Bennwihr were so devastated by the war that it took years before they were again productive. Most growers had to start from scratch, soon deciding to collaborate by establishing a cooperative in 1950. With a production of about 4 million bottles a year, this is now one of the most important in Alsace. It has some 230 members who jointly work between 860 and 990 acres. In Bennwihr itself only three growers are not members of the cooperative. The manager, Pierre Gressner, told me that his members receive a planting plan recommending which varieties should go where. The plan is based on extensive soil analyses (limestone, flint and gravel all occur) carried out for the cooperative.

Modern plant

The Société Coopérative Vinicole de Bennwihr has very modern equipment for quick processing of enormous quantities of grapes. After selection, the grapes are automatically tipped into the correct press; the six large presses have a combined capacity of 600 metric tons a day. The *cave* is built on several floors so that the must is transferred to the fermentation tanks by

force of gravity, having first been centrifuged. After fermentation it is twice filtered and then given a cold treatment. In the vast bottling area the wine is then bottled at the rate of 10,000 bottles an hour. The qualities of the cooperative's wines are in keeping with this massive scale of operation: generally they have little refinement or personality, but they are

certainly not bad — witness the large number of customers at home and abroad. Most customers have their own labels; Victor Preiss and Réal are subsidiary brands. The cooperative also runs three fairly modest restaurants: the *Relais Hansi* in Bennwihr (next door to the wine business), *Chez Hansi* in Colmar and the *Relais des Moines* in Riquewihr.

The Sigolsheim cooperative regularly takes part in fairs and competitions, with some success. Once a quarter of its total annual production won awards. In 1980 I tasted an award-winning Muscat 1976 and found it quite delicious, with a distinct nutmeg bouquet. The Tokay of various vintages appealed to me: usually gently spicy, pleasant and relatively full. I have also enjoyed serving and drinking the top category Riesling.

The better, usually award-winning Gewürztraminers from the Sigolsheim cooperative have a mild, amiable taste that tends towards the sweet, but lack depth. There is more subtlety and richness in the Gewürztraminer Mambourg, which is also mild. When the weather plays its part, the quality is truly first class. In 1946 the cooperative had a storage capacity of 7,000 hectolitres, at present 60,000 (over 11,000 in stainless-steel tanks), the SICA store included.

The firm of Pierre Sparr owns about a quarter of the Altenbourg vineyard (about 10 acres), where it produces a successful Riesling. In a sunny year such as 1976 this can be aromatic, powerful, with plenty of alcohol, but a modest elegance; in a rainy year such as 1977, slightly thinner and rather fresh. Not a wine with great breeding, but still extremely agreeable as a table companion, and much better in quality than the more ordinary Rieslings from this firm.

Pierre Sparr's Gewürztraminer Mambourg has more body and subtlety than other Gewürztraminers from this firm. The 1979 is a good example of the level this wine can attain; also the 1976. In these good years the wine has strength and fullness. Pierre Sparr owns 15 acres of the Mambourg. Another good, full-flavoured, broad wine from the Sparr range is the Tokay Cuvée Particulière: its better vintages can be served with game.

Ringenbach-Moser was established in Sigolsheim in 1936 by Guillaume Ringenbach, father of the present owner Jean-Paul Ringenbach. This small family firm has 16 acres of its own, the grapes from which are not vinified separately. Both grapes and wine are also bought from other growers. The speciality is the Gewürztraminer: rounded in taste without being too sultry, sweet or heavy. It is a good wine, perhaps only lacking somewhat in depth and length.

Vineyard acreage
Sigolsheim: 798

Below, left:
Sparr's bottling plant (firm founded 1892).

Below, right:
The Romanesque relief above the church door. The grower on the right is offering St Paul a barrel of wine.

Facing page, top:
Sigolsheim's roofs once won an award for being some of the best in France.

Facing page, below: Charles Sparr (left) and co-director René Sparr of the firm of Sparr. They buy grapes from some 100 growers in 10 communes.

The cooperative produces a little kosher Alsace wine.

Sigolsheim Alsace

The village of Sigolsheim, the third biggest wine commune in the *département* of Haut-Rhin, with about 815 acres, probably came into being in the 6th century AD. The founder was Sigolt or Sigwalt, a Frankish warrior. An old deed shows that wine-growing was already practised here in 783. Sigolsheim suffered severely in World War II. The first shells fell on 6 December 1944. Time and again the village was liberated, then retaken by the Germans. Not until 28 December was it finally freed, but by then practically nothing remained of the old village. Some bottles in the cellar of Pierre Sparr suggest the inferno that must have raged. Despite the fact that they were full and stocked underground, they were totally distorted by the heat. Only parts of the 12th-century church remained standing, but it was later possible to restore the fabric. A Romanesque relief over the door shows a kneeling farmer offering a barrel of wine to St Paul.

Vines and crosses

Behind Sigolsheim a broad, high hill stretches for about two miles. It is entirely planted with vines, except on the top where there is a national war cemetery with the graves of 1,590 soldiers of the 1st French Army. The Germans too lost many men at Sigolsheim — so many that they dubbed the hill *Blutberg*. A religious foundation here, the Couvent des Capucins, was captured and recaptured at least 15 times.
Happily, there is now no trace of these horrors. The village with its 100 inhabitants looks neat and peaceful, and its 127 or so growers generally do well enough. They each cultivate an average of 5 to 10 acres (7½ is enough to live on). Eight estates exploit 25 or more acres, and one, Pierre Sparr, owns about 50 acres.

Warmest vineyard

At one time Sigolsheim, like many other places in Alsace, was mainly planted with varieties of black grapes. Until the end of the 19th century the village even had a small area of 'Beaujolais'. A variety that once dominated the scene was the Trollinger, a black grape with white juice. At first it was made as a white wine, later mainly as red. Today the Trollinger has completely disappeared, like the Knipperlé and other varieties. Sigolsheim is nowadays noted chiefly for its Gewürztraminer, and successfully produces other superior wines. The best-known vineyard is the Mambourg or Mamburg, with a lot of limestone. In the spring of 1980 it was enlarged from 160 to 220 acres. The people of Sigolsheim claim that the Mambourg is the warmest vineyard in Alsace as the snow melts earliest here. The Altenbourg also enjoys a good reputation; its soil contains both clay and limestone. This vineyard is in fact a 40-acre enclave within the Vogelgarten. Their combined area is 136 acres.

Cooperative with branches

In 1946 most growers decided that only by working closely together could they solve their problems and so they set up a cooperative. It now has 190 members working a combined total of 680 acres. This

Sigolsheim

cooperative is not only one of the biggest but also one of the best equipped in Alsace. Working areas are tiled and clean, as much stainless steel as possible is used, and corks and bottles can, if necessary, be sterilized. On various occasions I have tasted really good wines from this cooperative, such as a Muscat, Tokay d'Alsace and Gewürztraminer. The cooperative only buys grapes from its members, but a subsidiary enterprise with another 800 members takes wine exclusively. This is a so-called SICA (*société d'intérêt coopérative agricole*) and it was founded in 1968, for two reasons: firstly, due to the fact that after World War II replanting consisted of such high-quality vines, creating a shortage of more ordinary wines; secondly, in poor years growers can still fulfil their contracts via the SICA. The cooperative owns two other enterprises. One supplies wines from cooperatives outside

Alsace to domestic and foreign customers; the other has a souvenir shop in Kaysersberg.

The family firm of Pierre Sparr

In Sigolsheim there are several shippers, the best-known being Pierre Sparr et ses Fils. This family has been involved in wine-growing for some three centuries. The medium-sized business is run by Charles Sparr, his brother René and their respective sons Pierre and François. They own 74 acres of vineyard, about 50 in Sigolsheim, the rest divided between Kientzheim and Turckheim (10 acres of the Brand vineyard). In addition, they buy grapes from 110 growers who

jointly cultivate 370 acres. All the grapes are divided into three classes of quality and then vinified separately in concrete vats. In general, the Pierre Sparr wines have a firm, almost robust constitution. The quality of the simpler sorts can leave something to be desired, but a number at the top of the range are well worth attention, namely the Tokay Cuvée Particulière and Mambourg, and the Riesling-Altenbourg. Other Pierre Sparr brands are Alsace Tempé (Jean-Pierre Tempé), Zigler and Pierre Dumoulin.

Cuvée des Comtes de Lupfen
BLANCK
APPELLATION ALSACE CONTROLEE
ALSACE
Domaine des Comtes de Lupfen 0,70 l
Mise en Bouteilles au Domaine des Comtes de Lupfen.
Propriété de Paul Blanck et ses fils à Kientzheim (Kaysersberg)
Haut-Rhin - France

Tokay d'Alsace
RESERVE SPECIALE
BLANCK
ALSACE
Domaine des Comtes de Lupfen 0,70 l
Mise en Bouteilles au Domaine des Comtes de Lupfen.
Propriété de Paul Blanck et ses fils à Kientzheim (Kaysersberg)
Haut-Rhin - France

Riesling Schlossberg
ALSACE GRAND CRU
APPELLATION ALSACE GRAND CRU CONTRÔLEE
BLANCK
Domaine des Comtes de Lupfen 0,70 l
Mise en Bouteilles au Domaine des Comtes de Lupfen.
Propriété de Paul Blanck et ses fils à Kientzheim (Kaysersberg)
Haut-Rhin - France

PINOT
Vin d'Alsace
APPELLATION ALSACE CONTROLEE
e70cl
CAVE VINICOLE DE KIENTZHEIM-KAYSERSBERG HAUT-RHIN - FRANCE

MUSCAT
Vin d'Alsace
APPELLATION ALSACE CONTROLEE
e70cl
CAVE VINICOLE DE KIENTZHEIM-KAYSERSBERG HAUT-RHIN - FRANCE

One of the best estates in Alsace is in Kientzheim and belongs to the Blanck family (Marcel, his brother Bernard, his brother-in-law Jacques). They own nearly 52 acres in five or six communes, the main part in Kientzheim itself. They reclaimed a lot of this themselves by hand, buying up pieces of good wine land that were lying fallow which other growers found too difficult to work. The class of the Blanck wines is evident in the Edelzwicker Cuvée.

Tasting with Marcel Blanck I was amazed at the excellent quality of the Sylvaner Réserve and the Klevner Réserve, both from the limestone. The Tokay d'Alsace Réserve Spéciale comes from the same type of soil: a mouth-filling, soft, fairly subtle wine of excellent quality. It should usually be allowed a year or two.

The Blanck family owns 8 acres of the Schlossberg. This provides a nice, balanced Riesling, usually firm in constitution with nuances of bouquet and taste. The wine retains its freshness for years. The Riesling Furstentum (of which a lot less is made) is quite different. This is harsher, almost metallic, yet fuller in flavour. Only after two years does this rare Riesling begin to show its class. The Blancks also produce a harmonious Gewürztraminer from their Furstentum vineyard (about 15 acres).

At the cooperative in Kientzheim-Kaysersberg they try not to process more than two varieties of grape each day during the vintage so as to select with due care and give each type maximum attention. After pressing, the must is only partly centrifuged so that the yeast cells stay in the juice. It then starts to ferment of its own accord. A wine I tasted on various occasions was the almost juicy, very delicious Pinot Blanc. The Sylvaner too is often good.

The first Muscat that I drank from the Kientzheim-Kaysersberg cooperative was the 1977, of which only 3,300 cases were made. I thought the quality was very successful in view of the difficult year. The class of this sometimes very slightly sparkling wine was confirmed by later years. The cooperative also makes a Tokay d'Alsace which is full of character, not too overpowering or alcoholic. The Riesling Schlossberg is definitely the least of Blanck's wines.

Vineyard acreage
Kientzheim: 205

*Below left:
Kientzheim, with the castle on the left and the white buildings of the cooperative on the right. Ammerschwihr is in the background, very close by.*

*Below centre:
Marcel Blanck, one of a handful of independent growers in the village. He carries out various official functions in addition to his vocation.*

*Below right:
Kientzheim in earlier times as painted on the wall of the cooperative. The village was recorded in 785, as Cönesheim.*

The village fair usually takes place at the end of June.

Kientzheim

The visitor arriving in Kientzheim from Sigolsheim is welcomed by the 'Lalli' or 'Lallekoenig', a grotesque face that sticks out its tongue high on the gatehouse and whose throat once served as an embrasure. The gargoyle is deceptive, for this is a hospitable village. Several times a year the *chapitres* and banquets of the Confrérie Saint-Etienne, the Alsace wine fraternity, are held here, always attended by several hundred people. These festivities take place in the château, close to the gatehouse. The castle was built by the counts of Lupfen, for centuries the owners of the village, and improved in the 16th century by Baron Lazare de Schwendi. He is the man said to have brought back the Tokay d'Alsace from his Hungarian campaigns. Both he and his son were buried in Kientzheim church. The Confrérie Saint-Etienne now owns the château and has its headquarters there; as previously mentioned, a wine museum and a 'bottle library' have been set up in the château.

Schlossberg: the first grand cru

Although a World War II tank stands on the western side of the village, Kientzheim suffered less damage than Sigolsheim, half a mile away. Many of the half-timbered houses in the winding main thoroughfare and narrow side streets remained intact. Nearly all the 925 inhabitants are involved in one way or another in the wine industry, documented here since the 8th century. Behind the village the vineyards climb some fairly steep slopes, and on the south they are virtually an extension of those of Sigolsheim. The best-known is the Schlossberg, which on 25 November 1975 was the first Alsace vineyard to be granted *grand cru* status. It covers 148 acres, largely on the granite, and extends on the east side of the village almost to the castle at Kaysersberg. The Riesling is the most commonly planted vine, and farther east in the Furstentum, where there is some limestone, a lot of Gewürztraminer and Tokay are grown.

A superior cooperative

Near the walls of Kientzheim is the Cave Vinicole de Kientzheim-Kaysersberg. This cooperative has 130 members, 20 of them in Kaysersberg, who between them cultivate 370 acres. It is managed by André Hauss, who makes a stringent selection of grapes. By not transferring the wine too often, it is kept as fresh as possible. During the whole vinification process, the wine comes into contact only with neutral materials such as stainless steel and glass. For quality I would rank the Kientzheim-Kaysersberg high among the cooperatives of Alsace, by virtue of its Sylvaner, Pinot Blanc, Muscat, Tokay, Gewürztraminer and Gewürztraminer Kaefferkopf.

(H) Gewurtz + Tokay

Domaine Weinbach, named after the little 'wine stream' that flows across the site, lies just outside Kaysersberg, towards Kientzheim. In 1885 it was bought by the Faller brothers. The efforts of Théo Faller, born on the estate in 1911, extended the vineyards and improved the wines. Théo died in 1979 and is buried in his beloved estate. His work is continued by his wife Colette. Her Sylvaner is excellent.

Colette Faller sells one of her best Rieslings under the name Cuvée Théo. The 1979 had a mildly fruity bouquet and a pure, supple, almost juicy taste with again a lot of fruit — and a great purity. Both the Riesling Schlossberg (from Kientzheim) and the Riesling vendange tardive are successful. There is a relatively low yield from Domaine Weinbach, and the wine is mainly fermented in wood. Colette is assisted by her son-in-law Edouard Leiber and her daughter Catherine.

During my visit to Domaine Weinbach I tasted five different Gewürztraminers from different vats, all of an immaculate quality. The richest was the vendange tardive harvested on 14 December 1979, a truly splendid wine with a long aftertaste. I can also recommend the Pinot Blanc and Tokay d'Alsace from this remarkable estate.

Vineyard acreage
Kaysersberg: 133

Kaysersberg is the birthplace of the great Albert Schweitzer (1875-1965), who received the Nobel Peace Prize in 1952. The parental home is now a museum. Kaysersberg and Lambaréné in Gabon (where Schweitzer worked) are now twin towns.

Kaysersberg has just under 3,000 inhabitants. The village has been mentioned in records since 1227.

There is a fountain (c. 1500) with a statue of the Emperor Constantine in front of the church.

Right:
Madame Colette Faller of Domaine Weinbach.

Below left:
Pickers' mealtime at Domaine Weinbach. In World War II the house was hit by 17 incendiary bombs, but Théo Faller put them all out, thus saving most of the building.

Below right:
One of Kaysersberg's beautiful old houses.

Kaysersberg

Alsace

Kaysersberg lies three-quarters of a mile west of Kientzheim and dominates the Weiss valley, one of the routes into Alsace. This strategic position was recognized in Roman times: the name is said to derive from *Mons Caesaris*. Later rulers took great interest in the village, which had defensive walls and a castle at an early date. Both are now in ruins. The remains of the castle are on a hillside and it is well worth making the short walk up to them. From the tower, with its 13-foot-thick walls there is a magnificent view over the village.

A charming village

Kaysersberg is one of the most attractive little villages in Alsace and has retained its charms in spite of past violence. It is obvious from the many half-timbered houses and Renaissance buildings that from the 15th to the 17th century the inhabitants led a prosperous existence. Despite the surrounding warfare, the village flourished as a busy trading centre. Wines were despatched to various countries and the place also had a reputation for vats, leather and pottery. Some points of interest from this period are the *hôtel de ville*; the church, partly Romanesque, partly Gothic, with a 19th-century clocktower, and Gothic treasures that include an altar dish from 1518; the chapel of Saint-Michel with its two storeys; the Oberhof chapel in which there is a statue of Christ holding a bunch of grapes; and the fortified bridge over the Weiss, unique in Alsace. Then there is the well opposite number 54 Grand' Rue. On it there is an inscription in 17th-century dialect that says, roughly, 'If you have drunk more than your fill at table, freezing your stomach, I advise you to drink an old, subtle wine, in moderation, and to leave me my water.'

The flying grape-picker

Wine-making has been practised for centuries in Kaysersberg, as is shown not only by the inscription on the well, but also by the legend of the flying man. A couple of centuries ago, so the story goes, a picker who ate an extremely sweet grape was carried into the air and set down some way off, close to a little chapel. The *chapelle de l'homme volant* still stands as a reminder of this miraculous journey and is reached from Kaysersberg — on foot — in 35 minutes. Nowadays, Kaysersberg's importance as a wine commune is very limited. Only 136 acres are cultivated and most of the growers take their grapes to the cooperative at Kientzheim. There is only one wine estate of significance, the Domaine Weinbach, with 58 acres in Kaysersberg and Kientzheim. Wine-making is a secondary activity in Kaysersberg, which is essentially a centre for tourists.

Kuehn's Pinot Blanc is one of the best I know. It is often of such quality that it surpasses theoretically superior Rieslings from less conscientious producers. It is a balanced wine with a rich taste, a vague hint of spices and terroir, soft tone, fruity and elegant in character. The Sylvaner is another simple, very successful wine from Kuehn.

To my mind, Kuehn's Riesling Kaefferkopf is way above the vast majority of wines of its kind. It is every inch a Riesling: great refinement, elegance, and breeding, freshness and pleasantly nuanced. The balance is extraordinarily good, the purity perfect. Kuehn often does not bottle it until August because it needs time to settle. Once bottled, it should preferably only be drunk 1½ to 2 years after the vintage.

Kuehn's Muscat, Tokay, Pinot Noir and Gewürztraminer are averagely good. However, the standard rises to excellent with the Gewürztraminer Cuvée Saint-Hubert. This wine, with its silver label, has a much more complex taste than the usual Gewürztraminer, and has more to offer. It is full without being heavy, mild without tasting sweet. The bouquet is soft and fairly broad, with suggestions of soft fruit. The 1978 and 1979 were very representative.

My notes on much of the Adam wine I tasted were critical. Most of the wines were correct but rather flat. The Kaefferkopf was an exception with a certain modest finesse. It is made exclusively from Kaefferkopf grapes, Gewürztraminer and Riesling. The proportions vary with the harvest, but the Gewürztraminer always predominates. The wine is supple, spicy and agreeable.

The ordinary Gewürztraminer from the Kientzheim-Kaysersberg cooperative (see page 118) is a very pleasant wine, but the Gewürztraminer Kaefferkopf is of a higher standard. The scent and taste are finer and also a little drier. The Kientzheim-Kaysersberg cooperative produces on average only 30,000 bottles annually of this wine.

René Schneider and his son Bernard own about 11 acres in Ammerschwihr, 2 acres being in the Kaefferkopf. Their two best wines are the Riesling Kaefferkopf and the Gewürztraminer-Kaefferkopf; I have a distinct preference for the latter. In good years this has the characteristic Gewürztraminer spiciness without being excessively sultry or heavy.

Ammerschwihr

Alsace

Ammerschwihr used to be a lovely, wholly 16th-century place, contented and colourful. For the visitor its charm was immediate and enduring. Unhappily, the old Ammerschwihr disappeared forever during the fighting of 1944. About 85% of all the village houses were destroyed. The fire raged so fiercely that at times there was no water left to put them out and wine had to be used, as at the wine firm of Adam. The people hid in the cellars. It must have been an appalling experience to have seen one of the most beautiful of Alsace villages reduced to ruins. Fortunately, however, Ammerschwihr has been rebuilt with taste and care; it is now an attractive, proud little place that is certainly worth a visit. Here and there reminders of the old Ammerschwihr still stand, such as the 13th-century Porte-Haute and the nearby Tour des Bourgeois, the 16th-century l'Homme Sauvage fountain, parts of the 16th-century church, the Tour des Fripons, and the 16th-century 'Rogues' Tower', next to the *Aux Armes de France,* one of the most famous restaurants in Alsace.

Desirable property

Ammerschwihr is first recorded in 869, in the form Amalricivilare. There was a period when the place had three different owners: the German emperor, the lord of Ribeauvillé and the lord of Hohlandsberg. At that time, too, Ammerschwihr had three mayors, three magistrates and three towers. Ammerschwihr's excellent wine may have had something to do with the fact that it was clearly a much-prized possession. Furthermore in the 13th and 14th centuries no fewer than 70 religious houses and noble families owned land there — wine-growing

René Sick and Pierre Dreyer, who live in Ammerschwihr, own about 25 acres, 30% planted with Pinot Blanc/Auxerrois, 30% with Gewürztraminer, 25% with Riesling, 15% with other types. These wine makers rightly consider the Gewürztraminer Kaefferkopf their best wine. It is sound, generous and very good. The Sick and Dreyer families own 5 acres on the Kaefferkopf, 90% planted with Gewürztraminer.

Henri Ehrhardt works 12 acres in Ammerschwihr on the Kaefferkopf, planted with Gewürztraminer and Riesling. The fragrance of his Gewürztraminer Kaefferkopf evokes memories of summer flowers. The wine has a fruity, almost too agreeable, mildly broad taste that is not exceptionally heavy or complex, merely delicious — and pure.

Vineyard acreages
Ammerschwihr: 870

Opposite page, centre:
Picture postcard of the old Ammerschwihr.

Opposite page, below:
The village of Ammerschwihr. The first wine fair of the season, in April, has been held here since 1922.

Left:
The Kuehn sign.

Below:
Kuehn's Cave de l'Enfer (Cellar of Hell). People were hidden down here during World War II, as well as statues of Saints from the church. Locals still speak of this as the time 'when the saints went to hell'.

Ammerschwihr

land. The village obviously took its wine-growing seriously, as is evident from the establishment in the 14th century of the *Herrenstubengesellschaft*. This voluntary association of citizens regulated the sale of all wine leaving the village. On 31 May 1947 this body was revived as the Confrérie Saint-Etienne. We find a clear indication of the quality of the local wine in the words of Nicolas Klein of Colmar, who wrote in the 17th century that the best wines of the country came from Ammerschwihr.
The vineyards of Ammerschwihr still represent a desirable possession. Approximately 112 acres, including 247 acres that produce wines without an *appellation contrôlée*, are divided among more than 700 different owners, of whom only 120 or 130 live in the village. After a costly ten-year study, all owners were asked in a referendum in 1975 whether they wanted a redistribution. A large majority rejected the proposal — and the 3,225 different plots remain. The people here are individualistic and conservative by nature: for example, despite the many small properties, there is no cooperative. Nor is everyone happy about the new estate where many commuters from Colmar have settled.

The famous Kaefferkopf

Ammerschwihr is the second largest wine commune in Alsace (after Dambach-la-Ville) and the biggest in Haut-Rhin. In quality, too, it has always been in the front rank. The Kaefferkopf vineyard, with Beblenheim's Sonnenglanz, was the first to be legally delimited and recognized by the Colmar tribunal, in 1932. Kaefferkopf wine had, in any case, been sold under that name since 1834, as is apparent from an old label at the firm of Adam. The 155-acre vineyard lies on a gently sloping hillside south of the village. The pattern of local land distribution is typified by the fact that 220 growers — no less — possess plots. The Gewürztraminer has been planted on 80% of the Kaefferkopf, which has a granite subsoil, but the Riesling,

too, does extremely well here. Only these two grapes and Pinot Blanc, Pinot Gris (Tokay) and Muscat may be used in a Kaefferkopf wine — never, for instance, a Sylvaner. Other Ammerschwihr vineyards are on the limestone.

Kuehn's rare quality

Kuehn is the leading Ammerschwihr shipper when it comes to quality. This house with its traditional methods — a lot of oak casks in the ancient cellars — produces gracious, pure wines, some of which, notably the Pinot Blanc, the Riesling Kaefferkopf and the Gewürztraminer Cuvée Saint-Hubert, have been among my favourites for years. With good reason, the wines from Kuehn are often given the seal of approval of the Confrérie Saint-Etienne; and the diplomas that cover the walls of the rather spartan tasting room are fully merited. The house owns about 12 acres of the Kaefferkopf, and 7 acres elsewhere in Ammerschwihr. In addition it buys grapes from growers who cultivate a total of 49 acres. Kuehn is in the happy position of occupying the same building as the restaurant *Aux Armes de France*, and being opposite another, the pleasant *À l'Arbre Vert*. The cooperative of Kientzheim-Kaysersberg has a majority share in the firm, but the vineyards are still owned entirely by the Kuehn family.

Les Caves Adam

With its annual production of 1.7 million bottles, Les Caves J.-B. Adam sells about three times as much as Kuehn and is by far the biggest firm in Ammerschwihr. The Adam family has been making wine since 1770, and the family tree can be traced back to 1614. Memories of its past are to be found in the house of owner-manager Jean Adam, which is full of imposing wooden furniture, most of it beautifully carved. Below and beside the house are some of the cellars, and there is also a modern complex on the edge of the village. About two-thirds of the wine ferments in stainless steel or glazed concrete, and the rest, mostly the finer sorts, in wooden casks. Adam owns 17 acres in Ammerschwihr (7 in the Kaefferkopf) and 11 acres in Ingersheim. In general, the wines are of decent quality, the most interesting being the Kaefferkopf made from Gewürztraminer and Riesling.

Katzenthal

Katzenthal and Ammerschwihr are separated by the hump-backed Kaefferkopf vineyard. Tiny Katzenthal, with its 550 inhabitants, is surrounded by vines, lying in the midst of rolling slopes half a mile from the *route du vin*. It can be recognized from afar: the white of its tall church tower contrasts strongly with the green of the vines and the grey of the Vosges. This little village did not escape the violence of 1944, when 95% of the buildings were destroyed, including the church. One of the few to survive was a finely preserved Renaissance house in the centre of the village. Towering above Katzenthal are the remains of Château Wineck, a historic monument that seems to be besieged by vines. It dates from the 11th and 12th centuries and was already in ruins by the 16th century. Since 1971 it has gradually been restored by volunteers (Les Amis de Wineck). A medieval evening is held once a year at the foot of the Wineck, on *Quatorze Juillet*, France's national day.

Cake and wine

Although the Katzenthal *kuchen*, a cinnamon cake, ranks as a local speciality, life in the village is almost wholly dominated by wine, and has been for centuries. The wines of Katzenthal were praised around 1560 by the German poet and satirist, Johann Fischart. Today the village has about 420 acres of vineyards, mainly worked by local growers. In 1980, there were 33 active growers, comprising 18 *manipulants* making, bottling and selling their own wine, ten cooperative members, two sellers of grapes, two sellers of wine in bulk, and one *négociant*. You can get a good impression of Katzenthal's wines at the wine festival which for some years has been celebrated in mid-August rather than during autumn.

No connection with cats

Even though some growers display a cat on their labels, the name Katzenthal has nothing to do with the German word for cats. The precise origin is not known, but there are several theories. Jean-Paul Ecklé — chairman of the *syndicat viticole* — told me that there were three possibilities: Katzenthal is either derived from the name of a Frankish landowner Kazo; or from Caïdinthalo, meaning 'Valley of the hills'; or from Kastellthal, in direct reference to the local castle. Somebody else added a fourth suggestion — that it could have been named after Katharinenthal, a convent founded here in the 13th century.

The earliest known name for Colmar is Villa Columbaria; the second word means either 'dovecot' or 'burial ground'. The name later became corrupted to Columbra, then to Colmar.

In 1359 there was already a guild of wine growers in Colmar.

There is a museum in Colmar dedicated to the local artist Bertholdi (1834-1904) who designed the Statue of Liberty.

In October Colmar celebrates 'sauerkraut time', which is then very fresh and at its best.

Right:
Evening in La Petite Venise. The name is derived from canals, now grassed over. The famous Fontaine du Vigneron is also here.

Below:
Shopping streets in the centre of Colmar are pedestrian precincts.

Bottom:
Saturday market in Colmar.

Despite fierce fighting nearby during World War II, Colmar was miraculously undamaged. The town was liberated on 2 February 1945.

Colmar

Alsace

For hundreds of years Colmar has been the wine capital of Alsace. Local wine-growing and the associated wine trade have spelt prosperity since the 14th century. Colmar lies on the Lauch, a tributary of the Ill. Large quantities of wine were formerly shipped via these waterways to the Rhine and farther in Europe. Much more traffic was carried by water than by road. Although the local wine industry has been drastically reduced, Colmar still plays a large part in the viticultural life of Alsace. Among the many authorities, institutes and associations concerned with wine-growing are the Comité Interprofessionnel du Vin d'Alsace, the Association des Viticulteurs d'Alsace, the Fédération des Coopératives Vinicoles d'Alsace, the Groupement des Producteurs-Négociants du Vignoble Alsacien, the Institut Viticole Oberlin and the Centre de Recherches Agronomiques d'Alsace (with its own department for wine-growing and technology). In addition, the biggest wine fair of Alsace takes place here annually in August. This Foire Régionale des Vins d'Alsace lasts for about a week and attracts tens of thousands of visitors.

A beautiful town

Colmar is more than a wine centre: it is also a town of great beauty. Voltaire did the place no justice when in 1754 he described it as 'half German, half French and wholly odd', for in the centre of the town there were already many fine houses that still survive today. Perhaps he was not referring to the town's architecture. At all events, though dismayed at the absence of good coffee, he pronounced the wine to be *fort bon*.
In its architecture, art and history, Colmar perfectly symbolizes Alsace. The heart of Colmar is a well-stocked treasure house. Its finest jewel is the Pfister house, built in 1537 by a chaplain from Besançon. The outside is adorned with a wooden gallery, frescoes and medallions. It is rivalled by the Maison des Têtes, which dates from 1608 and has a number of carved heads on the gable and the

figure of a wine grower on its roof. Then, too, there is the late 15th-century Koïfhus, once the centre of the city's trade, and La Petite Venise (Little Venice), a romantic canal district. The town has many other gems, and a leisurely walk through it offers great visual delight.
Art-lovers are likewise attracted to Colmar for its Unterlinden Museum, opened in 1850; the only museum in France to receive more visitors is the Louvre. It is housed in a 13th-century Dominican friary and exhibits very early as well as contemporary art. There is much here about the history of Alsace, along with displays of many articles connected

with the wine industry, such as beautifully carved vats, old tools and 17th-century presses.

Defiantly French

Like many of the towns and villages of the region, Colmar was founded by the Franks. In the 12th century it received its charter and constructed its fortifications. In 1353 it took the initiative in setting up the Décapole, an alliance of ten Alsace towns that sided with the German emperor and against the nobles. The town became French in 1673, during the reign of Louis XIV. The

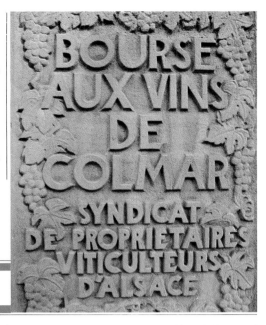

The SYNVA (see main text) uses stars on its labels to indicate the quality of the various wines, starting with one star and rising to four. My experience is that you reach an at least acceptable quality only with the three-star wines such as Riesling, Muscat, Tokay and Gewürztraminer. The Gewürztraminer from this collective enterprise is often a successful wine, particularly in the four-star category. I recall a 1976 with soft fruit in the bouquet and a rather elegant taste.

Alsace Monopole is a brand name used by the SYNVA, for the same range of wines. The tasting committee first chooses the wines by type, then the various qualities within each type. Besides a four-star Gewürztraminer (the label on the left) I have also tasted three- and four-star Rieslings and Tokays that were pleasant but not particularly subtle. Other wines were sometimes very disappointing.

The brand name Schwendi Monopole was thought up by the former Colmar firm of Charles Jux. By means of exchanges and purchases, Charles Jux succeeded in building up a 74-acre site in the Harth vineyard, with a further 136 acres elsewhere. Proportionally, a lot of Pinot Noir was planted. Only the name Charles Jux now remains: the firm and its vineyards are owned by Dopff & Irion of Riquewihr — which is also responsible for the bulk quality.

Vineyard acreage
Colmar: 388

Right:
Board on the front of the Syndicat de Propriétaires Viticulteurs d'Alsace, one of the wine organizations established in Colmar.

Below:
The splendid Pfister house in the centre of Colmar, built in 1537 by a priest from Besançon.

The wine shippers' syndicate, the SYNVA, used to sell nearly all Alsace wine up to about 1930. Then the various houses selling their own wines came along.

Colmar

Sun King immediately had the walls razed to 'break the pride of Colmar'. During the enforced 47-year German occupation of Alsace after 1870, Colmar remained very French in spirit. A leading figure of this period was Hansi (Jean-Jacques Waltz), the artist, writer and poet whose colourful and charming work is still to be seen all over Alsace.

The Harth vineyard

Colmar has long ceased to depend on wine for its income. This town of 68,000 inhabitants has many factories and is steadily expanding its boundaries with housing and industrial estates. In 1980 Colmar had only 388 acres of vineyard; there were some 20 villages in the Haut-Rhin *département* with more acreage. It is possible, however, that the Harth, Colmar's only important vineyard, will be extended by 110 acres; the decision was taken in April 1980. The Harth consists of rather flat, alluvial ground with light gravelly soil that warms up quickly in the sun — hence the name, which means 'hearth'. The vines planted here benefit from the fact that Colmar is, after Perpignan, the driest town in France. On the other hand, soil composition and general situation are inferior to those of vineyards in other wine communes. In addition, the growers have to contend with night frost. During the spring they sometimes try to counter the cold by burning motor tyres and producing vapour from sulphur plus ammoniac.

Collective wine enterprises

In terms of output, the CEVA or Centrale des Vignerons d'Alsace is the largest wine business in Colmar. It markets wines, mostly of simple quality, that it bottles for seven Alsace cooperatives. Various labels and brand names are used, including La Cigogne. The shippers too have a joint enterprise in Colmar — the Syndicat des Négociants en Vins Viticulteurs du Vignoble Alsacien (SYNVA) — set up in 1919. This

association had a dual aim: to encourage the highest possible quality (which was essential after the German occupation) and to promote Alsace as a wine region, for many Alsace wines had previously been blended anonymously with those from Germany. Around 1920 the syndicate created its own selling organization with the brand name Alsace Monopole. It began by selling wine to the Parisians. Later, SYNVA was also used as a brand name. Today the association has about 60 members, including all the large wine houses. Every year a 15-strong tasting

committee makes a selection of bottled wines: in 1980 no fewer than 540 samples were submitted. Profits are pumped back into the business or invested elsewhere. In this way the syndicate has become the owner of the vineyard at Château d'Isenbourg at Rouffach (see page 134) and of the Hôtel l'Alsace at Guebwiller, and has a share in the Hôtel Champ de Mars at Colmar and the Grand-Hôtel, Les Trois Epis. The syndicate's wines are usually of average quality, with a few rising above or falling below this level.

The first wine from the Ingersheim cooperative I encountered was an undated Sylvaner in a small restaurant in Alsace. It had a juicy, vaguely spicy taste and was decently full. Later I got to know the Pinot Blanc, a wine with a great deal of fruit and terroir. I found it delicious despite its somewhat rustic character, with a long aftertaste. The Gewürztraminer also has class and a rich, concentrated taste. Despite Ingersheim's limestone soil the Tokay and Pinot are quite good.

Marcel Mullenbach lives in Niedermorschwihr and owns 12 widely scattered acres. The wine ferments and matures in wooden vats. It has personality and good quality. I recall with pleasure Mullenbach's sometimes slightly spicy, earthy Riesling, his full-flavoured Muscat, and his rather intense, broad, spicy Gewürztraminer.

Albert Boxler and his son Jean-Marc work about 19 acres in four different communes. They are based in Niedermorschwihr, at the west end of the main street. The Boxlers regard the Riesling as their speciality. It is normally a rather elegant, pure wine that requires time to lose some acidity.

Vineyard acreages
Ingersheim: 529
Niedermorschwihr: 257

Below:
Entrance to the Ingersheim cooperative.

Bottom:
Niedermorschwihr, with its striking spiral-shaped church spire. It is hard to imagine that 60% of this village was destroyed in World War II. Long ago it was owned by the Knights of Malta and later by the lord of Hohlandsberg.

Niedermorschwihr's wine festival is usually held in October, the village fair at the end of August or beginning of September.

The oldest woman in France, Josephine Steinlé, used to live in Ingersheim, where a street is named after her. Was it perhaps the local wine that kept her so lively?

Part of Ingersheim's old defensive walls still stand and there are remains of the Witches' Tower or Hexenturm next to a house in the Rue Maréchal Foch.

There are only six independent growers living in Ingersheim; all the others are members of the cooperative.

Ingersheim was first recorded in 768, a century before Colmar. Its earliest known names are Anngehiseshaim and Villa Annghishaim.

Ingersheim and Niedermorschwihr

Although Ingersheim owns 529 acres of vineyard, and has more people than, for example, Ribeauvillé, it is a rather forgotten wine commune. This is mainly because of its situation: Ingersheim is separated from Colmar only by the river Fecht and serves increasingly as its suburb, as is evident from the new housing and industrial estates. In addition, Ingersheim was largely destroyed in World War II so that its centre is not as attractive as that of many other wine villages that remained undamaged. A few ancient houses are worth seeing, as are the old and the new *hôtels de ville*; the former has an open belfry with the figures of three moustached men (Hungarian brothers, it is said) on the gable. Few tourists reach Ingersheim as through traffic is taken round a bypass.

Rustic wines

Ingersheim's vineyards stretch from low ground to high up the Florimont. The soil on this hill — a paradise for botanists because of its rich flora — is calciferous; elsewhere in the district clay also occurs. The wine growers of Ingersheim have had a *syndicat des vignerons* since 1910. When formed, it was by far the biggest wine organization in Alsace. The urge to work together is also apparent in the early establishment of a cooperative; dating from 1925, it was one of the first in the area. At present it has some 170 members, 60% of them from Ingersheim itself, owning a total of 544 acres. With handsome pink tiles on many of the fermentation tanks, the concern makes a very clean and tidy impression. It sells its wine both bottled and in bulk. I regard the Sylvaner, Pinot Blanc and Gewürztraminer as the best of the cooperative's wines. They usually have a distinct *terroir* in taste and aftertaste, which makes them almost rustic; great elegance or finesse should not be expected.

Spiral steeple

A delightful route leads from Ingersheim through the vineyards to Niedermorschwihr. This little village was called Morsvilre in 1214, and has the head of a Moor in its coat of arms. The streets are narrow, and there are numerous old houses, quaint fountains and picturesque corners. Two of the most striking buildings are the *hôtel de ville* with

its covered wooden outside staircase, and the 13th-century church tower with its spiral-shaped steeple. Niedermorschwihr lies sheltered in a pleasant valley full of vines. Its best-known vineyard is the Sommerberg. Most of the 50 growers have joined the cooperatives at Ingersheim or Turckheim.

The Turckheim cooperative uses quite a wide range of labels, sometimes with just Cave Vinicole, and sometimes, as on this Riesling Côtes du Brand, Les Propriétaires-Récoltants de Turckheim et Environs. The word 'cooperative' is carefully avoided. The wine is usually of a very good quality: better, more complete, subtler, and with a slightly deeper colour than the usual Riesling.

Besides a Pinot Blanc and a classy Klevner, Turckheim's cooperative produces a good Tokay d'Alsace. The 1976, for example, had a very distinctive taste, full of character, mildly firm, pure, balanced, with the slightest hint of honey. The grapes are immediately sorted on arrival into three qualities, as at the Bennwihr cooperative.

Gewürztraminer is one of the specialities of the Turckheim cooperative. The wines from the Brand, the vendange tardive and the Réserve du Baron de Turckheim, are particularly worth mention. The latter comes only from the commune of Turckheim. (The baronial coat of arms may only be used with the permission of the family.) The wine is always powerful (the 1978 had 13.5°) and usually has a broad, mild taste with a certain spiciness: a Gewürztraminer to drink with Munster cheese.

The Pinot Noir is nearly always made into rosé in Alsace, but the Turckheim cooperative also produces successful red wines. These are really pleasant red wines of high quality. Perhaps a still better quality is on the way: as an experiment, some of the 1979 wine is being matured in oak casks and the resulting Pinot Noir was so good — the best I have tasted in Alsace — that the experiment is to be continued.

The firm of Dopff au Moulin in Riquewihr owns 10 acres of the Eichberg, a Turckheim vineyard. It is largely planted with Gewürztraminer. The grapes, which are often picked late, usually give a full, soft and often almost sweet wine with a good amount of fruit and a long aftertaste. Occasionally I found this Gewürztraminer a little on the flat side, bouquet and taste seeming to lack depth and interesting nuances.

Charles Schleret works about 15 acres in Turckheim. He lives on the south bank of the Fecht and his up-to-date cellars have modern equipment (including a centrifuge and enamelled fermentation tanks). Schleret's wines are generally excellent. His Pinot Blanc can have a juicy, lively taste with sufficient freshness, a little terroir and an attractive fragrance.

Turckheim

The green valley of the Fecht links Colmar with Munster, and at the entrance to it lies Turckheim. Because of this strategic position, Turckheim was fortified at the beginning of the 14th century. Although they offered protection for the population, these defences repeatedly led to armed conflict, often with disastrous consequences, as is apparent from the fact that in 1648, at the end of the Thirty Years' War, only 18 families were left in Turckheim. The place lost most of its walls in 1673, but this did not prevent a great battle being fought there two years later. A force of 20,000 French troops under Henri de la Tour d'Auvergne, Viscount of Turenne, defeated an Imperial army of 60,000 men. Turenne is commemorated in Turckheim by an obelisk and a statue.

Night watchman

Despite so much warfare, including that of 1945, Turckheim has largely retained its character of a genuine old Alsace wine village. Three 14th-century gates give access to its centre, which is shaped like an elongated triangle defined by the Tour de France, complete with stork's nest, the Porte de Brand, near the vineyard of that name, and the Porte de Munster, through which eight condemned witches were led away to their deaths in 1572. Inside these gates there are many 16th- and 17th-century buildings, including a fine *hôtel de ville* and Maison des Bourgeois. Every evening in summer a night watchman goes the rounds at ten o'clock, clad in ancient costume, complete with lance and lantern. At every street corner he sings out a 'good night' and warns the citizenry to attend to their 'hearths and candles'. This tradition dates from 1540.

The dying dragon

Turckheim's best-known vineyard is the Brand. Someone once wrote; 'The Brand at Turckheim produces the king of Alsace wines.' According to legend, the vineyard got its name from a dragon, burned to death on this spot by the fierce heat of the sun. Its blood gave the soil supernatural potency. Certainly the Brand does usually produce firm, rounded wines. The vineyard originally covered only 8 acres, and in 1924 a number of surrounding vineyards were added, some of them even superior to the Brand. It now extends over 74 acres. Besides the original

MUSCAT D'ALSACE

Another delightful wine from Schleret is his Muscat. I found the 1979, for example, sound in all aspects and truly delicious, and it makes a good aperitif. About 40% of the 50,000 to 60,000 bottles Charles Schleret produces every year are Gewürztraminer, which also has a lot of character. Schleret's Tokay also merits mention. Then there is a very drinkable Riesling, and a Pinot Noir that distinctly tastes of its grape — which is by no means always the case.

VIN D'ALSACE

Domaine Zind-Humbrecht
GEWÜRZTRAMINER 1978
HERRENWEG TURCKHEIM

A lot of wine land in Turckheim is owned by people from Niedermorschwihr and Wintzenheim. The Domaine Zind-Humbrecht is in Wintzenheim and has 31 acres in Turckheim. The most important single grape variety here is the Gewürztraminer, planted in the Herrenweg, a flat vineyard with a lot of sand and gravel. The soil warms up quickly and sometimes the grapes ripen one or two weeks earlier than elsewhere in Alsace. A fruity, charming, early-mature wine, broad but not heavy in the mouth.

Turckheim

site, the following vineyards are covered by the Brand *appellation*: the Steinglitz, Kirchthal Schneckenberg and Weingarten, on the granite, and the Jesbal, on limestone. These vineyards rise steeply behind Turckheim, face south and are shielded by mountains from north and east winds. There is talk of including the Eichberg site in the Brand, particularly as the name occurs in other districts. The house of Dopff au Moulin, whose Gewürztraminer Eichberg is renowned, has protested strongly against this project. Turckheim, incidentally, used to grow mainly black grapes and today the village still produces one of the better Pinots Noirs of Alsace.

An up-to-date cooperative

Just west of the village is the Turckheim cooperative, nestling against a hillside. All but ten or so wine growers from the neighbourhood take their grapes there. The cooperative also has many members in other villages. An 18-year agreement has been concluded with the Soultz-Wuenheim cooperative, the Cave Vinicole du Vieil Armand, whereby its members, who cultivate a total of 198 acres, are also members of Turckheim, where all their wines are bottled. The total active membership of the Turckheim cooperative is 220 growers, who jointly account for about 544 acres. The enterprise, in operation since 1956, is modern and efficient in method, as can be seen from the push-button telephones and TV screens

in the office. The cellars have been built in three storeys, of which the top serves as the *vendangeoir* where the pressing is done. The must then descends by force of gravity to the *cuverie* for fermentation and storing. A few months later the wine descends another storey for bottling. The cooperative makes considerable use of stainless steel.

In many other cooperatives only about one-third of the production consists of superior wines, whereas in Turckheim these represent two-thirds of the total. The better wines made here are, in my opinion, of a strikingly good standard. They include Pinot Blanc, Klevner, Riesling, Tokay d'Alsace, Gewürztraminer, and Pinot Noir — many of which are good, others very good and some quite excellent.

Wintzenheim

Alsace

This village lies on the left bank of the Fecht, west of Colmar. On a hill high above the village are the ruins of the Hohlandsbourg, a 12th-century castle whose owners controlled large parts of Alsace. Wintzenheim itself lies on either side of a long street busy with traffic between Colmar and Munster. It preserves a few remains of 13th-century walls, a fountain of 1750 in the market square, an attractive council hall, and a fine half-timbered house in the Rue des Laboureurs. Wintzenheim is first mentioned in a document of 786, as Wingisheim; it is thought that wine-growing had by then already been practised here for centuries.

Virile wines from the Hengst

The wine-growing soils of Wintzenheim contain mainly limestone and sandstone. The biggest concentration of limestone is in the Hengst vineyard, the best site in the village. The name has been used at least since 1875, for a wine of that vintage appears on a menu of 1921. A distinction was formerly made between the higher part of the vineyard (the Oberhengst) and the lower (Unterhengst). This was quite reasonable as there was a difference in the soil, the upper section being mainly limestone, where the Gewürztraminer does best, the lower a mixture of limestone and clay, most suitable for the Riesling and Pinot-Auxerrois. Hengst comes from the Germanic word for stallion (it was *hengest* in Old English) and symbolizes the virile personality of its wines.

Jos. Meyer et Fils

In 1854 the grower Aloïse Meyer founded his own wine business at Wintzenheim. It passed from father to son and is nowadays called Jos. Meyer et Fils. The present owners are Hubert Meyer and his son Jean, who has had a thorough oenological education in Burgundy and who vinified his first Alsace wine in 1966. The Meyer family owns 30 acres of vineyard and also buys grapes, mainly from Wintzenheim and Turckheim growers. When the grapes come in they are colour coded for quality: green and red for 'very good', green for 'good', and white for the rest, which are destined for Edelzwicker. The wine ferments and rests in wooden casks, stainless-steel or enamelled tanks and glazed concrete vats. Characteristic of Jos. Meyer, with a production of 350,000 to 400,000 bottles a year, is the large number of different *cuvées* from which the customer can choose — six for the Riesling alone. In my experience the quality of the different wines is very variable. A number of those I have tried had an unpleasant sulphury element in scent and taste, whereas others possessed considerable class. My personal preferences are for Jos. Meyer's Pinot Les Lutins, the Pinot-Auxerrois Hengst, the Riesling Hengst and the Gewürztraminer Hengst; the Muscat from this firm — especially the Cuvée du Centenaire — can be excellent.

The firm of A. Gaschy exports about 90% of its wines to some 40 countries. The firm buys most of its grapes from others, and also wine, which it obviously selects carefully. One of the best wines in its collection is the Riesling from the Steingrubler, where Antoine Gaschy owns 2 acres. It usually has breeding and purity, with a gracious taste. I thought it much better than Gaschy's usual Riesling. F. Brucker is another Gaschy brand name.

The name Gaschy does not appear on the label of its Gewürztraminer Réserve Exceptionnelle Comtes de Martinsbourg. The grapes mainly come from the Pfersigberg in Eguisheim, where Gaschy owns just under 1½ acres. The Gewürztraminer 1976 was mild in character, full-flavoured with a luxurious bouquet, not in the very top class but still extremely good. A Riesling and a Tokay with the same label and practically the same quality are also offered.

Among the best of various Gewürztraminers produced by Wunsch & Mann are the Cuvée Steingrubler (soft, spicy, generously broad, full and yet not heavy) and the Cuvée Saint-Rémy (label illustrated). The latter is usually the more robust, but milder and heavier. The Tokay Cuvée de la Reine Clothilde is in the same category, a full-tasting wine that could even go with game. Wunsch & Mann has a large clientèle in Alsace and exports relatively little.

Freshness and finesse are decidedly not characteristic of Wunsch & Mann's wines; so I had some trouble with the Riesling. In contrast, the Edelzwicker Joie d'Alsace has more fullness than many wines of its type and often an agreeable, supple, almost juicy taste. In its category I also found the light-red Pinot Noir agreeable, rather full, supple, lively and sometimes almost mild. It is an amenable, light Burgundy, harmonious and of good quality. Les Fils de Joseph Mann is another brand name used.

In Wettolsheim they say that the Muscat from the Steingrubler vineyard is good for convalescents and elderly people. I can well imagine that with Victor Peluzzi's wine. This is strong, full and aromatic, a type of Muscat to drink in the evening after dinner or during a meal — I find it too heavy as an aperitif. Peluzzi owns about 7 acres in Wettolsheim, and half an acre in the Steingrubler.

Wettolsheim is one of the oldest centres of Christianity in Alsace — dating from the 4th century. The village is twinned with Fleurie in the Beaujolais.

In Wettolsheim over 40 families live exclusively from wine-growing; for about the same number it is a secondary activity.

The village has three music societies.

Wettolsheim

Alsace

It is possible that Wettolsheim was the cradle of wine-growing in Alsace. Vines were cultivated here in Roman times, and it has been suggested that viticulture spread throughout the region from this district. Excavations in the immediate neighbourhood of the village have provided certain clues; the remains of a Roman settlement were found here in 1874. The site was, in fact, so rich in finds that Wettolsheim was nicknamed 'the Pompeii of Alsace'. Furthermore, the place has a long religious history. One of the very earliest churches in Alsace was founded here in the 4th century. Wettolsheim also has an impressive facsimile of the grotto of Lourdes, 30 feet wide and 36 feet high, erected in 1911 at the behest of a citizen of Wettolsheim named Shoerer, who was archbishop of Lourdes between 1900 and 1924.

During World War II Wettolsheim lost a number of old houses through bombardment and in 1959 was compelled to dispose of the ruins of the Château de Martinsbourg. This castle, the scene of the romance between Vittorio Alfieri, the Italian poet, and the Countess of Albany, wife of Charles Edward Stuart, the Young Pretender, had fallen into such disrepair that the local council sold it to a developer, who built a housing estate on the site.

A variety of wines

The vineyards of Wettolsheim — after Ammerschwihr the biggest wine commune of Haut-Rhin — climb the slopes west of the village. They produce a varied range of wines. This is due not only to a dry microclimate and a sunny situation, but also to the subsoil, which varies in type, with a good deal of loess, limestone, sandstone, granite and other components. The best vineyard is the Steingrubler. Its Muscat and Riesling have a particularly good reputation. Wettolsheim's products are on display at the annual wine festival, celebrated on the last Sunday of July.

Two shippers

Wettolsheim has a few important wine houses. The largest of them is A. Gaschy, run by its owner, Antoine Gaschy. The firm is characterized by a quick turnover: it sells about 156,000 cases a year with a cellar capacity of only about one-quarter of that quantity. It owns 16 acres of vineyard in Wettolsheim and Eguisheim. The firm's best wines are sold as Réserve Exceptionelle Comtes de Martinsbourg, but the Riesling Steingrubler with the ordinary Gaschy label is usually also a very successful wine.

Smaller in scale — about half the size of Gaschy — is the firm of Wunsch & Mann. Established in 1948, this family concern is headed by Joseph Mann and his sons Jacques and Jean-Louis. They process grapes from their own 35 acres, and from 150 to 200 acres cultivated by other growers. In general the Wunsch & Mann wines are big and powerful — and therefore sometimes a little wearing. The wines that tasted best to me were those that benefit from strength, such as the Gewürztraminer, Tokay and Pinot Noir.

The Eguisheim cooperative uses large wooden casks for its best wines, and also for the Riesling Cuvée des Seigneurs, of its type a fairly firm but still elegant wine that is fresh without too much acid and with a pleasant bouquet. Not of exceptional depth or refinement, it is still an extremely enjoyable Riesling, and compared with other special cuvées the price is very reasonable. The cooperative exports about a fifth of its production, mainly to Belgium.

The 220 or so members of the Cave Vinicole Eguisheim (not including 90 from Dambach-la-Ville) supply a lot of Gewürztraminer from Eguisheim itself. The best grapes — mainly from the Pfersigberg — are used for the Gewürztraminer Cuvée St Léon. The wine has a sultry bouquet, but the taste is not sweet, and the quality is good. The Muscat Cuvée de la Comtesse (made almost entirely from the Muscat) and the Tokay Cuvée du Schlossherr are also worthy of mention.

About 25 years ago the ever publicity-conscious Léon Beyer organized a competition for the best oyster opener. This event now takes place annually under the auspices of the Club Prosper Montagné and others. The Riesling Cuvée des Écaillers is an adjunct of this event, a fresh type of Riesling (often with a lot of fruit and some subtlety) that tastes wonderful with seafood. The Riesling Cuvée Particulière is somewhat fuller and needs to age a little longer.

At Léon Beyer the Tokay d'Alsace never lacks alcohol. The Réserve quality (better than the ordinary) always has 13°. I have followed this wine in various years and never found it disappointing. It usually has a mild but sinewy, generous taste. The 1976 vendange tardive was a wonderful experience; a 14.5° wine with a captivating bouquet with traces of wood, honey and cream sherry.

Léon and Marc Beyer sell their best Gewürztraminer under the slightly flashy label of Cuvée des Comtes d'Eguisheim. It is a broad, full, substantial wine with a mild tone in the taste. It is usually only sold three to four years after vintage. Even more special is the Gewürztraminer vendange tardive. I was privileged to drink the 1971 — a luxurious, unique wine with an improbably long aftertaste. It had fermented for almost a year, in some miraculous way attaining 15.9° alcohol.

Grower Antoine Stoffel lives in a modern quarter just outside Eguisheim, towards the hills. He works about 15 acres mainly in his own commune. During the presentation of Eguisheim's new wines in March 1980, four of Antoine's products, the Riesling, Tokay, Muscat and Pinot Noir won awards. Of these I personally preferred the Muscat: a wine with an elegant bouquet and taste, and very pure.

Eguisheim

Eguisheim is on my itinerary whenever I visit Alsace. This is because of its splendid *remparts*, the concentric rings of the old defences around the village centre. These are no ordinary ramparts, however, but fine old houses, the most beautiful of which line a long, narrow street. All are occupied and lovingly tended, their balconies and windows ablaze with spring and summer flowers. The backs of these charming houses reveal the austere, stout walls which clearly at one time had a defensive function. To walk for an hour or so around Eguisheim is go back three or four centuries in time. Fortunately, Eguisheim does not yet attract as many tourists as Riquewihr. Though crammed with visitors, most get no further than the local cooperative or the village square, so that it is usually possible to enjoy the real beauties of the village in peace and quiet. Long may it remain so.

Birthplace of a pope

Eguisheim is first mentioned in the annals in AD 720, but people lived here much earlier. The remains of *Homo eguisheimiensis*, one of our distant ancestors who lived tens of thousands of years ago, were found here in 1865. The most prosperous period was probably under the rule of the Counts of Eguisheim. The first Count, Eberhard, built the castle around which the village grew up, and also three tall towers. Only the octagonal wall of the original castle remains; the buildings inside were completely restored in the 19th century. The three towers are in a fairly ruinous state, although one of them can be climbed. The castle of Eguisheim was the birthplace, in 1002, of Bruno, son of Count Hugon IV of Eguisheim and Countess Heilwige of Dabo. He was the first and only man of Alsace to become pope, as Leo IX (1048-54). His statue stands above a fountain near the castle. The dynasty of the Counts of Eguisheim disappeared in 1189, and that of the Dabo family in 1225. Eguisheim then passed into the possession of the archbishopric of Strasbourg, which fortified the village in 1257. Soon afterwards,

it successfully withstood a siege by the German emperor. In the 15th century it was ravaged by the Armagnacs. When the village was rebuilt, it received its present form: three concentric rings of houses around a small nucleus.

Limestone subsoil

The wines of Eguisheim have enjoyed a good reputation for centuries, and were exported to England and the Netherlands at an early date. The Gewürztraminer is excellent here — mainly because of the limestone, on which this variety thrives and grows so well. The most famous vineyards are the Pfersigberg and Eichberg. The sheltered situation of the slopes, together with the dry microclimate, also contribute to the quality. On the last Sunday of March, the village of Eguisheim — led by its mayor Léon Beyer, whose father and grandfather held the same office —

presents the wines of its latest vintage to press and public. A jury gives awards to the four best wines from each grape variety. Predictably, wine also flows freely during the *fête des vignerons* on the last Sunday of August.

Largest cooperative in Alsace

The Eguisheim cooperative draws its grapes from an area of 740 acres in Eguisheim itself, Wettolsheim, Herrlisheim, Hattstatt, Voegtlinshoffen, Husseren-les-Châteaux, Obermorschwihr, Orschwihr, Bergholtz and Bergholtz-Zell. In addition, it bottles all the wine from the Dambach-la-Ville cooperative, whose members cultivate a total of 370 acres. Eguisheim likewise sells most of the Dambach wine, and with a total output of four to five million bottles a year this cooperative is the largest in Alsace. Collaboration with Dambach-la-Ville started

The house and cellars of Joseph Freudenreich are in the centre of Eguisheim, almost opposite the restored castle. The buildings face a lovely courtyard. Immediately to the right of the entrance is where Joseph Freudenreich (who is assisted by his son Marc) usually receives his visitors. Across the courtyard can be heard the grunting of pigs. The Freudenreich estate covers 17-20 acres; its best wine is the Gewürztraminer Cuvée Exceptionnelle, a fragrant, strong wine with a long aftertaste.

Vineyard acreage
Eguisheim: 630

The best local restaurant is the Caveau d'Eguisheim, set up by the Société au Propagande pour les Vins d'Eguisheim at the instigation of Léon Beyer. The participants have the right to have up to ten of their wines on the wine list. The sauerkraut here is famous.

About 40% of Eguisheim's 1,500 inhabitants live mainly from wine-growing.

Eguisheim is twinned with the village of Hautvillers in Champagne.

In local dialect, Eguisheim is called Exa.

*Opposite page, below:
The Eguisheim cooperative. Besides wine, it produces more Marc de Gewürztraminer than anyone else.*

*Opposite page, bottom:
Léon Beyer and his son Marc of the firm of Léon Beyer.*

*Right:
The castle of Eguisheim illuminated; on the right, in front of the fountain, is the statue of Pope Leo IX.*

*Below left:
The narrow, flower-decked remparts of Eguisheim. The houses are on the right, the barns on the left.*

*Below right:
Wooden figure showing the opening times of the cooperative.*

Eguisheim

at a time when Eguisheim found itself short of Sylvaner and Riesling, wines produced in great abundance around Dambach. Although the *cave coopérative* of Eguisheim was founded in 1902, it remained somewhat in the doldrums until 1952, when its rapid expansion began. It carries a range of three quality categories: wine with no awards, wine with awards (medals at Paris, Mâcon and other shows), and the Cuvées (Riesling Cuvée des Seigneurs for example). Tastings of the first two have failed to produce much to my liking. The wines in question were at best correctly made and generally flat and characterless. In the Cuvée category, however, I found some interesting items, particularly among the Riesling, Gewürztraminer, Muscat and Tokay. The Eguisheim cooperative trades under various brand names, including Pierre Meierheim, Pierre Rotgold and Wolfberger. The last is also the brand name of its sparkling wines, including an attractive Crémant d'Alsace made from Riesling (see page 90), as well as

that of the cooperative's own distillates (in 1979 it took over Cointreau's Jacobert distillery), and its tinned *pâté de foie gras.*

Léon and Marc Beyer

The wine firm of Léon Beyer is nowadays accommodated in a former roadside hostelry at the entrance to the village. It sells its wine in France mainly to good restaurants, and abroad to quality-conscious importers. The Beyer family has been active in wine-growing since 1580 and became *négociants* in 1867. The firm has 37 acres of its own land, in Eguisheim only, which provides almost one-third of its grapes, and sells a total of about 800,000 bottles annually. Léon Beyer, his son Marc and their cellar master work on very traditional lines, but with modern equipment. The house has no laboratory: everything is tested by sampling and tasting. The Beyer range usually comprises some 25 different kinds of wine,

including four types of Riesling. I do not find all these wines equally appealing; even in the case of the really good kinds, the bouquet is not always convincing, and in taste, firmness sometimes seems to triumph over finesse. Nevertheless, Léon Beyer is one of the better houses and I can safely recommend its Riesling Cuvée des Ecaillers, Riesling Cuvée Particulière, Tokay Réserve, Tokay *vendange tardive*, and all the Gewürztraminers.

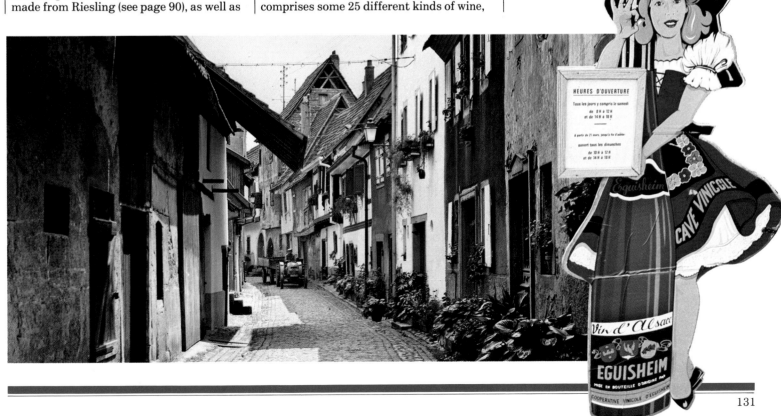

In 1979, at a blind tasting in the Netherlands of 31 Rieslings, the winner was the 1977 from Kuentz-Bas. This firm's Rieslings always have a great deal of elegance. They are fresh, possess breeding, and are typically Riesling — particularly the Cuvée Réservée and Réserve Personnelle qualities. The latter especially is a beauty, very fine and distinguished. Both Rieslings have an almost pale colour. They ferment and mature in casks; glazed concrete is for the simpler wines.

I have never yet tasted a bad wine from Kuentz-Bas. With this firm even a simple Pinot Blanc is of sound quality. I also have pleasant memories of the Muscat Cuvée Réservée, the Tokay Réserve Personnelle, the Pinot Noir Réserve Personnelle and the Gewürztraminer Réserve Personnelle. The last-named really is a wine to accompany a meal, usually fresh enough to serve with dinner, i.e. not too sweet, sultry or heavy.

Vineyard acreage
Husseren-les-Châteaux: 316

Right:
Some of the wine slopes are still tilled by horses.

Below left:
This sign stands at the entrance to the village and refers to the festival of the guinguettes. Husseren's coat-of-arms includes the three towers and a bunch of grapes. Grapes for wine have been grown here since 1648.

Below right:
Jean-Michel Bas from the firm Kuentz-Bas. The Bas family originated in Burgundy, the Kuentz's came from Switzerland.

In Roman times Husseren was an observation post. The village was destroyed many times — by the English, the Armagnacs and the Swedes, among others.

Husseren-les-Châteaux
Alsace

Set 560 feet above Eguisheim, this is the highest wine village in Alsace. The vines here are planted up to a height of 1,250 feet above sea level (1,300 feet is normally the absolute upper limit). For hundreds of years Husseren belonged to Eguisheim and today it still forms an enclave within the latter's boundaries. When it gained its independence in the 14th century, the owners of Eguisheim provided it with just enough land on which to make a living, which hardly guaranteed the inhabitants a prosperous future. Prior to that time, there were more distillers than wine growers: more could be earned from the fruits of the neighbouring woods than from those of the vineyard, and the villagers were long nicknamed *Les Bonbonnes* after the large bottles in which the spirits were kept.

Folklore weekend

Nowadays Husseren-les-Châteaux is genuinely a wine village; the majority of its hundred or so families are in some way connected with wine. The terrain here is excellently suited to growing grapes. The slopes face south and the subsoil contains both limestone and clay. The local wines are usually very lively and fresh.
One of the best times to visit Husseren is the weekend after 14 July. This is when the Fête des Guinguettes d'Europe is held, with French, German and Italian food and drink stalls, and performances by international dance and song groups. The village church with its 12th-century font is well worth a visit, and it is only five minutes' drive to the towers of Eguisheim; when they were being built the village provided labour. Husseren derives the second part of its name from these 'châteaux', adding it in 1919 to avoid confusion with another Husseren near Thann. Strictly speaking, although they are always referred to as *les trois tours d'Eguisheim* (see page 130), two of the towers actually belong to Husseren.

Kuentz-Bas: superb Rieslings

After his marriage to a girl surnamed Kuentz, André Bas set up his own wine business in Husseren in 1919. It still flourishes today, and is run by Jean-Michel Bas and his nephew André Weber ('best wine taster in Alsace' in 1970), with the assistance of Jean-Michel's son Hubert. The firm's wines are generally discreet and elegant, with a distinctly fresh character. I find the Kuentz-Bas Rieslings superb; indeed, you could hardly discover better ones in the whole of Alsace. The Pinot Blanc, Muscat, Tokay, Gewürztraminer and Pinot Noir also merit commendation. The house offers three qualities: Cuvée Tradition (the simplest, made up from bought wines), Cuvée Réservée (from grapes vinified by the firm), and Cuvée Personnelle (from grapes grown on the firm's own 30 acres).

Muscat is Voegtlinshoffen's speciality. It is therefore one of the best wines of Théo Cattin & Fils. The wine is made almost exclusively from the Muscat Ottonel, which is so sensitive that normally only one in three harvests succeeds. However, when this Muscat is produced, it is a delight: rich in fruit and freshness and absolutely pure — a perfect aperitif. It also usually keeps its fraîcheur for up to five years.

The Gewürztraminer Cuvée de l'Ours Noir is one of Théo Cattin's better wines: fairly well-defined, mild, slightly sultry. The Riesling Cuvée de L'Ours Noir is also usually quite pleasant, as is the Pinot Noir. I also found the Edelzwicker Ecume des Mers very pleasant in its simplicity. The ours noir (black bear) on the labels illustrated is part of the family coat-of-arms. The animal's paws are cut off: a Cattin supposedly protected the local lord against a bear.

The Stempfel family came from Württemberg, established itself in Obermorschwihr about 1650, and over the years became more and more involved in wine-growing. The X. Stempfel & Fils estate covers about 20 acres, 36% planted with Gewürztraminer, 28% with Riesling, 12% with Pinot Noir, 6% with Pinot Gris, 6% with Pinot Blanc, 5% with Muscat and 7% with other varieties. It is managed by the brothers François and Ulric Stempfel. I find the Riesling one of their best wines; subtle in taste with a touch of terroir.

Vineyard acreages
Voegtlinshoffen: 314
Obermorschwihr: 232
Herrlisheim: 104
Hattstatt: 188
Gueberschwihr: 430

Right:
Little grape lover on a fountain in Voegtlinshoffen.

Below left:
Giant bottles flanking a gate in Voegtlinshoffen. The one on the right depicts the local speciality, Muscat.

Below right:
Marcel Cattin (of Théo Cattin & Fils) with his family coat-of-arms.

The most famous vineyard in Voegtlinshoffen is the Hatschburg, part of it to the south of the village. The Hagelberg also has a good reputation.

Frankish sarcophagi were found in a wall near the church in Gueberschwihr.

In and around Voegtlinshoffen

Alsace

It is not far along the *route du vin* from Husseren-les-Châteaux to Voegtlinshoffen. For decades this village was at the end of a no-through road, which was not exactly a help in getting the place or its wines known. For centuries it was a poor village. The population was mainly employed in the neighbouring stone quarries and little income was derived from wine-growing. In fact the villagers did not acquire their own land until 1887. Nowadays, the tide has turned. About 315 acres of vines are cultivated, on clay soil that retains its moisture well in periods of drought, and the road runs right through to Gueberschwihr. The centre of the village has remained small and charming; the 12th-century church is worth visiting for its altars alone.

Théo Cattin et Fils

Repopulation of Alsace began in 1648, immediately after the Thirty Years' War. The newcomers were from Switzerland, and this is how the Cattin family arrived in Voegtlinshoffen. Their descendants are still wine shippers here: Théo Cattin et Fils. The management consists of Marcel Cattin and his son Jean-Bernard. The firm's own 44 acres provide sufficient grapes for about half the production (half a million bottles a year). The rest are bought from growers. Glazed concrete *cuves* are used exclusively for fermentation and maturing of the wine. Cattin et Fils generally makes supple, soft wines with sufficient strength but modest depth and refinement. The best qualities are sold as Cuvée de l'Ours Noir.

Old villages

Just east of Voegtlinshoffen is the village of Obermorschwihr, with its very unusual half-timbered tower and a golden statue of the Virgin over the village fountain. Wine-growing here dates from the 7th century AD. Farther into the plain is Herrlisheim, once a powerful centre, complete with walls and castle. In 1677, however, it completely burned down. All that remains of the earlier village is the ruin of the 'Witches' Tower', parts of the wall and a 15th-century belfry. Hattstatt too was at one period a place of some importance, as suggested by its sizeable *hôtel de ville*. It, too, was fortified with ramparts and a castle. In the very old church (first half of the 11th century) there is a symbolic mural with a vine. To the southwest is Gueberschwihr, recorded in 728 as Vila Eberhardo. Formerly it boasted no fewer than three castles, now all vanished. What does remain is the magnificent Romanesque tower of the church, a three-storey structure with windows on all sides. The church itself was built some seven centuries later. In front of it is a spacious square with shady trees, surrounded by old houses, a *caveau* and the signboards of various wine firms. Many of the local growers take their grapes to the Pfaffenheim cooperative.

Vineyard acreages
Pfaffenheim: 680
Rouffach: 403
Gundolsheim: 77

Rouffach has an agricultural and viticultural school with 30 acres of wine land.

Pfaffenheim, with Marlenheim, was the first village in Alsace to set up a walk through the vineyard area, a sentier viticole. Dambach-la-Ville also has one now.

Below:
Notches in the wall of Pfaffenheim church. These were made by growers who used to drive the Devil out of their pruning hooks every morning by striking them against the wall.

Bottom:
Pfaffenheim church with its 13th-century chancel.

Rouffach's name, first recorded in 770, derives from Rubeaquum, 'red water'.

Pfaffenheims Schneckenberg ('snails' hill') has long been known for its good Pinot Blanc. This wine is one of the specialities of the local cooperative. It is a mild, agreeable wine that should be drunk young. The cooperative's Gewürztraminer Bergweingarten is also very pleasant (aromatic, mild, pure but rather flat), like the best quality Riesling it offers. About 120 of the 190 members are from Pfaffenheim, the rest mainly from Gueberschwihr.

Joseph Rieflé is established in an old residence opposite the hôtel de ville. The owners are the brothers René and André Rieflé, and their estate covers 37 acres, including some land in Rouffach and Westhalten. I found their wines to be easy, uncomplicated, of a decent average quality. I have a slight preference for the Tokay, immediately followed by the Riesling.

The terraced vineyard Clos Saint-Landelin dates from the 8th century. It has been owned by the Muré family since 1926. There are still some very old vines in places. The vineyard has a low yield and produces very outstanding wines. To my taste the best is the Gewürztraminer, often mild and full of character. I have also drunk good bottles of Muscat and Pinot Noir. I have had more trouble with the Riesling (sometimes very clean and acidic in tone, sometimes with a very distinctive bouquet), just as with the Tokay.

The luxury hotel Château d'Isenbourg crowns a hill above Rouffach. It was built on the foundations of a bishop's residence in the last century. In front of the château there is a 14-acre vineyard owned by the SYNVA (see page 124), which sends the grapes to Dopff & Irion for pressing and vinification. The latter firm sells half the wines under an identical label. The quality is decent but not entirely convincing. I rate the Riesling and the Muscat among the better types.

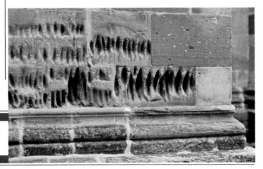

Pfaffenheim and Rouffach

Alsace

The busy Route Nationale 83 skirts Pfaffenheim, a small, ancient wine village where Frankish burial places have been found. With its many old houses, it has a very peaceful air. When I visited it on an April Saturday afternoon, all you could hear was the chink of bottles. Behind the high wooden doors and thick walls the villagers were busy bottling wine from the latest vintage.

Pfaffenheim, which until the French Revolution was governed from Rouffach, once had three castles. Nowadays, its most interesting building is the church, which lost the spire on its Romanesque tower in World War II. In one of the outer walls of the church you can see a number of deep notches. These were made by wine growers who observed the custom of 'beating the Devil' out of their pruning knives

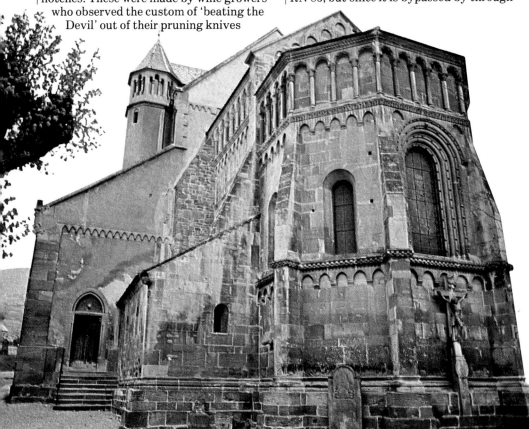

and other implements every morning. On the outskirts of Pfaffenheim, near the motorway, is the Cave Vinicole de Pfaffenheim, Gueberschwihr et Environs. This cooperative has about 160 members who cultivate a total 445 acres. The wines from this enterprise are pleasant, correctly made and intended for drinking quickly. I feel they rather lack depth and refinement. My three favourites, which often win awards, are the Pinot Blanc Schneckenberg, the Gewürztraminer Bergweingarten and the Riesling.

Avenging women

Rouffach is only a few minutes' drive via the RN 83, but since it is bypassed by through

traffic, it does not get many visitors. Yet Rouffach has a lot to offer. Around the Place de la République there is a church that looks more like a cathedral (late 11th century, altered in the 13th, 14th and 19th centuries), a fine corn exchange with stepped gable (late 15th or early 16th century) a beautiful hôtel de ville (16th century) and parts of the old walls, including a 'Witches' Tower' (13th and 15th centuries). All this indicates that Rouffach was formerly a place of some significance; and indeed it was once the seat of the archbishops who then controlled the Haut-Rhin.

The women of Rouffach gave early proof of their independent spirit on Easter Day, 1106, when the emperor Henry V had a beautiful girl abducted as she came out of church. The women immediately grabbed weapons from their menfolk (who apparently stood around not daring to do anything) and attacked the monarch, who made off in such haste that he left behind his crown, sceptre and cloak. In memory of that episode the women of Rouffach have since been allotted pride of place at all local official ceremonies. On the south side of the little town an enormous 13th-century press marks the premises of Armand & Oscar Muré. This firm is run by two young people, René Muré and his sister Marie-Thérèse. Muré-Ehrhardt is the brand name used for the ordinary qualities and Muré for the better wines, which together represent 500,000 bottles a year. The firm also has 42 acres of its own land, including the 37 acres of the Clos Saint-Landelin (approximately 100,000 bottles annually). This terraced vineyard lies towards Westhalten, on limestone. One-third, the lowest part, is planted with Riesling; above this comes another third planted with Gewürztraminer; the remaining third, mainly on the plateau, is planted with other varieties. The wines of the Clos Saint-Landelin should not normally be drunk until three years after the vintage. Despite the care which René and Marie-Thérèse take with their wines, not all of these appeal to me, because of their often strange bouquet. My first choice is the Gewürztraminer.

Vineyard acreages
Westhalten: 586
Soultzmatt: 507
Osenbach: 54

An expressive fruity bouquet and a pure, similarly fruity taste often typify the Muscat Cuvée Réservée from the cooperative in Westhalten. It is usually made from 70% Muscat Ottonel and 30% Muscat d'Alsace. The cooperative has had the latter variety planted to give the wine a little more fruit. The Pinot Blanc from the Strangenberg is agreeable, mild and very supple, and the Pinot Noir Cuvée Réservée is a very pleasant example of its type.

The Zinnkoepflé ('Sun Head') in Westhalten gives a good, surprisingly soft Sylvaner. This is due to the chalky soil which stores the warmth of the sun. The Westhalten cooperative produces a good example of this wine. However, I think the Gewürztraminer from the same vineyard is qualitatively even better, a mildly fresh, quite elegant wine, not too heavy or clinging, with a bouquet of roses and violets. The cooperative exports about a quarter of its production.

The firm of Heim owns about 2½ acres in the Strangenberg, all planted with Pinot Blanc. The resultant wine has a lively, very delicious and absolutely pure taste, and is excellent of its type. Alfred Heim did not set up under his name until after World War II. The firm originated with his wife's family and was first called Koehler. This remains as a brand name, along with Anne d'Alsace and Alsace Meyer.

The Riesling Les Eglantiers also comes from land owned by the firm of Heim. This wine has a soft, refined bouquet; the taste is rather mouth-filling but still graceful and fresh without being aggressive. The Muscat Cuvée Spéciale also affords much delight for the senses with its intense bouquet, sufficiently full and fresh in tone. The Tokay d'Alsace is also usually very good with sometimes a hint of smokiness in its perfume and a pure, not too pronounced taste.

Heim's technical director Marc Hagen considers the firm's Zinnkoepflé wines to be its best, particularly the Gewürztraminer. This I can well believe: the 1976 I drank about four years after vintage had a really excellent taste; not languid, sultry and rather wearing, like Gewürztraminers, but still having sufficient breadth and spiciness. A. Heim exports about a quarter of its production.

Below:
Members of Westhalten's cooperative queue to deliver their grapes.

Westhalten holds its Fête du Strangenberg in June with dancing, music, food — and wine.

The firm of Heim washes the returned empty bottles of a great many growers in Alsace.

Soultzmatt, near Westhalten, supplies mineral water as well as wine. The name means roughly 'salt-water meadow'. The Fête de la Truite takes place each year at the bottom of the Zinnkoepflé.

Westhalten

Until the French Revolution, the eastern part of Westhalten belonged to Rouffach and the western part to Soultzmatt. It finally gained independence in 1818. The village, with its 750 inhabitants, lies in a valley enclosed on one side by the vine-clad Strangenberg and Zinnkoepflé, both about 1,300 feet high, and on the other by the 1,180-foot Bollenberg. The vineyards are mainly on limestone and rainfall is sometimes lower even than at Colmar. This undoubtedly explains the local abundance of Mediterranean flora: botanists have discovered no fewer than 550 plants common to southern France, and consequently the slopes of the Zinnkoepflé have been designated a protected area. These slopes produce a superior Sylvaner and Gewürztraminer, and the Tokay can also be very good. The Strangenberg enjoys a reputation for its Pinot Blanc and Pinot Noir; and the Bollenberg's Muscat and Gewürztraminer are usually very successful. Westhalten itself is a picturesque village with old houses, narrow streets, two ancient fountains and a dungeon where drunks were once put to sober up.

A well-equipped cooperative

Just outside Westhalten, towards Soultzmatt, are the white buildings of the local cooperative. This was set up in 1955 by growers from Westhalten, Soultzmatt, Rouffach, Gundolsheim and Soultz. At that time their wines were selling so badly that many grapes were being left unvinified. Today these problems are past. The cooperative sells about 2.5 to 3 million bottles a year and is excellently equipped (ultra-low temperature treatment, membrane filters and so on). It receives the grapes from about 620 acres belonging to some 170 members. Good value for money is offered by the cooperative's Sylvaner Zinnkoepflé, Gewürztraminer Zinnkoepflé, Muscat Cuvée Réservée and Pinot Blanc Strangenberg. The Cave Vinicole de Westhalten, Soultzmatt, Rouffach et Environs, to give it its official name, also produces Crémant d'Alsace (see page 90). Brand names are Vieilles Caves de Cigogne and Mittnacht.

Quality from Heim

Westhalten is also the headquarters of Alfred Heim, a particularly attractive firm which generally produces flawless quality. The old, modest entrance to the premises in the centre of the village gives little hint of the extensive cellars behind the offices and reception area, from where 2 million bottles a year are despatched. Except for the ordinary (litre) qualities, Heim buys grapes from 170 small growers. There is strict control over selection and quality, and subsequently of the wines. Marc Hagen, one of the best oenologists in Alsace, handles the technical side of the business; and he has introduced membrane filters, which give better results than the conventional type, both to Heim and to the Westhalten cooperative. Of Heim's clean, fresh yet supple range of wines, I would recommend the Pinot Blanc Clos du Strangenberg, the Riesling Les Eglantiers (both from the 12 acres of the firm's own land), the Gewürztraminer Zinnkoepflé and the Réserve quality of the Muscat and Tokay.

Lucien Albrecht, with 49 acres of vineyard, is the largest grower in Orschwihr. His ancestors have been growing vines here since 1770. Lucien — assisted by his son Jean — produces 200,000 to 250,000 bottles a year, including his own Crémant d'Alsace (see page 90). I think one of the best wines is the Riesling from the Clos Himmelreich (4 acres) on the Pfingstberg: a balanced, lively, fresh wine with a nice suppleness — in short, delicious.

'In Orschwihr we have to make quality wines because we cannot sell to passing travellers, as they do in Riquewihr. People have to make special journeys to get to us,' says Lucien Albrecht, who works on this principle himself. His wines are made with a great deal of feeling for quality — as, for instance, the eminent Gewürztraminer Cuvée Martine (named after the daughter of the house), a pure wine with fruit, spices, softness and a spirited but not too heady taste. The Albrecht wines have a smooth balance.

Paul Reinhart is not only mayor of Orschwihr but has served as chairman of the Comité Interprofessionnel du Vin d'Alsace several times. He also works an 11-acre estate with his son Pierre. His Riesling comes from some 7 acres on the Bollenberg. The wine has a distinctive bouquet in which the coolness of the limestone can be detected. It is a type of Riesling that ages well and has really good quality.

Not every grower has a soil analysis carried out to determine which grape variety to plant where, but Paul Reinhart does. His Gewürztraminer comes mainly from loess soil on the Pfingstberg. The Cuvée Spéciale is usually notable for its pure bouquet and soft, excellent taste. This balanced wine is fresh and light enough to be served at table with the entrée or the main meal. I also found Reinhart's Klevner-Pinot a delicious wine; the Pinot Noir tasted fresh and spicy.

Martin Hartmann lives and works where once th castle of Orschwihr stood, cultivating about 15 acres. This is mainly in Orschwihr, but with some land in Rouffach and Westhalten. Martin Hartmann's wines are not memorable for outstanding quality, but they are orindarily good — particularly the Bewürztraminer. The old castle cellars contain mainly wooden casks.

Vineyard acreages
Orschwihr: 610
Bergholtz-Zell: 114
Bergholtz: 136

Below left:
Paul Reinhart, mayor of Orschwihr, was several times Chairman of the Comité Interprofessionnel du Vin d'Alsace.

Below right:
Pickers' lunch on a wine slope above Orschwihr.

The village was first mentioned as Otaleswilre in 728. The name became successively Alswilre, Orsweiler, Ohrschweier, and finally Orschwihr.

Many of the houses in Orschwihr were built with stone from the castle, destroyed in 1375.

Orschwihr

Alsace

'The master of the Maison des Trois Rois at Soultz must deliver to the Archbishop of Strasbourg each year two horses and a man to bring the wine from the Lippelsberg to Saverne.' These words appear in a document of 1578, indicating that Orschwihr wine was already quite famous in those days. The Lippelsberg, one of the first Alsace vineyards to have a name specifically associated with a particular wine, still exists. The village of Orschwihr also owns the sunniest part of the Bollenberg, the large hill that separates it from Westhalten. The soil is calciferous, and in addition to vines there are orchids and other rare plants here. One of the earliest churches of the district formerly stood on the Bollenberg and even attracted worshippers from Rouffach and Pfaffenheim. Today there is only a small chapel on this hill. According to local legend, witches used to gather on the Bollenberg for their macabre feasts. To drive away evil spirits before the vintage a 'witches' fire' (haxifir in the dialect) is still set up on a 50-foot stake in Orschwihr in mid-August. Two other well-known vineyards are the Pfingstberg and Affenberg.

A Gewürztraminer of renown

The village of Orchwihr was in existence before 728, when it was donated to the abbey of Murbach by Duke Eberhard of Eguisheim. The people have always been principally involved with wine-making. The population reached a peak of 1,350 in 1850, but then declined steadily for various reasons, including a high rate of infant mortality, the destruction of the vines by Phylloxera, and competition from industry and mining. Orschwihr now has about 820 inhabitants, most of whom make a living from wine, as testified by the signboards, paintings on gables, nameplates, shops and tasting rooms. The Gewürztraminer has long been a local speciality, attracting trade from far and wide. The Orschwihr Riesling can also be excellent.

A neat, friendly village

Although Orschwihr has little to offer the visitor — not even the half-timbered houses so prevalent elsewhere — it makes a neat and friendly impression. Atmosphere is provided by the Place Saint-Nicolas, where the local caveau is situated. Near the centre of the village there was once a castle, the Wasserschloss, but it was largely destroyed by fires in 1722 and 1934. Only the cellars and the bridge over the now dry moat remain. Leo IX, the Alsatian pope, lived here in the 11th century. He consecrated the church of the neighbouring wine village of Bergholtz-Zell. Southeast of Bergholtz-Zell is Bergholtz, where missionary monks from Ireland established themselves in the 8th century.

Usually I find the Schlumberger wines rather wishy-washy in character. They do not generally have much personality, or refinement. Many of the wines I tasted were correct, but also rather bland. They lacked 'bite', which is disconcerting in a wine like a Riesling. The Kitterlé Riesling from the vineyard of the same name was a happy exception. The wine also had refinement, although not to excess, and a rather rich, freshly soft bouquet and taste.

Schlumberger produces a Gewürztraminer Cuvée Christine Schlumberger usually only once every three years. In colour, bouquet and taste, the 1976 was just like a light type of Sauternes: golden yellow in colour, of a mildly sweet opulence. Another good Gewürztraminer is sold as Kitterlé Traminer: velvety and extremely agreeable. The Gewürztraminer Réserve is simpler but still acceptable. Two other pleasant wines are the Pinot Gris (from many old vines) and the Pinot Blanc.

Vineyard acreage
Guebwiller: 304

Because of its abundant flora, the valley to which Guebwiller forms the entrance was named Florival by a poetic monk in 1041. There is a Florival museum in Guebwiller devoted to crafts, in the church of Notre Dame.

The Schlumberger vineyards have 34 miles of terrace walls and 435 miles of vines.

Besides the name Knipperlé — part of the Schlumberger vineyard — the rather similar Kitterlé also occurs. This is now a vineyard (57 acres), but there also used to be a grape variety with this name.

Right:
Harvest in Guebwiller's terraced vineyards. The grapes are being simultaneously de-stalked and bruised by this small grower. This will not improve the quality of the wine because of too much oxidization of the juice.

Below:
The mile-long main street in Guebwiller with the hôtel de ville on the left. This Gothic building with its conspicuous bow window dates from 1514.

Guebwiller wines were called 'leg breakers' because of their potency.

Guebwiller

Alsace

It is highly probable that Guebwiller began as a Roman settlement, complete with its own vineyards. The village is mentioned for the first time in 774, as Gebunvilare. For centuries it belonged to the powerful abbey of Murbach, which provided fortifications. On the night of 14 February 1445, a valiant lady, Brigitte Schick mounted the walls to repulse single-handed a group of soldiers besieging the village. The ladders abandoned by the attackers all those years ago hang in the Saint-Léger church, where a special service is held annually on this day to commemorate the event. Guebwiller has two other churches, a fine Gothic *hôtel de ville* (1514), some old fountains and wells, and the Parc de la Marseillaise with its many attractive trees and flowers. The west side of Guebwiller is lined with factories, all bearing the name of Schlumberger, which, among other things, make machinery for the textile industry. Schlumberger employs nearly one-fifth of Guebwiller's population (about

11,000) and also owns practically all the local vineyard area.

Largest wine estate in Alsace

The Schlumberger family is of Austrian origin. Nicolas Schlumberger began his wine-growing and industrial activities here in 1810. Throughout the 19th century the Schlumberger vineyard remained modest in size, but grew in 1910, when Ernest Schlumberger bought up many plots that had been abandoned because of *Phylloxera*. Today the Schlumberger estate, with about 310 acres, is the biggest in Alsace. About two-thirds of the land lies on an oblong hill that dominates the whole northern side of Guebwiller. Because of the steepness of the slope, the vines are planted in terraces. The total length of the terrace walls is 34 miles. This hill consists mainly of pink sandstone, with some limestone in the lower parts. There is hardly any clay. Gewürztraminer

and Riesling, each with 30% of the area, dominate the vineyard. The Gewürztraminer and Riesling from the Kitterlé plot (37 acres at the southernmost point) are particularly well regarded. On the Schlumberger estate the vintage usually lasts up to five weeks and thus ends late. As Eric Beydon remarked: 'We have a *vendange tardive* practically every year.' As a rule, the wines are left to mature for 12 to 18 months in the *cuves* before bottling. This is done firstly in order to improve the quality of the wines, and secondly to avoid problems of supply in lean years. Besides the Schlumberger estate (about 600,000 bottles a year), there is a Schlumberger wine house that sells about 125,000 bottles annually, including some under other brand names. In addition, the concern has its own distillery which has a good reputation for its Marc de Gewürztraminer and other products.

Château Ollwiller
Riesling
APPELLATION VIN D'ALSACE CONTRÔLÉE

VIN D'ALSACE
APPELLATION ALSACE CONTROLEE
GRAND CRU
Saint Urbain
RIESLING du RANGEN 1978
de THANN

Château Ollwiller was rebuilt in the 18th century on old foundations. With its 40-acre vineyard, it belongs to the Gros family. The owners do not vinify the grapes themselves but have a contract with the Turckheim cooperative, which also sells the wines. I know the Riesling and the Pinot Noir: decent wines but definitely not memorable, lacking depth and character. The château is not open to visitors.

With 10 acres in the Rangen in Thann, the Domaine Zind-Humbrecht owns practically all the wine land in this commune. The grapes planted in the Clos Saint Urbain (named after a small chapel on the land dedicated to the patron saint of wine growers) are 7 acres of Riesling, 1½ acres of Tokay, 1½ acres of other varieties. The Riesling is a harshly dry, almost metal-cold, elegant wine with a discreet perfume. As the vines age, the wine will undoubtedly gain in depth of bouquet and taste.

Vineyard acreages
Soultz: 119
Wuenheim: 161
Thann: 11

Thann's Rangen vineyard has been in existence since the 12th century. It has been said of the wine 'it takes the feet from under you, but leaves the mind clear'. Above the Rangen are the ruins of Engelsbourd castle. They include a piece of round turret wall with a hole in it. This has been christened 'the Witch's Eye'. Across the valley on the Staufen stands the monument to the Alsatian Resistance of World War II.

Right:
Decoration in the church in Thann, with bunches of grapes. There was far more wine produced in the past than nowadays. The death blow to Thann's wine-growing was the growth of industry locally and in nearby Mulhouse.

Below:
The imposing Château Ollwiller in Wuenheim, built on the foundations of an earlier castle in the 18th century. In World War I it suffered a lot of damage. The Swiss used to order their communion wine from Wuenheim.

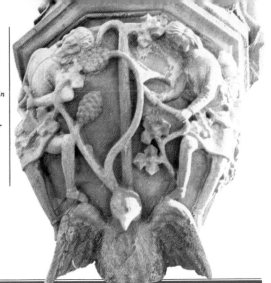

South to Thann

After Guebwiller the wine route runs south to its terminus. The last stage begins with a visit to Soultz, situated in the plain, which takes its name from salt springs. Although vines have been cultivated here since the 7th century, wine-growing is of little significance today. Lovers of wine need not spend long here, except perhaps to see the Place de la République with the church of St Maurice (13th and 15th century), the *hôtel de ville* with its covered outside staircase and its golden eagle (1856), and an attractive fountain. The route continues towards Wuenheim. Near the turning to the village stands the Cave Vinicole du Vieil Armand. This cooperative is associated with the one at Turckheim (see page 127). 'Vieil' is derived from the neighbouring hill of that name, the scene of eight months' fierce fighting in 1914-15. On the top of the hill stands a national monument to the dead. The village

of Wuenheim was badly damaged in this battle. Just outside it is the Château d'Ollwiller, which sends its grapes to the Turckheim cooperative for vinification and sale.

Vanishing vineyards

Vineyards are by now infrequent, and southwards they steadily thin out, disappearing altogether at Wattwiller, where they give way to meadows, orchards and woods. At Cernay, a few scattered plots are visible — but these probably produce only ordinary, anonymous wines. Like Wuenheim, Cernay was badly hit in World War I; and it happened again in World War II. The village of Vieux-Thann is reached by way of one of the few local reminders of the past, the Porte de Thann, and then comes the town of Thann, where the *route du vin* ends.

The Rangen revived

Thann is a busy provincial town with a famous church, regarded as a masterpiece of the Gothic period. The building was begun in the 14th century and was completed in the 17th century. The wine from the local Rangen vineyard used to be famous, and was even served at the Austrian court. In one year, so the story goes, the vintage was so abundant that wine instead of water was used in mixing the mortar for the edifice. Such a prolific harvest would be unthinkable today. Until the beginning of the 1970s, hardly any wine was, in fact, being produced. It is largely due to Léonard Humbrecht of the Domaine Zind-Humbrecht (see page 128) that part of the famous Rangen vineyard is again under cultivation. A titanic effort was needed to reclaim the slaty soil of the Rangen, for the slope here lies at an angle of 65°. Now that the first vines are fully grown it is clear that the labour was not in vain: the quality of today's Rangen wines is the proof.

Champagne

Champagne: the native soil

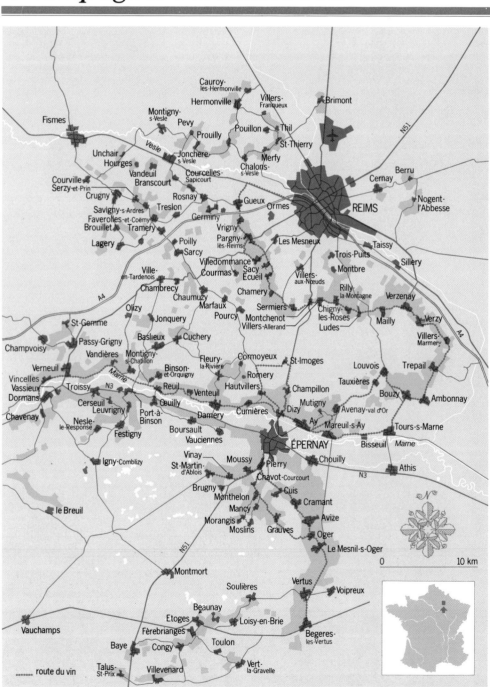

La Champagne is the home of *le* champagne: region and wine are indissolubly linked. The name 'Champagne' is derived from the Latin *campania*, 'plain'; and Champagne, in fact, comprises a series of broad, fairly flat areas, although in zones where vines are cultivated the terrain is usually hilly. The former province of Champagne comprised the present *départements* of Marne, Aube, Haute-Marne, Ardennes and part of Aisne. Wine-growing, however, is mainly concentrated in Marne (78%), with further vineyards in Aube (15%) and Seine-et-Marne (7%). The Institut National des Appellations d'Origine has ruled that a maximum area of 86,500 acres is suitable for wine-growing and of this about 59,300 acres has been planted. The vineyards are, as a rule, situated on gentle hill slopes, where the vines are better protected against damp and cold than lower down in the valleys.

The remarkable chalk

The unique character of champagne is explained by the subsoil, which consists of chalk. Within the belt that extends from Dover to Champagne, there are about 50 different zones of chalk. Of these, the Champagne chalk is best suited to wine-growing. The area was once part of a sea where conditions favoured the development of shellfish, sea urchins and cephalopods. For countless thousands of years these creatures lived and died here, and their shells and other hard parts built up into a chalk layer of exceptional quality, the *craie à belemnites*. Nowhere is there such a wealth of belemnite (extinct cephalopod) fossils in the chalk as in Champagne. Elsewhere chalk of this origin occurs only in the Paris basin, but in a lesser concentration.

Moisture and warmth

It is the chemical composition of this chalk stratum — 650 feet deep in places with only a thin layer of soil on top — that gives champagne its special organoleptic characteristics. Yet the chalk does more than

Champagne: the native soil

this. It drains off any surplus water in the subsoil, but retains enough moisture to supply the vines in the dry period — usually from the end of June to the beginning of August. (Irrigation is strictly forbidden in Champagne.) In addition, the chalk absorbs the heat of the sun during the day and radiates it to the vines on cool nights. That little extra warmth is very necessary, for the mean annual temperature in Champagne, France's northernmost major wine-growing region, is only 10°C. This is only just above the minimum at which the grape will ripen, so wine-growing here is practised under marginal conditions. Joseph Dargent, of the Comité Interprofessionel du Vin de Champagne (CIVC), once said: 'It is a law of nature that the best products always grow under somewhat unsuitable circumstances, because they are forced to surpass themselves; abundance is the enemy of quality.'

The chalk also helps to mature the wine. Many producers have perfect cellars in the chalk, especially in Reims. These *crayères* are often old Roman chalk workings.

Grands crus

The vineyards are in four zones: the Montagne de Reims, a plateau with wine growing on the northern, eastern and southern slopes; the Vallée de la Marne; the Côte des Blancs (mainly white Chardonnay); and Aube. The last zone, lying to the south of the others, is least important from the viewpoint of quality. In Champagne there is a very close connection between the quality of the soil and the quality (and price) of the grapes. Prices are fixed each year. The shippers pay the full price for grapes from the 12 best wine communes — the 100% *grands crus*. Then there are 41 *premiers crus* where soil and grapes are ascribed a quality rating of 90% to 99% and the price is proportionately lower. In the remaining wine communes the price drops further with a rating of 77% to 89%. The 12 *grands crus* are: Avize, Cramant (both white), Ambonnay, Aÿ, Bouzy, Louvois, Mailly,

Puisieulx, Sillery, Tours-sur-Marne, Verzenay and Vesle.

Dom Pérignon: cellar master extraordinary

It is a strange quirk of fate that the world's most festive wine was born in a region that has suffered as few others from the miseries of war. In AD 451 a bloody battle was fought near Châlons-sur-Marne, where the hordes of Attila the Hun were destroyed by the combined Roman armies: and during World War II the city of Reims was devastated. Wine has been made in Champagne from ancient times, although for centuries it was not white and sparkling, but red and still. According to the champagne expert Patrick Forbes, it was the English who discovered that champagne wine imported in the vat had a natural tendency to effervesce in spring, and they made use of this in bottling. In Champagne itself, however, it was Dom Pierre Pérignon (1638-1715) whose ideas were to have a decisive influence on the production of the wine. This remarkable cellar master of Hautvillers Abbey was probably the first person to succeed in making a completely clear white wine from black grapes. In addition, he discovered the principle of the *cuvée*: with careful blending of wines from different plots the whole became more than the sum of the parts. It is said that during the vintage Dom Pérignon — blind in the latter years of his life — would taste grapes from different locations before

breakfast and indicate how they should be blended. He also seems to have been the first *Champenois* to seal bottles with Spanish cork, which was then becoming available.

The great breakthrough

The great breakthrough for champagne came after 1740 when it created a sensation at the court of Louis XV. It was the ladies, above all, who were responsible for its popularity. Some of their verdicts are famous. Madame de Pompadour declared: 'It is the only wine that lets a woman stay beautiful after she has drunk it'; and Madame de Parabère affirmed: 'It brings a sparkle to the eyes without a flush to the cheeks'. The rest is history. No wine in the world so appeals to the imagination as champagne. Between 150 and 200 million bottles are sold every year and the champagne towns of Reims, Epernay and Aÿ attract hundreds of thousands of tourists from France and abroad, most of whom visit at least one cellar to learn how champagne is made.

Making champagne

Moët et Chandon

Emmagasinage des Vins - Le Soutirage

Phot. Em. Choque, Imp.-Edit., Epernay

Making champagne

No one in Champagne would dream of using the local grapes in a *tarte aux raisins*: they are much too expensive for that. Each year the Comité Interprofessionel du Vin de Champagne (CIVC) fixes the price per kilo for grapes from which champagne may be made. As mentioned, this price relates to *crus* rated at 100%; prices for lower-rated vineyards are based proportionately on it. This price applies to all grapes delivered on a contract basis to the shippers. For the remainder of the vintage there is a free market where the price is fixed by supply and demand. The price established annually by the CIVC is calculated from the average selling price of a bottle of champagne 'ex-shipper' during the previous 12 months. If the wine rises in price, so do the grapes, and the growers benefit. In Champagne, the 1980 price per kilo for 100%-rated grapes was 13.50 francs (and because of the very poor harvest the shippers in fact paid a further 10 francs a kilo). The people of Champagne are therefore thrifty with their grapes; each one is worth its weight in centimes.

Three grape varieties

The grapes from which champagne may be made are the Pinot Noir and Pinot Meunier (both black) and the Chardonnay (white). About three-quarters of the vineyard area is planted with black grapes, with the Pinot Noir in the majority. The Pinot Noir is a high-quality grape — basis of the great red Burgundies — a grape that provides its wine with backbone, strength and fullness. The Pinot Meunier is rather more rustic in character. It is more resistant to cold, damp and rot, and thrives in places where the Pinot Noir would have difficulties (i.e. in the Marne valley). This grape produces a wine with less bouquet and finesse; taste and aftertaste often have fruit and *terroir*. Like the Pinot Noir, the Chardonnay is a grape that produces splendid wines in Burgundy. In Champagne it imparts freshness, elegance and lightness. In many houses there is now a tendency to use more Chardonnay in their champagne, making them 'slimmer' and lighter. The problem is, however, that the area of Chardonnay planting cannot really be extended; in none of the champagne districts is the demand for grapes so great as in the Côte des Blancs, where the Chardonnay predominates.

Pressing

As quickly as possible after picking, the grapes are taken to the *vendangeoirs* for pressing. Great care attends this process. In the case of black grapes, any long contact between skins and juice, which would colour the must, has to be avoided. It is stipulated that 4,000 kilograms of grapes may produce 2,666 litres of must for making champagne — equivalent to 13 vats each of 205 litres. In pressing the grapes, three qualities are distinguished. The must and the subsequent wine from the first pressing comes to 2,050 litres and yields by far the best quality; this is termed the *cuvée*. The second pressing produces 410 litres, called the *première taille*; the third gives 205 litres and is termed the *deuxième taille*. Cuvée and *taille* will be frequently mentioned in the pages devoted to individual champagne shippers. The less *taille* is used, the better the wine. A number of houses process only *cuvée* and sell off the *taille* wines, or barter them with shippers who are not so particular. In general, the *taille* produces wines that flatter the taste and are fruity in their youth, but lack refinement, depth and serious potential for maturing.

First fermentation

After pressing comes the *débourbage*, when impurities present in the must are allowed to settle. The juice is then taken to the cellars for fermenting, usually in tanks of stainless steel, enamelled steel or glazed concrete. It is exceptional nowadays for the must to be fermented in oak vats, although this was the rule a generation ago. Nearly all the shippers practise a further, lactic acid fermentation after the first, alcoholic process. This

Making champagne

fermentation malolactique breaks down certain acids. Nevertheless, there are houses — such as Krug, Lanson Père & Fils, and Piper-Heidsieck — which specifically avoid this procedure; reasons for this are discussed in the appropriate sections devoted to these firms.

Phenomenal expertise

In the case of most French white wines, the work is nearly done when fermentation is complete. Not so, however, with champagne — for a number of processes ensue before the wine leaves the shipper. One of the most important is the blending or *assemblage*. Every year, specialists taste all the wines from the recent vintage in order to combine them into wines that typify the style of their house. The ordinary *brut*, or other non-vintage champagne, makes the greatest demands of their professional skill. This type of wine must maintain, as closely as possible, the same taste year after year. In many instances the desired result cannot be achieved with wines from the new vintage alone, and the *vins de réserve* have to be brought in. Every self-respecting house keeps tanks of wines from various vintages for later blending. Blending is an incredibly complicated affair, demanding a phenomenal degree of expertise. The work of the tasters in a sense combines that of both perfumer and master chef. They determine, and supervise, style, character and quality; or, as André Rouzaud of Louis Roederer put it: 'Un bon champagne est le résultat d'un assemblage.' These could have been the words of Dom Pérignon.

The best from the shippers

Because blending different wines determines the quality of a champagne, the finest quality is usually made by the shippers who have at their disposal an extensive collection of wines from the entire region and, in addition, their reserve wines. The small grower who produces his own champagne, the *récoltant-manipulant*, can only use the grapes from his private vineyard. He is, as it were, the prisoner of his own soil. Shipper and grower might be compared to two artists, the former with a full and rich palette from which he can mix all the colours and shades he wants, the latter restricted to a basic minimum. Champagnes from individual growers are nearly always less complete and subtle than those from the shippers. Although in virtually all the French wine districts the individual estates often produce the best wines, in Champagne this, by definition, cannot be the case.

Making champagne sparkle

Champagne remains a still wine until after it has been blended. The *mousse* or sparkle is produced by allowing the wine to undergo a

secondary, carbon dioxide, fermentation in the bottle. This is stimulated by adding yeast and sugar, a *liqueur de tirage*, at the time the wine is bottled. The carbon dioxide produced by fermentation remains trapped in the wine under enormous pressure, normally five to six atmospheres, and this causes the bubbles. It is very important that the wine should have ample time to mature after the *mousse* has been produced, for the longer this period, the smaller and more persistent the bubbles; large bubbles are undesirable.

Sufficient maturation is essential from another viewpoint. As a result of fermentation a sediment is produced. This feeds the wine, giving it many subtle elements of scent and taste. The bottles are stored horizontally while the *mousse* is induced and during the subsequent maturing period. In this way the wine has maximum contact with the deposit.

The law stipulates that non-vintage champagnes should have at least one year in the bottle before they are sold, vintage champagnes a minimum three years. All the quality shippers, however, allow at least three years for non-vintage, and four or five years for vintage champagnes. This period is regarded as essential not only for the reasons already given, but also to allow the champagnes to lose part of their acids as naturally as possible. Letting champagne mature for three years is an expensive affair, because for every bottle on sale there have to be three in the cellar. It is mostly the financially strong shippers who can afford this way of working; many small growers sell their champagne after one year.

Turning, shaking, tilting

Following the maturing period, the deposit has to be removed from the bottles. According to the traditional method, the bottles are placed upside down with their necks in the holes of the slanting racks known as *pupitres*. Specially trained

craftsmen, the *remueurs* ('movers'), then initiate the process of coaxing the deposit down to the cork. They start by giving each bottle a regular eighth of a turn. Subsequently they shake the bottles as well, steadily loosening the deposit. Finally they turn, shake and tilt each bottle, placing it at a steeper angle in the *pupitre* each time they make their rounds, until the bottle is practically on its head and even the smallest particle of deposit is lying on the underside of the cork. An experienced *remueur* can handle 30,000 to 40,000 bottles a day. His work, always in dank, gloomy cellars, is not enviable, yet every *remueur* has the pride of a craftsman. He always talks of 'my wine', for only he is permitted to touch his allotted quota of bottles. If he is ill, everything stops until his return.

The *remuage* process traditionally lasts two to three months. Most houses, however, find this period too long and costly: so for some years they have been employing methods that speed the deposit on its way down the bottle without adversely affecting the quality of the champagne. In many houses, *remuage* therefore lasts only five or six weeks. There is a good deal of experiment, too, with mechanical *remuage*, and certain firms have already largely accepted this. The most favoured system involves *gyropalettes*, metal baskets that can hold 504 bottles which are moved in the required manner every eight hours, day in and day out — including evenings and weekends. By this means Piper-Heidsieck, for example, has reduced the *remuage* to one week.

Disgorging

Once the deposit is resting on the underside of the cork, the bottle neck is dipped in a bath of freezing brine (usually −15 °C). The deposit freezes to a small plug, which shoots out when the bottle is opened. Some wine is also lost, but this is immediately replaced. The champagne is topped up with its *liqueur d'expédition* — a mixture of champagne, cane sugar and sometimes a drop of brandy. According to André Rouzaud of Roederer, half of the houses add brandy. I have not been able to check this statement, for many champagne firms are extremely vague, or evasive, on this subject. After the bottle has been topped up, it is given its definitive cork with metal plate and wiring, a 'muzzle' that holds the cork in place.

This process of freezing and removing the deposit is termed *dégorgement*, 'disgorging'. It used to be done by hand, but is almost always done mechanically today. The good firms customarily allow the bottles to rest for a few months before shipping. This enables the wine to recover from all the recent shocks, while the topping-up mixture marries perfectly with the champagne. Finally, the bottle is labelled and given its capping of foil.

Champagne producers

Types and tastes

The Champagne region has approximately 59,300 acres of vineyard: roughly 51,900 acres are owned by some 17,000 growers and about 7,400 acres by the shippers. The champagne firms, which produce about two-thirds of all champagne, but own only one-eighth of the vineyard area, are therefore very dependent on the growers. Many shippers have no land at all — in fact only 60 of the 140 firms have their own vineyards. For some years this situation has been causing problems. An increasing number of growers — about 4,000 of them so far — are beginning to produce their own champagne. In 1969 the shippers (*négociants-manipulants*) still produced 74.7% of the wine, the independent grower-producers (*récoltants-manipulants*) 25.3%. A decade later the respective figures were 65.7% and 34.3%. The result of this trend is that the firms are having increasing difficulty in obtaining the grapes they require. According to Bertrand Mure of Ruinart, there is only one solution: 'The champagne houses must share their profits with the growers.'

Undemanding home market

It is characteristic of the operations of the *récoltants-manipulants* that their success is almost exclusively limited to France, where there are fewer demands on quality than is the case abroad. This is not really so remarkable: after all, what is the point of a first-class champagne if it is served with a sweet dessert, as so often happens in France? Export is still firmly in the hands of the shippers. Of these 140 firms, many now exist only in name, or as part of larger concerns. The best of them are united in the Syndicat de Grandes Marques de Champagne, but as with many such groups, the fact that it is easier for a firm to get accepted than for a member to be expelled, means that it includes some lame ducks. (The complete list of members of Les Grandes Marques is given at the top of this page.)

Visible and invisible connections

The world of the champagne houses is small and exclusive, particularly that of the *grandes marques*. Many of them are formally linked: Moët & Chandon, Mercier, Ruinart and de Cazanove belong to the same group; Mumm, Heidsieck, Monopole and Perrier-Jouët to another. Veuve Cliquot and Canard-Duchêne form a group, as do Pommery & Greno, Lanson and Massé. The same applies to Henriot, Charles Heidsieck, Trouillard/de Venoge, and quite a number of other houses. Besides these visible corporate connections there are invisible ties — sometimes financial (Taittinger is a sleeping partner with a 30% share in Laurent Perrier, while Taittinger and Mumm own 5% of each other's shares), sometimes family (the father of Ruinart's Bertrand Mure has for years been a director of Louis Roederer and the name de Vogüé appears both at Moët & Chandon and at Veuve Clicquot).

Champagne tasting

A few years ago, a market research survey in Britain asked people what the word 'champagne' suggested to them. No one answered 'sparkling wine' or even 'wine'. The answers were all associated with abstract concepts such as pleasure, festivity, luxury, success, love, etc. This popular image of champagne is undoubtedly the reason why it is seldom the object of serious critical judgment. Tasting champagne is certainly no easy task. Firstly, it is often served too cold, and secondly, experience is needed to taste it through the effervescence. Even professionals who regularly examine still wines often have difficulty with champagne and other sparkling wines. For the purposes of this book, I have attempted to taste champagne seriously, both at the premises of all the houses visited and also in my own home. I deliberately restricted myself to the dry, and hence the purest, champagnes. The differences in quality and character proved greater than I had ever suspected — which will be clear from the following pages.

Champagne comes in a large number of types and tastes. Not only does each producer make a wine in his own style, but champagne possesses varying degrees of sweetness and also contains different kinds of wine. This sweetness is determined at the last moment, during *dégorgement* (see page 145): the wine receives its *liqueur d'expédition* and the more cane sugar this contains, the sweeter the champagne. Remarkably enough, the Champagne region has no legislation governing degrees of sweetness and terminology, even though this is an area with so many regulations that people complain 'they have liberty everywhere in France except here'. The *dosage* of cane sugar for the driest type of champagne, called *brut*, is usually between 6.4 and 12.8 grams per litre. Sometimes it is much less, as in the Brut Sauvage from Piper-Heidsieck; sometimes there is none at all (the wine is then called *brut de brut, brut zéro, brut 100%*, etc.). Dry champagne, or *sec*, generally contains 12.8 to 21.5 grams of sugar, and *demi-sec* between 21.5 and 34 grams. *Doux* is still sweeter. The *extra dry* quality, popular in Britain, comes between *brut* and *sec* in sweetness. The sugar has a masking effect; the best champagnes are those with the least *dosage*. Lesser wines are used for *demi-sec* and *doux*, most houses including a great deal of *taille* quality in them.

Champagne crémant

There are also differences in carbon dioxide content. Normally champagne has this gas at a pressure of five to six atmospheres. In the *crémant* type, however, it does not exceed three atmospheres. This less powerful *mousse* is obtained by restricting the sugar content of the *liqueur de tirage* (see page 145): 12 grams per litre are added instead of 24. Confusion stems from the fact that since 1975 other French regions have been permitted to use the word 'crémant' (the Loire, Alsace, Burgundy), where it refers to sparkling wines with a normal carbon dioxide content of about six atmospheres. In

Champagne, *crémant* is often a cheaper product of not too high a quality — except from certain firms, such as Abel Lepitre, that specialize in it.

White and pink

By far the majority of champagnes are made from black and white grapes, but there are also a number exclusively from white Chardonnay. The latter type is called *blanc de blancs*. *Blanc de noirs*, from black grapes only, also occurs but is rare. Pink champagne (rosé) nearly always consists of a blend of white and red wine — a practice that is strictly forbidden elsewhere in France. The red wine is usually added at the moment of bottling. Only a few firms produce champagne rosé by leaving the wine in contact with the black grape skins. As a rule, pink champagne is not particularly successful, except in appearance — white bubbles against a pink background. The added red wine usually reduces the finesse and freshness of the white.

Vintage and non-vintage

Champagne is sold with or without indication of vintage. In this book the former type is referred to as vintage champagne, although the term *millésimé* might also be used. According to EEC regulations, vintage champagne has to be at least 80% from a single vintage, which must be of good if not very good quality. Vintage champagnes are always *brut*. The so-called *cuvées de prestige* form a special category, the best possible wine from each firm. The first house to market one was Moët & Chandon with its Dom Pérignon. The other shippers have followed suit. Prestige champagnes almost always come in de luxe bottles and cost a small fortune. Whether they are worth their high prices is a matter to be discussed later in the pages on the various individual firms. A separate section is devoted to still champagne — Coteaux Champenois — on pages 190-1.

Serving and drinking champagne

Champagne is drunk cold, after the bottle has been in the refrigerator for about an hour, or for ten minutes in a bucket with cold water and ice. When opening a bottle, the idea is not for the cork to fly out with a bang. This is dangerous, 'startles' the wine and wastes some of it. A better method is to remove the foil and wiring and then very carefully turn or work the cork loose without letting it shoot out. Wipe the mouth of the bottle clean before pouring.

The best kind of champagne glass is the slender tulip-shaped design; this is the type most used in the region itself. The flat champagne coupe *à la* Hollywood ought to be banned, for neither scent nor *mousse* can be enjoyed properly in it. As already mentioned, the French drink (dry!) champagne mainly with the dessert — which in my opinion is the worst possible stage of the meal. The wine shows to far greater advantage as a festive aperitif or as a brilliant accompaniment to hors d'oeuvre or main course.

Veuve Clicquot-Ponsardin

Philippe Clicquot, banker and textile merchant at Reims, married in 1772 and in the same year set up a champagne business. His wife had brought a dowry of excellently situated vineyards in Bouzy and Verzenay. For many years Clicquot only sold his wine to friends and business relations. This situation changed when his son François joined the firm, for the young man was more interested in wine than in banking or textiles. In 1799 François married Nicole-Barbe Ponsardin, daughter of a wealthy citizen (later to become mayor of Reims). François was 23, Nicole 20. Their wedding was held in a cellar — perhaps symbolically — for the Revolution had not yet come to terms with the Church. In 1804 François decided to concentrate entirely on the wine trade; he wound up the bank and the wool business that his father had transferred to him in 1801. The following year both he and his father died. The family wanted to give up the champagne trade — but no one had reckoned with Nicole-Barbe's willpower. Against all advice, she continued the business. Four months after her husband's death, with two assistants (one of them, Bohne, later became her traveller and representative), she established the house of Veuve Clicquot-Ponsardin, Fourneaux & Co. She was then 27 and had a three-year-old daughter, Clémentine.

Russian successes

The early years were certainly not easy for the young widow, but thanks to Bohne, some important orders, mainly from Russia, were obtained. In one letter to his employer, Bohne wrote: 'The Tsarina is expecting a child. If a prince is born, copious amounts of champagne will be drunk in this vast country. Don't mention this to anyone — all our competitors would flood in.' Russia became Veuve Clicquot's biggest customer. The firm cleverly managed to get the first shipload of champagne there shortly after the fall of Napoleon. It arrived on 3 July 1814 and was soon followed by two more shipments. The wine became so popular that the Russian poet Pushkin reported in one of his letters: 'Madame Clicquot is drenching Russia. People call her wine *Klikovskoye* and drink no other.'

Important discovery

Besides her peaceful conquest of Russia, Nicole-Barbe took credit for another important achievement. It was she who laid the foundation of the present method of *remuage*. In her time, after completion of the secondary fermentation, the bottles were held upside down and shaken a few times. This treatment sent some, but by no means all, of the sediment down to the cork. Experiments showed that a more successful process was to invert the bottles at an angle and place them in holes cut in a table — these tables being the forerunners of the *pupitres*. In 1817 the widow's daughter, Clémentine,

Veuve Clicquot's brut usually has a light golden sheen in the colour, a liberal amount of little bubbles, an attractive, nuanced bouquet and a mouth-filling, classic taste, properly complete, sound and mildly fresh. For quality, this balanced, pure champagne is one of the best of its category. Vintage champagnes from Veuve Clicquot — they have a golden label — are also excellent.

In about 1815 Bohne wrote to Nicole-Barbe from Russia: 'They think Madame Clicquot's wines are perfect here. The pink is nectar.' Around 1912 a fashion collection was launched in Paris under the name 'Clicquot Rosé'. The present rosé from Veuve Clicquot is as good as ever, soft pink in colour, with white, extremely fine small bubbles, fruit in the bouquet, elegant and robust in taste. From 10% to 15% still red wine is added. The vintage year is always stated.

Veuve Clicquot's cuvée de prestige Grand Dame, launched in 1970, is made from grapes from the firm's vineyards in Verzy, Verzenay, Bouzy, Ay, Mesnil and Avize. It is a fully aromatic champagne with small, rapid bubbles, a robust, well-defined, but mellow mature taste and a nice aftertaste; truly a wine to accompany a meal. It lacks the finesse of some of the other de luxe champagnes, but still has great class.

Veuve Clicquot-Ponsardin

married a count who found it simpler to spend money than to earn it. His mother-in-law therefore refused to take him into the business, choosing instead a young man of German origin named Edouard Werlé. He began to sell Veuve Clicquot champagnes in other markets apart from Russia; as yet the firm had not sold a single bottle in France. Nicole-Barbe Clicquot-Ponsardin lived out her last years in the Château de Boursault, luxuriously furnished by her son-in-law. When she took over the business the production had been 50,000 bottles a year. At her death in 1866 annual output was near the three-million mark.

No filtering of the wine

Veuve Clicquot-Ponsardin is nowadays run by three direct descendants of Edouard Werlé. They and their families hold about 40% of the shares (quoted on the Paris Bourse). The firm owns 655 acres of vineyard with a quality rating of 97%, which supplies 40% of its requirements. Only wine from the first pressing, the *cuvée*, is used for vintage champagnes. Non-vintage *brut* includes second pressing (*première taille*) wine. The grape juice ferments in modern stainless-steel tanks at a temperature of around 22°C. An important point is that at Veuve Clicquot the must is filtered, not the wine, which is given only a 'cold treatment' and is sometimes clarified. The firm's cellars — 227 of them — extend for 12 miles and consist partly of old chalk workings. *Remuage* is still done by hand and takes two months. Veuve Clicquot sells about 6.6 million bottles annually, with a stock of between 20 and 24 million bottles.

Flawless quality

Veuve Clicquot deliberately aims at high quality. Alain de Vogüé, the chairman, told me: 'We work in a traditional way. Our *cuvée* contains a considerable proportion of black grapes, and our wines mature in chalk pits. For us the wine counts for more than the *mousse*. Champagne cannot just be *mousse* because then we would be no different from other sparkling wines. And I don't like the word "champagne". I would rather talk of "vin de Champagne".'
Veuve Clicquot champagnes are made with great care and are of flawless quality, and this applies to the whole range of dry wines, from non-vintage *brut* — one of the best of its class — to the prestige champagne La Grande Dame. All these wines have pinhead bubbles, a mouth-filling taste and a good deal of nuance and subtlety. They are the most delicate of champagnes and of a marvellous standard, equally acceptable when drunk at table or after the meal. Quite simply, Veuve Clicquot is an excellent firm.

G. H. Mumm & Co.

Like many other champagne firms, Mumm was founded by a German, P. A. Mumm, who came from the wine village of Rüdesheim in the Rheingau. His partner's name was Giesler and the business they started in 1827 traded as P. A. Mumm, Giesler & Co. The records show that after a few years Giesler left and set up his own wine business, and that a second split occurred in 1852. The firm was then run by two grandsons of the founder, George Hermann and Jules Mumm. They too decided to separate and both started up champagne businesses under their own names. Jules Mumm's enterprise today survives only as a brand name owned by G. H. Mumm & Co. In order to be able to continue using the name, the company ships five cases of Jules Mumm every year to Britain.

Confiscated as enemy property

George Hermann's firm (his descendants were always given names beginning with G or H) grew and prospered. Much of this success was due to the launching of Cordon Rouge in 1873. The importance of Cordon Rouge to Mumm is shown by the fact that this *brut*, non-vintage and vintage, makes up 65% to 82% of total sales. World War I, however, brought this favourable course of affairs to an abrupt end. No one in the Mumm family had taken the precaution of seeking naturalization and so the firm was confiscated as enemy property. In 1920 the French government offered it for public sale. The new owners comprised many different shareholders, including the firm of Dubonnet. From that concern came Mumm's new director, René Lalou, whose wife was a Dubonnet.

Bruts *from Mumm, vintage and non-vintage, have a red-banded label with the name Cordon Rouge. The vintage varieties distinctly show the most strength and personality, and have matured for a longer period. The successful non-vintage brut has a very soft type of bouquet and taste. It is certainly a quite pleasant, commercial champagne, a little milder than other well-known bruts. The Double Cordon is a sec, the Cordon Vert a demi-sec, and the Cordon Rosé a good, mild vintage pink.*

Mumm's prestige René Lalou is usually made from 50% white grapes. In character and finesse, this champagne falls short of many other cuvées de prestige, but still offers an attractive quality. It is the most nuanced of the Mumm champagnes, with grace in bouquet, and taste. Now and again — it varies with the vintage — the taste can be almost juicy, sometimes with hints of peach and apple. Mumm hopes to be selling around 450,000 bottles of René Lalou a year by 1984.

This gently foaming champagne, made exclusively from white grapes from the village of Cramant, is particularly charming: fresh, agreeable and light — a perfect blanc de blancs. The labelling of the bottle is very restrained, deliberately so 'to keep the wine as natural as possible, as close as may be to its terroir'. The dosage is 25% greater than for the René Lalou (at Mumm they say that otherwise the wine would be rather rough), but it is still 30% less than the ordinary Cordon Rouge.

G. H. Mumm & Co.

American succcess

Lalou worked hard to restore the fortunes of Champagne Mumm and was eminently successful. G. H. Mumm & Co. became one of Champagne's biggest shippers, with a present output of about 9 million bottles a year and a stock of 28 million bottles. The firm also established a strong foothold in the American market. Lalou had acquired a majority holding in the firm, but as he had no direct heirs, he sold his shares in August 1973 to the Canadian drinks giant Seagram, which already had a holding in Mumm. Mention has already been made of the interesting fact that Champagne Taittinger owns 5% of Mumm shares, and vice-versa.

The Mumm vineyards

Mumm owns more than 550 acres of vineyard, with an average quality rating of 97%, providing 20% to 25% of the firm's grapes. I have been informed that Mumm uses only wine from the first pressing (*cuvée*), at least for the non-vintage *brut* quality upwards. *Première taille* wine is only used for the sweeter types such as *sec* and *demi-sec*. Various types of vats are employed for the first fermentation; everything that glitters here is not stainless steel, as in some other houses. Mechanical *remuage* does not as yet interest Mumm. At the time of my visit in 1980, this new method had not even been tried.

Mild and commercial

Non-vintage Cordon Rouge is noticeably mild both in scent and taste, possibly because this is what Americans tend to prefer in their white wines. It also sparkles gently, almost creamily. Mumm's best-selling wine does not possess a very marked personality, still less much depth or nuance. It is no more, and no less, than a mild, commercial champagne whose success is demonstrated by the sales figures. Vintage Cordon Rouge always has more class and strength, although here again nothing too

exciting can be expected. Mumm's Cordon Rouge champagnes, like most *bruts*, are made principally from black grapes, albeit with rather more white than is usual among other firms. The *cuvée de prestige* René Lalou has a greater proportion of wine from white grapes — often 50%. This champagne is the most subtle of the Mumm range, with much grace of scent and taste. However, in character and taste it does not approach a Krug Grande Cuvée, a Dom Pérignon, a Bollinger R.D., a Taittinger Comtes de Champagne, a Roederer Cristal or others in this category.

Crémant de Cramant

The most striking wine from G. H. Mumm & Co. comes in a plain, unadorned bottle of green glass with no foil, and just a simple black-and-white label the size of a business card. The wine in question is Mumm's Crémant de Cramant, which thus has less *mousse* than ordinary champagne and comes exclusively from the village of Cramant in the Côte des Blancs. The grapes for this *blanc de blancs* come partly from Mumm's own vineyards. It tastes fresh, agreeable and light: an extremely pleasant and lively champagne. Only 105,000 to 110,000 bottles a year of this wine are produced. It is found mainly in good European restaurants.

The non-vintage Black Label brut *from Lanson Père & Fils has an appropriate label. It is a good wine, reasonably liberal in bubbles, pale in colour, with a mildly fresh, rather fruity bouquet, a substantial taste and a slightly acid aftertaste. For generations Britain has been the largest foreign importer of this and other Lanson champagnes.*

Vintage champagnes from Lanson are more robust and solid than the ordinary brut. The ones I have tasted had a rather disappointing bouquet. The taste was somewhat better: reasonably complex, softly mature and at the same time vitally fresh.

No more than 12% of red wine ever goes into Lanson's rosé, so there is always plenty of the freshness of the white in it. The soft pink wine with its miniscule white bubbles has an extremely pleasant dry taste. The bouquet too is agreeable. A very good pink champagne.

Lanson Père & Fils

The firm of Lanson was established in turbulent times. At some time in the early years of the 19th century — exactly when is not known — Jean-Baptiste Lanson became an employee of a champagne business dating from 1760. The French Revolution forced Lanson out of the country and he found refuge with a friendly German family called Kellerhof. The Kellerhofs later suffered a similar fate: because they refused to fight against the French (one of Jean-Baptiste's sons had married a Kellerhof girl) they had to flee in the opposite direction to Reims. In 1838 Jean-Baptiste Lanson took over the champagne firm in 1838 and gave it his own name. Lanson Père & Fils is still run by his direct descendants, although it no longer belongs to the family.

Artificial fertilizer and champagne

It was under the dynamic mangement of Victor Lanson — who was reputed to have drunk at least 70,000 bottles of champagne in the course of his life and lived to 87 — the firm brought in financial support from outside. In 1970 the *pastis* giant Ricard acquired a 48% interest. This financial marriage did not last long. Less than ten years later, the brothers François and Xavier Gardinier paid 65 million francs for the Ricard intrest. Since they had already bought up shares held by the family, this

Opposite page, above:
Reception corner in the Lanson
building in the Boulevard
Lundy. The cellars and offices
are elsewhere in Reims, next to
and in the buildings taken over
by Lanson from the firm of
Massé. On the right of the photo
there is the old pattern of
vintage bottle, replaced by an
ordinary type in 1976.

Opposite page, below:
About 80% of all the wine
ferments in stainless-steel tanks
at Lanson.

Right:
One of the cellar passages with
full pupitres. Lanson produces
no crémant or blanc de blancs.
The original firm was founded in
1760 by François Delamotte.

Below:
Salmanazars (with the capacity
of 12 ordinary bottles) of Black
Label.

Lanson Père & Fils

made them the owners of Lanson.
On the face of it, Gardinier and Lanson may
appear strange bedfellows, for the
Gardiniers are successful manufacturers of
artificial fertilizer: but, in fact, there are
long-standing personal connections between
the Gardiniers and the Lansons. These
became closer still in 1960 when Pierre
Lanson married Hélène Gardinier, sister of
François and Xavier. At present Pierre is a
director of Lanson Père et Fils, as is Etienne
Lanson. Other Lansons work in the business.
Overall supervision is in the hands of the
Gardiniers; and meanwhile Gardinier-
Lanson has acquired a majority interest in
the firm of Pommery & Greno. According to
Pierre Lanson, Pommery and Lanson will
continue to operate quite independently,
except for the exploitation of the vineyards.
Since 1969 Lanson has also owned 30% of
Laurent Perrier shares, and in 1976 it took
over Champagne Massé.

Post-war expansion

Until World War I Lanson did not own a
single vine. In 1918, however, Victor Lanson
and his brother Henri began to buy
vineyards. Now the firm has 507 acres,
providing about 40% of its grapes. The
average quality rating of the vineyards is
97%. The two most important holdings, each
of about 100 acres, lie near Chouilly, in the
Côte des Blancs, and close to Dizy, on the
slopes of the Montagne de Reims. After the
grapes have been pressed, the must is
fermented mainly in stainless-steel tanks.

No malolactic fermentation

A feature of vinification at Lanson is that
the wine is not subjected to malolactic
fermentation in the tank. The only other
major houses to follow this example are
Piper-Heidsieck and Krug. Lanson holds
fermentation malolactique to be undesirable
because, in its view, it does not improve the
wine. One reason is that in order to generate
this fermentation, the wine has to be slightly

warmed. Furthermore, according to Pierre
Lanson, malolactic fermentation is more
important for red wine than for white wine.
In Lanson's six miles of cellars the remuage
is still done by hand, taking two to three
months, but the firm is experimenting with a
mechanical system. In principle, wine from
the first pressing (cuvée) is used for the 5
million bottles that Lanson produces
annually, usually with some from the so-
called cuvée suite, the first vat of the second
pressing. Lanson's stock fluctuates around
10 million bottles.

By royal appointment

Most of the champagnes sold by Lanson —
80% to 85% — are Black Label non-vintage
bruts. The English name may reflect the fact
that Britain has long been Lanson's most
important foreign customer. Moreover, the
firm has supplied champagne 'By
Appointment' to every British monarch
since Queen Victoria. Black Label is a good
wine: pale in colour, with fruit and mild acids
in the bouquet, and a clear, pure taste in
which the fresh acids are enveloped by the
gentle sparkle. It is a substantial, well-made
champagne, pleasant to drink and stable in
character over the years.
Whereas in the ordinary brut there is a

certain elegance and lightness, this seems to
disappear in Lanson's vintage champagnes.
They are distinctly more solid in taste; and
they contain more wine from black grapes.
The examples I have tasted made a mild but
at the same time fresh impression. Their
reasonably complex taste — as in the 1971
and 1975 — appealed to me more than the
bouquet.
Lanson also makes a good, non-vintage
champagne rosé. This has a soft pink colour,
white pinpoint bubbles, and a pleasantly dry
taste. It represents only 5% of the firm's
total production. Lanson's red Coteaux
Champenois is equally interesting. This still
champagne is usually made up from three
different vintages and therefore has more to
it than the bulk of such wines. It is supple,
mild and fresh (see page 191), but does not
offer much scent or depth. A cuvée de
prestige champagne, thus far missing from
the house's range, was added to the Lanson
range in 1982. It is a rather elegant wine,
baptized Noble Cuvée.

It would not be surprising if the relatively low price explains the great success in certain markets of Pommery & Greno's ordinary brut and demi-sec, for the quality of the wine does not. The bouquet and taste are rather flat and the tongue sometimes encounters roughness. The character is fairly light and fresh. The vintage champagnes are slightly better, but still unimpressive.

Pommery's cuvée de prestige used to be its Avize Blanc de Blancs (10,000 bottles per year). This wine, however, will be replaced in the course of 1983 by a new one, Prestige de Pommery, marketed in a special bottle. It is a superior balanced blend of Pinot Noir and Chardonnay from Pommery's own vineyards, including those in Avize.

Pommery & Greno

On the southeast side of the city of Reims, a wrought-iron gate and large lawns lead to an impressive though somewhat muddled collection of buildings, with stone and brickwork in grey, reddish-brown and cream, a mixture of flat and pointed roofs, and an assortment of round and square towers. It looks as if someone had hired French architects to assemble a variety of British buildings from different periods: and this, in fact, is what actually happened. The buildings, largely based on two Scottish examples, Inverary Castle and Mellerstain House, were completed in 1878. The scheme was commissioned by Mme Louise Pommery, director of the firm of Pommery & Greno, who wanted premises that would not only catch the eye but would also flatter the vanity of the British, her biggest customers. Today the offices and cellars of Pommery & Greno are still undeniably eye-catching, though their architectural merit is more doubtful.

Cellars from chalk pits

Mme Pommery also made her mark on the business in other ways. In 1858, at the age of 39, she was left with the responsibility of running the firm after the death of her husband Louis, who had founded the concern 22 years previously with a certain Narcisse Greno. Pommery's widow decided from now on to place the emphasis on sparkling wine — until then the firm had specialized mainly in still red wines. She concentrated on winning the British market, where she introduced one of the very first dry champagnes — the Champagne Nature 1873, launched in 1874. Louise Pommery also converted the chalk pits under her land into champagne cellars. This fabulously expensive operation created 120 interlinked cellars where many millions of bottles could be stored. In 1882 and 1883 a local sculptor decorated the cellars with bas-reliefs. My favourite is 'Le Champagne au XVIII siècle', depicting a group of men and women around a table, drinking the sparkling wine with obvious enjoyment.

The Parc Pommery

In 1879 Louise's daughter married Count Guy de Polignac. Exactly a century later the de Polignacs sold the majority of the shares to the Gardinier family, already owners of the firm of Lanson. For a hundred years Pommery & Greno was run by a succession of de Polignacs, sometimes indirectly, as in the years following the death of Louise Pommery in 1890, usually directly. It was the Marquis Melchior de Polignac who opened the Parc Pommery in 1913. This lies across the street from the Pommery & Greno premises. It contains a swimming pool, tennis courts, an athletics stadium, etc, all free to the firm's staff. When Pommery & Greno was sold to the Gardinier-Lanson interest, Prince Guy de Polignac remained as chairman. The actual president of the board of administrators is Xavier Gardinier, who also holds a majority of the shares. In his office hangs a huge painting of Louise Pommery, who seems to be keeping an eye on the business she brought to greatness in the previous century.

The vineyards

Pommery & Greno sells roughly 3.8 million bottles a year and has a stock of some 12 million bottles. The firm is very successful in several markets, such as West Germany, Austria, the Netherlands, Switzerland and Japan. About half of the grapes come from the firm's own 740 acres of vineyards. About two-thirds of this area is in the Montagne de Reims, and one-third in the Côte de Blancs (with nearly 100 acres, the firm is the biggest landowner in Avize). Virtually the entire Pommery & Greno vineyard area has a 100% rating. Count Guilhen de Nattes, son-in-law of Prince Guy de Polignac, told me that second pressing wine — *la première taille* — is generally used. Mechanical *remuage* is being tested; by hand it takes up to 35 days.

Something lacking

Pommery & Greno champagnes are not conspicuous for their depth, nuances or completeness; and I have noted little remarkable about their bouquets. As a rule, the ordinary *brut* is yellow in colour, contains bubbles that are not of the smallest type, and has a rather ripe, indeterminate bouquet and fairly flat taste. There may be a little roughness, depending on the age of the bottle. The character of the wine is fresh and fairly light. There is sometimes a strange, not altogether pure, earthy element in the taste; and the sparkle tends to wear off rather quickly.

I would say that the Pommery & Greno *brut* is no more than adequate. The vintage champagnes offer rather better quality, although even they do not fill me with great enthusiasm. Here too is a certain lack of refinement and completeness; the taste sometimes seems a bit sharp. Nor does the rather flat and uninteresting pink champagne greatly appeal to me. My favourite wine in the Pommery range used to be the rarest: the elegant, delightful *blanc de blancs* from the firm's estate in Avize. This wine, however, has been discontinued in favour of Prestige de Pommery, a *cuvée de prestige*, made of carefully selected Pinot Noir and Chardonnay grapes, again from Pommery's own vineyards.

Heidsieck & Co. Monopole

In Reims there are three champagne shippers using the name Heidsieck: Heidsieck Monopole, Piper-Heidsieck and Charles Heidsieck. The foundations for all three were laid by one man, Florenz-Ludwig Heidsieck, originally a German wool trader. In 1777 he made his first business journey to Reims, where he got to know the wool merchant Nicolas Perthois, whose daughter he married eight years later. He then set up in business in Reims, under the name Heidsieck & Co., describing his wares as 'wines and fabrics'. In Reims, Florenz-Ludwig — whose name was gallicized as Florens-Louis Heidsieck — had, like so many others, fallen under the spell of champagne.

German nephews

Heidsieck & Co.'s wine was very successful and soon the textile side of the business disappeared entirely. Florens-Louis flirted with danger during the French Revolution. He managed to rescue the largest bronze bell of Reims cathedral from being melted down, and as a result was nearly arrested by the revolutionaries. He was lucky to escape; his neighbour ended up on the scaffold. Florens-Louis, whose only son died young, was assisted in the expanding business by German nephews. The firm passed to three of them when he died in 1828. They worked in partnership for only a few years before going their separate ways in 1834.

Arrival of Monopole

The eldest of the three nephews was Henri-Louis Walbaum. In 1834 he set up a champagne business with his brother-in-law Auguste Heidsieck which they called Walbaum, Heidsieck & Co. In 1846 Walbaum withdrew and August continued the business under the name Heidsieck & Co. The name was to change again several times. The longest form used appeared in 1889: Walbaum, Luling, Goulden & Co., Successeur de Heidsieck & Co., Maison fondée en 1785. The firm did not acquire its present name of Heidsieck & Co. Monopole

Opposite page, above:
Beneath Heidsieck Monopole's outwardly unimpressive premises there are 7½ miles of cellars. These are visited by 4,000-5,000 people each year (by appointment only). The firm's archives include a cellar book from about 1845 and a fine collection of menus back to 1923.

Opposite page, below:
Two symbols of Reims, champagne bottles (in this instance giant models of two types of Heidsieck Monopole) and the cathedral. The magnificent building was built amid a great deal of protest from the citizenry. At one point, when they had had enough of the taxes imposed by the local clergy, they rose up and expelled the builders and the bishops. The project, started in 1211, was at a standstill for many years and the city was even excommunicated. The cathedral was eventually finished in the 14th century, except for its towers: these were added in the 15th century. It is a wonder that the cathedral still stands — it was hit by some 30,000 shells in World War I.

Heidsieck Monopole owns a windmill dating from 1820 in Verzenay and uses it for receptions and dinners. The firm bought it in 1901 from the miller for the sum of 1,000 gold francs for each of his children — nine of them up to the day the contract was signed, when the tenth was born. The miller did not want the sails to turn after his death and so in 1904 Heidsieck Monopole blocked up the mechanism. In World War I the windmill served as an observation post.

Below: a young Champenois in traditional dress serving wine during lunch at the Verzenay windmill.

Heidsieck's Dry Monopole, made from two-thirds black and one-third white grapes, has no distinctive personality. It is a reasonably full champagne that is not striking in bouquet or taste, either in a positive or a negative sense. The scent sometimes has a slightly impure tone (worse as the wine becomes warmer), and the mildly acid taste is correct but does not captivate. Red Top is the sec, Green Top the demi-sec.

The vintage brut receives a dosage about one-third less than the ordinary brut, but the constituent wine is also softer due to longer ageing. You can clearly smell and taste that maturity. Yet the wine often preserves a freshness in the full-flavoured taste for some years. However, refinement and nuance are largely lacking.

Diamant Bleu (bottle and label were radically changed for 1975) is Heidsieck Monopole's cuvée de prestige. The champagne contains more white wine — 50% — than the other types in the range: fine, plentiful little bubbles, clean bouquet, refreshing taste that sometimes can be almost mineral-like. Nicely balanced, this is a good, fresh, prestige champagne, albeit not over-refined. I prefer to drink the wine seven to eight years after vintage.

Heidsieck & Co. Monopole

until 1923. The 'Monopole' part came into being in 1860, when the firm carried a brand called Dry Monopole. This champagne was so popular that it was decided to incorporate the name in the firm's title. The oldest surviving bottle with a Dry Monopole label dates from 1892. Henry Champman, in charge of Heidsieck Monopole's publicity, was given it as a present by Jean-Marc Heidsieck of Charles Heidsieck.

Canadian connection

On 11 March 1972, Heidsieck Monopole was taken over by Mumm. Both firms are now part of the Canadian Seagram group. Heidsieck Monopole owns 267 acres of vineyard, all with a 100% quality rating, which supply about one-third of the firm's grapes. Annual sales are nearly two million bottles, with almost eight million bottles in stock. Heidsieck Monopole's wine-making equipment is good, but not ultra-modern. Fermentation tanks are of glazed concrete, enamelled steel and stainless steel. The *vins de réserve* used to be stored in wooden casks, but tanks are now used.
There are few special features to note about Heidsieck Monopole's methods, unless it is that wine from the first pressing, with as a rule some from the second, is used in the vintage champagnes, the ordinary *brut* and the other varieties. Only in the prestige brand Diamant is this not the case.

Old windmill

The most delightful place to drink Heidsieck Monopole champagnes is the windmill at Verzenay. This old structure, built in 1820 and the only one in the Champagne, stands on Mont Boeuf in 106 acres of land that the firm owns there. Heidsieck Monopole sometimes organizes receptions and banquets in the windmill, which, during World War I, served as an observation post.

Elegant Diamant Bleu

I have visited the cellars and windmill of Heidsieck Monopole several times and have often drunk the champagnes. My recollections of the wines on those occasions appear to be more enthusiastic than the tasting notes I later made for this book. For many years I regarded Heidsieck Monopole *brut* as a good, middle-ranking champagne, but now I judge it less favourably. Both by itself and in comparative tastings, the Dry Monopole was somewhat disappointing. The *mousse* was not altogether consistent and there seemed to be something a little impure in the background of the bouquet. The taste I thought, at best, correct, not particularly engaging, with a certain mildness alongside some acidity at its core and in its aftertaste. It is simply a champagne without much personality. The vintage champagnes are

generally rather better, fuller and riper, but not, in my opinion, of top quality. However, the Diamant Bleu of 1969, 1971 and 1973 appealed to me greatly. These were elegant, generously sparkling wines, beautifully balanced. They are usually fairly light in weight and can have an almost mineral tone in their taste. It should be noted that Diamant Bleu is usually made half from white grapes, compared with the one-third white grapes that go into other Heidsieck Monopole champagnes.

Piper-Heidsieck

Like Heidsieck & Co. Monopole and Charles Heidsieck, Piper-Heidsieck is one of the offshoots of the wine business that Florenz-Ludwig Heidsieck started in 1785. Another of the three nephews who succeeded him and who in 1835 set up on his own, using the brand name Heidsieck, was Christian Heidsieck. Christian died only some eight months after starting his firm, and the business was continued by his widow, together with Christian's three assistants. In 1837 she married one of them, Henri-Guillaume Piper, and the firm's name was changed to H. Piper & Co. The wine, however, retained the name Heidsieck. The champagne thus became increasingly known as Piper's Heidsieck — particularly in America where J. C. Kunkelmann, another of the original assistants, settled, doing stalwart work for the firm.

Another change of name

In 1850 Kunkelmann returned from New York and in 1870, the year of Henri-Guillaume Piper's death, acquired the business. The name of the firm was changed to Kunkelmann & Cie, but not that of the champagne: Piper's Heidsieck had become an official brand name as Piper-Heidsieck, and this was to be perpetuated. The last of

CHAMPAGNE PIPER

ISOLDE

Piper-Heidsieck's ordinary brut is a fresh, light, uncomplicated champagne that foams softly and has no overpowering personality. It can sometimes taste a little 'green'. I have occasionally recognized a trace of yeasts in the bouquet and taste, although the champagne is correctly made.

Vintage champagnes from Piper-Heidsieck are generally made of 50% white Chardonnay wine. They clearly have more refinement and elegance than the non-vintage brut.

Piper-Heidsieck produces an excellent rosé champagne in which the added still red wine has not suppressed the fraicheur of the constituent wine (50% from white grapes). Light pink in colour, with a fine sparkle, and delicate, refreshing taste, it is best drunk when about five years old.

Piper-Heidsieck named its cuvée de prestige after the man who laid the foundations for the three Heidsieck houses, Florens-Louis Louis Heidsieck. This champagne (made from 60% white grapes), is rather light in character, with a fine bouquet and a stylish, unobtrusive taste. Very pure, it is made only in very good years.

After years of experimenting, Brut Sauvage was launched in 1980. This new Piper-Heidsieck champagne gets the smallest possible dosage and so it is very dry in taste. Quality and price are comparable to the Florens-Louis, although the champagne is made up not from one but from various good years. As it rather lacks substance (and also complexity) it is particularly suitable as an aperitif.

Piper-Heidsieck

the Kunkelmanns left the business to his daughter, who had married the Marquis de Suarez d'Aulan. He died a war hero in 1944. Later she married again, her second husband being General d'Alès. Her son, François d'Aulan, is now chairman of the firm. The shares of Piper-Heidsieck are quoted on the Bourse, but the d'Alès d'Aulan family owns a controlling (68%) interest.

Mechanical remuage

Piper-Heidsieck sells about five million bottles a year. Roughly one-quarter of this output goes to the United States, where the firm's interests are still represented by Kunkelmann (New York). In the extensive cellars, where visitors are driven around in little trucks, there is a stock equivalent to three years' sales. It may seem surprising that many of Piper-Heidsieck's cellars are standing empty; this is because of the almost complete change-over to mechanical *remuage*. By 1980 the firm had already invested five million francs in a *gyropalette* system — metal baskets that can hold 504 bottles. These baskets, as previously mentioned, turn and shake the bottles every eight hours. At Piper-Heidsieck *remuage* now takes one week instead of up to two months. This saves space as well as time, as the bottles no longer need to be put in wooden *pupitres*. I was told that one cellar of *gyropalettes* processes as many bottles as were handled in 70 cellars in the days of manual *remuage*.

No Piper-Heidsieck vineyards

The firm has no vineyards of its own and so all the wine has to be bought in. In principle, no second or third pressing wines are bought, except for *demi-sec*. As with Krug and Lanson Père et Fils, the wines undergo no malolactic fermentation. Cellar master René Menu told me why: 'We avoid the *fermentation malolactique* because the wine then stays fresher and ages less quickly.' Only in years when the wine is very acid does the firm allow some of it to undergo malolactic fermentation. Piper has not, in fact, used this process since 1972, and it is expected that other champagne firms will eventually follow suit. Piper-Heidsieck wine is given the so-called cold treatment (10 days at $-4°C$) and is clarified and filtered once.

Fresh, light and uncomplicated

In general, Piper-Heidsieck champagnes do not possess an overwhelming personality. The non-vintage *brut* tastes fresh, light and uncomplicated. The balance between acids and mildness is usually good, unless you chance upon a young bottle: the wine may then taste rather green. The *brut* usually contains about 30% wine from white grapes. Its bouquet is not remarkable, but pure; the *mousse*, though a little weak, consists of reasonably small bubbles. The vintage champagnes are finer and more elegant. They have a higher white wine content — usually 50%. One of my favourite Piper champagnes is the vintage rosé. Concerning the 1975, for example, I noted: 'Light pink colour, fine *mousse*, delicate, fresh taste — a flawless wine.' The basic wine for the pink champagne is made up from 50% wine from white grapes. Later 18% to 20% still red wine is added to this basis. As a rule, Piper's rosé tastes best four or five years after vintage.

Brut Sauvage

Piper-Heidsieck carries two *cuvées de prestige*. The older and better known is the Florens-Louis (always vintage). The white Chardonnay grape provides 60% of the wine so that this champagne, not surprisingly, has a fairly light taste. Other properties are a pale colour, fine bubbles, a delicate bouquet, a refined style and great purity. The second prestige brand was launched in 1980 and is called Brut Sauvage (non-vintage). It is very similar to the Florens-Louis, including its price, but tastes distinctly drier: it is given hardly any *dosage*. In my opinion this champagne is excellent as an aperitif, but as an accompaniment to food it somewhat lacks substance. Moreover, it does not have sufficient nuances to remain interesting for very long.

Charles Heidsieck's brut usually has quite a lot of colour, a not too pronounced bouquet and a full, rather solid taste. It retains its freshness for many years and is rather reserved in nature. Near enough the same label is used for the vintage champagnes. These have an extremely fresh taste for up to five years after vintage, with a detectable trace of lemon.

The vintage blanc de blancs (the label for which is currently unavailable for illustration)should not be confused with its much humbler, non-vintage equivalent (which bears a different label). It is not a really full wine, but no featherweight either. Here too the taste retains much of its fraicheur for many years after vintage; this truly elegant champagne usually remains vital for up to at least 10 years. The quality is very good.

La Royale with its golden label is firmly and soundly balanced. Its freshness is powerful and long-lasting: it can be left for about ten years old before drinking. The taste has an elegant firmness, with a cool undertone. It is a distinguished wine, but, personally I prefer a cuvée de prestige with somewhat more breeding and subtlety.

Charles Heidsieck

Champagne
Reims

Charles-Henri Heidsieck was the third of the German nephews Florenz-Ludwig Heidsieck brought in to assist him in the wine business he had set up in 1785 (see page 156). He arrived in 1805 and was later to travel extensively for the firm, particularly in Russia, where he and his white horse became almost legendary. Charles-Henri died relatively young, but evidently passed on something of his passion for wine and travel to his son, Charles-Camille, who, after a few probationary years at Piper-Heidsieck, started his own champagne firm in 1851. He too travelled a lot, especially to America. His baggage contained not only sample bottles of champagne, but also the latest makes of sporting guns, for he was a keen game hunter. This was the man who, as his success and popularity grew, acquired the nickname of Champagne Charlie, lending his name in 1869 to a music-hall ditty that took London by storm.

Out of the ashes

At the outbreak of the American Civil War Charles-Camille was in private and commercial difficulties. Sales were almost at a standstill and on one occasion he spent four months in a wretched jail near New Orleans. In addition, he lost large sums of money trying to get rich quick in the cotton trade. In late 1861 he returned to Reims almost destitute, to find that business at home was just as bad. The firm was still paying off some of its debts when his son, Charles-Eugène, took over in 1871. The company's problems were only solved when Charles Heidsieck, quite by chance, acquired a property in Colorado that greatly increased in value. Since the days of Charles-Camille and Charles-Eugène, the men of the family have continued to run the firm, all of them retaining Charles as one of their names. In 1976 Charles Heidsieck was taken over by Champagne Henriot, who acquired a majority interest; the present chairman of Charles Heidsieck is Joseph Henriot. History has thus more or less repeated itself: when Charles-Camille started his business in

Opposite page, above:
Charles Heidsieck is the only one of the three Heidsieck firms to have a Heidsieck working for it. This photograph shows Charles Jean-Marc Heidsieck, the export director.

Opposite page, below:
The champagnes of Charles Heidsieck mature in the same cellar complex of crayères as those of Henriot.

Left:
Some of the modern tanks used by the firm.

Below:
It is not true that pickers are served unlimited champagne at harvest time. As elsewhere in France, they have to quench their thirst with ordinary red wine or mineral water.

Charles Heidsieck has in its office engravings that 'Champagne Charlie' brought back from America.

Charles Heidsieck has kept some of the very first bottles it marketed. I saw one label with Russian text, another with 'Verzenay grand mousseux', a third with 'Grand Vin Premium Weisslack'.

Charles Heidsieck

1851 he had his brother-in-law Ernest Henriot as partner, who remained connected with the firm until 1875.

Shared vineyards

The merger with Henriot enabled Charles Heidsieck to obtain vineyards of its own for the first time. Henriot owns 270 acres, this being sufficient to produce about 20% of the firm's requirements. Production of Charles Heidsieck champagnes alone is some 3.5 million bottles. For every two bottles sold seven are stocked in the cellars. The Charles Heidsieck wines are vinified quite separately from those of Henriot. Both houses have their own champagnes with their own style. Traditional methods are employed at Charles Heidsieck, except that mechanical *remuage* is beginning to be adopted.

Different dosages

At Charles Heidsieck, malolactic fermentation is considered absolutely essential in order to make the wine rather more supple; or, as export director Charles Jean-Marc Heidsieck puts it: 'I would rather have little acid yet very dry champagnes, in preference to acid that you need to sugar.' At Charles Heidsieck the *dosage* sometimes differs according to destination: rather milder champagnes are sent to the United States and West Germany than, for example, to Switzerland. No brandy at all is used in the *dosage*.

Firm and austere

Charles Heidsieck champagne strikes me as being traditional, almost old-fashioned. The taste of the *brut* makes a complete, rather solid impression in which the freshness lasts a long time. It is not a lively, fruity wine, but firm and somewhat austere. The vintage champagnes retain an extremely fresh taste until a good five years after their vintage, sometimes with a hint of lemon. Only after

eight to ten years does a certain softness start to develop. I do not find the ordinary *blanc de blancs* of the Charles Heidsieck range terribly good, but the vintage variety is well worth while. This too keeps its *fraîcheur* for a long time. In 1980, for example, the 1971 was still extremely vital. La Royale is the firm's prestige *cuvée*. It was

launched in 1963, the vintage being 1955, and originally called Royal Charles. Made from about 75% wine from black grapes, it is generally a balanced, firm champagne with cool lemony tones in bouquet and taste. To me it seems less fine or subtle than many other *cuvées de prestige*. Nine or ten years' maturing is virtually essential for this wine.

Left:
Some of the modern horizontal presses into which the Henriot grapes are poured. As a deliberate policy, the firm has planted no Pinot Meunier vines.

Below left:
Inside Henriot's chalk cellars, which cover 12 acres. The firm sells around 1.5 million bottles a year and tries to hold an average 5.25 million in stock.

Below right:
Some Henriot champagnes. Doyen is a subsidiary brand, once sold a lot in Russia.

Although Henriot's blanc de blancs *tastes* rather thin, and the ordinary brut *seems* so mild to me that I once described it as demi-brut, quality rises significantly with the Souverain vintage champagnes: in 1980 the 1971 was a civilized, gently fresh wine, perfect to drink. The 1973 was slightly less attractive, with lemony tones in bouquet and taste. Henriot also produces a very decent vintage pink.

In about 1970 Joseph Henriot started to create a special cuvée for Baron Philippe de Rothschild, who wanted to be able to serve his own 'Château Mouton Rothschild' champagne; and it was not to be a petit champagne léger. *It was many years before the baron was satisfied: the first wine (the 1966) only came on the market in 1973. Exquisite little bubbles, fully foaming* mousse, *sprightly, graceful, yet with a mouth-filling taste and a decent aftertaste. Only modest in nuance, and sometimes also in bouquet.*

Henriot

'Our tools are tradition, technique and *esprit*,' says Joseph Henriot, chairman of Champagne Henriot. His family arrived in Reims in 1640 and has been in the champagne trade since 1808. The firm was founded by Apolline Henriot, née Godinot. After the death of her husband, she decided to exploit her father's vineyards. She called the business Veuve Henriot Aîné; it became Henriot & Co. in 1875 when her grandson, Ernest Henriot, who for almost 25 years had run the firm of Charles Heidsieck with his brother-in-law Charles-Camille Heidsieck, took over the family concern.
Henriot used to be one of the select group of shippers who belonged to Les Grandes Marques. However, the firm was expelled from the association in 1930 when Joseph's father took to transporting his grapes by lorry — an activity that was considered too 'industrial'.

Extensive vineyards

The Henriots have always attached great importance to owning vineyards, and the firm now has 271 acres with a quality rating of 94%. Nearly 60% of this land is in the Côte des Blancs, the rest in the Montagne de Reims. It was because of this large holding that Henriot sought a partner in the 1970s. The firm had more grapes than was justified by its champagne sales, whereas Charles Heidsieck had no vineyards and was struggling with a shortage of both grapes and capital. The merger — actually a take-over — was effected in 1976 (see page 160) when Joseph Henriot found financial backers. These are sleeping partners; the Henriot family owns 81% of the shares. A second acquisition was completed at the end of 1980 when Champagne Henriot took over the Trouillard/de Venoge group at Epernay. Probably only de Venoge will continue as a brand name.

High white wine content

Henriot uses both hydraulic and so-called balloon presses. Most of the fermentation tanks are of stainless steel and the *gyropalette* system has been introduced for the *remuage*. The essential character of the Henriot champagnes is affected as little as possible by chemical means. Joseph Henriot prefers biological and physical methods. A characteristic of these champagnes is that they contain at least 40% wine from white grapes, with up to 50% and sometimes 75% for the vintage varieties. In general, the firm produces fairly light, refreshing champagnes, the vintage types being higher, in my view, than the non-vintage kinds. For me the best champagne is the Réserve Baron Philippe de Rothschild in which sprightliness, grace, a quite persistent taste, and a fine, full *mousse* harmonize agreeably. The wine lacks only a little subtlety and could sometimes have more bouquet. I also have pleasant recollections of the Souverain vintage champagnes.

Right:
The premises in Reims, almost
next door to the Veuve Clicquot
cellars.

Below:
In Abel Lepitre's chalk cellars in
Reims there is a decorated wine
vat about 125 years old.

Abel Lepitre owns no vineyards
and so has no presses.

From Abel Lepitre's visitors'
book: 'If Cain had known
Lepitre he would have spared
Abel.'

At Abel Lepitre remuage is still
done entirely by hand, taking an
average of 2 to 2½ months.

Jacques's son Bruno is very
much involved in the business.

No more than 10% of Abel
Lepitre's champagne is
exported.

A good Abel Lepitre product is
the cuvée de prestige 'Prince A.
De Bourbon Parme', always a
vintage champagne. However, I
personally prefer the Blanc de
Blancs Crémant.

Abel Lepitre's crémant (always
vintage), which is made
exclusively from white grapes,
is the best of the entire range.
Very light, and refined, with a
spring-like scent and an almost
delicate taste with an
unobtrusive, mildly fresh hint of
lemon. A perfect champagne
(also delicious in the morning or
with a late breakfast). It has had
a special bottle since 1975.

Abel Lepitre

Champagne
Reims

The business premises of Abel Lepitre in
Reims stand between those of Henriot and
Veuve Clicquot. The firm was founded in
1924 in the village of Ludes by Abel Lepitre,
then 24 years old. Though successful, he was
not able to profit from it for very long: he
died, a prisoner of the Germans, in 1940.
After the war Abel's son Jacques continued
the business; he is still chairman and the
biggest shareholder.
The steady growth of the business forced
Jacques Lepitre to seek space elsewhere. He
found it in the village of Sacres, where the
firm invested heavily in facilities above and
below ground. When the Sacres complex was
bought, Abel Lepitre's production stood at
250,000 bottles a year; today it is about one
million. Not all the champagne carries a
Lepitre label. About one-third of the bottles
go out under the brand name of George
Goulet — a shipper taken over in about 1960
by Jacques Lepitre. The firm also owns the
Saint-Marceaux and Henry Goulet brands.

Young, fresh champagnes

In practically all the Abel Lepitre
champagnes, wines from the first, second
and third pressings are used. Cellar master
Germain Pithois claims that the second and
third pressings yield wines that are at their
best when young — and the firm aims at
producing youthful, fresh champagnes that
should be drunk within two years of leaving
the cellars. They will then already have
matured for about three years in the chalk
pits. With sales of 650,000 bottles a year
(Abel Lepitre alone) there is a stock of some
2.2 million bottles. The firm has no
vineyards of its own, the grape juice
ferments in glazed concrete tubs, and the
remuage is still done by hand.

Crémant the speciality

Although Abel Lepitre markets a good range
of very decent, though not remarkable,
champagnes, I must single out a speciality of
the house — the blanc de blancs crémant.
Crémant — as previously mentioned — is a
type of champagne with less carbon dioxide
pressure (about four instead of six
atmospheres); and with this wine Abel
Lepitre has secured an entrée to many high-
class French restaurants. It is always a
vintage champagne. The first vintage
launched, in 1952, was the 1949. With most
champagne shippers the crémant is a second-
rank wine, but in the case of Lepitre it is the
top-quality offering. This champagne is
usually distinguished by a light colour, a
fine, spring-like bouquet, and a subtle,
almost delicate taste with a fresh, judicious
impression of lemon. As an aperitif, Abel
Lepitre's Crémant Blanc de Blancs is
virtually perfect.

Left:
Henri (right) and Rémi Krug study the still cloudy young wines. At a later stage they will taste all the young wines two or three times a week over a three-week period in order to blend the cuvée. They nearly always call on the reserves of old wine too, of which Krug usually has about 80 types. Henri and Rémi taste all these as well. In terms of grapes, the Grand Cuvée is normally made up of about 50% Pinot Noir, 33% Chardonnay, 17% Pinot Meunier.

Below:
At Krug the wine ferments in wooden casks. Two coopers are employed to repair them.

Opposite page, above:
Transferring the wine to a clean cask.

'You don't play Bach today like they did in 1930' and 'Rolls-Royce too has moved with the times' are a couple of sayings the Krug brothers use to explain why the Grand Cuvée is lighter and more vital than its predecessor Private Cuvée. They also use more white grapes for this cuvée de prestige champagne. The Grand Cuvée (non-vintage) is a magnificent champagne with an exceedingly fine mousse, many nuances (particularly in the bouquet), great purity and magnificent balance. You could have none better.

This vintage champagne represents 15%-20% of Krug's sales, except in Britain, where it is 50%. It is a more traditional wine than the Grande Cuvée, firmer and fuller. You could describe the Grand Cuvée as a very sprightly champagne, the vintage as a really serious one. Its class is unmistakable — and obviously the year of vintage is much more influential. Recent wines are the 1975 (just a little) and the 1976 (available since the spring of 1982).

Krug

Joseph Krug, founder of the house of Krug, was born in Mainz in 1800 and eventually settled in Champagne; in 1834 he entered the employment of Jacquesson & Fils, an important wine firm at Châlons-sur-Marne. As the confidant and representative of the owner, Adolphe Jacquesson, he travelled abroad, including Russia. In 1843 Joseph set up his own business in Reims, initially with a partner, who died shortly afterwards. The direct descendants of Joseph Krug still run this champagne firm: managing director Henri Krug and commercial director Rémi Krug are brothers, representing the fifth generation of Krugs as champagne shippers. The sixth generation is already in the wings — Henri has three sons. He told me of a charming family tradition. After the birth of each of his boys he took a bottle of champagne and a silver champagne flute to the hospital to give the new babies *un petit*

Krug

goût. Henri himself had been given a sip of Krug as a baby, from the same little glass.

Help from Rémy-Martin

In the distant past, Champagne Krug owned a good deal of land, including 62 acres near Mailly. All this land was duly sold and it is only quite recently that the firm began buying vineyards again. In 1960 none of Krug's wine came from its own land, in 1970 a mere 2%. The really important purchases were made in 1971 and 1972. At present the firm has about 22 acres in Ay and 16 in Mesnil-sur-Oger; an additional 74 acres are rented in Avize and Oger, half the vintage going to Krug. Altogether these vineyards provide roughly one-third of Krug's grape requirements. Purchase of the vineyards was made possible by the financial backing of Rémy-Martin. This cognac firm took a minority holding in Champagne Krug, which has since grown into a majority interest, the other shareholder being the Krug family.

Aiming at perfection

Krug has always been a small firm. The present production of some 500,000 bottles annually shows little increase on the output of 1900. But quantity has never been regarded as important as quality: Krug champagnes are absolutely first class. Such perfection is obtained by a method so painstaking in every detail that many would dismiss it as old-fashioned. Naturally, Krug uses only best quality grapes, and a member of the family is often present when they are pressed. In principle, only must from the first pressing, the *cuvée*, is used. Like their forefathers, Henri and Rémi Krug ferment the entire vintage, slowly and at a low temperature, in oak vats. According to Henri, this gives them more bouquet. Thanks to the relatively small quantities of wine per vat, the firm has a wide range of options at its disposal for composing the eventual champagne. Henri and Rémi can introduce subtleties that would be impossible in larger units. Each vat can

obviously be judged on individual merits and less successful wines rejected.

Big wine reserves

At Krug there are no compromises in quality. Thus in years of poor harvests there is a heavy demand on the reserve wines. Normally these comprise 30%, but in 1978 (only a moderate year), 55% *vin de reserve* was added. Krug stores these reserve wines mainly in stainless-steel tanks. The firm has no cellar master: Henri himself usually makes the selection, assisted by Rémi and often by their father, Paul, as well. Krug wines undergo no malolactic fermentation. Henri points out that not only is it difficult to achieve in small units, but also maintains that the wines remain fresher without it. Any obtrusive acidity disappears quite naturally at Krug, for no bottle leaves the cellars before maturing at least five years. The stock fluctuates around 2.8 million.

No hurry

There is never any impression of hurry at Krug. The *remuage* is done by hand and lasts from two to three and a half months, and after *dégorgement* every bottle is given a further three to six months' rest. The wine is not filtered at all, just clarified once with isinglass. Among the other countless details that make Krug champagnes exceptional are bottling by gravity, a very limited *dosage* (the wine is after all mature) and as sound a cork as possible.

Only two wines

Krug produces only two champagnes, the Grande Cuvée and a vintage type, both exclusively *brut*. The Grande Cuvée was launched at the end of the 1970s as a successor to the Private Cuvée. There were two reasons: the Private Cuvée, even for connoisseurs, did not differ sufficiently from the vintage champagne to justify its existence; and the firm wanted to produce a

lighter, livelier and more contemporary champagne. This decision was made easier by the vineyards acquired in the Côte des Blancs, at Avize, Mesnil and Oger. In my opinion, the Grande Cuvée is a sublime wine. Its most striking features are ultra-fine bubbles, a bouquet full of subtle changes, a particularly beautiful, elegant, fresh taste (somewhat austere and wholly natural), a glorious aftertaste and a wonderful balance. This champagne, which accounts for 80% of Krug sales, is my favourite *cuvée de prestige*: every bottle is an experience. The vintage champagnes have a different character; they are more old-fashioned, more complete and rounded than the Grande Cuvée — and of course you can taste the vintage. If you were to seek an analogy with French cooking, the Grande Cuvée would represent the *nouvelle cuisine* with its light, inventive creations, while the vintage champagnes would represent the more classical style. But in both cases it is great champagne.

Taittinger

During World War I Champagne was once more a battleground. General Joffre's staff was accommodated in the Château de la Marquetterie, a beautiful old country mansion at Pierry, near Epernay. One young cavalry officer, Pierre Taittinger, was so captivated by the building that when the war was over he returned to buy it. Once settled in the region, Pierre Taittinger, not surprisingly, became a champagne enthusiast. As a result he took over the firm of Fourneaux Forest et Successeurs, founded in 1734, and subsequently started his own business under the new name of Taittinger-Mailly in 1932, dropping the latter part some 20 years later.

Growth and diversification

The success of Champagne Taittinger has been spectacular. Today, annual sales are around four million bottles (and increasing). The firm has also diversified. Taittinger owns the champagne house of Irroy; the firms of Monmousseau and Bouvet-Ladubey, specializing in Loire wines; a heating appliance factory; and the Concorde hotel group. Taittinger also acquired the splendid residence of the former Counts of Champagne — originally built for Thibault IV (1201-53), Count of Champagne and King of Navarre. It is said that Thibault

introduced the Chardonnay grape from Cyprus when returning from a crusade. This building, along with Taittinger's offices and cellars, is in Reims. Although Taittinger shares are traded on the Paris Bourse, 63% to 65% always remain in the possession of the family. The business today is run by Claude Taittinger.

Importance of white grapes

Taittinger's possessions include 617 acres of vineyards which provide about 40% of its grapes. About two-thirds are planted with Pinot Noir and about one-third with Chardonnay. There is hardly any Pinot Meunier. Most of the other grapes processed come through contracts with growers; Taittinger in fact boasts the most extensive purchasing arrangements in the Côte des Blancs. White grapes are important for this firm. Not only does it use rather more white wine in the ordinary *brut* than do most of the big houses, but its prestige *cuvée* Comtes de Champagne is a *blanc de blancs*. Production of this type is an estimated 600,000 bottles annually.

Old and new

Under the Taittinger offices in the Place Nicaise lie five chalk workings, now cellars,

dating from the 4th century. Yet in spite of its links with the past — symbolized, too, perhaps by the residence of the Counts of Champagne and the ancient Château de la Marquetterie, time has emphatically not stood still here. The four pressing areas are modern, most of the tanks for fermentation and storage are of stainless steel, and mechanical *remuage*, by the *gyropalettes* system, is on the increase. There is a great contrast, too, between the evocative chalk galleries and the austere modern cellars on the Rue de la Justice.

Sound, elegant wines

Taittinger is very quality conscious in everything, as is evident from its consistent policy of a three-year stock and also from the fact that it uses only wine from the first pressing (the *cuvée*). The *tailles* from subsequent pressings are exchanged with other shippers. Taittinger offers three vats of *taille* for one vat of *cuvée*. There are few shippers who could or would make such an offer.
Taittinger champagnes in general give an impression of soundness, elegance and purity. The ordinary *bruts* do not have a very pronounced or exciting bouquet, but they possess a mild, agreeable taste with a certain liveliness, and sufficient *fraîcheur*; they are indeed harmonious wines.

Comtes de Champagne

At the top of the Taittinger range is the *blanc de blancs* Comtes de Champagne, always a vintage champagne. I regard this as the best *cuvée de prestige* after that of Krug and the Dom Pérignon of Moët & Chandon. Its usual characteristics are plenty of small bubbles, a mild, elegant scent and a similarly mild elegant taste in which the freshness is restrained and never aggressive. Before it is sold, the wine is matured for five to six years. The *remuage* of Comtes de Champagne is always carried out by hand, and a real cork, not a crown top, is inserted

The Brut Resérve is a Taittinger standard: a soft, agreeable-tasting wine with a certain liveliness and ample freshness. A good, long-lasting mousse with sometimes a very vague green tinge in the colour and a not very pronounced but pure bouquet.

Taittinger makes and sells comparatively little vintage champagne, except the Comtes de Champagne. The vintage quality is usually a little more mature and milder than the brut. Not of the greatest refinement, but extremely agreeable and carefully made.

The Comtes de Champagne is a splendid champagne. It is made exclusively from white grapes — Chardonnay — and matured for five to six years. Characteristic features are a fine mousse, soft, elegant taste, refined freshness and perfect balance. One of the best prestige cuvées on the market.

Like the white Comtes de Champagne, the pink comes in a bottle copied from the earliest champagne type. It has less finesse than its namesake, this attribute being rather subdued by a fairly strong 'red' presence. The wine also tastes rather sweet for a brut. Good but not great.

Opposite page, above left: Château de la Marquetterie, bought by Pierre Taittinger, Claude's father, after World War I. It is still owned by the family. The Taittingers came to Reims after the 1870 Franco-Prussian war because Alsace-Lorraine, where they were born, was annexed by the Germans. Claude's grandfather, also called Pierre Taittinger, was at that time administrator for the Wagon-Lits company. He had an excellent knowledge of Greek, and was one of the greatest cheesemakers of France. At his 80th birthday party, 80 different cheeses were served.

Opposite page, above right: Claude Taittinger in one of the firm's vineyards; these have an average quality rating of 94%.

Opposite page, below: The head office in the Place Saint-Nicaise, Reims.

Below: Cellar figure.

Bottom: Part of the Taittinger cellars beneath the head office. There are modern cellars with gyropalettes elsewhere in Reims. Cellar capacity is being increased to approximately 15 million bottles.

Every year the firm organizes one of the most important gastronomic competitions for chefs, the Prix Culinaire International Pierre Taittinger. Chefs from other countries may also participate.

Taittinger

during fermentation in the bottle. Taittinger also makes a Comtes de Champagne Rosé. This is produced by the *cuvaison* method in which the colour comes from keeping the juice for some times in contact with the black grape skins. The rather pale hue that results is corrected by adding about 6% of red wine from Bouzy. The end product does not greatly appeal to me: the taste is too rounded, too sweet, and with less refinement than that of its white namesake. In 1982

Taittinger launched its Brut Absolu, a champagne *non-dosé*. The quality is excellent, the taste slightly round and mature, and the composition 60% Pinot Noir and 40% Chardonnay.

Louis Roederer

A stately patrician residence in the Boulevard Lundy in Reims, a large inner courtyard, an enormous stone staircase, high, mellow brown walls, a little office with 'Inquiries' above the window, and a waiting room with back numbers of magazines: these are the offices of Louis Roederer. The roots of this firm, in its handsome surroundings, go back to 1765, when the champagne firm of Dubois & Fils was founded. In 1827 the business was run by Nicolas-Henri Schreider who, having no sons, brought his nephew

Louis Roederer into the firm. Louis — a man of boundless energy — prospered. His wines became extremely popular in Russia and in America, the business grew, and so did his fortune and reputation. He sat on the Reims city council, and there is still a hospital in the city named after him. Louis died in 1870, leaving the business to his son, also named Louis, who was succeeded by his sister, Madame Jacques Olry-Roederer. Among other women who subsequently played key roles in the development of the firm, the

most legendary was Camille Olry-Roederer.

A wartime ruse

After the death of her husband in 1932, Camille continued to run the business with great determination. During World War II she gained local renown for the ingenious manner in which she held on to part of her champagne stocks (although some six million bottles had vanished by the end of the war). When the Germans began

This **brut** is a softly foaming, rather firm champagne that combines the strength of black grapes (about 60% Pinot Noir, half each from the Marne Valley and the Montagne de Reims) with the freshness of white (35%-40% Cote des Blancs) in a correct but not particularly exciting way. Avoid buying a bottle that is too old; the wine may have lost its attractiveness and become rather dull. I have been disappointed more than once, mainly in restaurants where the champagne had evidently been around for some time.

Louis Roederer's vintage champagnes are always very good: considerably better than the **brut**. They usually have a strong colour, a generous amount of small bubbles and a mature, respectably long aftertaste. The taste is distinctly more robust and fruity than the ordinary **brut**.

Power, class and freshness are combined in the Cristal into a harmonious, fine-tasting whole. A great champagne that can readily be served with red meat, poultry or game. I find it too heavy as an aperitif. The quantity of Cristal produced by Roederer each year can vary; in really poor years (1968 and 1972) it is hardly any. The label illustrated is also printed on the back because of the clear glass bottle.

'We want the champagne to remain and not to turn into red wine', said director Jean-Claude Rouzaud about his rosé. This is always sold as a vintage variety — often no more than 30,000 bottles a year. It has the lightest possible tint of pink: if you tasted it with your eyes shut you could not tell the difference from normal champagne. This wine has a little more Pinot Noir than the ordinary vintage and so tastes rather firmer. I rate this the best rosé made in Champagne.

Opposite page, above left:
Roederer's 60-100 hectolitre stainless-steel fermentation tanks, installed between 1967 and 1970. The wooden casks of reserve wines are elsewhere in the building.

Opposite page, above right:
A cellar guide serves visitors with a glass of wine. Roederer has about 2½ miles of cellar passages.

Opposite page, below:
The courtyard behind the offices in Boulevard Lundy, Reims.

Below:
Louis Roederer's offices are furnished in a restrained but stylish manner.

Roederer owns the world-famous Haras des Rouges-Terres stud farm in Normandy.

Part of the cellars and most of the business premises are in a turning off the Boulevard Lundy. Bullet holes in the metal nameplate are a reminder of World War I.

After dégorgement all the bottles are rested for at least 6 months at Roederer.

Roederer's chairman Jean-Claude Rouzaud was born in 1942 and since 1967 he has worked in all departments of the firm. He has been in his present position since 1979. He holds a pilot's licence and makes use of this for business trips.

Louis Roederer

plundering the champagne cellars in 1940, Camille Olry-Roederer confronted the officer responsible and announced: 'If you go on like this there will be no champagne left to celebrate your victory.' She also managed to secure extra supplies of sugar, allegedly for dosing her champagne. In fact, she distributed it secretly among the more needy local families.

After the death of Camille Olry-Roederer in 1975, the business passed to her daughter Madame Marcelle Rouzaud; her son Jean-Claude is the chairman, and her husband Claude vice-chairman.

Extensive vineyards

Louis Roederer is in the happy position of meeting about 80% of its requirements for grapes from its own vineyards. The firm has 457 acres at its disposal — mostly its own property, the rest under contract to the house — with an average quality rating of 98% to 99%. Half the acreage is planted with Pinot Noir, half with Chardonnay. The grape juice ferments in fairly small stainless-steel tanks. Only wine from the first pressing is used. The wine is, at most, lightly filtered; natural materials such as albumen are used for clarifying. The *remuage* lasts for four to six months and is done by hand, although the firm is experimenting with mechanical methods. Roederer holds a five-year stock: some 7.5 million bottles against annual sales of 1.5 million. The *vins de réserve* are kept in oak casks; altogether these represent one whole vintage. Such attention to detail, combined with other special features, result in some great champagnes.

Crystal-clear bottles

Louis Roederer's best and most famous wine is the Cristal, which derives its name from the clear bottles in which it has been sold for about a century. The bottle is said to have been created in 1876 for Tsar Alexander II. Only a new champagne in a new bottle was apparently considered worthy of an emperor, so Louis Roederer was instructed to make an

exclusive *cuvée* with its own bottle for the tsar. The present Cristal bottle still looks very much the same: thick, sturdy glass (to withstand the journey to St Petersburg) and a flat bottom, with no punt. This is the characteristic indentation which distributes pressure; but in this case, because of the solidity of the glass, it was unnecessary. The modern glass, however, shows one difference. It is reinforced against the disastrous effect of ultraviolet light, which can give the wine an unpleasant, fusty taste. As an extra protection, all bottles of Cristal are wrapped in tinted cellophane. Roederer's Cristal has a marvellous international reputation, and is rightly regarded as one of the greatest of all champagnes.

Balance

Only sound, ripe grapes are used for the Cristal *cuvée*, resulting in a potent wine. In fact, this basic wine is thought too strong at Roederer. To lighten it, Cristal is provided with rather more white wine than other Roederer champagnes. 'We start by giving the wine so much strength that it gets out of balance,' say the Rouzauds. 'We restore the balance with white wine.' Cristal is indeed a champagne that combines maximum firmness with maximum freshness. It tastes full without for a moment being leaden, seems well-matured, has long-lasting bubbles and lingers in the mouth. It is a real dinner-time champagne. I myself prefer rather more finesse in my wine, but I can well imagine that many regard Roederer Cristal as the very summit of champagne. It normally represents 20% to 25% of Roederer's production.

Other champagnes

As with most shippers, the best-selling champagne from this firm is the non-vintage *brut*. This has good bubbles and a mildly fresh, mouth-filling taste, sometimes with the merest hint of bitterness. This wine tastes best in the year after it leaves the Roederer cellars, when it is about five years

old. After that, in my experience, it quickly loses its attractiveness. Louis Roederer's vintage champagnes are always firmer and fruitier than the ordinary *brut*, bridging the quite enormous quality gap between the *brut* and the Cristal. Of the remaining wines the vintage pink in particular deserves attention: it is subtly coloured and almost perfect of its kind.

Ruinart Père & Fils

On 25 May 1728, Louis XV gave the city of Reims permission to transport the wine of Champagne in baskets of 50 or 100 bottles. Until that time only transport in vats had been allowed. The first *Champenois* to take advantage of the favourable trading conditions under the new decree and set up his own wine business was a cloth merchant, Nicolas Ruinart. For years he had given presents of champagne to his customers and created such a demand that he built up a modest but profitable sideline in wine. Now he was in a position to expand this by supplying wine in bottles. In a bulky accounts book we read that Nicolas Ruinart sold a consignment of wine on 1 September 1729 'in the name of God and the Blessed Virgin'. This document qualifies Ruinart as the earliest champagne shipper. The enthusiasm that Nicolas felt for champagne may well have been stimulated by his uncle, Dom Thierry Ruinart. This Benedictine monk, in his day a well-known man of letters, lived and worked in Paris but travelled to Champagne practically every year. At the abbey of Hautvillers, which accommodated one of the biggest libraries in the world, Dom Ruinart made the acquaintance of the legendary cellar master Dom Pérignon, and perhaps even assisted him in his work. It is a striking fact that his visits almost always lasted into the vintage. Dom Ruinart died at Hautvillers, and is, in fact, buried next to Dom Pérignon.

Cellars in the chalk

Descendants of Nicolas Ruinart expanded the business steadily. Claude Ruinart (1731-98) moved it from Epernay to Reims, to the part of the city situated above the old Roman chalk workings; and he was the first to start using these *crayères* as wine cellars. Nowadays, Ruinart owns 100 such cellars, extending 100 feet below ground for five miles, covering an area of 270,000 square feet. They have been classified as a historic monument. Edmond Ruinart (1796-1881) made a useful journey to America and presented a case of champagne to President Jackson in the White House. What the records fail to mention is that Edmond suffered from a stomach complaint and drank fresh milk every day, not champagne; so a cow, provided with a suitable amount of hay, accompanied him on board ship across the Atlantic.

The Rothschild connection

The house of Ruinart saw its premises completely destroyed during World War I and its cellars ransacked in World War II. Post-war expansion began in 1949, when Ruinart director Bertrand Mur came to an agreement with Baron Philippe de Rothschild whereby each was to distribute the other's wines. This collaboration lasted almost 14 years, during which period Ruinart sales increased from 150,000 to 600,000 bottles a year. The arrangement came to an end in 1963 when Moët & Chandon acquired 80% of the Ruinart shares. In 1973 the firm was wholly integrated with the Moët & Chandon group. During Ruinart's dynamic years of expansion, it was always Bertrand Mure who kept his finger on the pulse. Nephew of the last descendant of the Ruinarts, he is one of Champagne's great personalities. Bertrand's father, incidentally, ran the firm of Louis Roederer for 35 years.

The sales of Ruinart Père & Fils have continued to rise. Annual production is now around 1.2 million bottles, of which more than two-thirds is exported. The firm aims at a stock of some 4.5 million bottles, roughly equivalent to three years' sales. A modest proportion of the grapes comes from 35 acres of vineyard that Ruinart has owned near the village of Sillery for a couple of centuries. The land has a quality rating of 100%. The firm has invested in stainless-steel tanks for fermentation. Wine from both the first pressing (*cuvée*) and the second (*première taille*) is used in the non-vintage *brut*. The vintage champagnes, including the prestige *cuvée* Dom Ruinart, are produced exclusively from the first pressing.

Ruinart's Brut Tradition is usually made from two-thirds black and one-third white grapes. It is a rather mild champagne that lays no claim to greatness, but is still very pleasant and correct. The taste is fresh without any disturbingly sharp acidity. The bouquet often has slight indications of fruit and ripeness. The vintage champagnes are somewhat better and sprightlier, usually also with a fresh taste, and sometimes a hint of lemon. Ruinart's vintage rosé is nice but not remarkable.

The Chardonnay grapes for the white Dom Ruinart (there is also a rare rosé) come from the Côte des Blancs (Avize, Cramant, Mesnil-sur-Oger) and from the Montagne de Reims (Sillery, Villers-Marmedy). A very polished, balanced, fairly light champagne, with a certain delicacy and refinement is made exclusively from these white grapes. Its tone seems almost mild. I feel, however, that for a cuvée de prestige the wine is just a bit too short, too smooth, and lacking in depth.

Ruinart Père & Fils

Light, fresh style

Bertrand Mure described the style of his wines to me as 'light, fresh, and with a lot of finesse'. These qualities certainly apply to the Dom Ruinart, a *blanc de blancs* that is always a vintage champagne. This wine is indeed quite light and fresh, with a certain delicacy and refinement, but to my mind the taste (in which I have detected a trace of lemon) has little depth or personality. Dom Ruinart is undoubtedly a balanced, civilized champagne, but I would like it to be more complete and more exciting. The firm does not disclose how many bottles of Dom Ruinart it produces, but it must be a considerable quantity, certainly for a *cuvée de prestige*; the United States, the largest overseas customer, buys only this item from the range. The ordinary vintage champagnes from Ruinart Père & Fils possess less class than the Dom Ruinart, but are nevertheless of good quality. The non-vintage *brut* is usually blended from 15 to 20 different wines; a quarter or more of these consist of mature reserve wines. The Brut Tradition is sold after about two and a half years. It often has a soft, not particularly subtle bouquet with judicious hints of fruit and ripeness. The taste, fresh without obtrusive acids, matches the bouquet. It is a fairly mild champagne, neither too heavy nor too light — not great but certainly correctly made.

About 60% of all Canard-Duchêne champagne is sold in French supermarkets. It is relatively low priced, and this is reflected in the quality. It is made from 85% black grapes, which may explain the occasional reddish glint in the colour. It has a flat bouquet (sometimes with a hint of stewed apples), and the taste is rather mild and undemanding. Precisely the same wine is also sold in France under the label Cuvée Royale. The vintage brut is a little finer and fresher.

The cuvée de prestige Charles VII was launched by Canard-Duchêne in 1968. This champagne is made from about 66% white grapes. Bouquet and taste are reasonably refined and rather fresh, but the Charles VII could not be called truly great. The special bottle is slightly tinted because it has been treated to screen out ultraviolet light.

*Right:
Jean-Pierre Canard, director of Canard-Duchêne.*

*Below left:
Canard-Duchêne's buildings almost hide the little village of Ludes.*

*Below right:
The mouth of this grape-festooned cherub is a fountain.*

*Bottom right:
Some pupimatics, mechanically worked racks. This system is considered less efficient than the gyropalette system where 504 bottles can be moved, shaken and turned at the same time.*

Since the mid-1970s Canard-Duchêne has had stainless-steel tanks as well as concrete fermentation vats.

Canard-Duchêne has 37 acres of vineyard, in Ludes, Taissy and Verzenay, the grapes providing 3%-4% of requirements.

In 1972 Canard-Duchêne took over the champagne firm Chanoine Frères in Epernay. This was one of the oldest firms in the region, founded in 1730. Chanoine Frères is now only a brand name.

The 33.6% of the Canard-Duchêne shares Veuve-Clicquot took over in 1978 were held by Piper-Heidsieck at that time.

Two other quite pleasant champagnes from the Canard-Duchêne range are the Blanc de Blancs and the Rosé, both vintage.

Canard-Duchêne

The firm of Canard-Duchêne is in the little wine village of Ludes, on the north side of the Montagne de Reims. The most striking feature of its premises is the angular, bunker-like cellar that rises above surrounding rooftops. This above-ground cellar — in Bordeaux it would be a *chai* — was completed in 1974 and has 25,800 square feet of floor space. Opposite is an older group of buildings and underground there is a three-mile system of passages. In the 1970s Canard-Duchêne also invested in stainless-steel tanks and two systems of mechanical *remuage*.

Veuve Clicquot in control

Victor-François Canard, who married Françoise-Léonie Duchêne, founded the firm in the previous century at Ludes. He owned vineyards and in 1868 set up as a champagne shipper. His descendants brought the firm to great prosperity after World War II. Annual sales rose from 287,000 bottles in 1946 to 853,000 in 1960, to 1,650,000 in 1970, and to 2,300,000 in 1980. More than 80% of all the champagne stays in France. In 1978 Veuve Clicquot Ponsardin acquired 33.6% of the shares, and another 33% shortly afterwards. That signalled the end of Canard-Duchêne as a family concern — although it is still run by François and Jean-Pierre Canard.

Moderate prices

Canard-Duchêne aims at a range of moderately priced wines offering good value for money. About 90% of the basic wine is bought in the Aube *département*, wine from the second pressing is used in the ordinary *brut*, and from the third pressing in the *demi-sec*. The *brut* often has a reddish tinge, a flat bouquet, with sometimes a hint of stewed apples, and a rather mild, easy taste without much breeding or subtlety. The vintage champagnes are somewhat better and fresher (they contain more white grapes), but the quality only becomes really interesting with the prestige *cuvée* Charles VII. Blended from two-thirds Chardonnay wine, this is sometimes, but not usually, a vintage champagne. Bouquet and taste are quite fine and fairly light, and fresh without being acid. It lacks real greatness, falling miles short of a Dom Pérignon, but it is the most distinguished champagne in the Canard-Duchêne range.

Joseph Perrier's non-vintage brut is made from approximately two-thirds black grapes and one-third white: the traditional Champagne ratio. This champagne normally has a rather firm taste in which there is an almost chalky cool freshness. However, in some countries a much softer version is sold which has had a sweeter dosage. The ordinary brut is not an exciting champagne, but it is a solid, very correct product. The vintage champagnes have slightly more class.

The Cuvée de Cent Cinquantenaire is a reminder that Joseph Perrier has been in existence for over 150 years. This is a champagne made up of the best wines from various good years into the subtlest, most attractive wine from the firm. A champagne that substantially fills the mouth, it contains a larger proportion of wine from black grapes than many other prestige cuvées.

Right:
Export manager Jean-Claude Fourmon, nephew of the managing director Georges Pithois.

Below:
The entrance to Joseph Perrier. The firm was founded in 1825 by Joseph Perrier (1795-1870) and his portrait hangs in the reception hall.

Below right:
All the cellar passages end in this long gallery. Daylight enters through slits. They call it la cloître, 'the cloister'.

At Joseph Perrier, fermentation takes places in bottles up to Methuselah size (= 8 ordinary bottles). Most firms only go up to the magnum (= 2 bottles) and fill the larger sizes under pressure (transvasage) from ordinary bottles.

Joseph Perrier

Champagne
Châlons-sur-Marne

Most of the *grandes marques* welcome large numbers of visitors to their cellars every year, but at Joseph Perrier things are rather quiet. The firm lies outside the actual wine-growing area and off the wine routes, in the city of Châlons-sur-Marne. For this reason, perhaps, Joseph Perrier Fils & Cie has remained small and relatively unknown. It sells about 600,000 bottles a year and has a stock of some two million bottles; and until 1980 it had not invested heavily either in stainless-steel tanks or mechanical *remuage*. The firm was founded in 1825 by Joseph Perrier; his father already had a wine business and his uncle started the champagne firm of Perrier-Jouët. After Joseph's death, the firm was run by his uncle, Gabriël Perrier. He had no children and sold the business in 1888 to Paul Pithois. This family has remained in charge ever since, the present managers being Georges Pithois and his nephew Jean-Claude Fourmon.

A dash of brandy

About 40% to 60% of the grapes come from the firm's own 50 acres of vineyards in the communes of Hautvillers, Cumières and Daméry. The wine undergoes its first fermentation in enamelled metal and glazed concrete vats. It is filtered a number of times, clarified once and given a 'cold treatment'. As a rule, the champagnes are blended from the *cuvée* (first pressing), the *première taille* (second pressing), and sometimes the *deuxième taille* as well. At Joseph Perrier they freely admit that the *dosage* contains a dash of brandy: many houses refuse even to discuss this.

Mild freshness

In the large reception room, with its old beams, big fireplace and stone floor, and to a background noise of bottling, I tasted five Joseph Perrier champagnes. I tried some of them again later at home. The non-vintage *brut* had a yellowish colour and a not too sweet, gently fresh taste. Cool freshness and mouth-filling firmness characterize Joseph Perrier's vintage champagnes. The Cuvée du Cent Cinquantenaire occupies pride of place in the range. This prestige *cuvée* possesses more nuances in bouquet and taste than the other champagnes from this house, and is at the same time firmly constituted. It is blended from various good vintages, such as the Grand Siècle from Laurent Perrier. The Cuvée du Cent Cinquantenaire, like the other Joseph Perrier champagnes, matures in cellars cut into the 7-acre slope on which the business premises are built.

Moët & Chandon's Brut Impérial is the most widely drunk champagne in the world. Despite the fact that many millions of bottles are produced annually, the quality is correct in every sense. It is a beautiful, mildly fresh, good champagne that charms a large public without any hint of vulgarity. It usually contains 15% wine from white grapes and comes from vineyards with a quality rating of 86%-87%. The vintage version of this champagne is fuller, finer, more subtle.

In 1980 I held a comparative tasting of 16 different prestige champagnes. I put the Dom Pérignon (1973) in second place after the Krug Grande Cuvée, while others gave it first place. Dom Pérignon is an eminent champagne with an almost creamy foam, a pale colour, refined in bouquet and ultra-civilized in taste. It has a lot of nuance and a sublime balance. It retains its freshness for at least ten years.

The Dom Pérignon rosé is the rarest wine from the Moët & Chandon collection. In the years when it is made, only 300-400 cases are produced. This champagne was first served at the banquet to celebrate Persia's 2,000 years of existence. Maxim's in Paris is an important customer. The taste is softer and fuller than that of its white namesake, but it still lags behind as far as pure class and refinement are concerned.

Moët & Chandon

Champagne
Epernay

Claude Moët, a commission agent descended from a Dutch family that had settled in Champagne in the 14th century, set up his own wine business in about 1743. Two centuries later it has grown into the biggest in the region. Everything about Moët & Chandon is impressive. The firm has 16 miles of cellars, maintains a stock of some 50 million bottles, sells about 18 million bottles a year and employs more than 1,200 people — excluding almost 1,500 pickers. In Europe, America, Africa and Asia, Moët & Chandon is the most extensively drunk champagne; it is said that somewhere in the world, every two seconds, a bottle of Moët & Chandon is uncorked. In addition, the company is linked with the firm of Hennessy; together they own the champagne firms of Ruinart, Mercier and de Cazanove, as well as wine businesses in Germany, America, Argentina, Brazil and Portugal. They also have interests in many other concerns, including

Dior (perfumes) and Roc (cosmetics). Moët & Chandon is, indubitably, a giant.

Imperial customer

Claude Moët was succeeded by his son Nicolas-Claude, who in turn passed on the business to his son Jean-Rémy Moët. Under Jean-Rémy the firm grew in spectacular fashion. This expansion was largely due to Jean-Rémy's friendship with Napoleon. The emperor visited the firm on various occasions and ordered Moët's champagne for his court. Jean-Rémy put up two identical buildings to lodge Napoleon and his entourage. These still stand, diagonally opposite Moët & Chandon's main building in the Avenue de Champagne, and are referred to as l'Hôtel Moët. Adjoining them is an elegant garden with a rectangular pond that leads to an orangery — a copy of the one at Versailles.

Napoleon evidently valued Jean-Rémy's flattering attention, for on 17 March 1814 the emperor personally decorated him with the cross of the Legion of Honour. This was the last such award that Napoleon made. The medal has been carefully preserved by Moët & Chandon, along with a hat once worn by the emperor and other objects belonging to him. Jean-Rémy's friendship with Napoleon caused him no difficulties after Waterloo: indeed, from then until 1839, Moët's reputation and sales flourished as never before.

Modern equipment

Jean-Rémy left the business to his son Victor and his son-in-law Pierre-Gabriël Chandon; the latter changed the name to Moët & Chandon. Expansion continued, not least because of excellent management. Over the years, wine-growing land has been purchased and at present Moët & Chandon has no less than 1,150 acres of productive vineyard, supplying about 20% of its grapes. There is also continuous investment in equipment: from the technical viewpoint, everything is perfectly planned at Moët & Chandon. In 1978 a new *cuverie*, consisting of a great battery of enormous stainless-steel tanks, came into operation. In these all the *crus* are vinified and controlled separately. The firm has its own laboratories both for analysis and research, but has not yet adopted mechanical *remuage*.

Mass production, high standards

Despite the impressive quantities processed by Moët & Chandon, wine from the third pressing (*deuxième taille*) is not used. I understand, for example, that in 1979 all the *deuxieme taille* was exchanged for better wine from other firms, Moët & Chandon making up the difference in price. The firm's general approach in this and other particulars results in an ordinary *brut* which despite the massive scale of production is generally a good, correct champagne (although I have come across bad bottles). It

Moët & Chandon

is mildly fresh and appeals to a wide public. The vintage wines are fuller and finer, and more subtly nuanced. Only wine from the first pressing is used for these. The only dry champagne that has actually disappointed me is the vintage pink: as a rule it lacks freshness and refinement.

Dom Pérignon

The concept of Dom Pérignon came from the legendary André Simon, who in 1936 suggested that Moët & Chandon should bring out a special *cuvée* to celebrate the centenary of the firm's agency in Britain. (Moët & Chandon had bought the Dom Pérignon brand name from Mercier in 1930, but had not yet used it.) This prestige *cuvée* occupies a special position in the Moët & Chandon canon. Dom Pérignon is an excellent, lively champagne with a great deal of refinement and subtlety — one of the best of its kind. It is produced exclusively from Moët's own vineyards and is in such demand all over the world that there can never be enough of it. How much Dom Pérignon is sold is a secret, but I believe it to be less than one million bottles a year. The available quantity fluctuates considerably, because after some harvests only a little vintage champagne can be made, sometimes none at all.
Besides the white Dom Pérignon there is also a pink; it is much rarer but has much less class.

This label has a black band in remembrance of Pol Roger's most famous customer, Winston Churchill. Champagnes with this label are shipped only to Britain. Both the ordinary brut and the vintage champagnes are balanced, reliable wines that substantially fill the mouth but are not clumsy or heavy. They always have sufficient freshness. The wines are usually made from about 60% black grapes and 40% white, but variations are possible.

Blanc de Chardonnay is the name Pol Roger gives its blanc de blancs. It was launched in 1959. Top quality grapes are used. The wine has a nice, delicate mousse, a soft, elegant bouquet, a pure sophisticated taste and a smooth balance: sublime as an aperitif or on a late Sunday morning. The 1971 still tasted perfectly fresh nine years after it was made.

Pol Roger

Champagne
Epernay

'Pol Roger won splendidly today so there is a small profit for you on both races, best love, Winston' — so reads a telegram sent by Winston Churchill to Odette Pol-Roger. The Pol Roger in question was Churchill's racehorse. The British prime minister met Madame Pol-Roger at a reception in Paris in 1944, and relished her champagne so much that it became his favourite drink and he named his horse in its honour. Churchill publicized the champagne on many occasions. The firm's scrapbooks contain dozens of photographs and articles featuring Pol Roger and Churchill, who always took a supply of the champagne with him on his travels. After Churchill's death, the firm decided to add a permanent black edge to the label of its Extra Dry quality, which was specially reserved for Britain. This followed the example of Rolls-Royce: when Sir Henry Royce died in 1933 the red R-R initials on the cars were changed to black.

Notary's son

Odette Pol-Roger was one of those legendary champagne widows, a good-looking, intelligent woman who attracted all eyes at receptions the world over. Pol Roger (1820-99) was her husband's grandfather; son of a notary, he had founded the firm in 1849. When he started his champagne business he had neither vineyards nor cellars, and restricted himself initially to making wine for others. Later he launched his own brand. We read that the first bottles of Pol Roger were shipped to Britain in 1876. Pol left the business to his sons Maurice and Georges. They obtained permission from the President of France to change their surname from Roger to Pol-Roger, an exceptional concession. Today the firm, strictly a family business, is run by grandsons of Maurice and Georges: Christian de Billy and Christian Pol-Roger.

Back in time

The Pol Roger cellars extend along the Avenue de Champagne in Epernay and the offices are just behind in the Rue Henri Lelarge. They are modern and austere, in sharp contrast to the adjoining reception room. To enter this is to take a step back in time. The visitor is welcomed by a crackling open fire, comfortable armchairs, antique furniture, old paintings, two elegant clocks and a claret-coloured carpet with a flowered pattern. It is a cross between a French country house and a London club. This salon, in a way, symbolizes the style of Pol Roger, a style that Christian Pol-Roger described as 'Classicism in the noblest sense'. He explained that the house endeavours to preserve the traditional values of its champagne, but in a suitably modern context. Christian pointed out that Pol Roger champagnes were formerly fuller and heavier, but that, like the French haute cuisine, they have evolved and become lighter, more youthful. 'Nevertheless,' he added, 'Pol Roger champagne still retains its classically high standard.'

Traditional methods

Pol Roger therefore operates on traditional lines. The wine — 30% of which is derived from the 160 acres owned or rented by the firm — ferments in fairly small concrete and enamelled steel vats, and is then stored in large tiled tanks. Wine from both first and second pressings is used in the non-vintage champagnes; all vintage champagnes are made exclusively from the first pressing. During their fermentation in the bottle, Pol Roger vintage champagnes are provided with proper corks, not crown tops — which is very unusual. *Remuage* is done by hand, and a stock of 4 to 5 million bottles is kept to maintain annual sales of 1.2 to 1.5 million bottles.

The basis for Pol Roger's rosé is a cuvée usually from two-thirds black grapes and one-third white. A further 10% still red wine from Bouzy is then added. The final result — after five years' ageing — is a most pleasant champagne: light browny-pink in colour, an attractive bouquet, a creamy foam and a first-rate taste. At the table, particularly with white meat and poultry, this beautiful champagne is a delight.

The PR is only made in very good years from the best black and white grapes (usually half and half). The wine then matures for at least five years. It has a yellowish colour, delicate little bubbles and a full bouquet that is sometimes almost robust, as is the often pronounced taste. In some years (like 1971) the PR lacks refinement and I then prefer other vintage champagnes. However, some people are very fond of this type of champagne.

Opposite page, above;
The headquarters of Pol Roger in Rue Henri Lelarge, Epernay.

Opposite page, below:
Directors Christian de Billy and Christian Pol-Roger.

Right:
During the second fermentation, the bottles of the prestigious PR are sealed with real corks, not crown caps.

Below:
Photograph of the horse Pol Roger with its famous owner, Winston Churchill, on the left.

Pol Roger has 5 miles of cellars. In 1902 500,000 bottles were lost in a subsidence. The firm still fears a repetition, so there are many arches and reinforced sections of wall.

Pol Roger

Exceptional range

The traditional, painstaking way in which this firm works is naturally reflected in the champagnes. The vintage and non-vintage *bruts* have a generous *mousse* with quite small bubbles, a fairly firm, pure bouquet and an equally firm taste that gives an impression of maturity while retaining its freshness. There is an excellent balance between strength, fruit and acids, and a lingering aftertaste. The ordinary and vintage *bruts* of Pol Roger perhaps lack striking personality, but they are well-groomed, classic champagnes of an utterly reliable standard. Other wines in the range also merit praise. I have enjoyed the mild, elegant Blanc de Chardonnay, a stylish aperitif champagne, and the very successful pink; both are vintage wines. Pol Roger's *cuvée de prestige* is simply labelled 'PR' with the year of vintage. It is generally made half from Chardonnay and half from Pinot Noir, and is not sold until it has matured for at least five years. This is a so-called *vin gastronomique*, an accompaniment to food, full in the mouth and well-defined in taste. To my mind it is sometimes rather too full and robust, but others may prefer this style. Be that as it may, the generally high quality of the Pol Roger range fully justifies the epithet exceptional.

Perrier-Jouët

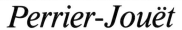

Champagne
Epernay

EPERNAY (FRANCE)
CHAMPAGNE
PERRIER·JOUËT

Nicolas-Marie Perrier, son of a cork manufacturer, and married to a Jouët, set up his own champagne business in 1811 at the age of 25, in Epernay. Things were not easy at first, for the Napoleonic wars were raging. But when peace was restored, the firm immediately spread its wings beyond the frontiers of France. In 1815, after Waterloo, Perrier-Jouët was the first champagne served at the British court. Britain was to remain an important customer, and Perrier-Jouët enjoyed a triumph in London during the *Belle Epoque*. Charles Skinner, who for more than half a century managed the wine business of the Savoy group, told the trade journal *Wine & Spirit*: 'The Savoy was a champagne house in those days. If you went into the restaurant, there'd be hardly a table without a bottle of champagne on it. Perrier-Jouët was the number one champagne then.' Parisians, too, drank a lot of Perrier-Jouët. Toulouse-Lautrec is said to have been inspired by it, and Sarah Bernhardt reputed even to have bathed in it!

Château Perrier

After the death of its founder, the business was continued in Epernay by his son Charles. He made so much money out of champagne and politics that in 1863 he could afford to build a château for himself opposite his business premises. Today Château Perrier houses a pleasant museum and the local library. The Perrier-Jouët cellars — six miles of them — still extend under the château. Charles was the last Perrier-Jouët and when he died the business passed to a nephew, who bequeathed it in turn to another nephew. He left it to a brother-in-law, and so on. Today Perrier-Jouët, like Mumm and Heidsieck Monopole, belongs to the Canadian Seagram group.

The style of this firm is clearly shown by the Perrier-Jouët brut: fine, vital champagnes, usually with a lot of fraicheur. *The non-vintage* brut *is of a reasonably good quality: light yellow in colour, spiralling bubbles, a decent bouquet and a lively taste with sometimes a vague hint of lemon in the freshness. The vintage champagnes offer slightly better quality and are also reasonably good in their category, but no more.*

Perrier-Jouët produces one of the most attractive pink champagnes I know of. The wine has a pale tint of orange-pink, a rather modest bouquet and a delicate, fresh almost 'white' taste in which the added red wine only accentuates and does not mask the taste (as often happens).

I consider the Blason de France to be Perrier-Jouët's best white champagne. It has freshness, lightness and a certain refinement. The aftertaste is rather short, the bouquet not usually impressive. The high proportion of white grapes often gives this wine a trace of green in the colour.

Perrier-Jouët's Belle Epoque has a transparent label on the splendidly decorated Emile Gallé bottle. (The actual label is not illustrated, but one very like it.) The bottle is nicer than the champagne, which is far from poor, but not of the best quality for a cuvée de prestige. *Bouquet and taste are rather at odds, and also rather flat. Compared to the Blason de France, the Belle Epoque is a little fresher and more aggressive in taste.*

Perrier-Jouët

A remarkable bottle

In 1840 the firm began to buy vineyards, and nowadays it owns 290 acres, including 99 in the Côte des Blancs (about 72 acres in Cramant, 27 in Avize). This land provides some 40% of Perrier-Jouët's grapes. Annual production is approximately 2.2 million bottles, with a stock of 8 million. Roughly one-half is exported, Britain still being the biggest foreign customer, followed by Italy and the United States. America imports mainly the Belle Epoque, a vintage champagne in a splendid bottle decorated with an Art Nouveau flower motif. This bottle was designed in 1902 by the celebrated French artist in glass, Emile Gallé. It was rediscovered accidentally in 1969 when the *directeur des caves*, André Baveret, found five of them in a corner of the cellars. It was Perrier-Jouët's managing director, Pierre Ernst, who had the idea of reintroducing this type of bottle; about 300,000 bottles are now produced annually.

Vital champagnes

The Perrier-Jouët buildings on the Avenue de Champagne in Epernay overlook three courtyards. The *cuves* are of glazed concrete and stainless steel. I was told that Perrier-Jouët utilizes all types of wine — from the first, second and third pressing. Slim, vital champagnes are the house style. The non-vintage *brut* is usually light yellow in colour, with spiralling bubbles, a decent bouquet, and a mildly fresh, lively taste with a discreet hint of lemon. By and large, this is a reasonably good *brut*, as are the vintage *bruts*.

A good pink

To my mind, the quality of the vintage rosé is very good. The Perrier-Jouët version has a particularly light shade of orange-pink, a modest bouquet and a delicate, fresh, almost 'white' taste. It is a very excellently made

champagne in which the added still red wine points up the character without masking the finesse of the basic wine.

The Blason de France is the firm's *cuvée de prestige*. Whereas the simpler *bruts* have 26% to 32% of wine from white grapes, the proportion here rises to between 48% and 52%. This gives the champagne a fairly light, fresh taste, plus refinement. For a prestige champagne it seems to me to be rather short in aftertaste, and often somewhat moderate in bouquet. Even more white grapes are used for Belle Epoque — always a vintage champagne in its unique

bottle. It seems lighter and less rounded than the Blason de France. It has a slightly more aggressive, racier taste — and is rather less sound. Moreover, for a *cuvée de prestige* it is somewhat flat, so I agree with a remark made during a champagne tasting: 'With Belle Epoque the bottle is nicer than the wine.'

Mercier

Champagne
Epernay

In 1858 Eugène Mercier united five
commercially linked small wine businesses
under his own name. He called the new
establishment Maison Mercier, Union de
Propriétaires, and it was originally located in
Paris, where the various concerns had a joint
sales office. In about 1930 the head office
moved to Epernay, where the cellars were
situated. Built to the specific requirements of
Eugène Mercier, they are, after those of
Moet & Chandon, the biggest in Epernay.
The cellar galleries, 11 miles long, were
opened by a carriage drawn by five greys,
and have since been the venue of a motor
rally. The 200,000 people who now visit them
annually are driven around, as at Piper-
Heidsieck in Reims, in electric trolleys.

Giant vat and hot-air balloon

Eugène Mercier had a great talent for
publicity. He commissioned an immense
wine vat for which whole oak trees were
especially felled and imported from
Hungary. Work continued for 20 years. The
completed vat weighed 20 tons, with a
capacity equivalent to 200,000 bottles. All
Paris turned out to see it brought in for
display at the 1899 World Exhibition.
Twenty-four oxen hauled it from Epernay on
an eight-day journey during which three
bridges on the route had to be widened and a
number of houses demolished. The
beautifully made vat is now back in the
cellars at Epernay. A year later, at the same
exhibition, Mercier showed the very first
advertising film, and gave people the chance
to drink a glass of Mercier in a balloon. This
was anchored by cable, and on one occasion
it snapped. Sixteen hours later, the 11
passengers were recovered in the Vosges.
Since the region was German at the time,
Mercier was fined 20 marks by the German
customs for the illegal import of six bottles
of champagne!

Collaboration with Moët & Chandon

For generations Mercier has concentrated its
advertising on the domestic market: 80% of
its champagne is sold in France itself.
Almost the reverse is true of Moët &
Chandon, which took over Mercier in 1970,
with about 70% going for export. Mercier's
annual sales amount to some 5 million
bottles, with 14 million bottles in stock.
Roughly one-fifth of the production is
covered by Mercier's 520 acres of vineyards.
The grapes are pressed at centres belonging
to the Moët group, but the must is fermented

Opposite page, above:
A battery of stainless-steel
fermentation tanks.

Opposite page, below left:
A relief in Mercier's cellars. The
firm receives over 200,000
visitors a year and they are
driven around in trains of little
pneumatic-tyred trolleys.

Opposite page, below right:
'La Vendangeuse Champenoise',
a statue in one of Mercier's
cellars.

Right:
Mercier's brut and Cuvée de
l'Empereur in one of the
reception rooms.

Below:
Another view of the complex of
underground passages. Mercier
employs about 400 people,
including some 150 in the cellars
and 80 in the vineyards. This
figure excludes a few hundred
pickers.

The Mercier family used to live
in the Château de Pékin, a small
castle near the cellars. It got its
remarkable name, so they say,
because it was in the extreme
east of Epernay. Eugène
Mercier had it built about the
same time as his wine cellars.
The last of the Merciers,
Jacques, also lived there.

France has Emile Mercier to
thank for its first deaf and dumb
institute, the Cercle de l'Abbé de
l'Epé.

Britain is the most important
export market for Mercier.

Mercier has its own museum of
winepresses. A collection of
about 40 different presses has
been assembled, dating from the
14th century to the present day.

Mercier

on Mercier premises. The stainless steel tanks are most impressive, occupying an entire tiled gallery. The wine is bottled by Moët & Chandon but the bottles are returned to Mercier for labelling and wrapping. Mercier and Moët & Chandon operate a joint computerized distribution centre on the Mercier site, and the two firms are linked by a 980-foot long passage under the Avenue de Champagne. But despite this close collaboration, the two houses have their own styles of wine.

Mass sales at moderate prices

Mercier's champagne is specifically geared to the demands of the home market. Much of it is sold in supermarkets, where price plays a crucial role. Furthermore, as has been noted, dry champagne is habitually drunk in France as an accompaniment to dessert. Consequently, high quality is not a main consideration, and with this in mind, Mercier's policy is to produce a reasonably

good champagne that can be sold in large quantities at moderate prices; this it does very successfully.

Easy to drink

Mercier champagnes are rather coarser of *mousse*, milder in taste and flatter in character than those, for example, of Moët & Chandon. I find them quite pleasant wines, sweeter than most *bruts*. The Mercier *dosage*, I was told, contains more sugar than that of Moët & Chandon. The champagnes are easy to drink, but not too much should be

expected of them. The vintage champagnes from Mercier usually contain more wine from white grapes than the ordinary *brut*, but are still somewhat flat. Mercier too carries a prestige champagne, its Réserve de l'Empéreur. This generally comes over as a mature, if not seasoned wine and in comparison with other *cuvées de prestige* distinctly lacks refinement and breeding. The name may be imperial, but the champagne is not.

Bollinger

Champagne
Ay

The foundations of the house of Bollinger were laid by Count Athanase de Villermont, an admiral who, when he retired, decided to restore his depleted fortune by exploiting an inheritance of 27 acres of vineyard. Since he deemed it beneath his dignity and social position to trade in wine himself, he engaged a young German, named Joseph Bollinger, who came from Württemberg and later took French nationality, calling himself Jacques. On 6 February 1829 Jacques set up a champagne firm that bore his name and that of his temporary partner, Paul Renaudin; the admiral's name never appeared on the labels, not even after Jacques married his daughter. Jacques Bollinger ran the business until his death in 1888, when it was continued by his sons, and later by a grandson, also called Jacques.

A great lady

Grandson Jacques died in 1941, before he was 50 years old; and as happens so often in the history of Champagne, a widow was left in charge. Five years younger than her husband, Elisabeth Bollinger, née Law de Lauriston-Boubers, tackled her challenging task with exemplary efficiency and unfailing charm.

I paid my first visit to Champagne and to Bollinger in 1969. My wife and I were somewhat wary when we were ushered into the living room of the already legendary Madame Bollinger. The old lady greeted us cordially, almost as if we were members of the family, addressing us affectionately as 'mes enfants': and as soon as she discovered that my wife was American, she switched to excellent English. At that time she still cycled regularly to the office and often around the vineyards. In 1972 she transferred the day-to-day running of the business to her nephews, but remained closely involved in all important decisions. The last time I met this great lady of Champagne was in 1975, again at her house. She looked tired, for she had undergone a number of serious operations; but she had lost none of her mental vigour and received us as warmly as always. We discussed the current economic troubles, and she remarked: 'I am not so young any more and I've been through a crisis before — in 1929. Today's problems are no worse than they were then, and we'll pull through. In life you must always hope.' Elisabeth Bollinger (always known as Lily) died in 1977, aged 78.

Search for perfection

While she was running the firm, Madame Bollinger managed to double the production of her champagne without a single concession on quality. Today Bollinger still retains her perfectionist attitudes. The firm owns nearly 350 acres of vineyard, of which about 295 are in production. The quality rating averages 97%, and this land provides about two-thirds of Bollinger's grapes. Wine from the first pressing is mainly used, supplemented, but only occasionally, by wine from the second. The wine is mostly fermented in small oak vats. The better the year, the higher the percentage of wine fermented in this way. In 1979, for example, 80% was fermented in oak, the rest in concrete *cuves*. Bollinger possesses some 4,500 casks and two coopers to maintain them. Because of these smaller vessels, the quality of the wine in each cask can be checked separately, and there is no need for filtering after fermentation. In addition, say the people at Bollinger, casks produce a firmer wine than can be obtained from ordinary fermentation tanks; the wine is also more resistant to oxidization and thus stays fresh longer in bottle and glass. With such relatively small quantities of wine in the casks, it is, of course, possible to blend champagnes with a great deal more refinement and precision than is normally the case.

Aristocratic air

Other noteworthy features of the Bollinger method include: the keeping of the reserve wines in magnums, so that the wine bubbles very lightly and keeps fresher; the use of a real cork for vintage wines undergoing secondary fermentation in the bottle; a gradual *remuage* lasting four months; and a five-year stock. For an annual sale of about 1.2 million bottles Bollinger keeps 6 million in stock. The result of all this attention is a series of remarkable, glorious champagnes. The ordinary *brut* has long-lasting, small bubbles, a reddish, pale yellow colour, a mature, charming bouquet, a taste that is complete, combining freshness, mildness and subtlety, and a beautiful aftertaste. It is a champagne of aristocratic grace, one of the best *bruts* I know. The vintage champagnes too are always excellent, sometimes with rather more *fraîcheur* than the non-vintage *brut*. Bollinger also produces a very successful pink champagne — always vintage.

The firm's *cuvée de prestige* has the initials

The Special Cuvée brut is given slightly less time in the cellars than Bollinger vintage champagnes — but, nevertheless, three to four years. It has a reddish tinge in its colour, small, long-lasting bubbles, a mature, charming bouquet, a full taste — fresh as well as mild, with some subtlety — and a beautiful aftertaste. This is one of the best non-vintage bruts I know.

Bollinger's vintage champagnes are, if possible, even better of their kind than the non-vintage brut. I always greatly enjoy their bouquet and their distinguished taste; depending on the vintage, this can be fresher than the ordinary brut. These vintage champagnes have the completeness so characteristic of Bollinger, a pleasant maturity (five years in the cellar) and complexity. Bollinger also produces a very good vintage rosé.

The deposit is not removed from bottles of Bollinger R.D. until seven to ten years have passed: R.D. stands for récemment dégorgé. When this champagne is eventually marketed, it has reached a perfect state of maturity and an exceptional refinement of bouquet and taste. 'Majestic' is a fitting description.

This extremely rare champagne (2,000 to 3,000 bottles in very good years only) comes from two small plots where the vines are cultivated exactly as in the last century. Since 1969 the grapes have been vinified separately, at least when the vintage offers good quality. This fragrant champagne is a blanc de noirs (from black grapes only). Its colour is distinctly reddish, its taste slightly less refined than other Bollinger vintage champagnes, but captivating and very sound.

Bollinger

R.D. on the label, standing for 'récemment dégorgé'. This champagne remains for seven to ten years in contact with the deposit (*lie*) formed during fermentation in the bottle. Only then is the deposit removed. During this long rest period the wine reaches a perfect state of maturity, and all manner of small, fine elements are released as a result of the interaction between wine and deposit. In my opinion, the Bollinger R.D. is a majestic, superbly balanced champagne with a particularly refined bouquet and taste.

The rarest champagne of the Bollinger collection is the Vieilles Vignes Françaises, made exclusively from black grapes grown on two small plots — one acre altogether — the plants being cultivated as in the previous century, without protection against the *Phylloxera* parasite. Bollinger always combined the grapes from these plots with all the others; but in 1969, a separate wine was made from these plots for the first time, on the occasion of Madame Bollinger's 70th birthday.

Deutz & Geldermann

William Deutz (1809-84) and Pierre Hubert Geldermann (1811-72) started this wine business together in 1838. Both came from Aix-la-Chapelle (better known today as Aachen), then temporarily French, and both married girls from Champagne. Later, the bond between the two families was further strengthened when William Deutz's daughter married Pierre Geldermann's son. The business did not become very big but won enough respect to be accepted as a member of the prestigious Grandes Marques.

Deutz & Geldermann went through an extremely difficult period just before World War I. During a riot by wine growers and cellar workers its premises, like those of Ayala and Bissinger, were practically destroyed. Deutz & Geldermann has been a public limited company since 1927, but remains family owned.

Other wine interests

The firm is run by André Lallier, great-great-grandson of William Deutz. He is also a joint owner of the business with his father Jean and brother James. The last Geldermann disappeared from the scene shortly after World War II. For a rather small champagne house, Deutz & Geldermann has acquired considerable interests in other wine-producing regions. It owns a Sekt factory in Germany, Château de l'Aulée in the Loire valley (see page 45), and the wine firm of Delas in the Rhône valley.

Cellars under a hill

The firm owns 82 acres of vineyard in Champagne providing 45% of its grapes. Except for a few small plots, this whole area has a quality rating of 100%. Anyone visiting Deutz & Geldermann can see that each generation of owners has made its contribution. André Lallier's grandfather installed concrete fermentation tubs, his father put in enamelled *cuves* and he himself introduced stainless-steel tanks. The cellars run from the level ground into the hillside for

up to 575 feet. There is normally the equivalent of four years' sales in stock: Deutz & Geldermann's annual production is usually between 600,000 and 700,000 bottles, about half of this being exported.

Careful processing

Exceptional care is lavished on Deutz & Geldermann champagnes. All the vintage champagnes are made exclusively from the first pressing (*cuvée*); a little wine from the second pressing (*première taille*) is added to the ordinary *bruts*. Third-pressing wine (*deuxième taille*) goes to the distillers. The

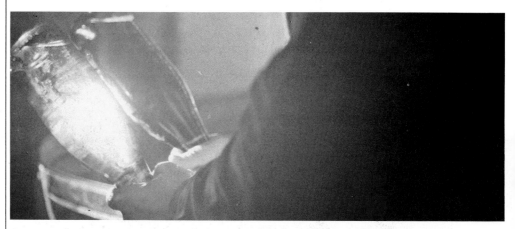

wine is subjected only to a 'cold treatment'; there is no clarifying or filtering. *Remuage* is still done by hand here, and after the bottles have finally been corked they are generally rested for five or six months in the cellars. Deutz & Geldermann sells a relatively large amount of vintage champagne: about 40% of the total.

Mild character

As might be expected from the foregoing remarks, Deutz & Geldermann champagnes (all sold under the name Champagne Deutz) are very correct in bouquet and taste. They

Opposite page, above left:
Chairman André Lallier. His features resemble those of William Deutz, as I was able to check from a portrait.

Opposite page, above right:
The two salons in the authentic Second Empire style, the period when Deutz & Geldermann's founder, William Deutz, was active.

Opposite page, below:
At Deutz & Geldermann, every bottle is held against the light and checked for flaws.

Opposite page, bottom:
Boxes of large-sized bottles (a speciality of this firm) being despatched.

Below:
This coat-of-arms appears on most labels.

Bottom:
Stainless-steel fermentation tanks; the firm also has cuves of other materials.

On the occasion of its 150th anniversary, Champagne Deutz engaged the celebrated French artist Georges Mathieu to design the label for a vintage champagne, the 1971. These modern graphics have also been used for a limited number of later vintage champagnes. (Mathieu designed the logo for French TV's second channel, and the 10-franc piece.)

Deutz & Geldermann's blanc de blancs 1971 was given no dosage at all — although this is not stated on the label.

CHAMPAGNE DEUTZ
Maison Deutz & Geldermann
FONDÉE EN 1838
BLANC DE BLANCS 1975   AŸ-CHAMPAGNE

Deutz and Geldermann has made a speciality of vintage blanc de blancs, selling about 50,000 bottles of it annually. It is fairly light, fresh, and with a creamy mousse. It has its merits, in particular as an aperitif.

CHAMPAGNE DEUTZ
Maison Deutz & Geldermann
FONDÉE EN 1838
ROSÉ 1975   AŸ-CHAMPAGNE

True to tradition, only red wine from the famous Bouzy commune is used in the Champagne Deutz rosé. This champagne usually has a soft reddish-brown colour with a tinge of orange, reasonably small white bubbles, a modest but pleasant bouquet and a correct, completely fresh taste with a mild aftertaste.

CHAMPAGNE DEUTZ
Cuvée William Deutz
CHAMPAGNE
VINTAGE 1973   Aŷ

Deutz & Geldermann's best champagne is named after one of the firm's founders, William Deutz. A lot is exported to America. Soft yellow colour, soft bouquet, soft taste. The wine does not possess a lot of breeding or character, but it has its charms. It usually tastes at its best five to six years after vintage because there is then still sufficient freshness present. Production is about 50,000 bottles per vintage year.

Deutz & Geldermann

are not notable for their breeding, refinement, depth or aftertaste. Most of them strike me as gently mature and mild, with no question of harshness or astringent acids. These champagnes are intended for customers who are not partial to austerely dry white wines. My favourite type is the Cuvée William Deutz, the firm's *cuvée de prestige*, with a special bottle. It usually has plenty of bubbles, a soft yellow colour, a mild, very mature bouquet and a rather mellow taste, though somewhat lacking the breeding similar champagnes from other shippers. Naturally, the champagne can vary in quality from year to year. In 1980, for example, I was more taken by the 1975 than the 1973, which may already have been losing some freshness. To my mind, Cuvée William Deutz should be drunk five or six years after its vintage; it seems to benefit little, if at all, from longer maturing.

Pink and pure white

Two other Deutz & Geldermann specialities are, according to André Lallier, the rosé and the *blanc de blancs*. The pink usually has a mild aftertaste, preceded by a not unattractive bouquet and a gently fresh taste, reasonably well constituted. The *blanc de blancs* is generally more elegant in bouquet and taste, fresher, and sometimes creamily mild in its *mousse*. This champagne cannot be described as great, but it makes a very creditable aperitif.

Napoleon III salons

André Lallier is, of course, proud of his products and stands by their quality. In a different way, he is equally proud of the great showpiece of his firm, two salons furnished in authentic Second Empire style. He himself collected the furniture, and craftsmen patiently executed walls, ceilings and woodwork in the style of about 1860. These rooms are a homage to William Deutz and Pierre Geldermann, both of whom lived and worked in Ay at this time.

Ayala owns the champagne brand of Montebello. This was once a firm of some standing, founded by the son of the Duke of Montebello in Mareuil-sur-Ay. The château of that name, once the property of the Dukes of Orléans, was stylish in its furnishing and decor. Montebello's glory is now entirely departed. The grapes from the 62 acres of vineyard (quality rating 98%) are nowadays used for Ayala champagnes.

Ayala's ordinary brut is made from two-thirds black and one-third white grapes. It is a champagne that in colour, bouquet and taste makes a well-aged impression. Within this maturity, however, there is a central core of fresh, cool taste. The wine seems reasonably full and firm, with a respectable aftertaste. Not an impressive personality and lacking much nuance or immediate charms, but a rather conservative champagne, undoubtedly made with care. The vintage version is in the same style.

Ayala's blanc de blancs, made exclusively from white grapes from the Côte des Blancs, is my favourite champagne from this small firm: a generous amount of bubbles, a pleasant bouquet, and a fresh, fairly light taste of an altogether decent standard. At worst, the champagne lacks some depth and substance. I like it best as an aperitif.

Ayala & Co.

Champagne
Ay

Ayala is situated in Ay, and it might be supposed that the firm's name was derived from that of the village. In fact, it takes its name from Edmond de Ayala, the son of a Columbian diplomat. Around 1860, Edmond was sent by his father to one of his political friends, Viscount of Mareuil, at Ay. The young man evidently enjoyed his visit and ended up marrying one of his host's nieces. His bride's dowry included a considerable area of vineyard — the basis for the champagne firm that Edmond set up soon afterwards. The descendants of Edmond de Ayala sold the business in 1937 to René Chayoux, a well-known personality in the Champagne region, who subsequently took over Champagne Montebello, with the Château de Mareuil-sur-Ay, and the *grand cru* Château la Lagune in the Bordeaux district of Médoc. Since the death of René Chayoux and later of his wife, the firm has been owned and run by Jean-Michel Ducellier.

No vineyards now

Although Ayala & Co. was originally based on its own vineyards, it no longer owns any, and merely has access to 62 acres that actually belong to Champagne Montebello. Ayala is not a large firm. It produces about 900,000 bottles a year and has some 2.7 million in stock. The wine ferments in glazed stone tubs. In blending the dry champagnes, only wines from the first and, usually, also the second pressing, are used. Third pressing wine goes to other shippers. Methods are very traditional, with manual *remuage*, and six to eight months' rest after corking. Ayala does not do much advertising and exports nearly half of its production.

Conservative style

After touring the cellars — 2 miles long, 80 feet deep under a wine slope and reached by a spiral staircase of 76 steps — I tried some wines from the Ayala range with the owner. I also tasted these and other champagnes later at home. I came to the conclusion that they were in all respects correct, but not very exciting. Ayala champagnes do not possess great refinement, generous fruit or irresistible charm. They are rather conservative wines that have been properly matured, exhibit a good *mousse*, fill the mouth well, and possess a fresh, cool taste and respectable aftertaste. Personally, I find Ayala's *blanc de blancs* the most appealing. This vintage champagne is a wonderfully fresh aperitif, rather lighter than the other, more conventional wines in the range.

Billecart-Salmon

Champagne
Mareuil-sur-Ay

The Billecart family has lived for hundreds of years in the little village of Mareuil-sur-Ay, as testified by two 16th-century tombs in the local church. In 1818 Nicolas-François Billecart, inheritor of the family vineyards, decided to start his own champagne business together with his brother-in-law Louis Salmon, who also owned vineyards. As his portrait suggests, Nicolas-François was a man of great resolve and enterprise. He travelled widely and introduced his champagne to Russia, which became his most important market, Jean-Roland Billecart, his great-great-grandson, now runs the business, which has remained family property. Billecart-Salmon's 7-acre site includes, in addition to a beautifully maintained little park full of flowers, underground cellars where an average of 1.6 million bottles are stocked. The firm sells about 520,000 bottles annually, of which only about 15% goes for export.

Vineyards split off

Billecart-Salmon no longer owns any significant wine-growing land, as it did in the 19th century. In 1911 the vineyards were separated from the champagne business. Jean-Roland Billecart buys exclusively Pinot Noir (40% in the Marne valley and 20% in Montagne de Reims) and Chardonnay grapes, and no Pinot Meunier. Only the first pressing, the *cuvée*, is used in the *brut* champagne and superior qualities. The wines ferment slowly at low temperature in modest-sized steel tanks. *Remuage* is still effected by hand and lasts at least 80 days. The firm maintains a 'strict minimum' of one month between the moment when the deposit is removed from the bottles and shipping; in practice it is often three months.

Cool chalk in the taste

Billecart-Salmon champagnes are characterized by a racily fresh, tingling sensation as soon as the wine comes in contact with the tongue; another feature is a cool, almost chalky taste that comes over as rather austere, but not unpleasant. I find that only the ordinary *brut*, including its aftertaste, is somewhat too mild. The true character of the Billecart-Salmon champagnes is to be found in the *blanc de blancs* (always vintage) and in the special *cuvée* N.F. Billecart. The latter wine has small, spiralling bubbles, a clear colour with a tinge of green, and a somewhat cool bouquet and taste. This prestige champagne also has a certain elegance. Billecart-Salmon, one of the Grandes Marques, may not be reckoned among the leaders in quality, but it certainly holds its own in the middle ranks.

Laurent Perrier

Champagne
Tours-sur-Marne

Growth is the dominant characteristic of the hard-working firm of Laurent Perrier. In 1949 production was about 100,000 bottles, in 1959 it was around 400,000 and by 1979 it had reached some 6 million bottles. In less than a generation the house had grown from an insignificant little business to one of the four most important shippers of the region; and expansion remains the keynote. At the time of my visit in 1980, the firm had fermentation and blending tanks with a capacity of three million litres; this was to be increased to eight million.

The firm was established on 28 December 1812 by the widow of Laurent Perrier, who had died in 1808. The Perriers were originally coopers. Later they were employed as bottlers, and eventually they decided to bottle wines on their own account as well as for others. Little is known about the lady who founded the house, but her name still appears in the firm's official title, Veuve Laurent Perrier & Cie. Business was languishing in 1939 when Bernard de Nonancourt's family bought the small company, and it was he who put Laurent Perrier on the map.

Still champagne

The firm made its great leap forward in the 1960s. There seemed to be little scope for yet another brand of champagne, still less one from an unknown shipper; nevertheless, doors opened for Laurent Perrier. The key was the still (i.e. non-sparkling) champagne now known as Coteaux Champenois. Most houses tended to look down on this product, but Laurent Perrier made a speciality of it. At one period the firm was selling half of the total amount of still champagne marketed by all the champagne houses combined. Thanks to an incisive marketing policy, sales rose so sharply that Laurent Perrier was soon seriously short of space. In the early 1970s, a comprehensive project was launched; the casualties were the firm's own small vineyards near the cellars, the cherry orchard and most of the garden. These made way in 1971 for a battery of stainless-steel fermentation tanks (Laurent Perrier was one of the first shippers to invest in these), modern bottling plant, and a number of large new buildings and cellars. In the same year Laurent Perrier took over a small champagne firm owning 22 acres of vineyard. Two years later the company added more fermentation tanks and purchased 37 additional acres of vineyard. Laurent Perrier now owns 222 acres of wine-growing land, good for about one-fifth of the grapes required, and there are 1,235 acres of vineyard under contract to the firm.

Human relations

The almost explosive growth of Laurent Perrier has not dehumanized the firm. There is still an excellent, friendly relationship among all levels of employees. Bernard de Nonancourt does a great deal for his workers. When annual sales reached five million bottles, he marked the event by hiring a Boeing and flying the whole staff, plus dependants, for a few days to the Canaries. At harvest time Bernard de Nonancourt and two colleagues are always out with the growers, for whom entertainments are regularly held. This policy of friendly informality with the producers can only result in better quality grapes.

Hygiene

With the exception of the *crémant*, the firm's simplest wine, all the champagnes are made from the *cuvée*, the first pressing. The wines ferment at 20°C in the steel tanks. I was greatly struck by the clean conditions at Laurent Perrier. Both the *cuverie* and the bottling hall have tiled floors that are kept spotless all the year round. This is a good sign: hygiene is a prime requirement when making quality wines.

Since 1957 Laurent Perrier has organized the annual Diner Grand Siècle in Paris, always held in honour of individuals, groups or institutions who have done good work. A jury of 12 makes the selection. Those chosen include the French Red Cross, the late Lord Mountbatten, and the people who carried out the restoration of Versailles. The event is always attended by hundreds of guests.

Together with the American firm National Distillers, Laurent Perrier created a subsidiary in America called Caves Laurent Perrier. This produces a still white wine exclusively from the Chardonnay. The first vintage of the California Chardonnay Blanc de Blancs was 1981. The grapes and the material are furnished by Almadén Vineyards, wholly owned by National Distillers.

Laurent Perrier's non-vintage brut has a pale colour, a lively mousse, a not over-emphatic bouquet and a taste that is neither too acid nor too light: a good all-round champagne, therefore, with a clear, almost metallic-cool taste and a sprightly personality. It is made from half black and half white grapes. With a vintage brut the wine is somewhat firmer, more elegant and rather more fully matured.

As Laurent Perrier is perfectly equipped for making red wine (Coteaux Champenois), it can produce rosé in a way that is usual elsewhere in France but not in Champagne: allowing the wine to acquire its colour naturally by leaving the must in contact with the black grape skins. The result is a delightful pink champagne, refined and fruity (sometimes with a hint of blackcurrants). The colour is soft pink.

Laurent Perrier's Grand Siècle is not blended from a single vintage, as are most de luxe champagnes, but from two or three different years. This method results in an exquisite wine, consistent in quality, fragrant, quite firm, yet elegant. Within its mature mildness it has a scintillating, vital core. This champagne is made from 80% white grapes. With the rosé, 500,000 to 600,000 bottles a year are sold.

History repeats itself: in 1900 a Laurent Perrier 1893 grand vin sans sucre was on the wine list of the Paris restaurant La Tour Eiffel. In the spring of 1981 the same house launched its Ultra Brut, again sugarless. A good champagne, naturally very dry, yet not meagre or too acid: thanks to the maturity of the wines from which it is blended, Ultra Brut takes on a certain softness. Soft yellow colour, generous mousse, fine small bubbles.

Laurent Perrier

The *remuage* is done by hand here — the capital cost of a mechanical system is regarded as too high — and lasts up to two months.

Clear, bright taste

The ordinary Laurent Perrier *brut* is a good all-round champagne, generously sparkling, pleasant of bouquet, and with a taste that is neither too acid nor too light for wide acceptability. Laurent Perrier champagnes seem to possess a strikingly clear, bright taste. They are not rich wines but sprightly, scintillating, slightly austere, and of reliable quality. The vintage champagnes have even more to offer than the ordinary *brut*; and this applies in particular to the Grand Siècle, the firm's *cuvée de prestige*. Always blended from two or three different vintages, and therefore fairly constant in character and quality, this is an exquisite wine. I also have a high regard for Laurent Perrier's champagne rosé, which is made not by adding still red to sparkling wine, but by leaving the black grape skins in contact with the must for a short time — an uncommon method in Champagne. The wine has a light, soft pink colour and a very good, elegant taste that sometimes suggests fruit, particularly blackcurrants. The Laurent Perrier still wines are discussed in the Coteaux Champenois section that follows (see pages 190-1).

Lamb steaks accompanied by a red Coteaux Champenois from Bonnaire. Photo taken in the excellent l'Assiette Champenoise restaurant at Chalons-sur-Vesle, where the owner, Jean-Pierre Lallement, does the cooking.

Below:
A wine grower of Avize shovelling the marc out of the press.

Opposite page:
Marc from white grapes.

Moët & Chandon makes an undisclosed amount of Bouzy of a very respectable taste. The wine is not sold but served exclusively at the firm's receptions, etc.

Many Coteaux Champenois bottles are sealed with an agraffe, a sort of metal clip that holds the suitably grooved cork in place. This is seldom seen on champagne — except for champagnes that are given a cork rather than a crown cap for their bottle fermentation (see illustration on page 177). Agraffes are also used for Mumm's Crémant de Cramant.

Coteaux Champenois is more difficult to bottle than champagne because of the danger of secondary fermentation. Laurent Perrier therefore uses sterilized bottles.

Georges Vesselle, well-known Coteaux Champenois producer and mayor of Bouzy, makes wine at Château d'Arly in the Côtes du Jura, where he supervises production, as well as in Champagne.

Coteaux champenois and other drinks

Besides its world-renowned champagne, the region also produces still wine. Until 1952 this was termed Vin Originaire de la Champagne, and from 1953 to 1974 Vin Nature de la Champagne. On 21 August 1974 this was changed, on the insistence of the EEC, to Coteaux Champenois. The wine has an *appellation contrôlée* and occurs mainly as red and white, though I have also tasted a rosé. Coteaux Champenois can only be made in Champagne, from the Pinot Noir, Pinot Meunier and Chardonnay grapes. These have to be cultivated in the manner prescribed for champagne. In the Champagne area the absolute maximum yield is 13,000 kilograms per hectare. Within this limit, the quantity of grapes that may be used for champagne is fixed every year; the rest can then be used for producing Coteaux Champenois. Thus in 1975 a total maximum of 10,000 kilograms per hectare was prescribed, with a maximum 7,500 kilograms for making champagne. Therefore, 2,500

kilograms per hectare remained for Coteaux Champenois. In 1979 the maximum for champagne was fixed at 12,000 kilograms, leaving only 1,000 kilograms for Coteaux Champenois. Sometimes the amounts are even less. The 1978 and 1980 harvests were so small that hardly any grapes were left over for Coteaux Champenois. Production therefore fluctuates strongly from year to year.

Mostly sold in France

Sales of Coteaux Champenois obviously vary according to production. From 1974 to 1978 inclusive they rose from 1.1 million to 4.2 million bottles a year. In 1979, however, because of the poor 1978 harvest, they were practically halved, to 2.3 million bottles. Between one-half and two-thirds of all Coteaux Champenois is handled by the shippers, the rest by *récoltants-manipulants* (growers who make and sell their own wine)

and cooperatives. More than 70% of this still wine is drunk in France itself.

Image better than quality

Compared commercially with champagne, Coteaux Champenois is a minor product, although some two to four million bottles a year cannot be altogether discounted. Indeed such annual figures are quite remarkable, considering that the price of Coteaux Champenois is relatively high, and the quality generally not comparable to similarly priced wine from, say, Burgundy (including Mâconnais and Beaujolais). Yet it is served in a surprising number of French restaurants. Its success can be explained by its rarity. It is a little-known wine from a well-known region, something with which to surprise your guests at home or in a restaurant; but it is not a serious wine to challenge one's tasting skills. Indeed, careful tasting is likely to prove a disappointment. Coteaux Champenois is bought principally because of its image and its label, hardly for any notable quality.

Rare rosé

I recall even being disappointed by the Chouilly Blanc and the recommended Ludes Rouge at the marvellous *Boyer* restaurant in Reims, mentioned in the *Guide Michelin*. On many other occasions I came across poor-quality, flat and thinly acid Coteaux Champenois. The *aficionados* will not agree with me. One of them explained: 'Coteaux Champenois is not an easy wine. Patience is needed to discover its qualities and subtleties, often through a very high degree of acidity.' I have tried to follow this advice, but have drunk very few Coteaux Champenois with real pleasure. Among the best-tasting and most reliable I would select the Chardonnay and the Pinot Franc from Laurent Perrier, the white Saran from Moët & Chandon and the white Coteaux Champenois from Pol Roger. I have also tasted decent white Coteaux Champenois from Veuve Clicquot and Billecart-Salmon,

Saran, Moët & Chandon's white Coteaux Champenois, comes from the 10-acre vineyard of Château de Saran in Chouilly, where the firm entertains its VIP guests in a most impressive manner. Production is limited to about 70,000 bottles annually: any Saran made is at the expense of the Dom Pérignon. The wine is usually blended from three different vintages. It has a sound, fresh, lively taste and is among the best white Coteaux Champenois.

Among a group of five white Coteaux Champenois, including the Lanson and Veuve Clicquot products, the Pol Roger is the brilliant best, with a quite elegant bouquet of great purity, a good taste with a chalk-rooted freshness, character and some fruit. A beautiful wine, excellent of its kind. Production is about 15,000 bottles a year. Not quite of this standard, but still decent, are the white Coteaux Champenois of Veuve Clicquot and Billecart-Salmon.

Laurent Perrier was the first shipper to give much attention to the production of still champagne — and with success. This non-vintage white Coteaux Champenois is a good wine made exclusively from the first pressing. Its bouquet and taste are extraordinarily pure; the taste is pleasant and very fresh without too much acid.

Laurent Perrier launched its Pinot-Franc in 1977, alongside the Bouzy ('we thought we were working more for Bouzy than for Laurent Perrier'). This wine is made only from very sound Pinot Noir grapes and is supplied almost exclusively to restaurants. It is a supple wine, fairly fresh in taste, without great depth but nevertheless very pleasant; 45,000 to 60,000 bottles are sold annually. Bouzy sales are around 60,000 bottles.

As with its champagnes, Lanson blends its Coteaux Champenois, red and white, from different wines. I find the white only moderate, but the red is interesting. This is usually blended from three different vintages, which means there is more to the taste than with most red Coteaux Champenois. It is supple and mild, too, but great depth or fragrance should not be expected.

For many years Georges Vesselle has been mayor of Bouzy (population 1,000; 865 acres of vineyard) and has also made successful use of his own 42-acre wine estate. As well as champagnes, Vesselle produces still red wines. His Bouzy Rouge (Coteaux Champenois) can be a very pleasant wine, especially from sunny years. Given its initial 'angularity', it is recommended that the wine be left to mature for a few years. A superior quality is sold as Cuvée Véronique-Sylvie, in a special bottle.

Coteaux Champenois and other drinks

and I have sampled quite good reds from Lanson, Bollinger, the Barancourt group (wine growers in Bouzy), and Denois Père & Fils in Cumières. I am told that other interesting Coteaux Champenois are made by, among others, Roland Lapie in Chouilly, André Clouet in Bouzy, and Vadin-Plateau in Cumières. One of the nicest rosés, in my opinion, is Nectar des Noirs from the Ambonnay cooperative.

Rosé de Riceys is comparable to Coteaux Champenois rosé. It comes from the Aube *département*, is made only from the Pinot Noir and has a very austere taste, often with a touch of bitterness. Originating in the communes of Riceys-Bas, Riceys-Haute-Rive and Riceys-Haute, its annual production does not exceed 550 to 1,100 cases.

Ratafia and distillates

Another alcoholic drink of the region is ratafia. This consists of freshly pressed wine juice to which wine alcohol (often cognac) is added. The result is a rather sweet drink, comparable to Pineau de Charente, suitable as an aperitif. The alcohol content is usually 18° to 22°. One of the best ratafias is made by Veuve Clicquot. The region also produces Marc de Champagne, a distillate with at least 40° alcohol, made out of the juice from *marc* — the mass of skins, seeds and stalks left after the last pressing. Scent and taste are generally rather fiery. Finally there is Fine Marne, a drink of at least 40° proof, which is simply distilled wine, usually white, from the Marne *département*. The quality is generally higher than that of Marc de Champagne, production much lower.

The fact is, nevertheless, that by far the best product of Champagne remains champagne.

Other champagne producers

On the following pages brief profiles of a number of other champagne producers are given, in alphabetical order. The selection, on grounds of quality rather than quantity, is strictly personal and by no means exhaustive. It would take many years to visit and describe all the makers of champagne.

Alfred Gratien

The Saumur firm of Gratien, Seydoux & Cie (sparkling wines) opened a branch in Epernay known as Alfred Gratien in 1864. The methods of this firm are extremely traditional. The wine still ferments in small oak vats (as at Krug and, to an extent, at Bollinger). Mature, mild champagnes are the speciality. This type is very popular in Britain, which buys most of the 200,000 bottles produced. Some even carry the label of the House of Commons. I find Alfred Gratien's champagnes rather too mature and somewhat lacking in breeding, refinement and depth. In other respects, the quality of the three types produced by the firm — non-vintage *brut*, vintage *brut* and rosé — is very correct.

Barancourt

The properties of three growers, Brice, Martin and Tritant, are united under the name of Barancourt. Together they work 116 acres with a 100% rating, mostly in the commune of Bouzy, with additional land in Cramant. Jean-Paul Brice told me that Barancourt is registered as a shipper because 10% of its production comes from grapes bought in. Total annual production averages around 600,000 bottles, and Barancourt stocks a two-year supply. Specialities are the Bouzy Rouge (a Coteaux Champenois) and Bouzy vintage champagne.

The latter usually has a slightly reddish colour and an agreeable, not particularly nuanced bouquet in which, to my mind, the mildness of the predominantly black grapes rather masks the freshness of the white; the same applies to the taste. The firm was established in 1969, and its wines, including the Bouzy Rosé and the Cramant, have a good reputation in France.

Besserat de Bellefon

Between 1968 and 1971, the firm of Besserat de Bellefon moved from Ay, where Edmond de Besserat founded it in 1843, to Reims. The firm's dynamic director, Paul Bergeot, had an ultra-modern complex of cellars, offices and reception halls built on the outskirts of the city. The largest of these reception areas measures 230 by 394 feet. This enormous investment was made possible by the fact that Besserat de Bellefon is part of the powerful Pernod-Ricard group. By and large, the firm produces rather superficial and light champagnes, sometimes tasting a little sharp. I would, however, except the rosé, a vintage champagne, excellent of its kind, often with a pale, orange-pink colour, a pure bouquet and a lively, refreshing taste. I also like the Brut Intégral, the *cuvée de prestige*. The house produces the own-name champagnes of the *Maxim's* restaurants. Sales about 1.8 million bottles; average stock three years.

Boizel

The small, friendly Epernay firm of Boizel, founded in 1834, is run by Erica Boizel-Hötte, who comes from Amsterdam, where her family owns the games manufacturing firm Hausemann & Hötte. For a not-too-expensive champagne from an unknown firm, Boizel's *brut* is very simple and very agreeable: with a ruddy glow in the colour, it is a fully mature and complete wine.

Other champagne producers

F. Bonnet

In 1922, wine grower Ferdinand Bonnet started his own champagne firm at Oger, which has been continued by his descendants. The business is now run by Mademoiselle Nicole Bonnet, who owns it jointly with her sisters. The firm has 22 acres in the Côte des Blancs, yielding enough grapes for two-thirds of the annual production of about 120,000 bottles. The average quality rating of all the grapes used by Bonnet exceeds 95%. Another characteristic is the very large proportion of white grapes in the *cuves*, in contrast to almost all other shippers, where black grapes predominate. Traditional, careful vinification and an average maturing time of four years are other factors that give Bonnet champagnes their fresh, light character and immaculate quality. One of my favourites from the range is the vintage Blanc de Blancs: good, generous *mousse*, excellent, fruity bouquet and a pure, pleasantly fresh and mild taste.

Champagne de Castellane

De Castellane's cellars are in Epernay at the foot of an impressive but disused water tower. Viscount Florens de Castellane founded the firm in 1893. The majority of Champagne de Castellane's shares are held by the Mérand family, with Mme Francine Mérand as managing director. The wine here ferments in the large, wooden 600-litre vats known as *demi-muids*. De Castellane owns some 2,500 of these. Only the first pressing is used. This house does not aim at the very topmost quality but produces good champagnes at reasonable prices — excellent value for money in their various categories. Worthy of note are the ordinary, fresh, perfectly respectable *brut*, the somewhat lighter *blanc de blancs* and the *cuvée de prestige* Cuvée Commodore: fine bubbles, mild bouquet, gently fresh, properly full and sound taste with a hint of *terroir*. A stock of roughly four times the annual sales (1.5

million bottles) is maintained. The cellar complex has 6 miles of passages situated as much as 130 feet below ground.

A. Charbaut & Fils

The public limited company of A. Charbaut & Fils in Epernay was founded by the present director, André Charbaut. He is assisted by his sons René and Guy. The Charbaut champagnes (2.5 million bottles annually) are to be found in a number of high-class French restaurants, and may bear the latter's or Charbaut's own label; Gaston Lenôtre, for example, carries Charbaut champagnes with the restaurant name on the label. The quality of the wines is, in my opinion, usually very decent, albeit a little flat. The *brut* I tasted had a distinctly mild taste, as well as a certain fullness and some fruit. The pink, on the other hand, was mediocre.

Duval Leroy

In Vertus, in 1859, the firms of Jules Duval and Edouard Leroy were combined as Duval Leroy. Today this concern is run by Charles Roger Duval. The firm boasts 225 acres of vineyard supplying more than one-quarter of its grapes. Duval Leroy sells about two million bottles a year, and usually keeps three times this amount in stock. I find that the Fleur de Champagne and the Cuvée des Roys are the best champagnes of the range, although even these are not particularly memorable for refinement or depth. They are decent champagnes without a great deal of personality, as is the firm's rosé.

Georges Goulet/Saint-Marceaux

These two brands represent completely identical champagnes marketed by Abel Lepitre of Reims, the owner of the eponymous firms. The Saint-Marceaux brand has existed since 1837, the George Goulet since 1867. The latter firm was taken over by Abel Lepitre in about 1960. It once

had a great reputation and supplied champagnes by appointment to the courts of Sweden, Spain, Great Britain and the Netherlands. The house makes refined, mild champagnes, in no sense great, but very pleasing in taste. To my mind, the non-vintage *brut* is rather thin; the vintage champagnes are more mouth-filling. The most interesting of these is the Cuvée du Centenaire in a special bottle, from George Goulet.

Gosset and Philipponat

The Gosset family has been firmly established in Ay for hundreds of years, providing three mayors, four aldermen, as well as fourteen generations of wine growers. The origin of the house goes back to the 16th century, when Pierre Gosset was making and selling wine in Ay. Today the firm owns some wine-growing land in Ay, Bouzy and Rilly-la-Montagne, which provides 7% to 8% of its grapes. Director Etienne Gosset sells some 200,000 bottles annually, and the cellars usually hold a stock of four times this quantity. A Gosset speciality is its pink champagne: a good wine, delicious and fresh in taste, with pin-point bubbles, and the scent of grapes in the bouquet. The non-vintage and vintage *bruts* are not exciting champagnes, but generally respectable. From time to time Gosset puts a limited amount of old vintage champagnes on the market. In the spring of 1980 Gosset took over the firm of Philipponat at Mareuil-sur-Ay, owning 27 acres of vineyard (including the Clos des Goisses, which produces an expensive but not very interesting wine). Philipponat turns out approximately half a million bottles a year.

Leclerc Briant

The Leclerc Briant estate was created in 1872 by an ancestor of the present owner-director Pascal Leclerc. The label shows Cumières as the company address, but the cellars and office are in Epernay. The

Other champagne producers

Other champagne producers

estate's 74 acres are spread over six communes. Production averages 200,000 bottles a year, and almost three times this amount is kept in stock. Some of the champagnes in the Leclerc Briant range disappointed me greatly. The estate's ability to make a very successful champagne is shown, nevertheless, by the Cuvée Spécial Club, a vintage dry. The *cuvée* (still wine) for this, and eventually the final product, both have to be approved by a jury. Only then can the round label of the Club de Viticulteurs Champenois be carried. This club was founded in 1961 and has members, who work independently of one another, in some 30 Champagne communes. The firm's Cuvée de Réserve is also often a good champagne.

The Mailly cooperative

This is the best-known and oldest cooperative in Champagne. It was set up in 1929, six years after a group of growers had started pressing their grapes collectively. At that time the all-powerful champagne shippers refused to accept the new collective enterprise, which was unable to market its wine. So the members embarked on the seemingly impossible task of making and selling their own champagne — and still do so today. Annual sales are about 600,000 bottles, with an average stock of 1.5 million. Mailly champagnes, containing 80% Pinot Noir, are respectably mouth-filling, but lack nuances — hardly surprising, as all the grapes come from the same commune. The Mailly vineyards have a 100% quality rating, but this, as the wines prove, does not count for everything. Most Mailly champagnes have struck me as rather mild in taste. The Cuvée des Echansons is the best and most expensive of the lot.

Massé

The firm of Massé, in Reims, was bought by Lanson Père & Fils in 1976. The champagne is cheaper and more neutral than Lanson's: output about 700,000 bottles a year.

Oudinot

At the beginning of 1982 the Trouillard family took over Champagne Oudinot. Earlier the Trouillards sold their own firm and the Trouillard name; these now belong to the Henriot/Charles Heidsieck group. The Trouillard vineyards, however, remained a family possession, and champagne was made under the name Lucien Beaunet. After the Oudinot takeover, the two houses were merged. The total vineyard acreage comprises about 150 acres with an average quality level of 90%. In principle, the new firm will only make wine from its own vineyards, which means an average of 400,000 to 450,000 bottles per year. The Oudinot cellars have always been located in Avize. There are plans, however, to move to the old de Venoge establishment in Epernay (see illustration, page 194). Subsidiary brands of Oudinot are Jeanmaire Royal Onzane and A. & S. de Perrot.

René Brun

René Brun started his own champagne firm in 1942. He died in 1976 but the business is continued by André and Roger Brun. Of the 200,000 to 220,000 bottles that the firm produces annually, about two-thirds comes from its own 37 acres at Ay, quality rated 100%. A stock of two to three years' supply is kept. In my experience, the vintage and non-vintage *bruts* are of really good quality. I was particularly impressed by the vintage wines, which were neither too heavy nor too light, very pure, sufficiently fresh and pleasant in taste. The blend usually contains 80% wine from the Pinot Noir. If I have one criticism, it is that the corks are sometimes impossibly short. This small family business has a subsidiary brand, Charles Doutey.

Salon

Eugène-Aimé Salon was a successful entrepreneur who around the turn of the century started making champagne just for himself and his friends. Gradually, however, the word spread, demand increased, and he began to produce on a commercial scale. Because he maintained rigorous standards of quality, his small firm only marketed wines from good years, and this tradition is still upheld today. The 1911 was the first champagne. In 1928 *Maxim's* in Paris picked Salon as its champagne of the house; the wine of that year was, in fact, one of the most legendary of this century. From the start, Salon wine was made exclusively from white grapes from Mesnil, where the firm owns 2 acres with a quality rating of 100%. Salon keeps wine from those years in which both still and sparkling champagnes are produced. The stock represents 10 to 11 times the number of bottles sold in a year; normally no more than 30,000 bottles annually are marketed. The firm is run by Paul Bergeot, who is also the head of Besserat de Bellefon. Like the latter house, Salon also belongs to the Pernod-Ricard group.

I know only the 1971 champagne from Salon, which was still being sold in 1980. Despite its mellow maturity, it still had a respectable *fraîcheur*. However, in my opinion, it distinctly lacked nuance and refinement. The years in which Salon has produced champagne are: 1911, 1914, 1915, 1917, 1921, 1923, 1928, 1929, 1932, 1937, 1942, 1943, 1945, 1947, 1949, 1950, 1952, 1953, 1955, 1959, 1961, 1964, 1966, 1971, 1973.

Left:
Mural showing a vintage scene, from a café in Cheverny. (For Cheverny wines see page 54.)

For information on the vintages I am most grateful to, among others: Gaston Rolandeau (Muscadet); Joseph Touchais (Anjou); Jacques Puisais (Tours); Jean-François Olek (Chinon); Gaston Huet (Vouvray); Alphonse Mellot (Sancerre); Hubert Heydt-Trimbach (Ribeauvillé, Alsace); and the Comité Interprofessionel du Vin de Champagne (Epernay).

When applying these characteristics of the various vintages the reader should realize that only the most generalized judgments, a rough-and-ready average, are given here. Quite awful wines can be made in a year described as 'good'; and a 'moderate' vintage can produce many attractive, really good wines. The best wines from a moderate vintage may be of better quality than the poorest examples from a good year.

Loire, Alsace & Champagne vintages

Loire

1959 A great, historic year, the strongest wines of which (Coteaux du Layon, Vouvray, etc.) can mature for a long time yet.

1960 A lot of wine, quality varying from ordinarily good to middling.

1961 Generally a good year; strong wines for keeping in Vouvray.

1962 Excellent in Coteaux du Layon; merely good elsewhere.

1963 Moderate to frankly bad.

1964 Moderate for Muscadet, but a great year from Anjou to Pouilly.

1965 Acceptable dry white wines, the rest rather poor.

1966 Great variation: a small vintage of very good wine in Muscadet; generous wines in Layon; dry, light wines in Touraine; good wines in Sancerre.

1967 From correct to good in quality.

1968 Unsuccessful.

1969 A wonderful year except for Muscadet.

1970 Abundant vintage, generally with pleasant, successful wines.

1971 Small vintage with good wines, except Muscadet; initially very acid here and there, including Vouvray.

1972 Middling, often rather meagre wines.

1973 Much wine of correct quality; rather lacking acid. Really good in Sancerre and Pouilly, often fine in Anjou (Coteaux du Layon, etc.).

1974 Sometimes great (Chinon), sometimes good (Sancerre), sometimes average (Vouvray, Muscadet).

1975 The farther up the Loire, the better the wine.

1976 Quality and quantity at a high level; almost too powerful in Muscadet.

1977 Night frosts: little wine, of varying but never memorable quality.

1978 A great year for Sancerre and Pouilly; dry and fruity in Vouvray; dry and aromatic in Touraine; good and distinctive in Chinon and Bourgueil; somewhat harsh but long in taste in Anjou; just above average in Muscadet.

1979 Good, balanced, charming wines that will mature quickly. Very fine in Sancerre and Muscadet, average in Vouvray.

1980 Rain during most of the harvest so that the quality is mostly not very high. Pleasant surprises, however, in Sancerre, Pouilly, Anjou and elsewhere.

1981 Quantity meagre, quality fairly decent.

1982 In most districts a big crop of very good quality.

Alsace

1959 Excellent in quality and quantity; the great wines are lasting well.

1960 Average quality, large quantity.

1961 Great, balanced wines that mature well and long.

1962 Correct, initially rather harsh wines.

1963 Very similar to 1960.

1964 Very good, especially for Gewürztraminer and Tokay. Abundant harvest.

1965 One of the worst ever Alsace vintages.

1966 Good year, fine wines, normal harvest.

1967 Very good year with some exceptional late-picked wines. Good yield.

1968 A little better than 1965; far from great.

1969 Average in all respects.

1970 A lot of wine, with the Riesling especially successful; a lot of wines for keeping.

1971 Magnificent, strong wines, small yield.

1972 As bad as 1965, but more wine.

1973 Record quantity, quality in all respects acceptable.

1974 Small yield; reasonably good, especially the Gewürztraminers.

1975 A good year, characteristic wines.

1976 Exceptional year with some extraordinarily good wines, including the Gewürztraminers.

1977 Average quality and quantity.

1978 Average quality; the wines are developing well. Small quantity, especially of Gewürztraminer.

1979 Elegant, charming, good wines in considerable quantity.

1980 Hardly any Gewürztraminer and Muscat. A modest yield with light, fruity wines, better than originally expected.

1981 Quantity and quality above normal.

1982 Very successful in all respects.

Champagne

1959 Supple, well-constituted, fragrant wines; an excellent vintage.

1960 Abundant vintage with rather light wines.

1961 Fine and fragrant wines, perhaps a little weak in acids, but good. Super-abundant quantity.

1962 Irregular quality.

1963 A lot of very acid wine, but fragrant.

1964 Good vintage with pleasant, firm, supple wines.

1965 High acid content, too little alcohol.

1966 Elegant, balanced and firm wines in good quantity.

1967 Wet autumn, with rotted grapes and rather light wines.

1968 Too much acid, too little strength and bouquet.

1969 More acidity than usual, but a successful year. Good yield.

1970 Considerable quantity of good wine, sometimes fuller than 1969, sometimes lighter.

1971 Fairly strong wines, fine bouquet, pleasant — but a middling yield.

1972 Unripe grapes, acid, poor wine.

1973 Super-abundant quantity with, thanks to good weather conditions, full, aromatic wines of excellent balance.

1974 Rainy and cold in the second half of September. In general, few wines of note. Acceptable yield.

1975 Fine, nuanced wines of often high quality. More wine than in 1974.

1976 Thanks to a dry, hot summer, an early harvest with a lot of good-class wine.

1977 Rather light, very acid wines.

1978 Disastrously small vintage, but the wine that was made is generally firm, fruity and strong.

1979 An adequate year with too little acid; considerable quantity.

1980 More wine than in 1978 but still a quite modest yield. Good quality because of a sunny autumn.

1981 Small vintage of reasonable quality.

1982 Enormous quantity, very good quality.

Bibliography

The Wines of The Loire, Alsace and Champagne

Loire

Pierre Bréjoux, *Les vins de Loire*, Paris 1974
Raymond Dumay et al., *Les vins de Loire*, Paris 1979
Jean de Malestroit, Gaston Huet et al., *La route du vin des pays de Loire*, Colmar-Ingersheim 1972
Michelin & Cie., *Châteaux de la Loire*, Clermont-Ferrand 1975
Georges Montorgueil, *Monseigneur le Vin*, 4th edn, Paris 1927
Henri Raimbault, *Les vins d'Anjou et de Saumur*, Angers 1967
R. Vivier, *Le Pays de Bourgueil*, 2nd edn, Bourgueil

Alsace

André Billich, *Histoire d'une ancienne ville impériale, Turckheim*, Colmar 1975
Gabriel Braeuner et al., *Ingersheim, 150e anniversaire du corps des sapeurs-pompiers*, Ingersheim 1977

Jacques-Louis Delpal, *Alsace Vosges*, Paris 1980
Raymond Dumay et al., *Le vin d'Alsace*, Paris 1978
Patric Fournial, *Chronique du vin et du vignoble de Mittelbergheim, Le Weinschlag*, Mittelbergheim/Sélestat 1980
Jean-Louis Gyss, *Le vin et l'Alsace*, Rosheim 1978
S. F. Hallgarten, *Alsace, its Wine Gardens, Cellars and Cuisine*, London 1978
Pierre Huglin, *Le vignoble d'Alsace et ses vins*, Colmar 1975
T. A. Layton, *Wines and People of Alsace*, London 1970
Jacques Legros, *Guide Kronenbourg de l'Alsace authentique*, Paris 1980
Michelin & Cie., *Vosges*, Clermont-Ferrand 1976
Marcel Pfister, *Zellenberg, témoin du passé*, Colmar 1975
Henry Riegert, *Où mûrit le vin d'Alsace*, Strasbourg 1969
Lucien Sittler, *La route du vin d'Alsace*, Colmar-Ingersheim 1969
Lucien Sittler et al., *Sigolsheim*, Colmar 1958
Oksana Willer and Fernand Woutaz, *Circuits touristiques en Alsace*, Paris 1975
Christian Wolff, *Riquewihr, son vignoble et ses vins à travers les ages*, Ingersheim 1967

Champagne

John Arlott, *Krug, House of Champagne*, London 1976
Paul Bergeot, *Champagne: la coupe est pleine*, Paris 1980
Raymond Dumay et al., *Le vin de Champagne*, Paris 1977
Patric Forbes, *Champagne: The Wine, the Land and the People*, London 1967
Patrick Forbes, *The Story of Moët & Chandon*, London 1972
Henri and Rémi Krug, *L'art du champagne*, Paris 1979
G. Marc, *La route du Champagne*, Colmar-Ingersheim 1971
Cyril Ray, *Bollinger*, London 1971
Robert Tomes, *The Champagne Country*, New York 1867

Index